Improvisation in the Arts of the Middle Ages and Renaissance

Improvisation in the Arts of the Middle Ages and Renaissance

Timothy J. McGee, Editor

Early Drama, Art, and Music
Monograph Series 30

Medieval Institute Publications

Kalamazoo, Michigan 49008

WESTERN MICHIGAN UNIVERSITY

2003

Library of Congress Cataloging-in-Publication Data

Improvisation in the arts of the Middle Ages and Renaissance / Timothy J. McGee, editor.
p. cm. -- (Early drama, art, and music monograph series ; 30)
Includes bibliographical references and index.
ISBN 1-58055-044-4 (casebound : alk. paper) -- ISBN 1-58044-045-2 (paperbound : alk. paper)
1. Improvisation (Music) 2. Improvisation in dance. 3. Improvisation in art. 4. Performing arts--History. I. McGee, Timothy J. (Timothy James), 1936- II. Series.
ML430.7 .I46 2003
791'.094'0902--dc21

2002015087

ISBN 1-58044-044-4 (casebound)
ISBN 1-58044-045-2 (paperbound)

Cover illustration by Marianne Cappelletti after Lorenza Costa, *The Court of Isabella d'Este* (detail).

Printed in the United States of America

Cover design by Linda K. Judy

This book is dedicated
to Audrey Ekdahl Davidson

Contents

ART

ILLUSTRATIONS

Foreword

This volume of essays on improvisation in the arts during the early centuries has resulted from a common interest in the subject that I share with my University of Toronto colleague, Domenico Pietropaolo. We had discussed the subject over a number of years and eventually realized that, although improvisation is generally agreed to be an important part of some of the arts—usually music and drama—its presence in early dance and painting is rarely discussed. As well, there had not yet been an attempt to approach the subject itself in an interdisciplinary manner. Our preliminary discussions revealed that there were several concepts and techniques that our two specialties, music and drama, had in common, and we decided to cast a wider net to see how broadly based these elements were.

Our original effort resulted in a conference on the subject which took place in May of 1999 at the University of Toronto. At that time the topic was not restricted in terms of centuries, and therefore the conference included addresses and presentations on improvisation from the Middle Ages to the present day. All in attendance were impressed with the quantity of information that resulted, and specialists in each area were surprised to see how much the arts had in common, which suggested how vast was the subject. It was clear from that experience that the subject of improvisation in the arts was very much in need of further academic exploration and publication, but that it was far too large a subject to treat adequately in a single volume. Our first effort, therefore, has been to limit this study to the time period preceding 1700, and we solicited individual academic papers from noted scholars in the various arts, some of whom had participated in the 1999 conference.

The present book does not pretend to be either comprehensive or evenly distributed in its scope and coverage. Its advantage is that it brings together, under a single cover, essays on all of the arts. But this is only a beginning and needs to be followed by many additional studies within the areas and time periods covered here as well as the centuries up to the present day. With the exception of Domenico Pietropaolo's opening essay which treats the subject as a whole over a large period of time, the papers included here are rather tightly focused. But although some concentrate on a single art with only occasional references to one or more of the others, several of the subjects by their very nature involve more than one art. Medieval drama included singing; Jane Freeman's title, "Shakespeare's Rhetorical Riffs," indicates a music-drama association; and it would be difficult to discuss dance without detailed reference to music. In fact, the three dance historians are musicologists, and thus their papers quite naturally approach the arts of dance and music as inseparable in many details; and Keith Polk's article on musical practices centers around music intended for dancing. Jennifer Nevile's association of dance and gardens is an interesting enlargement of the subject area, as is Randall Rosenfeld's paper which provides a model taken from experimental archaeology that would be of enormous assistance to the scholarly investigation of improvisation in all of the arts. The set of essays as a whole, therefore, can be regarded as models or seeds for further growth.

Considered from a different perspective, these essays also form a bridge between academic study and practical performance. The increased interest over the past fifty years in recreating the performing arts of the early centuries has led to exciting discoveries and has broadened our understanding of our ancestors from the Middle Ages and Renaissance. Because of the remoteness of the early cultures and their differences with those of the present day, it has been necessary to involve scholars to uncover the historic details and interpret them so that performers could put them into practice. The papers in this volume add to that fund of knowledge. They explore the subject of improvisation in the early centuries from a scholarly basis, which is to say that the conclusions are based on academic research and historical facts. This should be of assistance both to those wishing a broader understanding of the arts in the early centuries and to performers who are involved in recreating some of these works.

It is an advantage that all of the authors presented here are themselves closely connected with performance, and thus have a first-hand understanding of the practical details and demands of improvisation. This is no small matter given the paucity of detailed information which is a result of the very nature of the topic. Further, the limited information that has come down to us over the centuries often appears to be confused or even contradictory. The ephemeral nature of improvisation has resulted in historical records and accounts that are often unclear or ambiguous in matters of detail in such a way that could easily lead a non-performer to conclusions that may seem reasonable and/or logical from an academic point of view but which prove to be impractical and incorrect when actually attempted. The advantage of these papers having been written by scholar-performers is that each writer is able to subject the available information to close scrutiny in terms of whether it would make practical performance sense. For the reader this lends to the essays an additional level of authority and adds an aura of confidence that the information is not only firmly founded in scholarship but practically sound as well.

One impression that stands out from this collection as a whole is the extent to which improvisation was an important factor in all of the arts. Although each of the authors assembles a case by ferreting out small bits and pieces of information having to do with a single art, when the subject is viewed in its entirety the weight of all of the assembled material lends additional strength to each case. By considering the overall picture that results from the volume as a whole as well as that made by each of the individual studies, the reader should be able to see much more clearly the role played by improvisation from the late Middle Ages through to the time of Shakespeare and beyond. The idea of improvisation—the extent to which the performing artist was not only allowed but expected to improvise—was basic to the concept of the performing arts during this period. A surviving text, whether it be literature, music, or choreography, is incomplete and requires unwritten additions by the performers in order to bring it to life in terms of the expectations of the early centuries. To consider any artifact without this ingredient is to see only part of the product. When viewed with the addition of improvisation, the texts take on the freshness that made them a vibrant part of their contemporary culture. This conclusion, which will become all the more apparent as the reader scrutinizes the following essays, brings with it the awareness that to ignore improvisation is to distort the art in a major way. For anyone wishing to recreate an historical performance, it presents an apparent contradiction: to bring the performance to life requires the addition of something not present in the surviving text, whereas to perform only what survives is to ignore one of the most vibrant parts of the original work. In light of the present volume the very concept of 'faithful historical recreation' takes on a much broader and more complex character. For this we offer no apology.

It is fondly hoped that this collection of essays will stimulate many more scholars and scholar-performers to investigate the area of improvisation, and that this will result in publications on the subject that will continue to clarify our understanding of the nature of the arts as well as encourage more artistically accurate historical performances that include the ever-present element of improvisation.

I am grateful to the Drama Centre and the Faculty of Music of the University of Toronto for assistance with the 1999 conference on Improvisation in the Arts that was the basis for the present set of essays, and to Scott Wilson for accurately producing all of the musical examples. My largest debt of gratitude is to Clifford Davidson who has been enormously helpful throughout the planning and execution of this project. His extraordinary editorial eye, boundless energy, and constant good humor have lent a level of excellence to the book that would not have been possible without him.

T. J. M.

Improvisaton in the Arts

Domenico Pietropaolo

In an early chapter of his *Useless Memoirs* (1797) the aged playwright Count Carlo Gozzi interrupts his autobiographical narrative with a digression on improvisation. The discussion is occasioned by the author's recollection that when he was a boy he liked to improvise on the guitar and to sing impromptu verses to his own accompaniment—a fact which now leads him to describe, and comment very negatively upon, the merits of improvisation in the art of poetry. As a playwright working in the tradition of the *commedia dell'arte* and in partnership with the great actor Antonio Sacchi, the last of a long line of distinguished improvisers in the professional theater, Gozzi had championed a unique form of the genre. He had provided scenes for Sacchi that were little more than narrative suggestions and stage directions while writing out in full the roles conceived for most other members of the company in whose ability as improvisers he did not have as much confidence but who were nonetheless honored to work under his literary tutelage. As a young man, when he was an amateur actor, Gozzi too had impressed his audience with his capacity to improvise dramatic monologue and dialogue as a farcical female impersonator. But having cultivated elegant writing throughout all of his mature life, Gozzi could not bring himself to appreciate as a serious cultural undertaking the art of publicly improvising poetry which had so fascinated him as a boy.[1]

Though written long after the end of the Renaissance, in a period which saw the demise of improvised drama as a commercial enterprise, Gozzi's digression is relevant in at least two ways to the conference at which some of the papers included in the present volume were originally presented. The first point of relevance is of a historical nature. Gozzi's commentary tells us that at the end of the eighteenth century, improvisation in the various arts could still be seen in the same purview, something which made it natural for someone to discuss improvisation in music, drama, and poetry without giving the impression that he was discussing things that had little more than a name in common. Such a purview is no longer possible in our time and was already starting to lose much of its appeal in the age of Gozzi, when improvisation was systematically attacked on various fronts for aesthetic as well as for ideological reasons. Gozzi belongs to a transitional period in the history of improvisation, a stage in its development located almost exactly halfway between our time and the Renaissance. Since his time, the status of improvisation as a compositional form has undergone several changes, chief among which are its radical decline in popularity and artistic dignity (virtuosity being now measured with different meters) and the lapse of the conceptual unity that previously sustained it across the borders of various arts—arts which nineteenth- and twentieth-century history has pulled further apart, in response, no doubt, to the ever increasing urge towards the total compartmentalization of culture. In each one of these separate areas of activity, improvisation has become susceptible of independent development at a pace and in a direction determined chiefly by the changing aesthetic relationship of performance to notation. In the twentieth-century theater, for example, improvisation largely became a rehearsal strategy. It departed, that is to say, as far as it possibly could from its prototype in the early *commedia dell'arte* tradition without ceasing, however, to be improvisation.

The second point of relevance in Gozzi's narration is methodological, for his observations lead us to think of how natural it is for scholars to look at improvisation in the practice of a given art through critical categories that are essentially alien to its nature. Gozzi was very careful not to make this error in the theater. He resisted for many years the temptation to publish his *commedia dell'arte* plays, which had been written to be staged and not to be read, and when he finally published them the magic was suddenly gone because they were now judged as scripted or literary plays.[2] But he easily lapsed into error when he examined improvised poetry, which he summarily condemned as inferior art. In the absence of an adequate theory of lyrical improvisation, Gozzi naturally assimilated oral and written poetry and used theoretical models of the latter to guide his reasoning in his appraisal of the former. This attitude, which has been greatly intensified since the age of Gozzi, is the result of a presumed hierarchy in artistic culture which places written words far above spoken words, written texts above their physical enactment, compositions above performances, concepts above designs, and designs above the objects that embody them. The modern world is a world of scripts and graphic metaphors, and the large body of theory that it has produced is in general rooted in writing, notation, and graphic symbols. A performance that is not the execution of a notated text, which precedes it in time and logic but is a self-sustaining creative act, remains always in danger of being radically altered by the theoretical categories through which it is examined if these categories were originally developed for the analysis of a scripted or notated work.

As a technical term 'improvisation' originally denoted only the art of impromptu verse-making, at first in Italian but then in the other romance languages as well, especially Spanish. As late as 1636, in Lorenzo Franciosini's Italian and Spanish dictionary, *improvisare* was defined only as unpremeditated poetical composition, "comporre versi senza pensarvi," and was rendered periphrastically as "hechar coplas de repente," for there was not yet an equivalent word in Spanish.[3] In the course of the seventeenth century, the term was also used to describe the impromptu composition of dialogue on stage, and what we now call *Commedia dell'Arte* was called *commedia all'improvviso* at least until 1750.[4] The term entered the English language in 1765 (earliest example in the *Oxford English Dictionary*) by way of *improvisatore* to describe a person with the talent of composing verses in extempore recitation. Since verses were at times improvised to a musical accompaniment, the term became especially relevant to musicology, and it is in that acceptation that it entered the English musical lexicon.[5] The scholarly use of "improvisation" to describe the process of unpremeditated composition in the other arts, in which it was either not used or used derivatively or descriptively in a non-technical way, is the result of a more recent analogical expansion of the original category. In the disciplines that study the verbal arts, for which the very idea of "oral literature" is, strictly speaking, a contradiction in terms, the practice of improvisation continued to be regarded for a long time as a form of artistic crudeness and therefore on the fringes of literary history. In contrast, the analogous practice in Western music, which mostly concerns the singing of discant, the ornamentation of melody, and thoroughbass accompaniment, was for many centuries central to the art, which at times it entirely dominated.

These two lessons from Gozzi, the one in historiography and the other in method, are good indications of the type of work that we must do in order to understand correctly the phenomenon of improvisation in the Middle Ages and the Renaissance. The history of improvisation has not yet been written, but the ambitious scholar who is attracted by the prospect would do well to reflect on the usefulness of writing it regressively, starting with the present and proceeding rearward to the earliest instances of the phenomenon that are within his reach, always arguing from the effect to the cause rather than the other way round. An approach of this nature would enable us to see both the continuity and the discontinuity by which one stage in the development of improvisation as a form of cultural practice is related to the other. Our descriptive language is similar to that of earlier periods of history, but our artistic forms and our cultural contexts are different, and so we risk being prevented from understanding earlier instances of the phenomenon by the words that apparently best equip us to grasp its essence. On the other hand, regressive analysis would automatically force us to unite theory and history, since its practice would require us to develop distinct theoretical models for each stage of development of the idea of improvisation, each new model representing a revision of the one that is closer to us in history, and simultaneously to explain the changes that we are compelled to make in response to the historical parameters that define each earlier period.

In a regressive history of improvisation, it makes sense to locate the initial perspective in the second half of the eighteenth century, for the period between the later Middle Ages and the Enlightenment, representing as it does the first phase of development of capitalism and liberalism in Europe, can be fruitfully grasped in a single purview. This is a period in which a new social division of labor caused the middle class to advance to a position of dominance in intellectual and artistic life and in which the professions that have come down to us, each with its degree of cultural dignity and commercial value, were founded and allowed to grow in adherence to the logic of their own technical development while responding to trends in the middle class markets of Europe and to the preferences of aristocratic patrons. In the sphere of the arts, these changes are traceable through the emergence and history of the entertainment industry, the chief distinctive features of which were the discovery of the commercial value of artistic entertainment and the professionalization of the performers. In the age of feudalism, a performer was either a marketplace showman intent on pleasing the audience to whose generosity he would appeal for compensation by passing his hat around at the end of his act, or a court performer charged with satisfying his lord's need for diversion. In the early centuries of European capitalism, these two kinds of performers coexisted alongside a third category of musicians, dancers, and actors who catered mostly to the social strata between the court and street audiences. These were skilled performers who offered their labor on a par with other productive activities in the new market economy and who strove to rise to a position of dominance in the developing entertainment industry. Their history in this age—mostly the fifteenth, sixteenth, and seventeenth centuries—is largely the history of their professionalization and rise to stardom. The chief force behind this rise, which saw the transformation of medieval minstrels, tumblers, and mimes into the celebrated virtuosos of music, dance, and drama, was virtuosic improvisation. Towards the end of the eighteenth century, the performance practice whose development had been propelled by improvisation began to change, and at that time the performer, though he may have been a star of the first magnitude, began to lose the right to contribute to the creation of the text during the performance itself.

When we move backwards from the present to the late eighteenth century, and from that time to the early Renaissance, we find our purview becoming, very rapidly, more densely populated with distinguished improvisers, and we discover that our concept of improvisation becomes progressively more inclusive and that its parts become more closely integrated. If in our mental image of Gozzi, twanging his guitar and singing impromptu lyrics for sport, we replace his eighteenth-century clothes with a late medieval or early Renaissance costume, and if we furthermore trade in his guitar for a lira da braccio, the Renaissance instrument of improvisation, we have the famous icon of Orpheus taming wild beasts with his song—the picture by means of which Renaissance iconography frequently represented the self-understanding of humanism, perceived as centered on the civilizing function of art as performance. And if we should then want to divest this image of the abstract quality that comes to it from contemporary woodcuts in which the figure of Orpheus is not meant to resemble anybody in particular, we could easily visualize it with the countenance, real or imaginary, of a number of actual performers who in the early Renaissance achieved considerable distinction in the art of singing *ad lyram*—that is, of improvising on the lira da braccio. Our first choice would probably be Leonardo da Vinci, who, according to Vasari, was a great master of the art of impromptu verse-making and who extemporized magnificently on the lira. Our second choice might be the celebrated improviser Baccio Ugolini, who performed the title role in Poliziano's pastoral drama *La favola di Orfeo* in 1480, or Atalante Migliorotti, who, having learned to improvise from Leonardo himself, performed it in the second production, remounted for the pleasure of the Duke of Mantua in 1491.[6] But other historical figures would no doubt suggest themselves to our minds, commensurately to the frequency with which the image of Orpheus finds its way into our field of view from the contemporary iconographic tradition.

Nor is it likely that a performance on the lira would present itself to us in isolation as the sole attraction, for the Renaissance delighted in multidimensional shows involving all the performing arts. Music, dance, and drama came easily together as components of the same production. Among the many examples possible, none is perhaps more illustrative than the banquet offered on 20 May 1529 in the ducal garden of Belfiore by Ippolito II d'Este, future cardinal of Ferrara who was then still archbishop of Milan. This was a seventeen-course supper in which each course was accompanied by a different type of entertainment. The event began with the performance of a farce, at the end of which, while the guests washed their hands with perfumed water and sampled hors d'oeuvres prior to the first course, four dancers performed *balli alla gagliarda*, a dance susceptible of considerable variation. During the fifth course, *buffoni alla bergamasca,* that is to say, the archetypal clowns from which the stock characters of *commedia dell'arte* were later fashioned, improvised antics around the tables. During the twelfth course, five performers sang *canzoni alla pavana in villanesco*, while during the fourteenth course a group of dancers imitated peasants mowing grass with scythes to the sound of a *moresca*. At the beginning of the fifteenth course, a young man emerged from the pergola singing *ad lyram* in the likeness of an Orpheus reborn to new life in a refined Renaissance garden.[7]

Insofar as improvisation remained in the realm of mechanical skills to be used with measure in the service of art and the social order, the growing popularity of improvising performers was not an especially troublesome phenomenon. There had always been, after all, a tradition which encouraged the public exhibition of skill. However, the professionalization of the performer and his claim to stardom came together with the claim that, in the first place, performance was not an instrument for the execution of previously conceived art but itself art of the highest caliber, equal and possibly superior to the art of composition, and, in the second place, that improvisers were performers in possession of a vocabulary and of a grammar of direct composition that enabled them to generate coherent text in the act of performance itself—and therefore outside the range of control by other interested parties such as composers, playwrights, and, as we shall see, the authorities. This, of course, had always been present in latent form, but what was potential in feudal society was quickly becoming actual in early modern capitalism, and that provoked some opposition.

On the theoretical front, the source of the most formidable antagonism was the Aristotelian tradition following the Renaissance discovery of the *Poetics* and hence the large body of literary and dramatic theory which developed under its influence. This theoretical obstacle concerns drama specifically rather than all the arts in general, although the degree to which Aristotelianism penetrated the whole of Western culture, especially in the later Continental Renaissance, makes the issues contextually significant to all of them. Moreover, the *Poetics* has clear theoretical importance for all the imitative arts—and we need not agree with the details of Samuel Henry Butcher's celebrated and influential interpretation of the treatise as a "theory of poetry and fine art" in order to establish the connection.[8] Read in the context of Aristotle's other works and under the general categories described in the opening chapter, the *Poetics* has much to say that is philosophically relevant to all the arts without thereby implying that they are not essentially distinct from each other. Aristotle is not concerned with the formulation of a general aesthetic but with the theoretical and practical issues involved in the process of art-making, and therefore with problems determined not by universal principles but by the nature of the intended artificial product.[9] The question of improvisation is one of those which, though addressed by Aristotle specifically to the art of making drama, have a wider sphere of theoretical validity quite simply because the arts of making dances and music have a number of analogous problems to solve and, in any case, frequently find themselves working in intimate collaboration with the art of drama as they did in the plays that Aristotle himself saw in Athens and to which his reflections on tragedy were firmly anchored.

Now Aristotle describes improvisation as an early phase of the productive activity which led to the development of drama as an art form while remaining itself pre-artistic. "Rude improvisations gave birth to poetry."[10] Art was governed by precise theoretical principles and rules of structure and was guaranteed longevity by notation; improvisation was devised to produce unforeseen and unforeseeable text, which is the etymological meaning of the Latin term *improvisus*, and was limited moreover to the brief life of single performances. For Aristotle improvisation had been historically necessary for the development of art but was not itself art. Much Renaissance theory tacitly presupposed or explicitly restated this idea without question. "Little by little, from improvisations, there arose what is called Old Comedy," wrote Robortellus, certain of the fact that what came before Old Comedy was not quite art.[11] One way to reconcile Aristotle's view of improvisation with the rising professional and cultural status of the performer was to obfuscate the concept in a reading of the *Poetics* sympathetic to both sides of the issue. In the early sixteenth century, when the language of access to the *Poetics* was still largely Latin, Lodovico Ricchieri gave the phrase "ex rudi principio" as equivalent to Aristotle's statement on the improvisational stage of poetry, while later in the same century, when the *Poetics* was also being studied in Italian, the anonymous translator whose manuscript of Aristotle's work is preserved in the National Library of Florence explicitly rejects the Italian phrase "allo improviso" (sic) in favor of "co' versi rozzi," thus speaking of primitive attempts at art without specifying that the cause of their crudity was improvisation and showing at the same time that, in this tradition, the very idea of drama is in the domain of the writer rather than the performer.[12] The *playwright*, a term in which the practical maker (*-wright*) of drama is explicitly mentioned, has become for the Renaissance the play-writer.

Outside the circle of Aristotelian classicism, at whose center we might place playwrights, composers, and choreographers whether or not they are aware of working under the influence of the *Poetics,* the domain of theory included much that did not run counter to improvisation and much that favored its rise to prominence. The tradition of medieval rhetoric as it was handed down through the schools was especially supportive. A great legacy of the second sophistic with its celebrated emphasis on virtuosity, improvisation was for medieval rhetoric a skill to be mastered after long hours of practice. A good description of what was understood by the concept is "fluency of rehandling"[13]—that is to say, the ability to treat the same point extempore from a variety of perspectives by making quick and clever use of arguments and turns of phrase that are potentially applicable to many situations. Geoffrey of Vinsauf teaches, chiefly under the rubrics of amplification and ornamentation, a number of techniques for achieving proficiency in this practice.[14] Since training in rhetoric was basic to all education, the mental apparatus for improvisation, though acquired linguistically, could be easily carried over into the arena of the non-verbal arts. It is safe to generalize that, in the verbal as well as in the non-verbal arts, the apparatus consisted of two fundamental skills: the ability to generate by means of stock phrases and variations a rich and vibrant segment of text within a given theme or structure, and the ability to deliver it effectively to the audience. The first of these entails knowing how to determine in its particulars the not-given substance of the performance text—a facility that can be acquired principally by means of training in the rhetoric of *copia*, which, according to Erasmus whose classicism is deeply rooted in the medieval Christian tradition, contributes greatly to the development of "skill in extemporaneous speaking or writing." Erasmus, of course, is concerned with language and ideas, but it is with little difficulty that we can extend to the other arts—arts which deal in notes and tunes or in steps and dances rather than formulas and speeches—his statement asserting the ease of "divert[ing] even a rashly begun speech in any desired direction" when "so many formulas [are] prepared in readiness for action."[15]

The second skill consists in the ability to articulate every segment of the performance by using the rhetoric of body language most appropriate to it and simultaneously most accessible to the audience. Throughout the Middle Ages, when the level of literacy was low, reliance on gesture was high in all spheres of life, and, as a consequence, theoretical reflection on the nature of gestures was a more frequent occurrence than in other periods of history. As society became increasingly diversified with the decline of feudalism, "the pedagogy of gestures became a necessity," each social group seeking automatically to identify itself by means of a visible body language and code of behavior.[16] These teachings on gesture have significant implications for our appreciation of the role of unrehearsed performance in all communicative transactions. Roger Bacon, for example, stressed the importance of physical performance in all forms of serious oratory and pointed out the need for the speaker to determine an appropriate performance style when he first faces his listeners. The speaker, he says, should take stock of his audience, determine quickly their sensitivities and mental disposition to what he has to say, and then choose on the spot from the repertoire in his control the gestures and postures necessary to captivate them, for the audience "should be moved more by the movements of the mind expressed by the body than by the teaching or language."[17] The same argument, or, for that matter, the same narrative, is differently colored when it is presented to different groups, since the body language is automatically adjusted in the direction of the gestural code familiar to the group.

There is no great risk of error in assuming that this situation obtains in all the performance arts of the late Middle Ages and Renaissance, not only because in the contemporary consciousness they were all theoretically, if circuitously, retraceable to the rhetorical matrix, but also because, like oratory, they all included delivery to an audience as the final creative moment. The analogy between rhetoric and music was commonplace and explored on various fronts. With respect to the rhetoric of gestural expression, which is of special interest to us, it is sufficient to recall that in 1575 Giustiniani could lavish great praise on singers performing at the courts of Mantua and Ferrara, not only for the exquisite way in which they enriched the compositions with sophisticated ornamentation but also for having "accompanied the music and the sentiment with appropriate facial expressions, glances and gestures, with no awkward movements of the mouth or hands or body which might not express the feeling of the song."[18] As for dance, we may recall that Arbeau described it as a "mute rhetoric" in which movement and gesture can be used not only to elicit an emotional response from the spectator but also to convey to him ideas of discursive complexity.[19] At a higher level of generality, therefore, Roger Bacon's statement says, in the first place, that the performance language in which an artistic act is expressed is determined by the performer in response to the perceived performance culture of the audience, and, in the second place, that the gestural language of performance is not a mechanically added physical layer, preconceived in the mind of the performer and separable in the perception of the spectator, but the material dimension of the very soul of the text, from which it could not be separated without dissolving away its uniqueness.

In the art of dance, of course, physicality was the only perceivable dimension, everything else belonging to the realm of the intellectual or emotional connotations of the body in motion. It might seem, therefore, that once this dimension is determined by artistic preconception, improvisation has little more than a decorative role to play. But that is far from being true since it is chiefly through improvisations in the act of performance that preconceived structural elements are transformed into a signifying text. A clear illustration of this idea is found in the little-known French legend of *Our Lady's Tumbler* from the beginning of the fourteenth century. Tired of the worldly context of his art, a penitent tumbler sought refuge among the monks of Clairvaux, but, untutored as he was, he could neither read the hours of Our Lady, to whom he was profoundly devoted, nor chant to her as the other brothers did. Hence he decided to honor her secretly with his body. He started with high and low leaps and with a reverence, which was probably begun even then on the left foot, because, as Caroso would observe two centuries later, "one shows reverence to someone close to one's heart,"[20] and there can be no doubt that the tumbler's act was a gesture of great love, conceived as a spiritual parallel of the profane one in the contemporary courtly love tradition. Having reverenced to the Virgin, the tumbler then proceeded by doing first the somersault of Metz, then "the French vault, then the vault of Champagne, then the Spanish vault, then the vaults they love in Brittany, then the vault of Lorraine. . . . Afterwards he did the Roman vault, and then, with hands before his brow, danced daintily," whereupon he concluded his performance by walking on his hands, twirling his feet, and weeping with his eyes until he swooned with exhaustion. The reverence and all of these vaults and leaps, preconceived structures of movement from the dance repertoire of the tumbler's secular life, had no previous relation to Marian devotion, but they were arranged in a pattern and performed with such ornaments and variations that they became a silent orchestic chant of praise, parallel to the vocal one which the tumbler could hear rising from the choir even as he danced alone in the crypt and which served him as a distant accompaniment. The Abbot and a fellow monk who were spying on his secret performance were deeply impressed by how "he varied so cunningly" his vaults—that is, by his skill in improvising around them—but not more so than the Virgin, who was so moved that she came out of her statue on the altar and gently stepped down to succor her devoted tumbler, who had used all the signifying power of his art to sing silently his love to her.[21]

These examples lead us to consider that improvisation may be understood in at least two senses. In the first sense it refers to the creation of a complete and previously unscripted performance text, using only the vocabulary of the repertoire and the logic of the genre, while in the second sense it refers to the addition of supplementary material to a scripted but incomplete text, using again the vocabulary and logic of the genre but adhering throughout to the structure of the work given. In the first sense, it applies principally to the art of impromptu verbal performance, which includes extemporizing rhymes, telling stories, and delivering sermons and orations, but it also covers the improvisation of folk dances.[22] To be sure, it may also apply to music and to other forms of dance but in an extremely limited way and probably only to describe a precomposition exercise meant to lead to a score or a choreography. On the other hand, it does not apply at all to drama. The second sense of improvisation applies principally to drama, music, and choreographed dance but generally not to folk dance and to verse-making or other forms of impromptu literary composition.

The textuality of performance can be conceived as if written on three separate lines. On the first line, we find the dance steps in sequence, the musical melody, and the dramatic plot, all specific versions of the artistic action in the Aristotelian sense of the word and perceivable as a structured unit with beginning, middle, and end: this establishes the matter of the dance, the music, and the play. On the second line, we find the accidental dance steps and variations, the musical ornamentation (if not a discant or thoroughbass), and the verbal substance of a play: this is the dimension of the action that would be found in the articulation of the text using the specific medium of the art in question, if the text had been fully written as a choreography, a complete score, or a dramatic script. On the third line we may imagine the physical and vocal gestures involved in the delivery of all three arts: this is the gestural dimension of the action that would be contained in the stage directions, if every segment of the performance text had a detailed stage direction to prescribe it.

In *commedia dell'arte*, the material on the first line is called the scenario, and it is given in its entirety by an author to the company prior to production, whereas the materials for the second line, which includes the dialogue and speeches, and for the third line, which includes the physical articulation of speech and action, are improvised by the performers acting within the constraints imposed by the scenario on the first line. In playwright-dominated traditions, the material on the first and second lines is normally given in its entirety by the author to the company, but the substance of the third line is left largely to the performers, who must produce it in their physical interpretation of the material on the other two lines. In early vocal music, the composer provides in the score only the material in the first line, the essential melodic structure, whereas the notes for the second line, including discant and ornamentation by diminutions and passagework, and the material for the third, including the gestural expression of emotion and spiritual disposition as well as of the uniqueness of the performance experience, are left for the singer to contribute in his interpretation of the music given on the first line. In early baroque music, the thoroughbass is improvised on the second line, whereas the singer's coloratura in virtuosic aria repetitions would be found on both the second and third lines of performance textuality. Similarly in dance, the choreography does not extend beyond the first line, and there it is at times no more than a list of step sequences, transition markers, and starting positions, whereas the ornamentation and the expected pattern and rhythm modifications—which at once embellish the choreographed movements and turn them into specific signifying structures—and the gestural articulation that accompanies the total flow of the body in motion are improvised respectively on the second and third lines.

In producing the material for the second line, the performer was expected to be both faithful to what he had received and creative in his own contribution. Just how this was done is too complex for me to explore in detail in this essay since it involves technical issues in the theory of artistic form, in contemporary training programs, and in audience expectation for each of the arts under consideration. For our purposes it is sufficient to generalize what Herman Finck observed with respect to the performance of vocal music: "you receive all sounds from your mind and intelligence."[23] Now in the mind the late Middle Ages and the Renaissance distinguished the operation of two kinds of imagination: a reproductive imagination, by which previously memorized materials are retrieved to presence, and a productive imagination by which new ones, distinct from those already given, are brought to consciousness. The reproductive imagination is a near synonym of memory, but it is active rather than passive and includes a sense of purposeful agency which memory does not.[24] Performance by means of improvisation involves both forms of imagination in a ratio that varies continuously along the temporal axis of the text. In the medieval rhetorical tradition the special distinction of an improviser is his "readiness to draw upon a store,"[25] where the readiness may be interpreted as his productive imagination, which knows what new objects, beyond those already given in the text, must be brought materially into textual existence, and the act of retrieval as his reproductive faculty, which provides him with a choice of objects from the repository deep in his memory. For this reason instructional programs in all the performing arts emphasize the conscious retention and accumulation of minimal segments of text for later use in appropriate performance contexts. Jerome of Moravia would prescribe precisely this to a singer in training: "when he will have heard a pleasing note, let him diligently retain it, that he might make use of it."[26] The principle is the same in drama, as we can see from a very similar comment by the distinguished actor Niccolò Barbieri, who observed that performers "study and fortify their memory with a wide variety of things such as sayings, phrases, love-speeches, reprimands, cries of despair, and ravings, in order to have them ready for the proper occasion."[27]

In this connection, it is useful to consider in detail a statement from a later period (but fully in alignment with the tradition just described) on the difference between impromptu and script-based performance by the seventeenth-century *commedia dell'arte* actor Evaristo Gherardi, who had dazzled Parisian audiences as Arlecchino at the Comédie Italienne for many years. In the introduction to his collection of scripts in French he makes the following observation:

> One must not expect to find in this collection finished comedies, because Italian pieces cannot be printed in their entirety. The reason for this is that the Italian comedians learn nothing by heart, and because, in playing comedy, it is enough for them to

> have seen the subject of it only a moment before going on the stage. . . . Anyone can learn a part by heart and recite on the stage all that he has learned; but to become an Italian comedian something quite different is necessary. For to speak of a "good Italian comedian" means a man with a foundation, who acts more from imagination than from memory; who, in acting, composes everything that he speaks; who stimulates the players he finds opposite him on the stage; that is to say, who so successfully marries words and action with those of his comrades that he enters immediately into the play and into all the movements that the other demands of him, in a manner to make everyone believe that it has all been prearranged.[28]

An impromptu performer "acts more from imagination than from memory"—or, in the terminology that we have already introduced, more from the productive than from the reproductive imagination—because he memorizes the story outline and the configuration of the scenes, but he composes the actual text during the performance itself by tapping into his own creative power. But though he makes up the material being of the text on stage by drawing it out at an amazing speed from some mysterious place in his imagination just as it begins to take shape in it, he is not exclusively an improviser since he must adhere very closely to the guidelines of the scenario in order to avoid chaos. All performances involve the productive and the reproductive imagination as combined sources, but what distinguishes the extempore acting of *commedia dell'arte* players is that the ratio by which the two faculties are united is by far in favor of the productive imagination, whereas in script-based acting the weight is on the side of the reproductive faculty. The logic of impromptu acting is grounded in the reproductive imagination insofar as the narrative structure of the performance and the actor's repertory of phrases and gestures are concerned, but it is grounded only in the productive imagination in what pertains to the textuality needed to sustain that structure. One cannot be a successful impromptu performer without a fertile imagination, for one must be alert to all subtle turns of the action and be quick in bringing forth the most appropriate text for the situation.

Like all other skills, impromptu performance requires years of training, the right disposition by itself being (as a mathematician would say) a necessary but not a sufficient condition. It has always been assumed, and the assumption is entirely reasonable, that, as far as drama is concerned, the training took place within the troupes themselves, where children learned the art of improvising from older members of the company. But it is a fact, albeit still totally unexplored, that there were training programs in Naples, Bologna, Palermo, "and many other cities of Italy," as we read in Andrea Perrucci's treatise on acting.[29] Well-trained impromptu actors make their work appear effortless, so much so that observers unaware of the discipline and training which is required convince themselves that stage improvisation is not a very sophisticated art, and so they allow themselves to speak of it with contempt. Prominent in this group of critical observers are, according to Perrucci, "poets, scholars, and literary men," all paladins of the written word and hence of memory-based performance, men blinded by their own art to that involved in unrehearsed impromptu composition, until they are put to the test themselves and are allowed the opportunity to fail miserably. True enough, impromptu actors always say no more than "whatever comes to their lips," but, in the case of talented and well-trained performers, what comes to their lips from their imaginations is usually the right thing.[30]

In the above quotation Gherardi makes plain one of the most difficult aspects of all acting from imagination, and that is acting with a partner. Each actor must marry his utterances and gestures with those of his partner in such a way that the resulting combination contributes naturally to the development of the action outlined in the scenario. The equivalent situation in dance occurs when the lady performs graceful *passeggi* around her partner's virtuoso display of a fundamental variation. As for music, this is one of the areas in which there is considerable difference, given that in Early Modern music improvisation generally concerns solo performance, whereas in drama soliloquies are much less numerous than dialogue. The medieval *giullare*, performing always alone, played all the roles himself and made use of improvisation from the first to the last scenes of the performance. But as the *giullari* were replaced by companies and narrative performances by dialogical ones, the issue of acting from the imagination became much more complex. The process involves, as I have shown elsewhere, the formation of binary units of vocal and gestural speech, each in the form of a stimulus-response combination, by performers constantly assessing the range of appropriate expressions available to each other and simultaneously interpreting the audience's reaction in terms of the development most likely to be expected at that point in the exchange.[31] With a minimum of terminological adaptation, this model can also represent communicative transactions in the other arts such as that between two performers in competition or in a duet. In all cases, dialogical improvisation is the result of intimate collaboration and presupposes that each performer has, on the one hand, complete knowledge of the range of his partner's skill and, on the other hand, an intuitive sense of whether with each response it is desirable or not to fulfil the audience's expectation.

It follows from these considerations that the conception of improvisation that obtained in early modern Europe is quite removed from the various techniques that the term designates in our times. The chief differences can be usefully summarized by negative determination—that is, by indicating what Early Modern improvisation was not. It is clear that dramatic improvisation was not then a rehearsal exercise in character discovery, which is what the term principally designates for much twentieth-century theater practice. Nor was it a compositional exercise aimed at the full development of a script through an impromptu exploration of a given situation or theme, which is what the term represents for many script-development programs in our times. Equally clear is that, in this early period of its history, stage improvisation was never a spontaneous form of creation *ex nihilo,* mysteriously progressing towards aesthetic fullness without the aid of predetermined constraints, as has been occasionally fantasized on the basis of various pseudo-romantic notions of primitive creativity. On the contrary, improvisation in this period would be inconceivable without rigid constraints. In the oral composition of lyric poetry, for example, control over the material to be expressed extempore is ensured by the semantic field of the theme selected, which represents for the impromptu poet the limits of his available vocabulary, while control over the aesthetic shape of the product is exercised by means of the metrical patterns and rhyme schemes to which the improviser consents to adhere before he begins his performance. In longer poems, the story and the characters must also be factored in with the theme as part of the initial conditions. Analogous statements can be made with respect to drama in which the scenario, the conventional functional value of the stock characters in the plot—plot-building in the case of Brighella, rhythm maintenance in the case of Arlecchino, and so on—the logic for the distribution of key virtuoso numbers (known as *lazzi* in the *commedia* tradition), and pre-established scene divisions define the region in which the performers may legitimately move on their own without running the risk of becoming grossly unintelligible.[32]

Musical improvisation is likewise conditioned by structural conventions which were at times codified into very precise rules. Thus, to cite an early example, the fourteenth-century musician known as Anonymous XII gave very precise instructions for the governance of improvisation in the performance of *contrapunctus supra librum*, complete with a taxonomy and description of possible intervals and clear rules for the production of the movement of the improvised discant in relation to the rising and falling pattern of the tenor in the various sections of the text.[33] Similarly in the late Renaissance, Giovanni Camillo Maffei provided a comparable set of rules for the number and placement of diminutions in a madrigal —not more than four or five in all, in cadences, on the penultimate syllable of a verse, and preferably on the vowel *o*, since diminutions on other vowels usually "sound like laughter."[34] In the course of the sixteenth century the performance of diminutions and ornamental figurations was codified by a number of writers to a degree of sophistication that has no parallel in the improvisatory practices of the other arts.

Similarly in the theory of dance, performance can be regarded as a combination of steps memorized from a choreographer's plan and steps dictated to the dancer solely by his productive imagination, working in unison with his reproductive faculty and interwoven by him in extempore fashion with the steps in the choreography. As in drama and poetry, improvised dance steps had to occur within a precise framework of rules. In both popular and art dances, improvisation took chiefly the form of imaginative embellishment and variation within the horizon of expectations that surrounded each dance as determined by the style, music, and tradition. Unlike the history of music, the history of Early Modern dance generated very few treatments of the subject, and these are not very detailed studies by any means. But the factors which in the performance practice of the time were meant to condition the improvisatory impulse of the dancers are equally clear. For example, some movements are gender-specific and cannot be performed indifferently by male and female dancers. The basic pattern and the choreographed sequence of steps may be modified but not to an extent that would change the perceivable identity of the dance. Variation dances such as the *gagliarda* can be performed in a number of ways, but the timing must be tightly controlled. *Passeggi* can be inserted only at certain points and normally signal that the partner is engaged in a virtuosic display of variation.[35] The operational principle involved is the same as the one that obtains in music and drama, and that is that the fluency of improvisation is never a matter of free and spontaneous exuberance but always a matter of disciplined movement within the limits demarcating the range of creative legitimacy available to the performer.

In drama, this range becomes even more restricted in the performance of plays which are partly scripted and partly left for the performers to improvise on stage, and becomes relatively narrow in the case of plays for which the script exists in full. That improvisation is necessary in the first of these cases is obvious and requires no further comment—the scenes to be improvised in dialogical form are sustained by the same model of binary combinations into elementary segments of text. In music partly-scripted plays correspond to incomplete scores—missing discant, ornamentation, basso continuo, or coloratura, as the case may be—which are as common as incomplete dramatic dialogues are rare. Moreover, incomplete scripts come relatively late in the *commedia dell'arte* tradition—in the age of Gozzi, in fact, when the end of dramatic improvisation as a professional practice was clearly visible on the horizon—whereas the tradition of the virtuoso ornamentation of melody, which is the form of musical improvisation most closely related to this type of dramatic texture, is long, well documented, and, to a considerable extent, taken for granted by composers, many of whom "intentionally wrote in an austere manner, relying on the singers' ability to improvise the necessary ornamental figurations."[36] But that a degree of improvisation is also inevitable in fully scripted plays may not be obvious to everyone. The situation is perhaps clearer in music. With reference to Gherardi's approach, we can say that in the execution of scripted plays and full scores the art of performance is grounded chiefly but not exclusively in the performer's memory of the script or of the notes. The productive imagination contributes to the degree that the text requires interpretation or invites enrichment.[37] The actor must then assume the responsibility of making explicit what is only implied by the text, and to do so he must improvise, physically if not verbally, while the musician must respond to the score's expectation that at the right places he will supply the proper embellishments in the appropriate style. In such a performance context, actors and musicians who do not make use of their imagination as a source of performance textuality are ultimately mediocre performers who add nothing to the luster of the artistic team and generally bring down the level of production. Gherardi had stern words to say about them: "I compare a comedian of this sort to a paralytic arm, which, though useless, is still called an arm."[38] All good performance has improvisational elements in it, and these range from the few needed to make clear the meaning of a play text or score, to the more numerous ones required to complete a partly scripted work, to the continuous ones found in the impromptu performance of works that did not have a prior existence in any form. And as we move from a scripted work to a non-scripted one, we note that the pivotal point of the reproductive-productive imagination continuum shifts from a position that favors one extremity to a position that favors the other.

Gherardi's elevation of the imagination to the status of chief explanatory principle of improvised drama can be applied with relative ease to extempore creation in the visual arts as well. We are not accustomed to the idea that the figurative arts can make use of impromptu techniques except, perhaps, with reference to non-representational modern art. But as Leslie Korrick has shown in her contribution to the present volume, sixteenth-century Italian theory of art was well aware of the importance of unprepared extempore production of images. Drawing on the same binary source of individual creativity—that is, productive and reproductive imagination—the artist quickly filled his page with tangled sketches of different figures, each presumably drawn from memory of real appearances in response to the criterion of verisimilitude and joined into the creation of a new figure, swiftly shaped in the mind and on paper almost simultaneously. The issue for the theorist who was most keenly aware of the practice of visual improvisation, Giovanni Battista Armenini,[39] was whether improvisation should be regarded, as he proposed, to be a studio technique, a useful first step in the slow development of a compositional idea, or a technique for a visual performance meant to produce a finished work without preparatory sketches—a meaning which he rejected. The contrast was probably due to the fact that improvisation was normally practiced in drawing, and drawing was then regarded as the preliminary stage of painting—something like the workshop process in the composition of a play. However, even Armenini had to admit that, when it was practiced by a skilled artist, impromptu drawing was frequently a finished product of distinction.[40]

In all these acts of improvisation, the performer's awareness of the structural parameters in which he must contain himself must be coupled with an equally clear awareness of the degree to which the audience is familiar with the verbal, visual, and musical vocabulary with which he is about to fashion his product—that is, pushing his art somewhat beyond the limits expected by the audience and yet remaining sufficiently within them to preclude any sense of obscurity. When this is done with the required skill, the final product observed by the audience is seamless and totally free of signs that may indicate uncertainty of development. In fact, the audience should not be able to distinguish an improvised performance from one based on a fully scripted score, choreography, or play text. What, then, is the difference between an improvised and a non-improvised performance? From the perspective of the phenomenology of perception, the only answer possible is that there is no difference at all: the performers enable the audience to experience their living art in exactly the same manner as they would experience a performance based on a previously scripted work. From the perspective of the performers' perception of themselves in action, the answer is that in improvisation they have authorial status, whereas in non-improvised performances they are instruments of another person's artistic intent and must bend their creativity in order to serve a predetermined artistic vision. Insofar as the performers are the authors of the performance, the show is linked to them in an essential way, and they cannot be replaced without prejudice to the performance text.

The problem, however, is that in addition to performers and audiences there are frequently also readers in the picture, and readers are not concerned with the perception of a living art form but with the written documents that describe in detail the intended performance, generally viewed by them as a more or less successful realization of the author's intention. Readers, in other words, are primarily interested in scores, details of choreography, and complete scripts and only secondarily in performances. For readers, a play text is the fixed artistic matrix that can engender many performances. On the other hand, performances are ephemeral and difficult to study even with the aid of the text but are altogether impossible if the matrix itself is created during the performance and vanishes with it in the final applause. The readers who have been most preoccupied with the transitory nature of the type of performance texts of interest to us fall into two categories: members of the board of censors or officials otherwise concerned with ways of controlling the transmission of ideas to audiences, and historians from later periods of history concerned with extrapolating from written and graphic sources a narrative of the status and development of the performing arts during a given time. As I have already suggested, historians may be able to overcome, in part at least, the obstacle of unrecorded performance texts if they write their histories regressively and from the inside in a process designed to force them, little by little, to rid themselves of anachronistic and alien thought forms. But unless they are writing in a period that is reasonably close to the period of performance, various essential aspects of impromptu performance texts are likely to escape them in their entirety, while a number of other aspects would at best be available to them only through the filter of conjecture.

Censors are a different matter altogether since for them improvisation is no more than a strategy for the avoidance of ideological screening. This is especially evident in the case of *commedia dell'arte*. Soon after the appearance of the first companies in the early decades of the Counter Reformation, religious authorities denounced *commedia* because its texts, being only performance texts, could not be screened for orthodoxy and propriety prior to the production itself. In an official report to the Roman Curia dated 1578, Cardinal Gabriele Paleotti went as far as to call for the complete suppression of *commedia* since in the art of improvisation its practitioners had found a way of circumventing authority with impunity.[41] Prior to the performance the censors had nothing on which to rehearse their authority in order to determine whether the performance was intended to be an innocent display of art or a devious stratagem for the dissemination of dangerous ideas. After the performance it was already too late, and in any case there was no recorded evidence of wrongdoing that could be adduced in a police investigation. In such a profoundly repressive age as the Counter Reformation this is how the *commedia dell'arte* managed to thrive on themes of irreverence, satire, and subversion. Improvisation was an artistic technique designed to safeguard the freedom of the theater to comment on the values and institutions of society in a manner that occasionally ran counter to the sources of authority that sustained the status quo. Playwrights were generally dependent upon some form of patronage and belonged to a higher class than that of the street audiences sought out by early *commedia* troupes. As a consequence the ideological perspective from which play texts were composed—that is, for carnival celebrations and for the periodic gatherings of academic organizations—was in perfect alignment with official policy. Discrepancies were unlikely and in any case would not get through the screening process of the Inquisition. A playwright-dominated theater, in which the script must be licensed before production, is as easy to control as its performer-dominated counterpart is difficult.

Among the characteristics that distinguish popular from literary drama is its proclivity to address to the audience members' perception of their social location and to remind them of the fact that it is within their power to reject ideas and values designed further to weaken their position in the hierarchy of authority. As a consequence *commedia* players, who, having received admittance to court theaters and wanting to assure themselves the comforts and security of patronage, would surely present the same play differently in an aristocratic setting. Improvisation allowed them that flexibility, for it enabled them to give the same repertory items a different political turn, transforming denouncement into legitimation. The history of the *commedia dell'arte* shows that what in the market places of its early history was subversive actually became reactionary and repressive by the age of Gozzi, largely under his influence. Improvisation is a slippery compositional tool since it can endow any dramatic form with an enormous potential to adapt to different social settings and political circumstances.

This capacity for adaptation is a good point of access to the economic significance of extempore performance in all the arts. However, on this score it is to the history of the stage that we must turn for the clearest evidence since in drama the economic circumstances of the first professional players are very well documented. In the staging of scripted plays, the conventional hierarchy of creative forces puts the author invariably above the performers on the principle that the unperformed text has chronological, logical, and aesthetic priority over its performance. But this principle of subordination also has serious economic implications, especially in the Renaissance, the period in which performers first achieved professional status and incorporated themselves into a guild or *arte*, which is what the term alludes to in the expression *commedia dell'arte.* Now, according to contemporary sources, the production process of a literary play from conception to staging was extremely long, for it involved several months for the composition of the script and several others for its rehearsal. This did not constitute a problem in the amateur environments of court and academic drama, but it would have been disastrous in the newly formed professional setting in which the livelihood of players and production crew depended entirely on the market value of their work. A product that takes so long to prepare has for the company that produces it a higher budget value than actual earning potential. On the other hand, a stage product created impromptu without the services of a playwright, a work requiring, moreover, less than an hour of total preparation time for each full performance[42] and, what is more, a work susceptible of sufficient variation to justify long runs and repetitions in other venues, has a much greater market value than a playwright-centered production could ever have in Early Modern Europe. Improvisation, cultivated to the point at which companies can venture confidently into the entertainment industry without the aid of a dramatist, is a tool for the economic emancipation of the common player from the subordinating tutelage of literature and simultaneously a condition for the professionalization of the performer in the difficult market economy of early European capitalism.[43]

While functioning as a source of performance textuality, the imagination enabled skilled performers to vindicate their ideological, economic, and artistic autonomy in a world otherwise intent on keeping them anchored to a role of subservient dependence. The discovery that the power to improvise was a commercial commodity as well as an artistic faculty emboldened them with visions of cultural and social dignity previously unavailable to them. By cultivating their skills methodically and by marketing them shrewdly, they embarked on a journey that would soon transform them from the instruments of the art of others into the great virtuosos of their own.

NOTES

[1]Carlo Gozzi, *Useless Memoirs*, trans. John Addington Symonds, introd. Harold Acton (London: Oxford University Press, 1962), 16–18.

[2]Ibid., ix.

[3] Lorenzo Franciosini, *Vocabolario italiano spagnolo* (Geneva: Pietro Marcello, 1636), 320.

[4]The term *commedia dell'arte* occurs for the first time in Goldoni's *Teatro comico* (Venice, 1750), act 1, scene 2; see also the modern edition by Guido Davico Bonino, *Il teatro comico & Memorie italiani* (Milan: Mondadori, 1983), 38.

[5]See, for example, *The Oxford Companion to Music*, 10th ed. (1970; reprint Oxford: Oxford University Press, 1986), *s.v.* "Improvisatore."

[6]Giorgio Vasari comments twice on Leonardo's ability to improvise: "sopra quella [lira da braccio] cant divinamente all'improvviso," and "fu il migliore dicitore di rime all'improvviso del tempo suo" (*Le vite de più eccellenti pittori*, ed. Gaetano Milanesi, 9 vols. [Milano: Sansoni, 1906], 4:18, 28). See also Emanuel Winternitz, *Leonardo da Vinci as a Musician* (New Haven: Yale University Press, 1982), xxiii. On the dating of *La favola di Orfeo*, see Nino Pirrotta, *Music and Theatre from Poliziano to Monteverdi*, trans. Karen Eales (Cambridge: Cambridge University Press, 1982), 6; originally published as *Li Due Orfei da Poliziano a Monteverdi* (Turin: RAI, 1969), 8.

[7]For other details concerning the banquet, see the account by Cristofaro da Messinburgo, *Banchetti, composizioni di vivande e apparecchio generale* [Ferrara, 1549], ed. Fernando Bandini (Venice: Neri Pozza, 1960). The relevant sections are quoted by Francesco Luisi, *La musica vocale nel Rinascimento: Studi sulla musica vocale profana in Italia nei secoli XV e XVI* (Turin: Edizioni RAI, 1977), 65–67. See also the discussion in Howard Mayer Brown, "A Cook's Tour of Ferrara in 1529," *Revista Italiana di Musicologia* 10 (1975): 216–41.

[8]Samuel Henry Butcher, *Aristotle's Theory of Poetry and Fine Art* (1894; reprint New York: Dover, 1951).

[9]See Kenneth Telford's analysis in his edition of Aristotle, *Poetics* (Chicago: Gateway, 1961), 62–63.

[10]*Poetics* 1448b23, in Butcher, *Aristotle's Theory of Poetry,* 17. See also 1449a9 (19): "Tragedy—as also comedy—was at first mere improvisation."

[11]Franciscus Robortellus, *Explicatio eorum omnium quae ad comoediae artificium pertinent* (1548); I have used the English translation in Marvin T.

Herrick, *Comic Theory in the Sixteenth Century* (Urbana: University of Illinois Press, 1964), 229.

[12]Lodovico Ricchieri, *Lectionem Antiquarum Libri XX* (1516), and Florence, Biblioteca Nazionale, MS. Magliabechiano VII–437, both cited in Bernard Weinberg, *A History of Literary Criticism in the Italian Renaissance*, 2 vols. (Chicago: Chicago University Press, 1961), 1:368, 589.

[13]Charles Sears Baldwin, *Medieval Rhetoric and Poetic* (New York: Macmillan, 1928), 15.

[14]Geoffrey of Vinsauf, *Poetria Nova*, trans. Margaret F. Nims (Toronto: Pontifical Institute of Mediaeval Studies, 1967), chaps. 3–4.

[15]Desiderius Erasmus, *On Copia of Words and Ideas,* trans. Donald B. King and H. David Rix (1963; reprint Milwaukee: Marquette University Press, 1982), 17.

[16]Jean-Claude Schmitt, "The Rationale of Gestures in the West: Third to Thirteenth Centuries," in *A Cultural History of Gesture,* ed. Jan Bremmer and Herman Roodenburg (Ithaca: Cornell University Press, 1992), 67.

[17]Roger Bacon, *Moral Philosophy,* 5.3.20 and 5.4.15, 18, for convenience cited from *Medieval Political Philosophy*, ed. Ralph Lerner and Muhsin Mahdi (Ithaca: Cornell University Press, 1963), 384. For that reason the sacred orator should weep if weeping is the best gesture to use in a particular occasion (387) and should in any case "colour" his argument in a manner determined by his perception of the sensitivities of his listeners (388).

[18]Vincenzo Giustiniani, *Discorso sopra la musica*, trans. Carol MacClintock, Musicological Studies and Documents 9 (Rome: American Institute of Musicology, 1972), 70.

[19]Thoinot Arbeau, *Orchesography*, trans. Mary Stewart Evans (New York: Dover, 1967), 16.

[20]Fabritio Caroso, *Rules and Directions for Dancing the "Passo e mezo"*; quoted for convenience from the selection translated by Julia Sutton in *Dance as a Theatrical Art: Source Readings in Dance History from 1581 to the Present,* ed. Selma Jeanne Cohen (New York: Dodd, Mead, 1975), 11.

[21]*Our Lady's Tumbler*, trans. Eugene Mason, in *Women from the Greeks to the French Revolution,* ed. Susan Groag Bell (Stanford: Stanford University Press, 1973), 135, 137.

[22]In folk dances, as Barbara Sparti observes in her essay in the present volume, "creation and performance (process and product) are simultaneous."

[23]Herman Finck, "On the Art of Singing Elegantly and Sweetly," trans. Carol MacClintock from *Practica Musica* (1556), in *Readings in the History of Music in Performance* (Bloomington: Indiana University Press, 1979), 62.

[24]For the productive imagination the *Oxford English Dictionary* cites an example from Chaucer's *The Miller's Tale* ("men may dyen of ymaginacioun, / so depe may impression be take") and, for the reproductive imagination, an example from Shakespeare's *All's Well that Ends Well* 1.1.82–83 ("I have forgot him. My imagination / Carries no favor in't but Bertram's").

[25]Baldwin, *Medieval Rhetoric and Poetic,* 16.

[26]Jerome of Moravia, *Tractatus de Musica,* chap. 25; I quote from the selection trans. MacClintock, in *Readings in the History of Music in Performance*, 7.

[27]Niccolò Barbieri, "What is a Buffoon?" trans. from *La supplica* (1634), in *Actors on Acting*, ed. Toby Cole and Helen Chinoy (New York: Crown, 1970), 53.

[28]Evaristo Gherardi, "On the Art of Italian Comedians" (1700), quoted for convenience from *Actors on Acting*, 58.

[29]Andrea Perrucci, "Introduction to Impromptu Acting," from *Dell'arte rappresentativa premeditata e all'improvviso* (Naples, 1699); quoted from the translation in *Actors on Acting,* 57.

[30] Ibid., 56–57.

[31]See my "Improvisation as a Stochastic Composition Process," in *The Science of Buffoonery: Theory and History of the Commedia dell'Arte*, ed. Domenico Pietropaolo (Ottawa: Dovehouse, 1989), 167–76.

[32]Nor is this true only of farce. In addition to the plentiful examples of tragicomedy, one can also find scenarios of tragedy, though these are decidedly rare; see, for example, *La regina d'Inghilterra, tragedia* and *I quattro pazzi, opera tragica* in *Scenari inediti della commedia dell'arte*, ed. Adolfo Bartoli (1890; reprint Bologna: Forni Editore, 1979).

[33]Anonymous XIII, *Treatise on Discant*, trans. MacClintock, in *Readings in the History of Music in Performance,* 8–11.

[34]Giovanni Camillo Maffei, *Letter on Singing,* trans. MacClintock, in *Readings in the History of Music and Performance*, 52–53.

[35]See the essays by Yvonne Kendall and Jennifer Neville in the present volume.

[36]Frederick Neumann, *Performance Practices of the Seventeenth and Eighteenth Centuries* (New York: Schirmer, 1993), 517.

[37] In the third of his *Dialogues on Stage Affairs*, the sixteenth-century director Leone de' Sommi states that performers of scripted drama must provide on stage "actions which the author has not been able explicitly to indicate in his script" (quoted from the selection translated in *Actors on Acting,* 47).

[38] Gherardi, "On the Art of Italian Comedians," 58.

[39]Giovanni Battista Armeini, *De' veri precetti della pittura* (Ravenna, 1586), on which see the detailed commentary by Leslie Korrick in this volume.

[40]See the essay by Barbara Sparti in this volume.

[41]Ferdinando Taviani and Mirella Schino, *Il segreto della commedia dell'arte* (Florence: Usher, 1982), 319–20.

[42]Andrea Perrucci, "Introduction to Impromptu Acting," 56.

[43] On the economic significance of improvisation in drama, see Cesare Molinari, *La commedia dell'arte* (Milano: Mondadori, 1985), 40–41.

MUSIC

Cantare all' improvviso: Improvising to Poetry in Late Medieval Italy

Timothy J. McGee

There has never been any doubt that a large share of the music heard in Italy throughout the Medieval and Renaissance periods was improvised. Instrumentalists improvised music for dancing and processing, singers improvised melodies to accompany their poetry, and on some occasions the poetry too was improvised.[1] In recent years we have come to a fuller realization of the extent to which this tradition permeated daily life in Italian cities and courts. As Nino Pirrotta demonstrated in numerous articles over the past forty years, our perception of the musical life in Italy during the early centuries has been distorted by our reliance on the surviving written repertory.[2] Whereas the Italians thought very highly of the written polyphonic repertory, they also revered their tradition of improvisation. Some work has been done in the area of reconstructing the way in which instrumentalists improvised,[3] but research into improvised singing has not resulted in a clear impression of what exactly was done or how it was accomplished, and in some cases has produced a somewhat confused view of the practice.[4] The goal of the present essay is to investigate the many facets of improvised singing and to propose a probable musical model for the tradition of improvised singing in the late Middle Ages.

Cantare all'improvviso was a tradition of long standing in Europe where the village bard functioned as an important element of cultural identity. The poet/musician was far more than an entertainer; he was the person entrusted with passing on the history of the tribe—including its myths, beliefs, and tales of good and evil—and he did this by setting his stories to music. In Italy during the late Middle Ages there were many such singers in each community, and there are numerous literary references to improvised song and music for dancing that describe some of the occasions on which improvisation would have been heard. In Dante's *Vita nuova*, Amore counsels the poet that his *ballate* should be adorned by sweet harmony,[5] and Giovanni Boccaccio's *Decameron* makes it clear that improvising a melody for poetry was something that a member of the educated upper class could be expected to do. In the *Decameron*, set on the hillside outside of Florence in 1348 where ten young nobles went to escape the Black Death, each evening after dinner one of them was called upon to improvise a dance song, as for example on the third day:

> Filostrato, per non uscir del camin tenuto da quelle che reine avanti a lui erano state, come levate furono le tavole, cosí comandò che Lauretta una danza prendesse e dicesse una canzone; la qual disse: "Signor mio, delle altrui canzoni io non so, né delle mie alcuna n'ho alla mente che sia assai convenevole a cosí lieta brigata; se voi di quelle che io ho volete, io ne dirò volentieri." Alla quale il re disse: "Niuna tua cosa potrebbe essere altro che bella e piacevole; e per ciò, tale qual tu l'hai, cotale la di'." Lauretta allora con voce assai suave, ma con maniera alquanto pietosa, rispondendo l'altre, cominciò cosí: Niuna sconsolata, da dolersi ha quant'io. . . .[6]
>
> (When the tables had been removed, Filostrato, instead of taking a walk as had those who were in command before him, decreed that Lauretta lead a dance and sing a *canzona*. She responded: "My lord, I do not know any *canzonas* that the others do, nor do I have in my head one that would be respectable to this esteemed *brigata*; but if you want one that I know, I will happily sing it." At which the king responded: "Nothing of yours could be other than beautiful and pleasing; and so whatever you have, present it to us." Then Lauretta responded with a voice rather soft but with an affective manner, beginning thus: "No disconsolate one has as much sadness as I. . . .")

Simone Prudenzani, in poetry describing a grand feast around the year 1400, also has his character Sollazzo improvise dance songs in various styles.[7] The tradition continued to have a very high profile in the fifteenth century as witnessed by the contest that took place in the Duomo of Florence in October of 1441—a contest sponsored by L'Accademia Coronaria, in which a number of literary figures sang their poetry over a period of several days in front of a distinguished audience.[8] Later in the same century the title role in Angelo Poliziano's *Orfeo* was sung *all'improvviso* by Baccio Ugolini, one of the most famous improvisors of his day.[9]

The extent to which the ability to improvise was considered to be an important mark of a professional musician can be seen as late as 1623, when it became the only test in a controversy over who was the finest soprano in Rome. The incident, reported in a letter to the Grand Duke of Tuscany,[10] took place during an evening gathering of notables at the palace of Cardinal Orsino where the singer "La Cecchina" (Francesca Caccini, daughter of Giulio Caccini) was performing. During conversation the poet Gian Battista Marino asserted that in his opinion the most gifted singer of the day was "L'Adriana" (Adriana Basile), whereas others stated their preference for "La Cecchina." After some discussion the participants decided that the issue was to be settled by a trial: the poet sent for some of his *ottave rime* and presented them to "La Cecchina," who was asked to improvise both a melody and accompaniment to them at sight. On the next night the same verses were presented to "L'Adriana," and the matter was judged to be settled in favor of "La Cecchina." The letter states that following the contest Marino "celebrated throughout all of Rome the ability of Signora Francesca."

As in the earlier centuries, entertainment was not the only function of sung poetry in late medieval Italy: *cantare all'improvviso* was also a traditional vehicle for social and political commentary, both formal and informal. There was an official post of "civic herald" in many communities that required someone who could improvise. In Florence, civic pay documents record this position from as early as the 1320s, and the duties required of the herald provide us with an impression of the importance accorded to such an activity. The office of "civic herald" could be described in modern terms as "Master of Ceremonies." It was the herald's job to see to all of the official ceremonial details for the civic government which included writing and singing poetry to honor a distinguished visitor to the city and to celebrate an important accomplishment such as a military victory. On these occasions the government mounted rather elaborate public celebrations, and the civic herald was expected to sing his poetry as a part of the ceremony.[11] There was also another role played by the Florentine herald—a role similar to that of a court jester in which he sang *canti morali* (moral songs) for the executives of the government in the special dining room where they took their meals together. The subject matter of the herald's songs ranged from praise to criticism; he was the civic conscience, and he was free to comment on all important matters that concerned the city and its government.[12]

The civic herald was the only *official* singing/rhyming political commentator in Florence, but he was certainly not the only one who spoke out in this manner. Another, less official part of this tradition was practiced by private individuals who sang in various piazzas all around the city. They were referred to as *cantimpanca*, the *panca* being a platform from which they sang.[13] From iconographic as well as literary sources we know the singer usually accompanied himself with a musical instrument. The instrument most often depicted is a lira da braccio, a seven-string bowed instrument with symbolic ties to the traditional lyre of David and the singing poets of ancient times.[14] There are also references to the use of a lute or a harp as an accompanying instrument, although the lira da braccio came to be symbolic of this kind of presentation.[15] Each *cantimpanca* had a favorite weekly time and venue for his performance, and developed a loyal following. In the last half of the fifteenth century, for example, the favorite *cantimpanca* of Lorenzo de' Medici was Antonio di Guido, who performed on Sundays in the piazza in front of the church of San Martino.[16]

The poetic forms chosen by the improvisors were quite varied, with some types more popular during particular decades or in certain locations: all of the poems in the *Decameron* are *ballate*, the Florentine civic heralds sang *canti morali* and *sonetti*, and most of the surviving poems of the *cantimpanca* are *ottava rime*. In Ferrara during the mid-fifteenth century, Giovanni Cieco di Parma wrote and sang *capitoli* and *sonetti petrarcheggianti*, whereas in Naples the preferred form was the *strambotta*.[17] It would seem, therefore, that with few exceptions the improvisors felt free to choose any of the popular poetic forms for their art.

Commentaries from the fourteenth and fifteenth centuries suggest that the performances of certain of the more famous improvisors were quite spectacular. In 1375, the singing of the Florentine civic herald Jacopo Salimbene was described in the civic records as "dilettevole armonia" ("delectable harmony") and "delectabili sonoritate" ("delightful sound").[18] In an elaborate tribute written in 1459, the poet, statesman, and dancing master Antonio Cornazano described the performances of Pietrobono, the famous lute virtuoso and singer from Ferrara, by comparing him to Apollo and Orpheus[19] and claiming that "his music rivals the heavenly harmonies, can revive the dead, turn rivers and stones, and even change people into statues."[20] According to the fifteenth-century Florentine historian Luca Landucci, Antonio di Guido, the singer at San Martino, "Passato ognuno nell'arte di cantare" ("surpassed everyone in the art of singing"),[21] while a contemporary account of his performance makes a comparative reference to both Orlando and Petrarch;[22] and Angelo Poliziano, in describing a performance of a boy improvisor he had heard in Rome, speaks of the performer's power to enthral, exalt, or soothe the souls of listeners.[23]

The quality of the poetry undoubtedly was the cause of much of the adulation, but many of the statements make it clear that the praise also referred to the lavishness of the musical setting: Pietro Bembo wrote that the early fifteenth-century Venetian poet Leonardo Giustiniani "was held in greater esteem for the manner of song with which he sent forth his poems than for his mode of writing."[24] In the mid-sixteenth century, Alfonso de' Pazzi, a popular Florentine poet, was praised in prose and poetry for his improvisatory skill. In de'Pazzi's sonnets attacking the noted Florentine chronicler Benedetto Varchi, he contrasts his own ability as improvisor with that of musicians who sing "by note"—that is, music that is composed and written down. The text of de'Pazzi's works, as well as that of a canzona by "Il Lasca"[25] and a prose diatribe by Pasquino Patritio Romano, verify that in certain intellectual circles in Florence and in Rome improvisation was considered to be the "true Italian" style as opposed to the written repertory, which was associated with the foreign composers from Northern Europe.[26]

There is extensive testimony concerning the existence of the unwritten *cantare all'improvviso* tradition, but what is missing, unfortunately, is a clear indication of exactly what type of music the musician-poets actually performed on these occasions. Although some of the performers wrote down their poems, not one of them left a single note of music to show us how they set the lines.

From the material presented above it is obvious that there were numerous kinds of improvisors, ranging from amateur to professional, in the late Middle Ages and Renaissance and that there was a variety of occasions on which it was appropriate to improvise music to poetry. It would seem to follow, therefore, that more than one style of singing was involved, and that the singer probably would have chosen a style for his improvisation that would fit the poetry and the occasion. Although this last point would seem to be a logical consequence of the preceding discussion, most of the attempts to reconstruct what could possibly have been the style of improvised singing have begun with the assumption that there was a single style, one that would have been comparatively simple—perhaps close to the level of only one note for each syllable of text—and that the music would have been based on a traditional simple setting or possibly on commonly known formulae.

The only secure musical evidence we have is present in some sample settings published in the first years of the sixteenth century by Ottavio Petrucci in his books of *frottole*. Petrucci provides four-part musical settings for *strambotti*, *odi*, *capitoli*, and *sonetti* that could be used to set any poem in those poetic forms.[27] Each of his settings is formally constructed in order to provide music in a format that parallels the structure of the poetic type. I have reproduced his model for *sonetti* as Example 1, with indications of how any poem in *sonetto* form could be adapted to the format of the music.[28] A typical *sonetto* is comprised of two four-line stanzas, followed by two or more three-line stanzas. Petrucci's model provides three musical phrases with which to set the lines. For the first and second stanzas which have the rhyme scheme ABBA, the second musical phrase is repeated (as in Example 1)—mirroring the line rhyme. For the three-line stanzas no musical repeat is necessary.

A number of musicologists have dealt with the subject of setting poetry to these Petrucci models; most recently William Prizer has written on the relationship of these pieces to the Italian compositional style of the late fifteenth and early sixteenth centuries. He has demonstrated convincingly that the Petrucci models are identical in their musical structure—melodically, harmonically, and formally—to the surviving composed *frottola* repertory of the period.[29] There is no doubt, therefore, that by the end of the fifteenth century at least one of the musical models for setting poetry would be identical in sound to the written *frottola* repertory of the time.[30] What Petrucci provides, of course, is not a guide to improvisation but a collection of generic musical settings that can be used by anyone unable to improvise, although they undoubtedly also reflect the style in which one could improvise. But without denying this conclusion, one may still wonder to what extent Petrucci's models were related to the tradition of improvisation—that is, how widely they were used, and how far

EXAMPLE 1
Modo del Cantar Sonetti

Modo de cantar sonetti, from Antonio Petrucci, *Strambotti, ode, frottole, sonetti, et modo de cantar versi latini e capituli, Libro Quarto* (Venice, 1507), fol. 14r; text: Biblioteca Comunale di Mantova, MS. A.I.4, fol. 8r.

back in the century can we project this relationship between the improvised tradition and the style of the music that was eventually written down in the *frottola* repertory at the end of the fifteenth century.

My reasons for questioning the extent of the relationship are two: one is that the melodies of the models are all quite simple and not sufficiently flexible to be adjusted to specific texts in a manner that would inspire the kind of praise some improvisors received; the other is that the *frottola* style of the late fifteenth century, when it first emerges in written form, bears little resemblance to the style of the written repertory of the fourteenth and early fifteenth centuries; compare Examples 1 and 2. To state the most obvious differences between the two repertories: the early works, as exemplified by Example 2,[31] are for two voices instead of four; and they have extensive florid sections as compared to the rather sparse melodic material of the later *frottola* style. A more detailed musical analysis yields the information that the two melodic and harmonic practices are also quite different, with the earlier compositions far more closely related to the modal practices of the earlier centuries (a topic to which I will return). It has been suggested that the *frottola* style itself was a new musical form in the late fifteenth century, and therefore, although the Petrucci models are definitely a part of this new style, a direct relationship between the *frottola* and the traditional improvisational style cannot be established. Further, even allowing for the probability that singers improvised in the *frottola* style by the end of the fifteenth century, we should also ask if that would have been the only style of improvised poetry setting at that time.

Several scholars have looked at fourteenth-century composed music for possible models of the early improvisational style.[32] One possibility was suggested by Howard Mayer Brown, who cited the early *lauda* repertory (see Example 3).[33] Brown's choice was based on the assumption that the style of improvisation by an amateur probably would be quite simple and the only known simple musical style from the fourteenth century is the monophonic *lauda*. There are no existing musical models or instructions for setting a *lauda* text nor any secondary evidence that such a thing ever existed, but it is probable that *laude*, similar to most other types of poetry, were set to music by improvisors.[34] The singing of *laude* was part of the ritual associated with confraternities of lay people who gathered

Example 2
Bench'amar crudel donna

Bench'amar crudel donna. Anonymous ballata. British Library MS. Add. 29,987, fol. 59r.

together for devotional services,[35] and an impressive collection of texts written for this ceremony has survived.[36] Some music has come down to us as well (as in Example 3), but the tradition also included the adoption of melodies of well-known songs, the *cantasi come* tradition.[37] Usually the *laude* were sung by the entire membership of the confraternity, and in that context a simple setting would be quite understandable. Records from the early decades of the fifteenth century also indicate payments to a small group of special singers[38] for whom we might suspect the possibility of a more elaborate setting. In any case, it would seem highly probable that when required to improvise a melody for a *lauda*, a capable improvisor would have invented one in the style usually associated with that genre. The question posed earlier, however, can also be asked of this repertory: would this model have been adopted for *all* occasions of improvisation. In addition to being an obvious model for a *lauda* text, would this musical format also have been an appropriate choice for, say, a love song at a social gathering of well-educated aristocrats such as that depicted in the *Decameron*, for the civic herald to praise a distinguished visitor, or for a *cantimpanca* to set a text criticizing a government decision?

EXAMPLE 3

Regina Sovrana

Regina sovrana de gram pietada. Anonymous Lauda. Cortona, Bibl. Communale, MS. 91, fols. 24r–25v.

A somewhat different source of the early improvisatory style has been pursued by Nino Pirrotta, who suggested that clues may exist in the music of southern Italy and Sicily. Basing his argument on literary documents and poetic as well as musical analysis, Pirrotta identifies elements of southern Italian forms such as the *siciliana* in music found in North Italian manuscripts of the late fourteenth century, and he demonstrates that there are literary connections between the *siciliana* and popular Northern forms such as the *ballata, strambotto*, and *giustiniana*. He further establishes the fact that singing in the Sicilian style was popular in northern locations such as Ferrara and Venice.[39] It is interesting to note that the fourteenth-century *siciliana* was a completely improvised form and that one of its characteristics is a florid melody similar to that found in some of the composed northern repertory of the period such as those presented in Examples 2 and 4.[40] Pirrotta's conclusion that "a Sicilian style of singing was practiced and imitated in northern Italy"[41] suggests the possible existence of a basic traditional Italian musical approach that allowed refinement and adaptation according to regional style characteristics. Following this line of reasoning, I would like to explore the possibility of discovering just such a basic organizational idea by investigating some of the oldest surviving Italian secular repertory that appears to reflect an older practice.

Many writers have commented on the somewhat shapeless formation of the more florid Italian compositions of the Late Middle Ages that defy attempts at systematic analysis. The melodic lines do not have clearly shaped melodies in the sense that we have come to expect in the less florid compositions, nor do they follow the established rules of harmony and counterpoint as found in the theoretical treatises. It is clear even from a superficial observation of the Italian secular repertory that much of it does not reflect the compositional practices laid out clearly in numerous Northern theoretical treatises of the period and exemplified in the compositions of the Franco-Netherlandish composers. Further, the compositions to which I refer are not in accord with some of the statements of Marchettus of Padua, the most famous and widely read Italian theorist of the fourteenth century. James Haar has noted that certain of the early monophonic *ballate* seem to be elaborations of an outline rather than sculpted melodies, and he refers to the melodic style of many of the fourteenth-century secular compositions as "highly declamatory."[42] An analysis of this repertory following from those observations yields some interesting suggestions both about the orientation of these compositions as well as about the way in which the various improvisors of the period may have proceeded when setting their poetry.

The broad elements of Italian composition are well known: each piece takes a musical format that in some way matches the structure of the poetry, either *ballata* or *madrigale*.[43] The lines of text are usually set off by a long note on the last syllable, followed by a rest—a reflection of the poetic structure that is further emphasized by a melodic flourish over the initial and penultimate syllables of each line. Often the second musical section is marked by a very large upward leap from the last note of the preceding section. But other than these broad generalizations, it has proven difficult to explain the compositional approach in closer detail. *Per non far lieto*, a monophonic *ballata* by Gherardello da Firenze (Example 4), is a good example of the style;[44] its two-section formal

Per non far lieto. Ballata by Gherardello da Firenze. Florence, Bibl. Medicea Laurenziana, MS. Mediceo Palatino 87 (Squarcialupi Codex), fol. 28r.

structure reflects the ABBA structure of the poetry, with a final return of the opening text and music as a refrain to reflect its dance-song heritage.

Per non far lieto, one of the more florid compositions of the fourteenth century, consists of long passages of melodic motion that are almost completely stepwise. There are few recognizable melodic-rhythmic motives—an element that is responsible for the "aimless" appearance and sound of this style. But whereas the compositions in this repertory resist the kind of motivic analysis that can be applied to other late medieval European repertories (and to some of the Italian repertory as well), a modal analysis indicates that they were carefully formed according to a more basic set of organizational principles. On the broadest level, *Per non far lieto* can be described in terms of its conformity to the characteristics of one of the ecclesiastical modes: it ranges over an octave from g to g, and is oriented around the notes d and g. This and the presence of b♭ results in the tone-semitone distribution of mode 1 (transposed up a fourth), as described in the theoretical treatises of the late Middle Ages. More particularly, the composition also conforms to Marchettus of Padua's more detailed requirements of "species" in a perfect authentic mode 1.[45] As Marchettus requires, the first species of mode 1 consists of the notes within the interval of a fifth from final to reciting tone (in this example it is the fifth from low g to d, which is emphasized in the first musical section, but especially in the first seven bars), and those within the fourth from reciting tone to the octave above the final (d to high g, emphasized in the second section, especially in bars 34 to 49). In addition to fulfilling these modal requirements, Gherardello has structured his melody to single out the individual notes of the scale within their species and to emphasize the modally important notes of g and d by a combination of repetition, ornamentation, and omission. The opening bars, for example, center around the reciting tone d, emphasizing it by repetition and by ornamenting it with motion above and below. Once that is established, the line moves indirectly through the other notes of the upper species (c, b♭, and a) to g, the modal final. After the importance of g is affirmed, a sustained f♯ in bar 7 emphasizes g by omission—that is, by depriving the listener of the relaxation of the expected cadencing note.

Rather than following the Northern practice of writing a clearly structured melody composed of easily identifiable melodic-rhythmic motives, Gherardello has chosen to organize his melody as elaborations of its modal components. In light of that criterion, it can be seen that, instead of what at first appears to be aimless wandering around the scale, his melody is highly organized so that it highlights the notes of his modal scale in a hierarchical manner, delineating the two modal species and emphasizing the final and reciting tones. A survey of the repertory of compositions in this style indicates that the quantity of melodic elaboration varies from composer to composer and, indeed, from composition to composition. The element that the compositions have in common is that they establish a rhapsodic melodic impression by avoiding recognizable small melodic-rhythmic motives. To state this in more positive terms, these compositions have as their melodic goal the delineation of the scales that are the basis of their structure. Within the confines of the modal outline, the melodic practice adopted in most of the compositions is quite free, lending it the quasi-improvisatory appearance that Haar and others have observed.

It is significant to note that the compositional style I have just described has been found in one other European repertory from this period: the fifteen monophonic instrumental dances in an Italian manuscript from c.1400.[46] The melodic characteristics of these dances as well as their unusual lengths and formal construction have prompted several scholars over the past century to compare them to Middle Eastern traditional instrumental music and to note that this influence is unique in European music of the period.[47] In light of the present discovery of a similar technique in Italian vocal music, it would appear that this observation may be only partially correct. Rather than demonstrating an Eastern influence, the compositional style employed both in the dances and in some of the vocal music would seem now to have been one of the traditional Italian approaches to musical composition. This would not eliminate a connection with the Middle East, but instead of being an indication of an Eastern influence in Italy it is more probably evidence of a relationship between basic musical techniques used in both regions.[48] Additional similarities between the two melodic practices can be seen in the liberal use of accidentals in both the vocal and instrumental repertory, in which unexpected sharps and flats are inserted into a melodic pattern as a way of highlighting particular notes of the scale (see Example 4, bar 15), or for the purpose of contrasting one scalar pattern with another.[49]

Until now the general consensus has been that compositional practices for instrumental and vocal music were quite separate, but the discovery of such similar basic characteristics in the two repertories suggests a much closer relationship between them, both written and improvised. Wulf Arlt has speculated that much of the repertory of instrumental music that has come down to us from the late Middle Ages may be examples of an improvisatory practice. His analysis of the extant repertory centers around formal, melodic, and rhythmic relationships rather than modal orientation, but he draws interesting relationships between the instrumental and vocal repertories, especially between instrumental music and some of the earlier sacred repertory, that support the present hypothesis.[50]

Although an analysis of *Per non far lieto* establishes its compositional principles as different from other practices, it does not prove that this was the method chosen for *cantare all'improvviso*. In the absence of detailed statements in the contemporary treatises or literature as to what system was employed, such a claim will necessarily remain at the level of conjecture. There is some theoretical testimony, however, that unschooled improvisors were capable of singing correctly in the modes. A passage in the treatise *De musica*, written 1078 by Aribo Scholasticus,[51] states that minstrels employed the modes correctly even though they were not trained in the art. His word for minstrels, *histriones*, is one of the many synonyms for improvisors, and heralds, and performers generally.[52] According to Aribo, the schooled musician understands rationally what he is doing, but both types of musicians used the modes artfully.

> De naturali musico et artificiali. Quamvis nihil ars primo, nihil natura inveniat postremo, ut quidam asserit sapientium, expolitius tamen fiet per artem, quod incultum et hirtum naturae genitricis procedit ab utero. Ars enim ab arctis, quibus constringi conformarique debet, dicitur regulis. Nobis admodum consanguineam et naturalem esse musicam praecipue possumus ex hoc perpendere, quod quique histriones totius musicae artis [non] expertes quaslibet laicas irreprehensibiliter jubilant odas, in varia tonorum semitoniorumque positione nihil offendentes, ad finalem chordam legitime recurrentes. Unde quamvis non vere, verisimiliter tamen tractat Plato de animae genitura, dicens eam compositam musicis proportionibus. Cum enim dupla proportio, sesquitercia, sesqualtera, sesquioctava, iocunditatem

mentibus intonat, potest a gentilibus credi non incongrue animas ex eisdem proportionibus consistere, cum similitudo sit amica, dissimilitudo odiosa. Nam etiam boni bonos, reprobi diligunt perversos. Sed histriones et caeteri tales musici sunt naturales non artificiales. Artificialis autem musicus est, qui naturalem omnium specierum: diatesseron, diapente, diapason constitutionem intelligit subtiliter; qui dispositionem troporum naturae pedissequuam cognoscit rationabiliter; qui principalium chordarum operationem perpendit efficaciter; qui troporum proprietates, quae in sex chordis consistunt, tenet memoriter. Ipse quoque artis facultate optime sciat legitima comprobare, viciosa quaelibet emendare, irreprehensibiles per semetipsum cantilenas excogitare.[53]

(On Natural and Artificial Musicians. However much art should find nothing at first, so nature will find nothing afterwards. As a certain wise man said, "However more refined he may become through art, he proceeds rude and uncultivated from the womb of his natural mother." 'Art,' indeed, is derived from '*arctis'* [English 'confines'; this is a false etymology] to which it ought to be bound, and it ought to be fashioned according to rules, as it is said. In our opinion, we are especially able to judge from this that music is fully natural and transmitted through consanguinity, for every minstrel not experienced in the whole art of music can rejoice without fault in any layman's song. These minstrels offend not at all in the changeable placement of tones and semitones and can return properly to the pitch [*lit.* string] of the final. However much this may be found doubtful, nevertheless Plato treated the begetting of the soul in a more probable manner, saying that it is composed from musical proportions. When the double *proportio,* the *sesquitercia*, *sesqualtera*, and *sesquioctava* resound with delight in listeners' minds, those of better birth can hold (not incongruously) that souls are indeed composed from the selfsame proportions, considering that resemblance may be amicable, and difference displeasing. For the good also like the good, and false ones love the perverse. Yet minstrels and similar performers are natural, not artificial musicians. The *musicus* is an artificial musician, who understands precisely the natural composition of all species: *diatesseron*, *diapente*, and *diapason*. The *musicus* rationally recognizes the arrangement of tropes, the handmaid of nature. He effectually judges the effectual power of the principal notes [*lit.* strings]. He accurately remembers the properties of tropes, which depend on the hexachord [*lit.* six strings]. He is also the very one who knows best how to collect precepts by the faculty of art, to correct any faults, and to devise faultless songs through his own agency.)

Aribo, of course, was writing in Southern Germany in the eleventh century, but a passage written by the Italian humanist Paolo Cortese and published in 1510 attests to the fact that in the early sixteenth century the singing of poetry was still being described in terms of modal characteristics. In this somewhat obscure and difficult passage, Cortese associates Virgil and the poet Benedetto Gareth, known as Chariteo,[54] who improvised at the Aragon court of Ferdinando II in Naples at the turn of the sixteenth century. He then refers to another contemporary, the poet, composer, and improvisor Seraphino d'Aquilano, as having revived the style of Petrarch.

Canendi autem ratio tripartita descriptione scernitur, ex qua una phrygia, altera lydia, tertia dorica nominatur. Phrygia enim est qua animi audientium acriori vocum contentione abalienari solent, ex quo genere illa numeratur, qua Gallici musici in palatino sacello natalitiis exsuscitatiisque feriis, rituali lege utuntur, lydia autem duplex indicari potest; una quae coagmentata, altera quae simplex nominatur, coagmentata enim est qua inflexo ad dolorem modo animi ad fletum misericordiamque deducuntur, qualis ea videri potest qua novendilia pontificia ac senatoria parentalia celebrari solent, quo quidem lugubri canendi genere semper est natio hispanorum usa, simplex autem est ea, qua languidius modificata cadet, ut eos P. Maronis versus inflexos fuisse vidimus qui Ferdinando secondo auctore sunt a Caritheo poeta cani. Ut vero dorica ratio multo est aequali mediocritate temperali, or qual illud genus videri volunt quod est a Divo Gregorio un aberruncato, rio sacro statario canendi mensione institutum quocirca nostri omnem canendi rationem in litatoria, praecentoria et carmina comparando veniunt. Litatoria enim sunt ea in quibus omnia phtongorum prosodiarum, analogicarumque mensionum genere versantur et in quibus musicorum generi laus cantus praeclare struendi datur . . . Aut vero carminum modi hi numerari solent qui maxime octasticorum aut trinariorum ratione constant quod quidem genus primus apud nostros Fr. Petrarca instituisse dicit qui edita carmina canere ad lembum nuper autem Seraphinus Aquilanus princeps eius generis renovandi fuit a quo ita est verbum et cantum coniunctio modulata nexa ut nihil fieri posset eius modoque ratione dulcius. Itaque ex eo tanta imitantium auledum multitudo manavut in hoc genere Italia tota cani videtur.[55]

(The manner of singing can be perceived in a description of three parts. The first part concerns the Phrygian, the second the Lydian, and the third the Dorian, so named. In the Phrygian the souls of the listeners are usually spared the more violent exertions of voices. Included in this type is the singing of the French musicians in the Palatine chapel (according to religious usage) on saints' days and week days (when celebrated). The Lydian type can appear in two guises. The first is called "combined," the second is called "simple." In the "combined" the souls of the listeners are brought in an affecting mode to sorrow, tears, and pity, as can be seen where the pontifical *novendilia* and the senatorial *parentalia* are customarily celebrated. This type of plaintive singing has always been used by the Spanish people. The "simple" is measured more sluggishly, as we experienced when those affecting verses of Virgil were sung to Ferdinand II by the poet Chariteo. The Doric manner is in a much more temporally uniform mean, as in that type which they wish to be perceived as established by the holy Gregory, an *aberruncato*; a sacred brook calm in the meter of the singing, to which they come to procure the complete manner in which we sing *litatorial* and *precentorial* pieces and songs. *Litatorial* pieces are those in which are all the *pythongi* of proses in the type of analogical meters, and praise is given to musicians who can arrange these well. . . . These modes of songs are usually considered to correspond to the *octava rima* and *terza rima*, which are said to have been first established among us by Francesco Petrarch. Seraphino d'Aquilano, who sings the songs recently published *ad lembum*, is the foremost of those reviving this type of song. In his mode and manner he so joins text to music in measured conjunction that nothing appears more sweet. So great is the number of those imitating the accompanied singer that all Italy seems to be singing.)

Although Cortese's statement is too late to be directly connected to the compositional and improvisational practice of the fourteenth century, when seen alongside the earlier statement by Aribo it does suggest a continuity of performance style over the centuries. Cortese is still using the same frame of reference when discussing improvisation to poetry, and this brings the practice to Italy and affirms a continuum of the tradition. Additional support can be found in the connection between the monophonic *ballate*, the instrumental dances, and the melodic practices of early centuries which provides a past as well as context for the technique I have been describing.

Italian reverence for the preservation of tradition is well documented. The numerous rules that governed all formal behavior underline the importance of tradition in Italian society: the continuation of the office of civic herald, the lay confraternities over the centuries, and the existence of a myriad of other ceremonial events from the past together point to a society that placed a high value on its relationship with its heritage—one in which tradition and continuity played a very strong role.[56] In Cornazzano's poem, Pietrobono is referred to not as lutenist but as *cythariste*, affirming the connection between the fifteenth-century practice and that of the ancient *kithera* player.[57] Seen in this light the iconographic representations of the singing poets present additional evidence of a stable and long-lasting tradition. Scenes from the thirteenth through the sixteenth centuries that depict the improvising singer most often show him singing alone accompanied by his bowed instrument, which suggests an unchanged mode of performance that links the activity to a long and sustained tradition.[58] Should the format of the musical presentation have developed to include a more up-to-date setting, one might expect to see a similar evolution in the instruments found in the pictorial representation. That is to say, if the nature of the music for improvisation had changed in the late fifteenth century from lightly accompanied melody to the three- or four-part polyphonic texture of the *frottola* rather than depicting a solo singer with his lira da braccio, the later images should contain either a group of instruments or a single instrument that is more easily adapted to multiple polyphonic lines such as a keyboard instrument or a lute.[59] But it is from the sixteenth century that we have the largest number of representations of the lira da braccio. The singer of the title role in the first performance of Poliziano's *Orfeo* was praised by Lorenzo de' Medici for singing *ad lyram*, a term that not only refers to the lira da braccio but also affirms the existence of a tradition.[60]

All of these pieces of circumstantial evidence, when taken as a whole, provide a background that lends support to the conclusion that the *cantare all'improvviso* practice in the fourteenth through the sixteenth centuries was directly related to the same practice in the eleventh, twelfth, and thirteenth centuries. None of this, of course, establishes that the compositional technique I have described was the one in use. On the other hand, for a number of reasons discussed above and below, and in the absence of any other convincing model, it does emerge as the best candidate.

What I have done here is to provide analytical details that support the observations of others concerning the possible connection between one type of late medieval Italian secular monophonic composition and the improvisatory style. My purpose, however, has been somewhat different from that of earlier writers: whereas their interests were directed toward an understanding of the extant written repertory, mine has been to use the written repertory in order to discover the unwritten art of the improvisor. Since we know that improvisors often accompanied themselves while singing, I would like to continue along this line of investigation with a discussion of certain elements of the harmonic practices employed in the polyphonic repertory of this same era.

Analysis of two-part Italian compositions reveals that they follow the same basic construction principle of adherence to a modal outline as the monophonic compositions, although with some further refinements. For an example I have chosen a madrigal from one of the earliest sources of Italian secular music, the anonymous *Su la rivera* from the Rossi Codex (Example 5).[61] The most serious implication for modal analysis in this repertory derives from the fact that the two voices commonly occupy ranges that are a fourth apart. The reason for the separation probably is to allow flexibility within each of the lines without constant voice overlapping, but the result is that the two voices cannot equally express the same mode; to do that would require identical ranges. The modal consequence that results from the different ranges is exemplified in *Su la rivera*: the voices present both the authentic and plagal version of a modal pair (known as a *maneria*[62]). *Su la rivera* is in *maneria* III, sharing the final f; the upper voice is in the authentic mode 5 (range f to f with reciting tone c), whereas the lower voice is in the associated plagal, mode 6 (c to c, reciting tone a). Similar to the melodic style of *Per non far lieto*, the individual lines of *Su la rivera* proceed by decorating the notes of the modal species. The upper line exceeds its range by descending two notes below the final, thus fitting

Example 5
Su la rivera

Su la rivera. Anonymous madrigale. Rome, Bibl. Vaticana, MS. Rossi 215, fol. 6r.

Marchettus's classification of "pluperfect," whereas the lower voice limits itself to the lower notes of its mode, never rising above its reciting tone, and conforms to Marchettus's "imperfect" classification.[63] (Although the melody of *Su la rivera* is not as flamboyant as that of *Per non far lieto*, many of the other polyphonic compositions do have quite florid melodic lines—for example, the works of Lorenzo da Firenze.[64])

It is important to note that there is a limit to the extent one can use these lower lines as evidence of the kinds of details that might have been employed as an accompaniment line in improvisational practice. Nearly all of the lower lines of the polyphonic compositions in this repertory are texted and intended for vocal performance —characteristics that raise them above the category of mere accompaniment. They are melodically active and often include melodic-rhythmic gestures that mirror the upper line or are integrated with it. Because the composer wished to establish a close relationship between the lines, the upper line of *Su la rivera* exhibits a melodic-rhythmic control on a level not observed in the monophonic compositions, and a melodic relationship between the two parts that probably would not have existed should the lower part have been an instrumental accompaniment.

Even with this limitation, however, it is possible to extract the basic elements of the harmonic practices that could have applied to an improvised accompaniment. *Su la rivera*, similar to many of the early Italian two-part compositions, employs harmonies in a manner that separates them from the Northern practice. Although the hierarchy of consonant and dissonant intervals is similar to that found in all of the treatises of the fourteenth century and practised throughout Europe, the Italian compositions do not adhere to the principles of contrary motion. Parallel perfect intervals, such as those found in the first seven bars of *Su la rivera*, are commonly used, as are passages in which the two parts join in unison or octaves, such as in bars 44–45. What can be seen in the early two-part Italian compositions is a harmonic practice that intermixes on an equal footing contrary motion, parallel perfect and imperfect intervals, and unison passages. The lower line preserves the integrity of its mode by emphasizing the modally important structural notes, and at the same time it chooses from the common hierarchy of consonant intervals in accompanying the upper line, yet does not follow the other contrapuntal practices found in the treatises of the time. As a result, these compositions preserve the irregular texture common of twelfth- and thirteenth-century practices rather than the contemporary Northern practice in which a more homogenous texture was favored.

I hasten to note that this is not the only harmonic practice observed by Italian composers of the period. Many of the polyphonic compositions contain much closer observances of the Northern practice of contrary motion with avoidance of parallel perfect intervals and unison passages, and therefore produce a more homogenous harmonic texture; this is especially true of the music from the end of the fourteenth century. It is interesting to note that I was not able to choose a typical polyphonic *ballata* to demonstrate the above harmonic practice. Although the *ballate* conform modally and melodically to the descriptions above, in their harmonic execution they more closely follow the rules of Northern counterpoint (see Example 2). In this aspect they show a more studied, later compositional practice and therefore were not useful in establishing what might be an earlier and more improvisational approach to harmony. With the exception of the monophonic pieces, Italian compositions by the end of the fourteenth century more and more took on melodic practices that are similar to those found in the French repertory which have more sculptured melodic lines with clear melodic-rhythmic motives repeated throughout the composition—practices that thus provide a melodic unity not present in the more rhapsodic compositions. The Northern influence on Italian music gained momentum throughout the century, and by the 1390s the Italians had adopted French notation as well as Northern melodic and harmonic compositional practices.[65] We are fortunate that a few written compositions from the period retain what would appear to be an older system, preserving what must have been the local practice that was in vogue prior to the time when the Italians succumbed almost entirely to the Franco-Netherlandish domination of the field of written music.

My speculation from the preceding analyses is that the essence of the early improvisatory practice can be seen in the melodic orientation of the monophonic *ballate* and in the basic harmonic practices of the early madrigals. These characteristics have caused scholars in the past to speculate on their possible association with the improvisatory tradition as a way of explaining their variances from the "main stream" compositional practices. As the analyses reveal, these compositions are closely guided by the modal system, which provides a stable overall guide while leaving a great amount of latitude for invention. Each composition is guided by two principles: the form of the poetry that dictates the overall musical form, and the principle of the modal system that dictates which notes are to be emphasized. Within these constraints the details of each composition are quite free and can be described in terms of general, stylistic guiding principles rather than rules: the opening melodic flourish firmly sets either the final or the reciting tone of the mode by decorating that pitch with movement above and below; the other important notes of the mode are similarly emphasized by the use of decorative passages; and a complete feeling of cadence is avoided by the use of notes dissonant in the mode (often a step/half-step above or below the final or reciting tone).

Within this format, the stylistic elements vary widely from composition to composition. The particular melodic/rhythmic figures chosen for any one composition may or may not consist of sequential patterns, bursts of florid passages, or chromatic inflection. The amount of variation found in these details suggests that they were the choices left to personal preference and individual style. Given such clear general procedural guides, even a modestly talented singer should have been capable of improvising a composition in the basic style of those we have seen. The overall structure of a given poem would have been obvious to anyone familiar with poetry, and the principles governing modes were a basic part of every young musician's education. In that case, once the poem had been chosen, the singer need only select a mode in order to be in possession of all of the guiding principles necessary for improvising a setting similar to what we have seen in Example 4. If an accompaniment was to be added (which was often the case), it would be placed below the melody in the associated mode of the *maneria*. It would follow the basic rules of consonance, begin and end in unison with the melody, and employ the unison or fifth for internal cadences. Otherwise, the accompanying part could move freely around the notes of its mode without necessarily observing rules of contrary motion or avoiding parallel consonant intervals.

It is highly likely that these florid Italian compositions of the fourteenth and early fifteenth centuries, both monophonic and polyphonic, are direct reflections of the traditional improvisation practice of the Late Middle Ages and Renaissance. The simplicity of the basic melodic outline and the rudimentary harmonic practice would allow for the individual abilities of the singers; elaborating as much or as little as they wished, they could adapt their presentation to the needs of the occasion as well as to their own interests and talents. The essential ingredients are so flexible that once the basics of the modal system were learned, this improvisatory style could easily be adjusted and applied to any form of poetry and even to prose.

The examples I have chosen to illustrate my point about improvisation were, of necessity, not themselves improvised, and in order to accept this limitation it was necessary also to allow for the possibility that this compromise could distort the main point of my investigation. There is no doubt that certain specifics in the construction of the examples I have chosen may not have been likely in a situation where the composition was spontaneous; details such as the melodic coordination of the two parts in *Su la rivera*, for example, or the reuse of the melodic gesture up-a-third, down-a-third in bars 25–33 of *Per non far lieto*. The essence of the compositional technique, however, while allowing attention to such details, does not require it. The basic requirements are few but allow an enormous amount of flexibility on the part of an improvisor, who can adjust, elaborate, or extend the system to adapt it to any number of variables. It is an ideal musical outline to be customized according to evolving local taste as the artist sees fit. The simplicity of its basic tenets suggests a linear heritage that goes back to the historical origins of the village bard. The reliance of this system on a complete understanding of the scalar system would explain the inclusion of often lengthy and detailed descriptions of the modes even in the more advanced theoretical treatises. Previously this has been explained in terms of a reverence for earlier writings coupled with a tradition of stating the basics of the system before proceeding—which is undoubtedly true. But it is interesting to note that the treatises often do not differentiate between the instructions for written and improvised composition or between instructions for composer and performer, and from the above discussion it can be seen that for the improvisor a detailed understanding of the modes was the single most important tool.[66]

Further along this line it should also be noted that a similar understanding of the modes was the basis of the earliest Italian ornamentation instructions beginning in the sixteenth century. The manuals by Silvestro Ganassi (1535) and Girolomo dalla Casa (1584), for example, present hundreds of examples of how one could ornament various intervals, with different passages proposed depending upon the mode of the melody.[67] Even when ornamenting an existing melody, a musician had to be aware of the melodic implications of its mode and to choose the notes of his ornamental passage so that they would conform to the mode. The significance of this point is that throughout the medieval and Renaissance periods instructions for composition, improvisation, and ornamentation—all of the areas in which a musician was to create—were based on a firm knowledge of which notes in each mode were important.

The literature of the late medieval period informs us that within the improvisatory tradition, as with the written tradition, there were a number of local styles—a topic that brings us back to the findings of Nino Pirrotta's research. By establishing a connection between the Sicilian improvised tradition and attempts by late medieval North Italian composers to imitate that style, Pirrotta demonstrated the way in which North Italian composers adopted other styles into their repertory. What he identifies as recognizable elements of the southern style are details of vocabulary, text setting, melodic flourish, harmonic practice, and chromatic inflection—the kinds of considerations noted above as the elements of personal choice that could be applied to the basic framework in order to stylize a composition.[68] Another glimpse of the subject has been provided by

Walter Rubsamen with reference to two different versions of the *gustiniane Aime sospiri* by Leonardo Giustiniani.[69] In its earliest known version from c.1465, the composition is written in a simple and unornamented fashion.[70] It later appears in a highly ornate three-voice version in Petrucci's sixth book of *frottole*, published in 1505.[71] Rubsamen concludes that the later version establishes the continuation of the much earlier florid style and proposes this composition as an example of the local Venetian song style, the *aere venetiano*. James Haar has questioned how closely the Petrucci version actually resembles the *aere venetiano* and suggests that the ornate version may have been written for instruments rather than voice.[72] In any case, the Petrucci version does demonstrate a form of florid elaboration that is definitely related to the earlier practice —both vocal and instrumental—and Petrucci's inclusion in his publications of native Italian repertory of a *gustiniane* as well as a number of other regional forms illustrates the continued North Italian interest in that kind of formal and regional variety.

This investigation of the breadth and popularity of the improvisatory tradition as well as the variety of occasions on which *cantare all'improvviso* was practised expands and revises the conclusions of earlier investigations in that it suggests that there probably were many techniques as well as styles of improvisation. It also points out the need to refine what we understand by the term 'improvisation,' separating the long-lasting bardic tradition from the more ephemeral types rather than grouping all such events together as if they were a single phenomenon with a single background, technique, and purpose. The traditional style sought to preserve a legacy and therefore employed a musical format which was basically unchanged throughout the late Middle Ages and early Renaissance and which was used on formal and ceremonial occasions precisely to establish the link with the past. This is the improvisational technique that I have described above. At the same time, improvised music also would have been created in whatever were the contemporary styles of the time. Improvisation was associated with almost every occasion in which music was employed, and many of the instrumentalists and vocalists would have been capable of matching spontaneously whatever was the popular repertory and style of the time. On the occasion of a dance, for example, instrumentalists would have improvised a *saltarello*, *piva*, etc. in the latest style, which in the year 1500 would have been stylistically different from that of a century or even fifty years earlier. Since much of the popular repertory at any time was unwritten, the surviving written repertory provides only a very faint image of the variety of kinds and types of music in which a musician would have improvised.

When discussing improvisation, scholars also have included certain related traditions that were associated with specific repertory, for example the *cantasi come* practice, in which a new *lauda* text (or even an old one) was sung to the music of another composition. This custom continued over a long period of time, and therefore the choice of musical setting would have included whatever was the most popular secular music of the time as well as traditional material. A similar practice adhered to the *frottola* repertory. For those who could not improvise in the late fifteenth-century *frottola* style, a new text could be sung to music already existing, including the generic models provided by Petrucci for just such a purpose. The *cantasi come* and Petrucci models should not actually be regarded as *improvisation*, however; they more closely fit the musical category of *contrafactum* in which an existing musical setting is borrowed for a new text.

Contrary to the prevailing thought on the matter, the results of this study indicate that there does not seem to have been a direct relationship between the Petrucci models and the traditional improvisation practice. Instead, I suspect that Petrucci was providing stock settings for amateurs who wished to set poetry in the new style of the *frottola* but who were not capable of inventing a setting of their own—and who for some reason did not wish to adopt an already existing setting that was associated with another text.[73] There is no question that texts would have been set to these models; in printing them Petrucci undoubtedly was supplying a needed service, but I do not believe that they would have been the setting of choice for an improvisor. Talented musicians in every era are capable of imitating what they hear, and there is no doubt that such people existed in the late Middle Ages and Renaissance who could improvise a song or instrumental composition in the image of any known style. In his *Orlando innamorato* (1484), Boiardo describes an improvisation scene involving three performers: one sang the top, another the tenor, and the third the contratenor.[74] This, of course, would have been the newest popular style of the time, but it was probably unrelated to what was heard from the *cantimpanca*, the civic herald, or on any occasion in which it was deemed important to establish a connection with the traditional practice of *cantare all'improvviso*.

On those occasions that called for the traditional art of *cantare all'improvviso*, the singer most likely would have chosen the technique based on modal elaboration as described above. Having chosen that approach, the actual style of the improvisation undoubtedly would have been adjusted to fit the poetry, the occasion, and the musical ability of the improvisor. Because the basic format of that system establishes only the broadest of outlines, allowing the singer maximum flexibility in terms of style and performance considerations, a *ballata* text, for example, such as those sung after dinner by the aristocratic young people in the *Decameron*, could be simple or elaborate, depending on all of the criteria cited above. If the song was intended to accompany dancing, a regular rhythm would be employed, for otherwise the rhythmic flow could be less regular. If an accompaniment was desired, the singer could harmonize his melody by choosing notes from the harmonically acceptable intervals and appropriate notes of the related mode. Should the singer wish to perform in a fashionable foreign regional style such as *strambotti de Cicilia a la reale*, as did Prudenzani's Sollazzo,[75] the melodic style could be easily adjusted by adding regional style characteristics such as those described by Pirrotta in his delineation of the Sicilian style.[76] As for the civic herald and the *cantimpanca*, again the amount of elaboration and the style of presentation would have been adjusted according to subject matter (praise, criticism, love, whimsy) and the occasion (casual or formal), but the basic musical format for delivering the poetry probably would have been that of modal elaboration.

Although it may at first seem unusual to suggest that in the sixteenth century a *cantimpanca* would reject the Italian *frottola* and the Netherlandish style models in favor of a medieval format for his improvisations, I believe that is exactly what would have been done, and the documents mentioned above in conjunction with Alfonso de'Pazzi tend to support that belief. Tradition was an important and powerful influence, and the connection with the age-old role of the Italian improvisor would have been the most compelling reason for a sixteenth-century *cantimpanca* to improvise in the inherited style. As one of the few areas in which the foreign influence had been avoided, it therefore identified the singer with his

Italian heritage.

Cantare all'improvviso was a popular and well respected Italian tradition that flourished throughout the late Middle Ages and on into the seventeenth century and later.[77] It was a vehicle for serious commentary as well as entertainment, and was employed in a wide variety of social and political functions. No public ceremony would have been complete without verses sung in honor of the occasion, nor would Sunday be complete without the diversion of the *cantimpanca*. During those centuries the performances of the singing poets were probably the most frequently heard musical events in the lives of city dwellers. The ephemeral nature of the improvisors' art has deprived us of a clear impression of their presentation, but perhaps the foregoing discussion will aid us in a better understanding of the musical tools and techniques that they employed.

To take this investigation one step further, I would like to propose a practical model for the reconstruction of the format used for improvisation in Italy during the late Middle Ages and Renaissance. Rather than a complete polyphonic setting with all notes and harmonies as in the Petrucci models, what I propose is considerably simpler, allowing (and requiring) the performer to fill it in. It is an example of what I believe any trained musician could have invented in the early centuries without the need for such a written guide. Example 6 is applicable to the poetic form of a sonnet, and for purposes of clarity I have set the first stanza of a sonnet in praise of Cosimo and Lorenzo de'Medici, probably written in 1434 by the Florentine civic herald Anselmo Calderoni:[78] I have chosen *maneria* I, with the melody in the authentic mode 1 and the accompaniment in its plagal, mode 2. The first and third sections of the outline are intended to set one line of a stanza. For the first two stanzas, in which there are four lines, the second section must be repeated as marked. For the remaining three-line stanzas, no repeats are necessary. My outline suggests the range of notes (the modal species) that should be used in each section; the first and last notes in each section are those to be used to begin and end the section and are to receive the most emphasis through repetition and decoration. For a model of how to proceed melodically—the kinds of melodic, rhythmic, and ornamental gestures that would be appropriate to the style—I recommend the monophonic *ballate* of the fourteenth century such as in Example 4.[79] For the accompanying part I suggest the simplest possible line. Ideally both parts should be performed by

EXAMPLE 6
Cantare all'improvviso

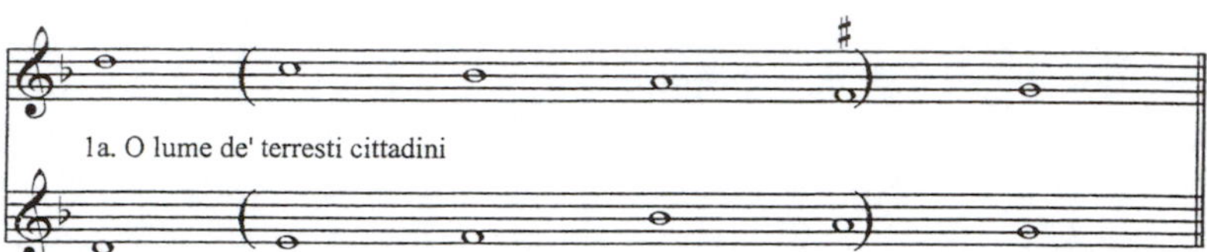

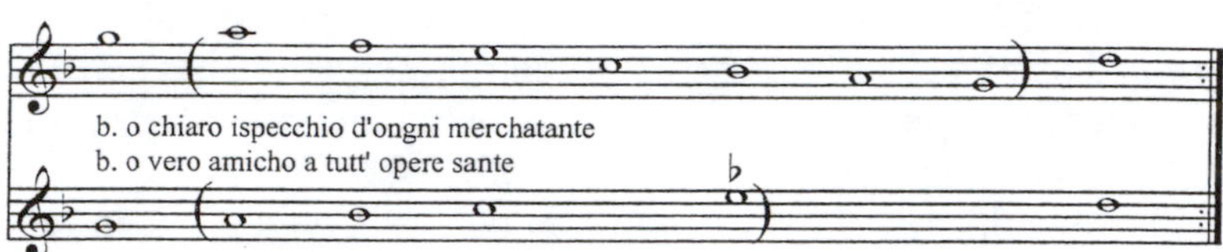

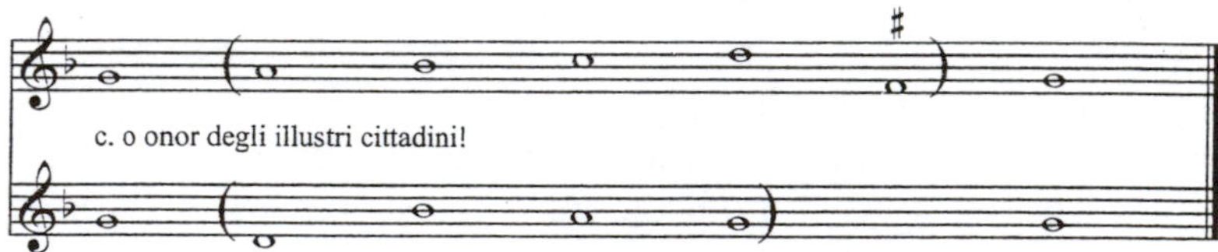

2a. O sperenza dei ghrandi e dei piccini
b. o socchoroso d'ongun ch'è bisongniante
b. o de' poprilli e vedove aiutante
c. o forte schudo de Toschan chonfini!

3a. O sopra ongn'altro a Dio charitativo
b. o prudente, o temperato, giusto e forte
c. o padre al buono, e patrigno al chattivo!

4a. O di somma pietate larghe porte
b. o aversario d'ongni atto lascivo
c. o tu che rendi per mal buone sorte!

5a. Dobbian fino alla morte
b. per Chosimo e Lorenzo tutti noi
c. poveri, preghar sempre Iddio per voi.

Author's proposed musical improvisation model for a sonnet in *maneria* 1. Opening and closing notes of each phrase establish the mode. Notes in parenthesis delineate the species of mode and therefore should be emphasized, although not in any specific order. Sonnet *O lume de'terrestri cittadini* by Alselmo Calderoni.

a single musician, but experimentation has demonstrated that with a bit of rehearsal it is possible to coordinate the efforts of two people who work from a common outline.[80]

NOTES

[1]Standard sources on the topic are Francesco Flamini, *La lirica toscana del Rinascimento anteriore ai tempi del Magnifico* (Pisa, 1891; reprint *La lirica toscana nei secoli XIII–XIV* [Bologna, 1977]); and Ezio Levi, "I cantari leggendari," *Giornale Storico della Letteratura Italiana*, suppl. no. 16 (1914).

[2]Nino Pirrotta, "Polyphonic Music for a Text Attributed to Frederick II," "New Glimpses of an Unwritten Tradition," "The Oral and Written Traditions of Music," and "Music and Cultural Tendencies in Fifteenth-Century Italy," all reprinted in *Music and Culture in Italy from the Middle Ages to the Baroque* (Cambridge: Harvard University Press, 1984), 39–50, 51–71, 72–79, 80–112. Pirrotta's ideas have been further explored by James Haar in *Essays on Italian Poetry and Music 1350–1600* (Berkeley and Los Angeles: University of California Press, 1986), "Arie per cantar stanze ariosteche," in *L'Ariosto, la musica, i musicisti*, ed. M. A. Balsano (Florence: Olschki, 1981), 31–46, and "Monophony and the Unwritten Tradition," in *Performance Practice: Music Before 1600*, ed. Howard Mayer Brown and Stanley Sadie (New York: W. W. Norton, 1989), 240–66; and by William F. Prizer, "The Frottola and the Unwritten Tradition," *Studi musicali* 15 (1986): 3–37.

[3]See Wulf Arlt, "Instrumentalmusik im Mittelalter: Fragen der Rekonstruktion einer schriftlosen Praxis," *Basler Jahrbuch für Historische Musikpraxis* 7 (1983): 32–64; Timothy J. McGee, *Medieval and Renaissance Music: A Performer's Guide* (Toronto: University of Toronto Press, 1985), 186–200, "National Styles in Fifteenth-Century Embellishment," in *Music Fragments and Manuscripts from the Low Countries; Alta Capella; Music Printing in Antwerp and Europe in the 16th Century*, Yearbook of the Alamire Foundation 2 (Leuven: Alamire, 1997), 131–46; Keith Polk, *German Instrumental Music of the Late Middle Ages* (Cambridge: Cambridge University Press, 1992), 163–213, and Polk's essay in the present volume.

[4]For a summary of earlier research into the topic as well as a presentation of a number of documents that refer to the practice, see Emil Haraszti, "La Technique des improvisateurs de langue vulgaire et de latin au Quattrocento," *Revue belge de musicologie* 9 (1955): 12–31. The most significant recent study of the tradition is Haar, *Essays on Italian Poetry and Music*, chap. 4.

[5]Dante Alighieri, *Vita Nuova*, ed. Fredi Chiappelli (Milan, 1965), 32: "falle adornare di soave armonia"; as quoted in Haar, *Essays on Italian Poetry and Music*, xvi.

[6]Giovanni Boccaccio, *Decameron*, ed. Cesare Segre (Milan: Mursia, 1966), 252–53 (translation mine).

[7]Published in Santorre Debenedetti, *Il "Sollazzo"* (Turin, 1922).

[8]See Flamini, *La lirica toscana*, 3–5.

[9]On the opera and its probable date of origin in 1480, see Nino Pirrotta, *Li Due Orfei da Poliziano a Monteverdi* (Turin: RAI, 1969), 8, translated as *Music and Theatre from Poliziano to Monteverdi*, trans. Karen Eales (Cambridge: Cambridge University Press, 1982), 6.

[10]Florence, Archivio di Stato (hereafter ASF) filza Mediceo 3645, from the Florentine agent Antimo Galli to the Florentine Secretary of State Dimurgo Lambardi, 11 November 1623. The letter is partially reproduced in Ellen Rosand, "Barbara Strozzi, *virtuosissima cantatrice*: The Composer's Voice," *Journal of the American Musicological Society* 31 (1978): 254, n. 51. Also see a short discussion of the incident in Warren Kirkendale, *The Court Musicians In Florence During the Principate of the Medici* (Florence: Olschki, 1993), 321–22.

[11]On public ceremony in Florence, see Richard C. Trexler, *Public Life in Renaissance Florence* (New York: Academic Press, 1980); and idem, ed., *The* Libro Cerimoniale *of the Florentine Republic* (Geneva: Droz, 1978).

[12]For a discussion of the function of the Florentine herald, see Suzanne Branciforte, "*Ars Poetica Rei Publicae*: The Herald of the Florentine Signoria" (Ph.D. diss., University of California at Los Angeles, 1990); and Timothy J. McGee, "Dinner Music for the Florentine Signoria, 1350–1450," *Speculum* 74 (1999): 95–114. For an account of a similar position in Siena, see Frank A. D'Accone, *The Civic Muse: Music and Musicians in Siena During the Middle Ages and the Renaissance* (Chicago: University of Chicago Press, 1997), 458–59.

[13]For a list of the many terms used to refer to the poet/musician improvisors, see Haar, *Essays on Italian Poetry and Music*, 78.

[14]For a discussion of the lira da braccio, its heritage, and its symbolism, see Emanuel Winternitz, *Leonardo da Vinci as a Musician* (New Haven: Yale University Press, 1982), chap. 4, and Sterling Scott Jones, *The Lira da Braccio* (Bloomington: Indiana University Press, 1995).

[15]Another tradition that appeared in the mid-fifteenth century was that of a *tenorista*, a second musician who performed an accompaniment for the improvisor. See discussion in Prizer, "The Frottola and the Unwritten Tradition," 10–12.

[16] For Antonio di Guido, see Bianca Becherini, "Un canta in panca Fiorentino, Antonio di Guido," *Rivista musicale italiana* 50 (1948): 241–47. It is likely that Lorenzo also improvised. His poetry is well known, and recently a

document has been found that indicates that he played the "viola," a term often used to mean the lira da braccio; see Frank A. D'Accone, "Lorenzo il Magnifico e la musica," *La Musica a Firenze al tempo di Lorenzo il Magnifico* (Florence: Olschki, 1993), 234. For an account of a *cantastoria* performing in Sicily as late as 1954, see Peter G. Evarts, "The Technique of the Medieval Minstrel as Revealed in the Sicilian *Cantastoria*," *Studies in Medieval Culture* 6–7 (1976): 117–27.

[17]Haar, *Essays on Italian Poetry and Music*, 85.

[18]ASF, Provvisioni Registri 65, fol. 102 (22 August 1375).

[19]Poem quoted in Pirrotta, "Music and Cultural Tendencies," 93–94.

[20]Pirotta, "Music and Cultural Tendencies," 94–95; see further Lewis Lockwood, *Music in Renaissance Ferrara 1400–1505* (Cambridge: Harvard University Press, 1984), chap. 10 ("Pietrobono and the Improvisatory Tradition").

[21]The remark was made when recording Antonio's death, 10 July 1486 (*Diario fiorentino dal 1450 al 1516 di Luca Landucci* [Florence: Sansoni, 1883], 51; *A Florentine Diary from 1450 to 1516 by Luca Landucci Continued by an Anonymous Writer till 1542 with Notes by Iodoco del Badia*, trans. Alice de Rosen Jervis [1927; reprint Freeport: Books for Libraries Press, 1971], 43).

[22]Letter from Michele Verino, published in Levi, "I cantari Leggendari," 2: "Audivi ego quandam Anthonium in vico Martini bella Orlandi canentem tanta eloquentia ut Petrarcham audire viderer, ut agi non referri bella putares. Legi post carmina eius, inculta ut alia crederes."

[23]Pirrotta, "Oral and Written Traditions of Music," 75.

[24]Quoted in Walter Rubsamen, "The *Justiniane* or *Viniziane* of the Fifteenth Century," *Acta musicologica* 29 (1957): 174.

[25]"Il Lasca" was the pseudonym of Antonfrancesco Grazzini.

[26]For documents and discussion, see Robert Nosow, "The Debate over Song in the Accademia Fiorentina," *Early Music History* 21 (forthcoming).

[27]For discussion of Petrucci's *frottola* publications see Prizer, "The Frottola and the Unwritten Tradition," 3–37.

[28]Ottoviano Petrucci, *Strambotti, ode, frottole, sonetti, et modo de cantar versi latini e capituli, Libro quarto* (1507; facsimile reprint Denmark: T. H. Jensen, 1991), fol. 14[r]. The sonetto is anonymous, found in Biblioteca Comunale di Mantova, MS. A.I.4, fol. 8[r], reproduced in Claudio Gallico, *Un libro di poesia per musica dell'epoca d'Isabella d'Este* (Mantua: Bolletino Storico Mantovano, 1961), 151.

[29]Prizer, "The Frottola and the Unwritten Tradition," 3–37.

[30]This connection between the *frottola* and the improvisatory tradition is also affirmed by Haar, *Essays on Italian Poetry and Music*, 87, and Anthony M. Cummings, "The Sacred Academy of the Medici and Florentine Musical Life of the Early Cinquecento," in *Musica Franca: Essays in Honor of Frank A. D'Accone*, ed. Irene Alm, Alyson McLamore, and Coleen Reardon (Stuyvesant, N.Y.: Pendragon, 1996), 72.

[31]British Library, MS. Add. 29987, fol. 59^r; for a facsimile, see *The Manuscript: London, British Museum Additional 29987*, introd. Gilbert Reaney, Musicological Studies and Documents 13 ([Dallas]: American Institute of Musicology, 1965). Only the first line of text is underlaid in the manuscript, and only in the superius. Additional lines of text, presumably those for the second *piede* and *volta*, appear at the end of the tenor. My speculation as to how these lines might be underlaid is marked off within square brackets.

[32]For a discussion of possible influences on the *frottola* style see Haar, *Essays on Italian Poetry and Music*, 45–47. Among the earliest publications to posit a relationship between Italian fourteenth-century written polyphony and improvisation are Kurt von Fischer, "On the Technique, Origin, and Evolution of Italian Trecento Music," *Musical Quarterly* 47 (1961): 41–57, and Marie Louise Martinez-Göllner, *Die Musik des frühen Trecento* (Tutzing: Schneider, 1963).

[33]Howard Mayer Brown, "Fantasia on a Theme by Boccaccio," *Early Music* 5 (1977): 329.

[34]Brown (ibid., 329) makes the point that most *lauda* texts were written in *ballata* form. There does not seem to be a connection between the surviving music for *lauda* singing and the extant composed repertory for *ballate*.

[35]On the *Lauda*, see Cyrilla Barr, *The Monophonic Lauda and the Lay Religious Confraternities of Tuscany and Umbria in the Late Middle Ages*, Early Drama, Art, and Music Monograph Series 10 (Kalamazoo: Medieval Institute Publications, 1988); Fernando Luizzi, *La lauda e i primordi della melodia italiana*, 2 vols. (Rome 1935); and Blake Wilson, *Music and Merchants: The Laudesi Companies of Republican Florence* (Oxford: Oxford University Press, 1992). On Confraternities, see John Henderson, *Piety and Charity in Late Medieval Florence* (Chicago: University of Chicago Press, 1994).

[36]Discussed in Henderson, *Piety and Charity in Late Medieval Florence*, 74–112.

[37]For a discussion of the tradition, see Giulio Cattin, "I 'cantasi come' in una stampa di laude della Biblioteca riccardiana (Ed. r. 196)," *Quadrivium* 19 (1978): 5–52.

[38]For documents and discussion, see Wilson, *Music and Merchants*, chap. 4.

[39]Pirrotta, "Polyphonic Music for a Text Attributed to Frederick II," 39–50, and "New Glimpses of an Unwritten Tradition," 51–71.

[40]Musical examples with southern characteristics are supplied in Pirrotta's articles.

[41]Pirrotta, "New Glimpses of an Unwritten Tradition," 66.

[42]Haar, *Essays on Italian Poetry and Music*, 12–20.

[43]The only other poetic form to receive written music was the *caccia*, which was given a special musical treatment owing to the interaction of the texted parts.

[44]Florence, Bibl. Medicea Laurenziana, MS. Mediceo Palatino 87 (Squarcialupi Codex), fol. 28^{r}; facsimile: *Il codice Squarcialupi: MS. Mediceo Palatino 87*, 2 vols. (Florence: Giunti Barbera, 1992).

[45]*Lucidarium* 11.2.22, 11.4.1–47. See Jan W. Herlinger, ed., *The Lucidarium of Marchetto of Padua: A Critical Edition, Translation and Commentary* (Chicago: University of Chicago Press, 1985), 378–79, 394–97.

[46]British Library, MS. Add. 29987, fols. 55^{v}–63^{v}. They are edited along with all other known medieval dances in Timothy J. McGee, *Medieval Instrumental Dances* (Bloomington: Indiana University Press, 1989).

[47]The earliest of the writers to notice the connection between this repertory and that of the Middle East was Jacques Handschin, "Über Estampie und Sequenz," *Zeitschrift für Musikwissenschaft* 12 (1929): 1–20; 13 (1930): 113–32. See a discussion of the subject in Timothy J. McGee, "Eastern Influences in Medieval European Dances," in *Cross-Cultural Perspectives on Music*, ed. R. Falck and T. Rice (Toronto: University of Toronto Press, 1982), 79–100, "Medieval Dances: Matching the Repertory with Grocheio's Descriptions," *Journal of Musicology* 7 (1989): 498–517, and *Medieval Instrumental Dances*, 23–24. Perhaps it was this resemblance to the instrumental compositions that led James Haar to remark that the florid vocal compositional style is "curiously unvocal" (*Essays on Italian Poetry and Music*, 16).

[48]A further extension of the relationship between European and Eastern Mediterranean musical practices is explored in Timothy J. McGee, *The Sound of Medieval Song: Ornamentation and Vocal Style According to the Treatises* (Oxford: Clarendon Press, 1998).

[49]For a more extensive discussion, see McGee, "Eastern Influences," 79–100.

[50]Wulf Arlt, "Instrumentalmusik im Mittelalter," 32–64; and, by the same

author, "Von der schriftlosen praxis und überlieferung zur aufzeichnung: kritisches zu den anfängen der Italienischen mehrstimmigkeit des trecento im stilwandel um 1300," *L'Ars nova Italiana del trecento* 6 (Certaldo, 1992): 127–44.

[51]The treatise was dedicated to Bishop Ellenhad of Freising in 1078; see Aribonis, *De musica*, ed. Joseph Smits van Waesberghe (Rome: American Institute of Musicology, 1951).

[52]The earliest records of the Florentine civic herald refer to him as *istrio*. See Branciforte, "*Ars Poetica*," 11.

[53]Aribonis, *De musica*, 46; translation by Randall Rosenfeld.

[54]His poetry is edited and discussed in Erasmo Percopo, *Le Rime di Benedetto Gareth, detto il Chariteo* (Naples, 1892).

[55]*Pauli Cortesii Protonotarii Apostolici Libros De Cardinalatu ad Julium Secundum Pon. Max., Proemium* (1510); quoted in Haraszti, "La Technique des improvisateurs" 27–28; translation by Randall Rosenfeld.

[56]The role of tradition and ceremony in Italian life is explored by Richard C. Trexler, in "Ritual Behavior in Renaissance Florence: The Setting," *Medievalia et humanistica* n.s. 4 (1973):125–44, and by the same author, *Public Life in Renaissance Florence* and "Ritual in Florence: Adolescence and Salvation in the Renaissance," in *The Pursuit of Holiness in Late Medieval and Renaissance Religion*, ed. Charles Trinkaus and Heiko A. Oberman (Leiden: Brill, 1974), 200–64.

[57]See Pirotta, "Music and Cultural Tendencies," 93–95, and n. 20, above.

[58]For a number of representations of the lira da braccio, see Winternitz, *Leonardo da Vinci as a Musician*, 25–39, and Haar, *Essays on Italian Poetry and Music*, pls. 2–5.

[59]The structure of the lira da braccio seriously limits its polyphonic performance capabilities to relatively slow-moving chords or drones. On the instrument see Jones, *The Lira da Braccio*; Winternitz, *Leonardo da Vinci as a Musician*, chap. 4; and Howard Mayer Brown, *Sixteenth-Century Instrumentation: The Music of the Florentine Intermedii* (Rome: American Institute of Musicology, 1973), 41–45; 223–25. Prizer, "The Frottola and the Unwritten Tradition," 8–9, believes that the instrument was capable of playing simple *frottola*-type polyphony. While this may have been possible, the difficulty in doing so suggests that it was not the type of music intended for the instrument.

[60]See Winternitz, *Leonardo da Vinci*, 30.

[61]Rome, Bibl. Ap. Vat. Rossi 215 (Rossi Codex), fol 6^{r}; for a facsimile, see

Il Codice Rossi 215, ed. Nino Pirrotta (Lucca: Libreria Musicale Italiana Editrice 1992).

[62]They are discussed by Marchettus as four modes, tropes, or tones which he calls *Protus, deuterus, tritus, tetrardus*. He then divides each of these into authentic and plagal (*The Lucidarium*, ed. Herlinger, 372–73). For a good summary of the medieval concept of mode and *maneria*, see Andrew Hughes, *Style and Symbol: Medieval Music, 800–1453* (Ottawa: Institute of Mediaeval Music, 1989), 120–26.

[63]Marchettus of Padua, *The Lucidarium*, ed. Herlinger, 382–87.

[64]Transcribed in Pirrotta, *The Music of Fourteenth-Century Italy*, vol. 3.

[65]See Michael P. Long, "Musical Tastes in 14th-Century Italy: Notational Styles, Scholarly Traditions, and Historical Circumstances" (Ph.D. diss., Princeton University, 1981), and, by the same author, "Francesco Landini and the Florentine Cultural Élite," *Early Music History* 3 (1983): 83–99; Timothy J. McGee, "The Pifferi and the Mensa of the Florentine Signoria," *Discordia concors: Perspektiven auf die Musik vor 1600*, Beiträge vom internationalen Symposion Neustift/ Novacella 1998, ed. Annegrit Laubenthal, Diskordanzen. Studien zur neueren Musikgeschichte 9 (Munich: Georg Olms Verlag, forthcoming); and Haar, *Essays on Italian Poetry and Music,* 1–21.

[66]On the intermingling of written and improvisational instructions, see the discussion in McGee, *The Sound of Medieval Song*, 4–11.

[67]Silvestro di Ganassi, *Opera intitulata Fontegara* (Venice, 1535; facsimile reprint Milan: Bolletino bibliografico Musicale, 1934); trans. Dorothy Swainson, *A Treatise on the Art of Playing the Recorder and of Free Ornamentation* (Berlin and Lichterfelde: Robert Lienaw, 1959); Girolamo dalla Casa, *Il vero modo di diminuir*, 2 vols. (Venice, 1584; facsimile reprint Bologna: Forni, 1970).

[68]Pirrotta, "New Glimpses of an Unwritten Tradition," 51–71.

[69]Walter Rubsamen, "The *Justiniane* or *Viniziane* of the Fifteenth Century," 172–84.

[70]Escorial, MS. a.24, fol. 85^{v}.

[71]Ottoviano Petrucci, *Frottole Libro Sexto: Frottole, sonetti, strambotti, Ode* (1505), fols. 85^{v}–86.

[72]See Haar, *Essays on Italian Poetry and Music*, 42–43.

[73]The adoption of a Petrucci setting would not necessarily result in the sterile performance that this might at first suggest. It was also the Italian practice to ornament whatever the musicians performed, and thus a musical singer would be

able to adjust such a stock setting to provide creative and fresh expression for each new text. For a discussion of the sixteenth-century ornamentation practice, see Howard Mayer Brown, *Embellishing Sixteenth-Century Music* (London: Oxford University Press, 1976); and Richard Erig, *Italian Diminutions*, Prattica Musicale 1 (Zurich: Amadeus, 1979).

[74]Cited in Haraszti, "La Technique des improvisateurs," 16.

[75]From the seventh day: "Quella sera cantaro ei madriale, Canzon del Cieco, a modo peruscino, Rondel franceschi de fra Bartolino, Strambotti de Cicilia a la reale" (Debenedetti, *Il "Sollazzo,"* 176).

[76]Analyses and descriptions of both the language and musical peculiarities of the Sicilian style are found in Pirrotta, "Polyphonic Music for a Text Attributed to Frederick II," 39–50, and "New Glimpses of an Unwritten Tradition," 51–71.

[77]References to nineteenth-century improvisors are cited in Haar, *Essays in Italian Poetry and Music*, 81. Bianca Becherini reports an improvised performance of *ottava rime* in a village near Pistoia as late as the first quarter of the twentieth century ("Un canta in panca Fiorentino," 241).

[78] *Sonetto di Messer Anselmo Chalderoni pur buffone, Mandò a chosimo de' Medici*; in Florence, Biblioteca Nazionale, Magl. II.II.40, fol. 114^r; Palatina 215, fol. 90^r; and Biblioteca Laurenziana Plut. 41, 34, fol. 75. Published in Suzanne Branciforte, "*Ars Poetica*," 380. The poem was possibly written to honor the Medici's return from exile in 1434. It would not have been written later than Lorenzo's death in 1440.

[79]Transcriptions of the entire repertory can be found in Pirrotta, *The Music of Fourteenth-Century Italy*, and *Polyphonic Music of the Fourteenth Century* (Monaco, 1956–), vols. 6–13.

[80]During the conference presentation of an earlier version of this paper, the technique of elaboration from an outline similar to that in Example 6 was illustrated by soprano Angela Brubaker and harpist Catherine Coyne, and I am grateful to them for their assistance. Also I wish to express my gratitude to Clifford Davidson, Andrew Hughes, and Randall Rosenfeld for assistance and advice.

Performance Practice, Experimental Archaeology, and the Problem of the Respectability of Results

Randall A. Rosenfeld

> Mr. Clibborn (the Curator of the Royal Irish Academy) informs me . . . that the late Dr. Robert Ball, of Dublin, entertained a different opinion, and believed that trumpets of this construction [*i.e.*, side-blown Irish Bronze Age horns; see fig. 1] were really musical instruments. By a strong effort of the lungs and lips, he was able to produce, on a smaller trumpet of this form in the Academy's Museum, a deep bass note, resembling the bellowing of a bull. And it is a melancholy fact, that the loss of this gentleman's life was occasioned by a subsequent experiment of the same kind. In the act of attempting to produce a distinct sound on a large trumpet . . . he burst a blood-vessel, and died a few days after.[1]

This "melancholy fact" occurred about a century and a half ago; at the time of its retelling in the early 1970s it was considered "the first and only fatality known to experimental archaeology."[2] Dr. Ball was, of course, improvising.

While there is inherent human interest in the "melancholy fact" issuing from "the subsequent experiment of the same kind," there is little in the scientific record of Dr. Ball's experiment that is of interest to current archaeology or to musicology. What is of interest, however, is that Dr. Ball thought there was something to be gained through the practical experience of sounding the Royal Academy's artifact; he believed he could prove its original function.

The nineteenth-century case of Dr. Ball—melancholy, picturesque, and perhaps pioneering—can, as a subject of reflection, bring us to the modern problem of presenting and using practical experience in a scholarly setting. The work of recent decades in recovering ornamentation and improvisation methods from medieval written sources is of greater value to performance practice than Dr. Ball's "note, resembling the bellowing of a bull," yet that

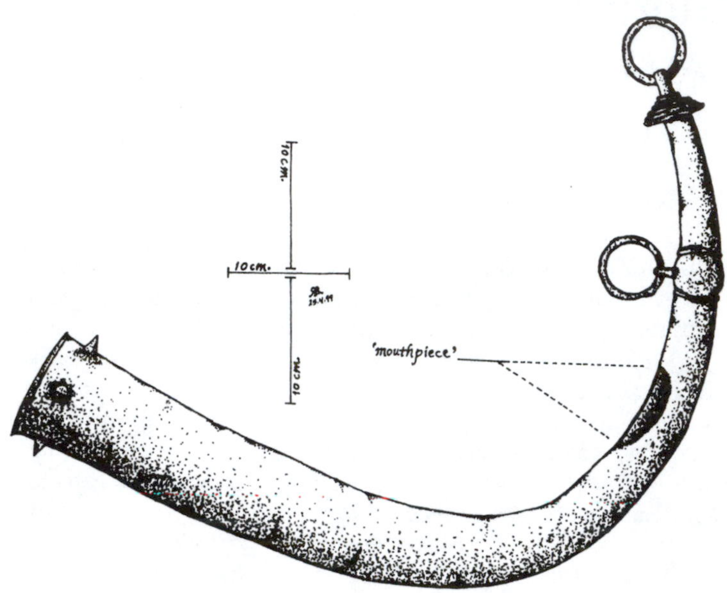

1. Irish Bronze Age side-blown horn. Copper alloy. Drawing by R. A. Rosenfeld after various examples.

note is not without resonance. Few research performance practice without the hope that their results will some day affect performances of the relevant repertoire. Musicologists can see themselves as benefactors of performers and their public. This is largely true. Do the performers benefit the musicologists? Can an historically informed performance be, as it were, a laboratory for a scholar of performance practice? The involvement of musicologists as consultants, transcribers, translators, and note writers for and even as initiators of concerts and recording projects would seem to argue that this is the case, although the desire on the part of performers and producers to legitimize a project through association with a *Fachmann* is certainly at play.[3] The Gothic Voices or certain groups from the Schola Cantorum Basiliensis can be heard as vehicles for presenting the research of, respectively, Christopher Page and Wulf Arlt. Paradoxically, there is virtually no literature on the exact goals, methods, manner of stating results or criteria for proof of any experiment in performance practice. The theory has yet to be written. This is partly due to the sheer difficulty of writing about these things. And no "experiment" in performance practice is just an experiment. There is also considerable unease about the evidential value of performances among musicologists who do not work on performance practice. A textual citation alone seems to carry far more weight in scholarly circles than does an insight gained from a performance.[4] There is, however, another discipline at the heart of which lies the practical experience of reconstructing past processes but which, unlike the performance of improvisation in historical musicology, is a standard technique in its scholarly milieu: namely, experimental archaeology. Can the methodologies, criteria for degrees of proof, and manner of stating results in experimental archaeology be applied with any success to the study of improvisation in performance practice?

I begin with a simple definition of experimental archaeology, then sketch the position of experimental archaeology within archaeology compared with that of the actual performing of improvisation in historical musicology. A brief treatment of an example of good practice in experimental archaeology leads to a consideration of how that discipline functions. I conclude by suggesting how the study of improvisation in performance practice can benefit from the example of experimental archaeology.

The matter with which I am dealing has a broader application than to improvisation in music alone; it is relevant not only to performance practice within historical musicology but also to improvisation and the performance practice of historical traditions in all the performing arts.

The artifacts we possess owe their appearance to human as well as to natural agency. Experimental archaeology is the reconstruction of the processes, man-made and natural, that culminate in the artifact in one of several states: a pristine original state, a present decayed state, or some state intermediate. An experiment may be focused not on the total artifact but on only one aspect of it—for instance, marks of wear on a single surface or the performance of a part under a particular condition. An experiment may be concerned with how an artifact may have been produced, and an experiment may be part of an array of such experiments. It is axiomatic that only those materials, equipment, and techniques either demonstrably—or at least probably—available to the original makers can be used for the reconstruction. Transparency of procedure must be maintained at all times and deviations from appropriate materials and techniques noted. I will revisit these features when considering

2. Caricature of Vere Gordon Childe. Aquarelle crayon on rag vellum, after M. Howard. Private collection, Toronto. Drawing by R. A. Rosenfeld. Reproduced by permission.

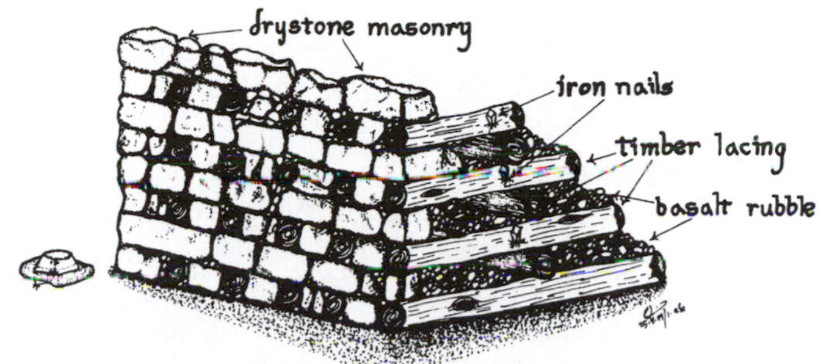

3. *Murus gallicus.* Drawing by R. A. Rosenfeld.

in more detail how experimental archaeology works. What, then, is the standing of this technique, or subdiscipline, in archaeology?

In 1937, a pre-eminent creator and annihilator of paradigms (fig. 2) and an accomplice set fire to a structure of timber-laced stone walls first at Plean Colliery, Sterlingshire,[5] and then at Rahoy, Morvern, in Argyll.[6] We know about this intentional act because it was reported in *The Proceedings of the Society of Antiquaries of Scotland* as "The Experimental Production of the Phenomena Distinctive of Vitrified Forts," by V. G. Childe and Wallace Thorneycroft.[7] Their aim was to see whether the vitrification of the walls of some Iron Age hill forts might have been due to a deliberate conflagration of their wooden elements (fig. 3).[8] Vere Gordon Childe (1892–1957), then the Abercrombie Professor of Archaeology at the University of Edinburgh, was the leading archaeological theorist of his time, and his name was a household word.[9] It is hard to think of a comparably placed musicologist, and a musicological

4. Portrait of Johannes Wolf. India ink on rag vellum. Private collection, Toronto. Drawing by R. A. Rosenfeld. Reproduced by permission.

analogue is unthinkable. It is as if Johannes Wolf (1869–1947) (fig. 4)[10] or Gustave Reese (1899–1977)[11] had decided to collaborate with God-knows-whom to provide an account of a major notational form by presenting a concert and subsequently writing it up.

Gordon Childe's willingness to seek answers through experimental archaeology is not unusual. The current archaeological textbook of choice in the English-speaking world, *Archaeology: Theories, Methods and Practices* by Lord Renfrew and Paul Bahn, lists the technique as something useful and ordinary in the professional's bag of tricks.[12] Two handbooks on the subject were published in Britain in the 1970s,[13] papers on experiments are included in prestigious journals such as *Antiquity*,[14] and monographs have appeared on everything from microwear studies of stone tools[15] or aspects of life in the Roman army[16] to the justly famous experimental earthwork project.[17] The Anglo-Hellenic trireme project alone has generated a number of papers and a series of book-length reports.[18] It is not unusual for experimental archaeology to be used to elucidate a select aspect of a modern excavation.[19] Some research facilities devoted solely to experimental archaeology are practically venerable.[20] The discipline has attracted some criticism, surprisingly little of it hostile and most of it concerned with improving procedure or theory.[21]

The investigation of improvisation through performance has no such sure place within historical musicology—yet. There are very good general texts on medieval music currently available;[22] many make some reference to performance matters;[23] none recommend the performance of improvisation as a serious research tool.[24] Works of varying degrees of usefulness on performance practice for performers have existed for some time.[25] These are, quite reasonably, directed towards providing musicians with answers to quotidian problems of performance rather than to framing research programs. Critical academic source-study of medieval vocal improvisation has only just begun.[26] An important recent monograph does acknowledge the benefit to be derived from experiment in understanding written descriptions and notation, although it is not the author's purpose to detail how this is done.[27] Work on instrumental improvisation will derive in important respects from that on vocal improvisation. For instrumental music proper, one of the best expositions of a particular tradition of improvisation is found in Keith Polk's study of late-medieval German music.[28] It would be relatively simple to base an experimental program on his admirably clear and detailed account. Ernst Ferand's pre-war *magnum opus* retains some interest, but, as with his other writings, descriptive and speculative, it shows its age.[29] Like the studies of Imogene Horsley[30] and Howard Mayer Brown[31] for the Renaissance, all these works are necessary *prolegomena* to the investigation of improvisation through performance, but they do not describe methodology, criteria for degrees of proof, limitations, or modes of stating results. Papers by Kenneth Zuckerman[32] and Lorenz Welker[33] satisfy the first requirement—and possibly the third—and in some respects are most promising, but they stand alone. There are no handbooks on the investigation of improvisation through performance and no institutions devoted primarily to that work.[34]

I now turn to experimental archaeology in action and will make use of a notable example from a particular area of the field. Over the last half-century underwater archaeology, particularly in its naval aspects, has seen much activity in speculative ship reconstruction. One of the most notable and recent examples is the Anglo-Hellenic project centered around the trireme Olympias and her projected successor(s).[35]

The exact nature of the warships of Greco-Roman antiquity has been the subject of controversy since the day antiquaries were abroad and stalked the land.[36] Learned disagreement seems scarcely avoidable, given the abundance of meager, imprecise, and perplexing textual references; the host of iconographic sources

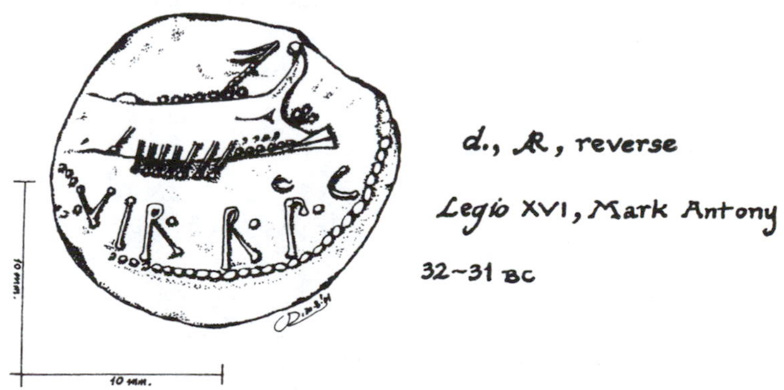

5. Solidus, Æ, reverse, Legio XVI (Mark Anthony), 32–31 B.C., showing late-republican Roman trireme. Drawing by R. A. Rosenfeld after various examples.

abbreviated through design, or damage (fig. 5); and the spectacularly scant remains of ancient warships, some possibly anomalous.[37] A principal mystery has traditionally been the internal disposition of the files of rowers;[38] but many other features of construction, techniques of operation, and levels of performance were and are not settled.[39] A British group, the Trireme Trust, was formed to investigate those very mysteries. One tool that was decided on was the Olympias, a hypothetical reconstruction of a trireme from the fifth or fourth century B.C.: "Owing to the sparseness of direct and reliable evidence from ancient sources, this [i.e., building and operating reconstructions of ships] is now virtually the only means of learning with any confidence how ancient warships could be worked."[40] The ship was designed by John F. Coates, a highly experienced naval architect formerly with the Royal Navy who benefitted from the extensive historical research and knowledge of his colleague in the Trust, John S. Morrison, and others. Every scrap of historical evidence they believed relevant was considered;[41] the techniques and materials of ancient boat building were respected to the extent that Morrison and Coates deemed reasonable and practicable;[42] and crews were recruited, selected, and trained.[43] The

6. "Scientific Method."

ship was constructed at Piraeus under contract to the Hellenic Navy. A program of trials was devised and pursued, and these led to adjustments and more trials.[44] The results of the major trials have been—or are in the process of being—published fully, promptly, and honestly.

Coates' general approach to design is worth quoting: "A naval architect attempting to reconstruct ancient Mediterranean warships is offered scanty . . . evidence on which to draw. It is, however, generally accepted that these ships were relatively fast for oared vessels, and when the demands of the laws of physics and our present knowledge of human ergonomics are brought to bear, the room for choice in features of their design affecting performance under oar is greatly narrowed. In many cases main hull dimensions, stability, oar power, lengths, gearing and rig, and longitudinal hull structure can be determined within quite close limits by such considerations."[45] To this can be added his evaluation of the ship's real importance: "Owing to the loss since antiquity of all practical knowledge of triereis, this ship [the Olympias] is virtually a prototype."[46] It is important to note that, for the most part, the principals in the Trust have not claimed that Olympias is anything other than a reconstruction of a trireme, a floating hypothesis;[47] she was the Trust's best solution at the time she was researched, designed, and built.

The many problems revealed through the course of the project represent a real advance in knowledge about this class of ancient warship. Some difficulties at the planning and construction stage concerned materials. Oak and Mediterranean pine or fir of the length thought to have been employed in ancient warships are not available today. Alternatives as close as possible to those species had to be chosen. These turned out to be iroko (*Chlorophora excelsa*) and Douglas fir (*Pseudotsuga menziesii*), which, incredible to say, could not be found of the desired "ancient" length.[48] An authentically tight fit for the tenons proved extremely difficult to achieve.[49] This is crucial, for without that feature a wood ship of "shell-first" construction measuring 36.8 meters in overall length and 5.45 meters in breadth will be subject to unavoidable longitudinal shearing of the hull (termed "hogging").[50] After the first trial it was clearly necessary to inject the mortices with epoxy because the fit of the tenons was not sufficiently tight. Coates, who labels this a "wholly inauthentic operation," believes that ancient shipwrights had no choice but to ensure the tightest fit for the tenons.[51]

The other problems which arose during the trials were equally instructive. I will mention one. To quote Coates again: "The sea trials of *Olympias* demonstrated the importance of an *interscalmium* (the oarsman's 'room') of adequate length to allow the full length of oarstroke. . . . In *Olympias* the *interscalmium* has the length of two cubits of 0.444 metres, understood from the evidence extant at the time of her design and building to be the length of an Attic cubit. More recent metrological finds have shown that the cubit in use in Peiraios and Salamis in the 5th–4th cent. BC was more likely to have been 0.490m in length. . . ."[52] It was not the new evidence of the longer cubit which indicated the problem, however, but something more interesting:

> The most striking feature of the performance of both crews was the ineffectiveness of the thalamians [the lowest file of rowers] . . . [for they] were quite simply afraid of the consequences of pulling hard. This was the case despite the provision for the Trireme Trust's crew of "preventer stays" whose function was to arrest the oarhandle to keep it from pinning the rower against a crossbeam if he or she should get into difficulties. The implication is that ship beams—the *zyga*—had powerful psychological effect, inhibiting the thalamians. . . .[53]

The practical experience of using the ship led to a re-examination of the ancient metrological evidence and of the ship's design. Using the larger cubit to increase the *interscalmium* is one possible way to bring the ship's performance closer to that of the Trust's reading of the ancient evidence.[54]

Several further features of the Olympias trials should be noted. Various results of the experiments, where quantifiable, were measured using modern scientific instruments—for example, the power in watts of a rower at a particular stroke rate over a particular time measured with an ergometer,[55] or the ship's speed measured with a land-based geodimeter or with a shipboard global positioning system (GPS).[56] Experiments were sometimes hampered by the limitations in the skills, preparedness, and attitude of the experimenters.[57] Finally, the reports are scrupulous not only in detailing unsatisfactory compromises regarding material, design, and building and trial techniques but also in recording results which revealed errors in the conceptions of the planners. Further, they are equally careful in declaring errors in data and interpretation in addition to recording changes and limitations in the trials.[58] It is this mature and critical approach to reporting which gives the record of their work its exemplary value.

The requirements for a successful archaeological experiment can now be set out. I base the following points on the Olympias project as presented here and on an expanded and systematized version of the suggestions for procedure given by John Coles in *Archaeology by Experiment*:[59]

> 1. Materials used should be those available to the original craftsmen, or craftswomen.
>
> 2. Techniques should be those of the time, place, and activity under investigation.[60]
>
> 3. Modern technicians should not be incompetent, inexperienced, or inexpert as regards 1 and 2 above.[61]
>
> 4. Modern technicians must be fully informed of the goals of the experiment, and be sympathetic to its aims, unless the experiment design requires them to be uninformed or unsympathetic.
>
> 5. Observing 1 and 2 above, modern materials and technologies should play as little a role as possible in the experiment. Where they are necessary, their use should be controlled, and recorded.[62]
>
> 6. Parameters, qualifications, and limits to an experiment should be clearly formulated.
>
> 7. Experiments in sequence should be consistent, for the sake of ease in making significant comparisons and observing cumulative effects.
>
> 8. Experiments should be developed and run with reference to previous trials.
>
> 9. All possible ways of achieving the result, provided they are in accordance with 1 and 2 above, should be investigated.
>
> 10. The experiment should be reproducible, where appropriate.[63]
>
> 11. Results must be stated as accurately as possible, with all necessary qualifications, chief among which is that *a successful experiment provides only one possible way something may have been done.*

12. The experiment must be published as fully, transparently, and rigorously as possible. Prompt publication is desirable, but ought not to be achieved through the sacrifice of rigor, transparency, or fullness.

13. Evidence from other cultures can be introduced in a controlled way when interpreting results, or even earlier in the planning and design stages of the experiment.[64]

Before returning to improvisation in performance practice, I should make one further observation. An experiment must be fit not only for the sort of questions the researcher wishes to explore, but it must also respect the nature of the materials and the area of research. The questions which prompt an experiment must be ones which can reasonably be asked of the materials and techniques. It is a naive misconception to expect that all trials must be conducted under the shelter of a single "scientific" method or that all experiments must conform to a formulaic and rigid recipe (fig. 6). This is a myth well known to those who work in labs or who think on the epistemology of science, but it seems less well known to those in the humanities.[65] There are as many "scientific" methods as there are experimenters; each takes account of what constitutes good practice in his or her field.

Reviewing the requirements for a successful archaeological experiment reveals that the method seems adaptable or adoptable for the investigation of improvisation in performance practice. There are, however, certain difficulties which have to be acknowledged. The first and possibly most serious is that the very artifact in which we are interested no longer exists.[66] We have vestiges of that artifact in manuscript sources, treatise references, iconography, remnants of instruments, and places of performance.[67] The situation is not unlike that faced by the investigators of ancient Greek warships; they have scarcely more in the way of direct artifacts than have the scholars of performance practice—and improvisation is among the most difficult of subjects to be investigated, whatever the method chosen.

Following the suggestions for procedure does pose problems. Authentic materials, appropriate techniques—these keystones to an edifice of experiment can prove difficult to discover or to put in place by those seeking to study improvisation. We will not always know where in the structures of medieval music improvisation happened and why.[68] Changes in human physiology which have occurred since the Middle Ages may have to be taken into account when planning an experiment, stating limitations, or interpreting results.[69] If improvising on instruments, are they indeed appropriate to time and place, and to that which is being attempted?[70] It is certain that we have virtually no direct information on many techniques,[71] and that which we do have on other practices can seem incomplete or confusing.[72] This is not a worse situation than that faced by those who investigate the trireme problem. If we had full information, there would be little point in investigation.

The competence of experimenters is a point worth much reflection. How do we know that someone is competent to perform an experiment in improvisation? The trireme investigators have ancient descriptions of voyage duration and distance—that is, of performance—and we have ours. There are examples of very ornate fifteenth-century intabulations,[73] and there are descriptions of performers such as Pietrobono (fig. 7).[74] One can expect that musicians of over half a millennium ago were more than competent, particularly if they were worth holding by d'Este money or with *fiorini d'oro*. Full control of the voice or of other requisite instruments should be expected of anyone who would stand in for one of the Signoria's musicians, then as now.[75] Non-Western classical traditions at their highest levels may provide some useful insights into this question.

7. Medal, Æ, obverse. Portrait of Pietrobono del Chitarino (de Burzellis, ?1417–97), "who surpasses Orpheus," by Giovanni Boldù, dated 1457. Drawing by R. A. Rosenfeld after various examples.

If concert performers who specialize in medieval music are chosen to participate in an experiment, care must be taken that they are sympathetic to the project (suggestion 4 above) and that they are flexible in their approach.[76] Concert performances of medieval music may not be the best venue for performing experiments in improvisation for a variety of reasons.[77] Nor are compact disks, at present, an ideal form for presenting the results of experiments.[78]

Could not the search for every possible and historically justifiable way of doing something involve endless experiment?[79] Yes, but reasonable limits should be set. Some ways may seem more likely than others, or some may accord better with the evidence; and some may not be practicable during a particular run of experiments. Only one reconstructed trireme has been built; although there are competing theories about trireme construction, funds have not been available to move other hypothetical triremes from the drafting board to the water.[80] This does not prevent the same test with different variables from being run on the trireme reconstruction that does exist.[81] Publish what has been assayed, and note what hasn't been tested in the current trials.

A requirement of reproducibility may appear incompatible with an experiment in improvisation. This view is erroneous. Variability, of one sort or another, is a characteristic—indeed an *authentic* characteristic—of musical improvisation. The requirement for reproducibility should be tailored to the phenomenon investigated. The requirement can be satisfied on various levels: by limiting a test and its replications to one genre of music or to a single piece; by limiting the mode of improvisation to a single style; or by running the test and its replications with the same forces or experimenters.

The benefits of adopting the procedures of experimental archaeology are many, but the chief one is that it offers a way to use critically controlled performances as evidence in the scholarly literature—evidence supplemental to that of more traditional sources, evidence which can be used when there is nothing from more traditional sources.[82] The clear formulation of parameters, qualifications, and limits to an experiment, the accurate statement of results with necessary qualifications, and full, transparent, and rigorous publication would make that possible. The respectability of results depends as much on how they are presented as on any other factor.

Performance practice viewed from within experimental archaeology has much to offer that science.[83] It could chiefly provide experimental investigations of process, which would help clarify the issues around reconstructing artifacts as evanescent as sound. Experiments in performance practice would be relatively inexpensive to mount compared to many other experiments in archaeology even if they involved specially commissioned hardware, instruments, or training. And presenting the range of possible ways of achieving a result is considerably easier in the field of improvisation in performance practice than it is in underwater archaeology where a different ship has to be built for every floating hypothesis.

I conclude with a suggestion for an experiment. Many descriptions of elements of improvisation in medieval sources can be interpreted in more than one way.[84] This may be due to an author's particular use of terminology, level of style, oddities of grammar, or syntax; or it could be due to some lack in the information available to us. It would be invaluable to explore the range of supportable interpretations through performing them. At the very least this will (1) vividly demonstrate our range of understanding of each of the elements of improvisation under investigation; (2) show what in the treatise descriptions seems clear as a performance indication and what does not, and will therefore require more philological work; and (3) demonstrate what music sounds like with the different interpretations of the elements of improvisation under investigation, and what those interpretations suggest was heard by contemporary auditors and transmitted. Each interpretation would have to be presented with a fully referenced textual explication and justification along with a clear description of how each is performed, an audio record of the trials, and, if desired, a visual record. This will reveal much that is not expected and certainly much that has so far not been heard—and, most valuably, much which could have been heard five hundred or more years ago. I for one am quite willing to live with indeterminate data, intelligently won.[85]

NOTES

I wish to thank Andrea Budgey for helpful comments on this paper, and Timothy McGee and Domenico Pietropaolo for the invitation to take part in this project. I should also mention help cheerfully rendered by the staff of the library of the Royal Ontario Museum.

While this paper was in course of publication, John S. Morrison and Peter J. Reynolds, figures who made capital contributions to the field of experimental archaeology, passed away. This paper is dedicated to their memory.

[1]Robert MacAdam, "Ancient Irish Trumpets," *Ulster Journal of Archaeology* 8 (1860): 101; John Coles, *Archaeology by Experiment* (London: Hutchinson, 1973), 165. In relation to another and more recent experiment, Owain T. P. Roberts has written: "Experimental archaeology should not include the possibility of killing people as a result of uncertain factors in vulnerable areas" ("The Sailing Rig of Olympias," in *The Trireme Project: Operational Experience 1987–90, Lessons Learnt*, ed. Timothy Shaw [Oxford: Oxbow Books, 1993], 31). Needless to say, under normal circumstances the hazard is greater in testing a reconstruction

of an ancient ship than in, say, improvising a *basse danse*. Dr. Ball's ill luck may have had as much to do with his technique as anything else. Peter Holmes, "The Manufacturing Technology of Irish Bronze-Age Horns," in *The Origins of Metallurgy in Atlantic Europe: Proceedings of the Fifth Atlantic Colloquium*, ed. Michael Ryan (Dublin: Stationery Office, 1978), 179–80, warns against applying the tight, compressed embouchure of modern brass playing to side-blown horns and suggests the didjeridu as a useful conceptual analogue.

[2]Coles, *Archaeology by Experiment*, 165.

[3]A desire not dissimilar from archaeologists calling upon their "bone man/woman" (osteopathologist/zoologist), "rock man/woman" (geologist/petrologist), "seed man/woman" (paleoethnobotanist), etc.

[4]Christopher Page is one of the few who have attempted to introduce insights from performance openly in scholarly analysis of medieval music; see his *Discarding Images: Reflections on Music and Culture in Medieval France* (Oxford: Clarendon Press, 1993), 103–10, 165; also see Lorenz Welker, "'Alta capella'—zur Ensemblepraxis der Blasinstrumente im 15. Jahrhundert," *Basler Jahrbuch* 7 (1983): 155–57, 162–65. A change seems to be occurring in the discipline as ever more reputable musicologists are willing to state that performance is of some value; see note 31, below. There seems, however, to be uncertainty over the way to introduce the "evidence" gained from performances into learned discourse.

[5]Now Sterling, Central Region.

[6]Now Argyll and Bute, Strathclyde.

[7]Vere Gordon Childe and Wallace Thorneycroft, "The Experimental Production of the Phenomena Distinctive of Vitrified Forts," *Proceedings of the Society of Antiquaries of Scotland*, 6th ser. 12 (1937–38): 45–55. Some of Childe's and Thorneycroft's conclusions have been verified through petrological analysis; see K. Fredriksson, E. Youngblood Anthony, and B. J. Fredriksson, "The Celtic Vitrified Forts," in *The Petrology of Archaeological Artefacts*, ed. D. R. C. Kempe and Anthony P. Harvey (Oxford: Clarendon Press, 1983), 154–70. A similar experiment, attempted fifty years later, met with only partial success; see Ian Ralston, "The Yorkshire Television Vitrified Wall Experiment at East Tullos, City of Aberdeen District," *Proceedings of the Society of Antiquaries of Scotland* 116 (1986): 17–40.

[8]It should be noted that fig. 3 does not show the complete wall structure. Omitted are the turf ramparts and other organic material which may have been included in the interior.

[9]For monographs on Childe, who later became the Director of the Institute of Archaeology at the University of London, see Bruce G. Trigger, *Gordon Childe: Revolutions in Archaeology* (London: Thames and Hudson, 1980); Barbara

McNairn, *The Method and Theory of V. Gordon Childe: Economic, Social, and Cultural Interpretations of Prehistory* (Edinburgh: Edinburgh University Press, 1980); and Sally Green, *Prehistorian: A Biography of V. Gordon Childe* (Bradford-on-Avon: Moonracker Press, 1981). The proceedings of four conferences devoted to Childe were published in the 1980s and 1990s.

[10]Lothar Hoffman-Erbrecht, "Johannes Wolf," in *The New Grove Dictionary of Music and Musicians*, ed. Stanley Sadie, 20 vols. (London: Macmillan, 1980), 20:502–03.

Daniel Leech-Wilkinson, "Yearning for the Sound of Medieval Music," *Mittelalter Sehnsucht?* ed. Annette Kreutziger-Herr and Dorothea Redepenning (Kiel: Universität Heidelberg, 2000), 295–317, argues that early twentieth-century performances of medieval music had some effect on European musicologists' perception of their subject, yet on the whole it was the writings of the musicologists which shaped the performances; and no musicologist cited evidence from a performance as "evidence."

[11]James Haar, "Gustave Reese," *The New Grove Dictionary of Music and Musicians*, 15:668–69.

[12]Colin Renfrew and Paul Bahn, *Archaeology: Theories, Methods and Practice*, 2nd ed. (London: Thames and Hudson, 1996), 49, 258–59, 301–11, 314–15, *passim*; 3rd ed. (2000), 53, 200, 274–75, 542. See also Philip Barker, *Techniques of Archaeological Excavation*, 2nd ed. (London: Batsford, 1982), 254–67 (the third edition of this work [1993] was not available to me).

[13]Coles, *Archaeology by Experiment*, and John Coles, *Experimental Archaeology* (London, New York, Toronto: Academic Press, 1979). To Coles's typologies of experiments can be added that of Peter J. Reynolds, "The Nature of Experiment in Archaeology," in *Experiment and Design: Archaeological Studies in Honour of John Coles*, ed. Anthony F. Harding (Oxford: Oxbow, 1999), 158–62.

[14]Paul Ashbee and Peter Jewell, "The Experimental Earthworks Revisited," *Antiquity* 72 (1998): 485–504.

[15]E.g., Irene Levi Sala, *A Study of Microscopic Polish on Flint Implements*, BAR Tempus Reparatum International Series 629 (Oxford: British Archaeological Reports, 1996); a rather different sort of study is John C. Whittaker, *Flintknapping: Making and Understanding Stone Tools* (Austin: University of Texas Press, 1994).

[16]The curious can read in Marcus Junkelmann, *Die Legionen des Augustus* (Mainz am Rhein: Philip von Zabern, 1986), of a first/twentieth-century "experience" of a centurion (Junkelmann), eight legionaries (his colleagues), two mule drivers and their charges equipped with accurate reproductions of appropriate military gear doing the milder sorts of things accurate and appropriate to Augustus's soldiers in a march from Verona to Augusta Vindelica (Augsburg). The

report contains much of real value, along with humor and occasional whimsy.

[17]*The Experimental Earthwork Project 1960–1992*, ed. M. Bell, R. J. Fowler, and S. M. Hillson, Council for British Archaeology Research Report 100 (York: Council for British Archaeology, 1996).

[18]*An Athenian Trireme Reconstructed: The British Sea Trials of Olympias, 1987*, ed. John S. Morrison and John F. Coates, BAR International Series 486 (Oxford: British Archaeological Reports, 1989); John F. Coates, Stavros K. Platis, and J. Timothy Shaw, *The Trireme Trials 1988: Report on the Anglo-Hellenic Sea Trials of Olympias* (Oxford: Oxbow Books, 1990); *The Trireme Project: Operational Experience 1987–90, Lessons Learnt*, ed. Shaw; *Trireme Olympias: The Final Report. Sea Trials 1992–4. Conference Papers 1998*, ed. N. Boris Rankov (forthcoming). For a convenient summary of the trials, see John S. Morrison, John F. Coates, and N. Boris Rankov, *The Athenian Trireme: The History and Reconstruction of an Ancient Greek Warship*, 2nd ed. (Cambridge: Cambridge University Press, 2000), 191–275. Papers, reviews, and controversies are best followed in *The Mariner's Mirror*, *International Journal of Nautical Archaeology*, and *Antiquity*.

[19]Levi Sala, *A Study of Microscopic Polish*, 20–27.

[20]E.g., Butser Ancient Farm (Nexus House, Gravel Hill, Waterlooville, Hampshire, P08 0QE: http://www.butser.org.uk: accessed 15 February 2002), and Lejre Historisk-Archæologisk Forøgscenter (Slangealleen 2, 4320 Lejre, Denmark: http://www.lejre-center.dk/: accessed 15 February 2002). Recent accounts are Peter Reynolds, "Butser Ancient Farm, Hampshire, UK," in *The Constructed Past: Experimental Archaeology, Education and the Public*, ed. Peter G. Stone and Philippe G. Planel (London: Routledge, 1999), 124–35; Marianne Rasmussen and Bjarne Grønnow, "The Historical-Archaeological Experimental Centre at Lejre, Denmark: 30 Years of Experimenting with the Past," in *The Constructed Past*, 136–45.

[21]E.g., Ruth Tringham, "Experimentation, Ethnoarchaeology, and the Leapfrogs in Archaeological Method," in *Explorations in Ethnoarchaeology*, ed. Richard A. Gould, School of American Research Advanced Seminar Series (Albuquerque: University of New Mexico Press, 1978), 169–99; Pascale B. Richter, "Experimentelle Archäologie: Ziele, Methoden und Aussage-Möglichkeiten," in *Experimentelle Archäologie: Bilanz 1991*, ed. Mamoun Fansa, Archäologische Mitteilungen aus Nordwestdeutschland 6 (Oldenburg: Isensee, 1991), 19–49. One of the few hostile treatments is Timm Weski, "Experimentelle Archäologie: Ausgewählte Beispiele experimenteller Archäologie aus dem Bereich der Unterwasserarchäologie," in *DEGUWA* [= *Deutsche Gesellschaft zur Förderung der Unterwasserarchäologie*] *Rundbrief* 12 (Feb. 1997) (http://www.abc.se/~m10354/bld/exp-beisp.htm; accessed 15 February 2002). On the other hand, Peter Reynolds's recent call for more rigorous standards in experimental archaeology is timely ("The Nature of Experiment in Archaeology,"156–57).

[22]E.g., Andrew Hughes, *Style and Symbol: Medieval Music 800–1453* (Ottawa: Institute of Mediaeval Music, 1989); David Fenwick Wilson, *Music of the Middle Ages: Style and Structure*, 2 vols. (New York: Schirmer, 1990).

[23]E.g., Hughes, *Style and Symbol*, 494–511; Wilson, *Style and Structure*, 6, 11–12, and *passim*.

[24]In fairness, fault should not be found with these authors for omitting a practice which is not part of the field they are presenting to neophytes. Interestingly, both Andrew Hughes and David Wilson have extensive experience in directing performances.

[25]E.g., *Performance Practice: Music Before 1600*, ed. Howard Mayer Brown and Stanley Sadie, New Grove Handbooks in Music 1 (London: Macmillan, 1989) (a most useful compendium); *Companion to Medieval and Renaissance Music*, ed. Tess Knighton and David Fallows (1992; reprint Oxford: Oxford University Press, 1998); Timothy J. McGee, *Medieval and Renaissance Music: A Performer's Guide* (Toronto: University of Toronto Press, 1985); *A Performer's Guide to Medieval Music*, ed. Ross W. Duffin (Bloomington: Indiana University Press, 2000).

[26]Timothy J. McGee, *The Sound of Medieval Song: Ornamentation According to the Treatises* (Oxford: Clarendon Press, 1998).

[27]Ibid., xi.

[28]Keith Polk, *German Instrumental Music of the Late Middle Ages: Players, Patrons and Performance Practice* (Cambridge: Cambridge University Press, 1992), esp. 163–213. The experiment reported by Welker ("'Alta capella'—zur Ensemblepraxis der Blasinstrumente im 15. Jahrhundert," 119–65) is an attempt at reproducing the improvisatory practices of musicians of the fifteenth century; it predates Polk's monograph by nearly a decade.

[29]Ernst Ferand, *Die Improvisation in der Musik: eine entwicklungsgeschichtliche und psychologische Untersuchung* (Zürich: Rhein-Verlag, 1938).

[30]Imogene Horsley, "Improvised Embellishment in the Performance of Renaissance Polyphonic Music," *Journal of the American Musicological Society* 4 (1951): 3–19.

[31]Howard Mayer Brown, *Embellishing Sixteenth-Century Music* (Oxford: Oxford University Press, 1976). That Brown considered performance an important technique in the effort to understand music is stressed by Victor Coelho, "Revisiting the Workshop of Howard Mayer Brown: [Josquin's] *Obsecro te domina* and the Context of Arrangement," in *". . . La musique, de tous les passetemps le plus beau. . . :" Hommage à Jean-Michel Vaccaro*, ed. François Lesure et Henri Vanhulst (Paris: Klincksieck, 1998), 47: "Whether he was editing a Florentine *chansonnier*, publishing images of *trecento* angel musicians, or provoking cross-

Atlantic furor for his cheeky observations about the 'English *a capella* heresy,' Howard Mayer Brown was convinced that performers held the secrets to understanding Renaissance music . . . since performance was essentially a large repertory of *solutions*." This sensible approach can be detected underlying much of what Brown wrote, although it was rarely, if ever, allowed to appear directly in his published work. Another statement on the value of performances is Theodore Karp, "Evaluating Performances and Editions of Aquitanian Polyphony," *Acta Musicologica* 71 (1999): 21, 49.

[32]Kenneth Zuckerman, "Improvisation in der mittelalterlichen Musik—eine Suche nach Lernmodellen," *Basler Jahrbuch für historische Musikpraxis: Improvisation in der Musik des Mittelalter und der Renaissance* 7 (1983): 65–83. This is a valuable contribution, although in many ways it does not come up to the standards recommended for archaeological experiments below. Zuckerman explores the problem of recovering and replicating the methods of instruction used by medieval instrumentalists through focusing on the processes of teaching and learning improvisation. He uses his experience of a particular classical tradition of North India as an analogical tool. The work of Lewis Binford suggests itself by way of an (ethno-)archaeological parallel.

[33]Welker ("'Alta capella'—zur Ensemblepraxis der Blasinstrumente im 15. Jahrhundert," 155–57, 162–65) serviceably and honestly reports an experiment to replicate the improvisatory practices of an *alta capella* ensemble performing the *basse danse* repertoire. Unfortunately, the results are uncomfortably far from surviving examples (and the analyses and suggestions for procedures offered in Polk, *German Instrumental Music*, esp. 163–213). Interestingly, though the rhythmic movement seems within the bounds of surviving models, the melodic motifs and direction are not.

[34]Both the Schola Cantorum Basiliensis and Indiana University's Early Music Institute offer training in improvisation as a component of their programs.

[35]See John S. Morrison, with contributions from John F. Coates, *Greek and Roman Oared Warships* (Oxford: Oxbow Books, 1996), 279 and *passim*; Morrison *et al.*, *The Athenian Trireme*, xvii–xxviii; and other work cited in n. 18, above. The best, and most accessible series of photographs of Olympias can be found on the *Perseus Encyclopedia*, Perseus Project: an Evolving Digital Library, editor-in-chief Gregory Crane (Tufts University), 'Trireme' entry (http://www.perseus.tufts.edu/cgi-bin/vorlookup=trireme; accessed 15 February 2002).

[36]J. Timothy Shaw, "A Summary of the 'Trireme Controversy'," in *The Trireme Project*, ed. Shaw, 1–3 (*breviter*); Morrison *et al.*, *The Athenian Trireme*, 8–24.

[37] My colleague Bryan Martin has kindly informed me of the announcement made several years ago (*Agence France-Presse*, Rome, 14 April 1999) of the discovery of a "fleet" of Roman ships near Pisa, at least one of which may be a

warship. This identification by the excavators has been challenged. The verifiable discovery and competent recovery of the remains of any Roman warship would be of considerable importance for the understanding of the equipment of Roman sea power. It could also be, in many respects, a more critical test of the validity of the (pre-Roman) Olympias hypothesis than any trial thus far used.

[38]See Shaw, "A Summary of the 'Trireme Controversy'," 1–3; Morrison *et al.*, *The Athenian Trireme*, 8–24. The works cited in n. 18, above, chronicling the Olympias hypothesis must be read in conjunction with the writings of Alec Tilley, e.g. his "Three Men to a Room—A Completely Different Trireme," *Antiquity* 66 (1992): 599–610; and Borimir Jordan and Alec Tilley, "Triremes" (http://www.atm.ox.ac.uk/rowing/triplebank.html; accessed 15 February 2002).

[39]E.g., the details of the arrangement and fitting of the *ὑποζώματα*, "pre-stressed tendons" of rope used to reduce bending stresses in the hull (hogging), are unknown; John F. Coates, "Reconstructions," in Morrison, *Greek and Roman Oared Warships*, 283, 328–29; Coates, "The Design of an Experimental Trireme," 25; Coates, "Development of the Design," 74; John. F. Coates and J. Timothy Shaw, "Speculations on Fitting Hypozomata," in *The Trireme Project*, ed. Shaw, 82–86; Morrison *et al.*, *The Athenian Trireme*, 196–99, 220–21. There were practical problems with fitting the hypothetical *ὑποζώματα* of Olympias for her 1987 and 1988 trials; Coates *et al.*, *Trireme Trials*, 8. Equally obscure is the rigging of a trireme; see Owain T. P. Roberts, "The Sailing Rig of Olympias," in *The Trireme Project*, ed. Shaw, 29; Morrison *et al.*, *The Athenian Trireme*, 175, 223.

[40]Coates *et al.*, *Trireme Trials*, 59.

[41]E.g., John Morrison, "*Triereis:* the Evidence from Antiquity," in *Trireme Project*, ed. Shaw, 11–20 (*breviter*); Morrison *et al.*, *The Athenian Trireme* (note in particular the index to passages in ancient authorities, 313–19) .

[42]The Trust's approach to these aspects has been questioned, as in C. Westerdahl, "The Trireme—An Experimental Form?" *International Journal of Nautical Archaeology* 22 (1993): 205–06; and defended, as in Morrison *et al.*, *The Athenian Trireme*, 233–36. As explained below, "authenticity" of materials and techniques is a matter for the experimenters' judgment; an aspect of "authenticity" which appears to have little to do with performance may be sacrificed due to tight financing. In such a case the experimenters' decision may be sound, but the particular test so affected may not prove that.

[43]Coates *et al.*, *Trireme Trials*, 13–19; Morrison *et al.*, *The Athenian Trireme*, 235–36.

[44]E.g., the 1988 trials were designed to investigate, among other things: the resistance of Olympias' hull and rudders; her speed under oar; her acceleration under oar; and the endurance of the ship and her crew; see Coates *et al.*, *Trireme Trials*, 1–2.

[45]Coates, "Reconstructions," 279.

[46]Coates *et al.*, *Trireme Trials*, 56.

[47]E.g., Shaw, "Is Olympias a Trieres," 105–07. Some have on occasion not successfully resisted the temptation to believe Olympias *is* an Athenian trireme of the "golden age"; although understandable, this is the best way to undermine the scholarly and scientific rigor of the project. In archaeological experiments it is probably better to underestimate the success of an experiment, lest one finds oneself placed in the company of the "inventors" of cold fusion and shunned by one's friends. The worst recent example of the incautious attitude of an experimenter towards his own creation is Ole Crumlin-Pedersen, "Experimental Ship Archaeology in Denmark," in *Experiment and Design: Archaeological Studies in Honour of John Coles*, ed. Anthony F. Harding (Oxford: Oxbow, 1999), 144, 146.

[48]Coates *et al.*, *Trireme Trials*, 3; Morrison *et al.*, *The Athenian Trireme*, 205–06.

[49]Coates *et al.*, *Trireme Trials*, 8–9.

[50]Coates, "Reconstructions," 279, 281. This is in addition to the protection offered by the *ὑποζώματα* mentioned in n. 39, above.

[51]Coates *et al.*, *Trireme Trials*, 9; Coates, "Development of the Design," 73–74.

[52]Coates, "Reconstructions," 281; also John S. Morrison, "*Triereis*: The Evidence from Antiquity," in *The Trireme Project*, ed. Shaw, 11–13, 18–19, and the same author's "Ancient Greek Measures of Length in Nautical Contexts," *Antiquity* 65 (1991): 298–305; Morrison *et al.*, *The Athenian Trireme*, 133, 245–46.

[53]Coates *et al.*, *Trireme Trials*, 77; also Boris Rankov, "Rowing Olympias: A Matter of Skill," in *The Trireme Project*, ed. Shaw, 51–52; Morrison *et al.*, *The Athenian Trireme*, 245.

[54]Coates, "Reconstructions," 281–82; Morrison *et al.*, *The Athenian Trireme*, 268–73.

[55]Coates *et al.*, *Trireme Trials*, 68; Shaw, "Rowing Olympias," in *The Trireme Project*, ed. Shaw, 63, 66.

[56]Coates *et al.*, *Trireme Trials*, 69–72; Shaw, "Rowing Olympias," 65, 67; Morrison *et al.*, *The Athenian Trireme*, 260–61. Unfortunately, the geodimeter readings did not correspond with those taken with the ship's log.

[57]E.g., in the experiment in station keeping "the crew did not fully understand

how to scull [in the seaman's sense]" (Shaw, "Rowing Olympias," 65); modern conditions (many financial) do not allow an ideal length of time to prepare crews (Rankov, "Rowing Olympias," 51; Morrison *et al.*, *The Athenian Trireme*, 235); some of the 1990 crew did not seem to realize the necessity for an extended experiment with the *αὐλός*, complaining of aural discomfort (Rankov, "Rowing Olympias," 55; Morrison *et al.*, *The Athenian Trireme*, 251). Similar difficulties are bound to arise in any experiment; they cannot always be foreseen; and they increase with the number of experimenters involved.

[58]See the references in n. 18, above. Equally impressive, the Trust invites its critics to deliver papers at the conferences it organizes; e.g., 19–20 September 1998, at the River and Rowing Museum, Henley-on-Thames, and at Corpus Christi College, Oxford (report available at: http://www.atm.ox.ac.uk/rowing/ttrankov2.html: accessed 15 February 2002). This is an indication of the health of the project.

[59]Coles, *Archaeology by Experiment*, 13–18. Coles' presentation in this earlier work is more complete than that offered in *Experimental Archaeology*, 46–48.

[60]The roles of improvisation and adaptability in an original technique, where recoverable, should be built into the experiment's design; see Coles, *Experimental Archaeology*, 47.

[61]Also see Crumlin-Pedersen, "Experimental Ship Archaeology," 141–42. Experimenters or technicians should also be aware of the roles of improvisation and adaptability in the original techniques they are recovering, where these can be known or estimated; see Coles, *Experimental Archaeology*, 47.

[62]Also see Crumlin-Pedersen, "Experimental Ship Archaeology," 141. Some have argued for the substitution of modern materials in areas which are not critical for the experiment; see Graeme Lawson, "Getting to Grips with Music's Prehistory: Experimental Approaches to Function, Design and Operational Wear in Excavated Musical Instruments," in *Experiment and Design*, ed. Harding, 135–36. Modern materials and techniques can and should be utilized for measuring, recording, and analyzing results. It would be good, however, if experimenters could force themselves to "analyze" results (as far as possible) as a contemporary of the process or object under investigation would have done.

[63]There are, of course, degrees of reproducibility. The Yorkshire Television vitrified wall experiment was, at least in part, an attempt to remount the Childe/Thorneycroft experiment of fifty years before; see n. 7, above.

[64]Also see Crumlin-Pedersen, "Experimental Ship Archaeology," 144.

[65]It is most unfortunate that Reynolds, "The Nature of Experiment in Archaeology,"157–158, 162, advocates the adoption of a "scientific method" resembling the caricature of science purveyed in secondary schools in North America in the

mid-decades of the last century—a view supported by citation of a text published in 1950. A more sensible approach, by a scientist, is Tony Waldron, *Counting the Dead: The Epidemiology of Skeletal Populations* (Chichester: John Wiley and Sons, 1994), 4–5: "outside the pages of learned journals and grant applications, science tends to proceed in a largely informal way, and the idea of *a* or *the* scientific method is something of a modern myth."

[66]So Coles, *Archaeology by Experiment*, 161: "the reconstruction and playing of the Sutton Hoo harp, now said to be a lyre, is visually and musically pleasing but contributes nothing to our knowledge of ancient music so far as can be determined. More satisfaction attaches to the reconstruction of a six-stringed lyre from the 'Grave of the Minstrel' at Cologne, dating from the eighth century A.D., *but its notes, its songs and its place in society are all lost*" (italics mine).

[67]This last remains imperfectly studied, although good treatments of particular spaces exist; see, for example, Craig Wright, *Music and Ceremony at Notre Dame of Paris, 500–1550* (Cambridge: Cambridge University Press, 1989), 3–18 and *passim*; Anne Walters Robertson, *The Service-Books of the Royal Abbey of Saint-Denis: Images of Ritual and Music in the Middle Ages* (Oxford: Clarendon Press, 1991), esp. 218–304; Tess Knighton, "Spaces and Contexts for Listening in 15th-Century Castile: The Case of the Constable's Palace in Jaen," *Early Music* 25 (1997): 661–77.

[68]E.g., does John of Garland (or, more properly, Pseudo-Garland) intend the *comminutio* to be used on every note of every conductus? See McGee, *The Sound of Medieval Music*, 72–73.

[69]More studies such as Simon Ravens, "A Sweet Shrill Voice: The Countertenor and Vocal Scoring in Tudor England," *Early Music* 26 (1998): 122–34, are clearly needed. Ravens attempts to use "laryngological and anthropometric research" to solve the problem of "the vocal scoring and pitch of Tudor sacred music." Physiological data from past populations is notoriously difficult to use, but it should not be ignored on that account. Evidence for the physiology of fifth- to fourth-century Athenian males has played a role in determining the "correct" *interscalmium* for a trireme (see nn. 52–54, above). Not unexpectedly, the evidence is subject to several interpretations.

[70]This problem is as old as the early music revival itself. The best makers often display more integrity in their approach than do many of their customers.

[71]E.g., bowing articulation in fourteenth-century Florence, use of the off-fingerboard plucked *bourdon* on vielles, etc.

[72]An example could be chosen from any medieval treatise that contains performance indications—e.g., some of Notker's significative letters, or aspects of Jerome of Moravia's *reverberatio*; see McGee, *The Sound of Medieval Music*, 32–33, 180–81 (Notker), 68–69, 172–73 (Jerome).

[73]E.g., the fifteenth-century Faenza Codex from North Italy; facsimile in *An Early Fifteenth-Century Italian Source of Keyboard Music: The Codex Faenza, Biblioteca Comunale, 117*, ed. Armen Carapetyan (American Institute of Musicology, 1961); transcription in *Keyboard Music of the Late Middle Ages in Codex Faenza 117*, ed. Dragan Plamenac, Corpus mensurabilis musicae 57 (American Institute of Musicology, 1972).

[74]Lewis Lockwood, *Music in Renaissance Ferrara 1400–1505: The Creation of a Musical Centre in the Fifteenth Century* (Oxford: Clarendon Press, 1984), 95–108. The medal struck in his honor with its inscriptions testifies to his fame. The obverse reads: ·PETRVS· BONNVS [sic.]· ORPHEVM· SVPERANS· ("Pietrobono, who surpasses Orpheus"); and on the reverse (front of the plinth): OMNIVM PRINCEPS ("Prince of all [musicians]"). For a good reproduction of the Ashmolean medal see Dora Thornton, *The Scholar in His Study: Ownership and Experience in Renaissance Italy* (London: British Museum Press, 1997), 122, fig. 73.

[75]Timothy J. McGee, "Dinner Music for the Florentine Signoria, 1350–1450," *Speculum* 74 (1999): 97, 112; Polk, *German Instrumental Music*, 77.

[76]In return they should (1) be treated with respect; (2) be kept fully informed of the course of the experiment; (3) be allowed to comment constructively on the experiment, and taken seriously when they do so; and (4) be acknowledged for their participation and contributions. These procedures should be adopted, irrespective of any remuneration agreed upon.

[77]Put simply, audiences attend concerts in the main to be entertained; few go to be challenged. Performers cannot afford to alienate the majority of their audience through trying a performance technique which, while authentic and common six or seven hundred years ago, is too foreign to the audience's listening experience; many in the audience might not return; and that would be a loss in more ways than one. While interesting work has begun to appear on the original audiences for and audience responses to some medieval music (e.g., *Early Music* 25 (1997): 591–701), writing a paper is a signally ineffective way to extend the listening limits of modern audiences.

[78]It is unlikely that any record company would risk investing in such projects (a possible exception is Harmonia Mundi, France, given its record of backing Marcel Pérès' Ensemble Organum; also worth honorable mention is EMI Reflexe, for recording the Allegri *Misereri* performance by Andrew Parrott and his Taverner Choir, originally issued as *Musica della cappella sistina* [1987], CDC 7476992, and reissued on Virgin Veritas [1996], VER 5613092). Compact disk booklets, as they are presently produced, do not afford a coverage even remotely sufficient to stand as interim reports on experiments (this is a particular problem with booklets provided with Ensemble Organum releases); and they are far from the basic minimum found in experimental archaeology. These circumstances could change for the better; the technologies of the enhanced compact disk and the CD-ROM are capable of providing sufficient space for the level of information required. And an

e-journal, such as Early Music America's newly launched *HPO: Historical Performance Online* (http://www.earlymusic.org/Content/HPO/HPOhome.asp: accessed 15 February 2000), may offer the technologically best mode of publication.

[79]It is worthy of note that some who work on historical musicology have begun to present alternative accounts of aspects of their subjects in the course of a single paper: e.g., *Hearing the Motet: Essays on the Motet of the Middle Ages and Renaissance*, ed. Dolores Pesce (New York: Oxford University Press, 1997), in particular Rob C. Wegman, "For Whom the Bell Tolls: Reading and Hearing Busnoy's *Anthoni usque limina*," 122–41, and Richard Sherr, "Conflicting Levels of Meaning and Understanding in Josquin's *O admirabile commercium* Motet Cycle," 193–212.

[80]The Trireme Trust would increase its scholarly and scientific standing, even beyond its success with Olympias, if it could aid in having full-scale mock-ups and trial pieces of Commander Tilley's trireme hypothesis produced and tested; see n. 38, above.

[81]E.g., Shaw, "Rowing Astern," 69–70; Shaw, "Rowing Olympias," 64–65.

[82]"Only the tendency of modern historiography to base its views entirely on written sources, rather than on these in relation to the larger landscape from which they emerge, could prevent our seeing Pietrobono, in his domain, as a figure comparable to the greatest polyphonic masters of the period" (Lockwood, *Music in Renaissance Ferrara*, 98). The implications of this are wider than they might first appear; for to achieve an accurate and true knowledge of medieval and renaissance music, it is necessary that improvised forms—and the role of improvisation generally—be incorporated into any serious account. The late Nino Pirrotta was a vigorous advocate of this approach; see his "Nuova luce su una tradizione non scritta," and "Tradizione orale e tradizione scritta della musica," in *Musica tra Medioevo e Rinascimento* (Turin: G. Einaudi, 1984), 154–84. An improvised form may have been as important as a written form, or even more so, to many contemporaries. Nor can the nature of written forms be ascertained, the forms analyzed, or written about without considering the improvised component in their composition and performance. The "experimental" performance of improvisation, as outlined here, would certainly be one significant tool in the effort to achieve a more balanced, exact, and valid account of medieval and renaissance music.

[83]Work on "music" within experimental archaeology has mostly been confined to prehistorical organology, and much of it remains unknown to those concerned with historical organology. This may be a good thing, for paradoxically a great deal of it is not among the best in experimental archaeology. An excellent paper, presenting a salutary warning, is Francesco D'Errico, Paola Villa, Ana C. Pinto Llona, and Rosa Ruiz Idarraga, "A Middle Paleolithic Origin of Music? Using Cave-Bear Bone Accumulations to Assess the Divje Babe I Bone 'Flute'," in *Antiquity* 72 (1998): 65–79. For those interested, the Study Group on Music

Archaeology, intermittently part of The International Council for Traditional Music (under the aegis of UNESCO), regularly publishes the proceedings of its symposia. Details are available on the *HARPA* website: http://www.odilia.ch/music-archaeology/index.htm: accessed 15 February 2002. The quality of the work is variable. Cajsa S. Lund, a member of the Study Group on Music Archaeology, offers mild criticism in "What is Wrong with Music Archaeology? A Critical Essay from a Scandinavian Perspective, Including a Report about a New Find of a Bullroarer," in *Hearing the Past: Essays in Historical Ethnomusicology and the Archaeology of Sound*, ed. Ann Buckley (Liège: Université de Liège Service de Préhistoire et Centre de Recherche Archéologique, 1998), 17–28. Also see Catherine Homo-Lechner, "False. Authentic. False Authenticity. Contributions and Failures of Experimental Archaeology as Applied to Music Instruments," in *Hearing the Past*, 29–64, who also deals with a few of the issues raised in the present paper. We are occasionally in agreement.

[84]See nn. 68 and 72, above.

[85] As a final note, the recent intrusion of "performance studies" into archaeology ought at the very least to have offered the latter discipline a valuable new approach to investigating the use and meaning of the remains of human activity. The practice of the former and its results have proven disappointing and have curiously belied expected affinities to the practice and results of cognitive and experimental archaeology. Perhaps the aridity, remoteness, and inutility of the discipline of performance studies is due to its diffuseness of concept, obscurity of jargon, and avoidance of empathy with the people whose personal remains, vestiges of activity, and physical and spiritual landscapes it objectivizes; e.g., Mike Pearson, "The Past Was Not Silent," http://www.theatre-wales.co.uk/critical/voice.htm: accessed 15 February 2002 (commentary on the 1997 Aberystwyth conference "An Archaeology of the Voice"); "Performance as Valuation: Early Bronze Age Burial as Theatrical Complexity," in *The Archaeology of Value: Essays on Prestige and the Processes of Valuation*, ed. Douglass Bailey and Steve Mills, BAR International Series 730 (Oxford: British Archaeological Reports, 1998), 32–41.

Instrumentalists and Performance Practices in Dance Music, c.1500

Keith Polk

Instrumental musicians in the courts and cities of Europe around 1500 faced a dynamic, rapidly changing professional scene. Performance practices had hardly been static for several decades, but their development through the fifteenth century had been reasonably smooth. With the beginning of the sixteenth century, though, instrumentalists faced what amounted to a crisis with particular impact on two of the areas of concern here: improvisation and music for dancing. It will be my purpose in this article to consider the set of conditions that arrived with the new century and to explore how performers responded to the challenges these conditions posed.

A detailed survey of the background of fifteenth-century developments would not be appropriate here, but it should be understood that by about 1475 a quite sophisticated set of musical practices in instrumental music was in place. By then professional instrumentalists incorporated three basic approaches in their performances: they would play a piece as written, they could add embellishments, or they could improvise. It is important to emphasize the first (playing a piece as written) because the works of major composers of the time formed a basic component of their performance practices. This represented a fundamental shift, for until the end of the fourteenth century instrumentalists evidently worked almost exclusively within an aural tradition. Surviving evidence from manuscript sources, though scanty, suggests that players drew increasingly on written music throughout the fifteenth century. By about 1480 compositions by Martini, Isaac, Agricola, Josquin, and Obrecht were fundamental to the instrumental repertory. This phenomenon was long veiled from modern view. The surviving musical manuscripts would appear to be almost exclusively vocal. Moreover, contemporary illustrations invariably showed that players did not use written texts in their performances. It now seems clear, however, that instrumentalists then did read music and were familiar with an international core repertory.[1] All performers in the late fifteenth century were trained in the second area, which involved ability to add decorations to simple melodic outlines. The third category, improvisation, formed a central element in contemporary instrumental performances, particularly those in providing music for dancing. In improvisation, especially involving three or more parts, some prior understandings had to have been in operation. One standard approach of the time was to take a preexistent tune into one part (usually the tenor) and weave one or two counterpoints around this borrowed tune. In short, by the last decades of the fifteenth century instrumentalists had command of mature and reasonably stable practices, with underpinnings which were widely understood.

The practices were international, as is suggested by the fact that stables of musicians, especially those in the most important centers, often included players from a variety of origins. Philip the Fair, the Habsburg archduke in the Low Countries and briefly Spanish king until his early death in 1506, maintained a corps of players at the turn of the sixteenth century that included Flemish, French, and German musicians. The court ensembles in Ferrara in the middle decades of the fifteenth century included French, German, and Italian instrumentalists and an English harpist as well. The Valois Dukes of Burgundy regularly supported French, German, and Flemish instrumentalists and in the mid-fifteenth century boasted a pair of chamber musicians who were evidently of Spanish origin. The instrumentalists supported by Henry VIII in England were an especially motley troop, for besides Englishmen there were Flemings, Germans, Frenchmen, and, beginning in the 1530s, Italians as well. Cities also could import talent. In Florence in the 1450s the civic ensemble combined Germans, Flemings, and Italians. At about the same time the town band in nearby Siena included Italian, German, and French musicians.[2] It must be said that mixed groups were by no means always the case. Venice seems to have engaged only Italian performers, while over the Alps membership in civic ensembles in such leading centers as Augsburg and Nuremberg were rigidly German throughout the Renaissance. Leading German courts such as those of the Dukes of Bavaria and Saxony were exclusively German until a wave of Italian violinists and cornettists began to sweep in about 1550. Of course German musicians were nonetheless international, as is demonstrated by the careers of members of the Schubinger clan. In the 1490s, one brother (Ulrich) was a key figure in the civic ensemble in Augsburg, another (Michael) was with the court band in Ferrara, and yet another (Augustine) was in the service of Philip the Fair in the Low Countries.[3]

The intermixture of talent and practices was reinforced by the intense interest in dancing which characterized the age. When Philip the Fair traveled with his retinue within his own lands or to France, Germany, England, or Spain, he was of course entertained. A focal point of such entertainment would be a banquet, inevitably followed by a clearing of the tables, and then dancing. If this was a court occasion his nobles would mix with the local aristocracy. If in a city such as Bruges or Antwerp, his courtiers might mingle with the local elites. The basis of the dance repertory about 1500 lay apparently in the courtly and very complicated *basse* dances. One did not simply wander around the floor shuffling through a basic two-step. The steps were highly complex and evidently carefully matched to the music. For this all to work there was a core repertory of dances with which courtiers and elites were familiar—as were, of course, the musicians as well. Though there were also dances which were more local, this core repertory was obviously international in character.

In sum, for musicians at the turn of the sixteenth century a variety of factors interacted to engender performance practices which were widely understood across national boundaries. Contemporary sources certainly give every indication that players from varied locations and backgrounds could merge smoothly and effectively. In fact this continued to be the case as changes began to unfold more rapidly after 1500 when a relatively stable set of practices began to unravel as their underpinnings began to collapse. Challenges came from several directions. Most important was the development of the idea of imitative counterpoint as the standard texture in composed music, for this introduced a completely different and much more flexible structural foundation. In a texture based on the tenor voice much is firmly established from the outset. Cadence points can be predetermined along with phrase lengths and much of the harmonic outline. With imitative counterpoint, relationships between voices are freer, less predictable, and therefore much more difficult to manage in extemporaneous performance. Another challenge came with an increased interest in greater sonority. The usual texture earlier was one of three parts, but by 1500 many ensembles consisted of at least four parts. By 1520 some groups included six and even more performers. Again, with three parts (with one of these being a borrowed tune) skilled improvising performers could negotiate around harmonic clashes with reasonable success. With added voices such clashes became very much harder to avoid.

The issue is: how did instrumentalists respond? And response was necessary, especially in dance music, for the conditions in the halls where dancing was done required improvisatory performances. These musicians had to play for several hours at a time, and the only really efficient way to do this in the early sixteenth century was through the use of various kinds of improvisations. Necessity, then, required a series of adjustments. Performers at the turn of the century were conservative in many ways, however, and these adjustments still required the basic three-way skills of earlier generations—that is, knowledge of written repertory, ability to decorate, and skill with improvisation—though the relative weight among the three altered.

One adjustment particularly involved instrumentalists performing dance repertory—and in fact emanated from changes in the nature of the dance itself. As suggested above, in the fifteenth century dance choreographies and their associated tunes, the *basse* dance as an example, were often long, quite elaborate, and characteristically asymmetrical. Each choreography was unique. The complexities of these dances made them very difficult for the dancers to learn.[4] For experienced professional musicians, on the other hand, once the length of the tune was established (this was a possible variable as a few notes might be cut from or added to a tune to make it fit a choreography), their task of providing the musical accompaniment was relatively straightforward. As described above, the melody would be placed in one voice (usually the tenor), around which counterpoints would be improvised. The players had to be skilled, of course, and they had to know the tune, but the procedures themselves were not overly complicated. With the early sixteenth century came a preference for a different kind of dance. Repetitions became more explicit, and phrases were often arranged symmetrically (often in pairs, and often, in modern terms, in four measure units). Moreover, choreographies became more standardized so that one set of steps could be applied regardless of which tune was chosen. This was a vastly less involved repertory and was much easier for the dancers to learn. The symmetries and the repetitions, of course, also made the repertory easier for the musicians to grasp as well.[5]

Another adjustment, with direct effect on dance musicians, was to favor a different set of sonorities and vertical relationships. Rather than either the older structure based on a tune in the tenor or even the newer textures based on imitation, for dancing the favored texture became one in which the top voice predominated. This changed stature of the soprano is reflected in the way in which borrowed material was incorporated. Much of the dance repertory in the early sixteenth century was created by adapting vocal pieces, as had been the case in the fifteenth century. What was borrowed earlier, however, was usually a tenor part, which was placed in the tenor in the dance version. With the sixteenth century, it was usually the soprano that was borrowed.[6] The preference for soprano-dominated texture was not, of course, limited to the dance. The emerging Parisian chanson as well as the Italian *frottola* were two vocal genres which had, like the dance, a very wide popular appeal in the early sixteenth century. For a dance version of this texture, the well-known *Ronde VI* (Example 1) from Susato's *Derde musyck boexken* (*Third Music Book*) of 1551 may serve as an illustration. In addition to the clearly prominent melody in the soprano, note also the regularity of the four-measure phrases.[7]

By about 1530 this texture was deeply rooted and was accepted as the prevailing one for all manner of dances. Most such pieces were evidently short and included two or more repeated sections. This kind of structure was in striking contrast to that of the Burgundian dances of a generation earlier and called for a different balance of performance techniques. In pieces like the *Ronde*, for example, with the repetitions the musicians would be expected to demonstrate their mastery of the art of embellishment. Compensation for relatively less emphasis on improvisation was provided by relatively more on decoration. Underscoring this change, which dates from the early sixteenth century, musicians such as Silvestro Ganassi of Venice produced treatises on how one might ornament a line artistically.[8]

To describe the new texture in terms of the top part is incomplete, of course, for in fact now the emphasis was on *both* of the outer parts. Clearly the bass was also thrown into particular prominence in the texture. As this happened players evidently quickly took advantage of yet another new approach which was to base an improvisatory scheme upon repetitions of a bass pattern.

EXAMPLE 1
Ronde VI

Ronde VI, from Tielman Susato, *Danserye (Het derde musyck boexken)* (1551), ed. Bernard Thomas (London: London Pro Musica Edition, 1993), 19; used by permission.

The earliest such patterns of which we know seem to be Italian, especially those associated with the *passamezzo.* Again Susato's *Derde musyck boexken* provides an example with a *Passe e medio* which is based on a pattern (in Example 2 in the bass: D–C–D–A//D–C–D–A–D) similar to the *passamezzo antico*.[9]

The piece (given complete in Example 2) is quite short and is intended to be repeated, undoubtedly many times, for dancing. The structure is again based on repetitive four-measure phrases, and it is with the repetitions that the bass pattern becomes especially clear. The repeats would have been enlivened by a variety of decorative techniques in the upper parts with the responsibilities for embellishment likely being passed from performer to performer. As the musicians did this they could also create a variety of textural contrasts. In a four-part fabric, for example, the player of the tenor might take over in rapid motion while the soprano and alto could drop out (which could result not only in a welcome change in timbre, but an opportunity of the players to rest). Susato published the *Passe e medio* in 1551, but he was probably familiar with the use of bass patterns during his career as an instrumentalist in the civic ensemble of Antwerp in the 1530s and 1540s. In fact, at least one ensemble version using a similar pattern is found in a set of dance pieces in the *Augsburg Liederbuch*, which has been dated c.1513 and which would indicate that such patterns were being put to use by the turn of the century.[10]

Ultimately this new emphasis on soprano and bass led to a kind of polarity between these two outside voices. That is, eventually musicians heard the outside voices as by far the most important with the inside voices as providing a kind of filler. Very soon with this texture what musicians would have heard would be a series of vertical sonorities—that is, a series of chord "progressions." With this development would have come, one assumes, an increasing awareness of the harmonic framework. And in turn one might further assume that players would have been quick to seize the advantage of such frameworks and incorporate them as flexible foundations for improvisatory performances. This would have been true especially for dance musicians, for we must keep in mind that these players were involved in providing music for dancing which was often noted as lasting through an entire night. Such long sessions were not only exacting in terms of physical stamina since

EXAMPLE 2
Passe de medio

Passe e medio, from Tielman Susato, *Danserye*, ed. Thomas, 37; used by permission.

the demand for musical raw material must indeed have been pressing. Despite such motivation, however, the musical evidence would suggest that musicians in the first decades of the sixteenth century did not avail themselves of the potential of repetitions of harmonic frames with any consistency. To the ear trained in the conventions of tonal harmony (that is, the practices governing harmony from Johann Sebastian Bach onward), once a melody with its chordal support is heard, we tend to hear the two (melody plus chords) as an entity. In jazz improvisation, for example, musicians refer to knowing the "changes" that go with a particular melody. But this consistent identification of a particular set of chords to go with a melody had not yet developed in the early sixteenth century. In two versions of *Mille ducas* (again provided by Susato), for example, no strong resemblance of harmonic structure seems to be shared between the two (Examples 3–4).

Some outlines of the top part are common to both settings, but even this voice is treated with considerable freedom (it is at least close enough at the beginning to establish a relationship between the two versions). The bass part, however, seems only vaguely related, and the harmonic structures are hardly linked at all. In short, in these pieces—and in some others of the earlier sixteenth century discussed by Daniel Heartz—the soprano/bass complex did not appear to generate a framework of chords which would have provided the basis for further improvisation.[11] Of course the soprano/bass texture ultimately did lead to greater harmonic awareness. Indeed, early on a number of pieces do share a harmonic framework between different versions. Susato, for example, based a *Salterelle* on *Ronde VI* in which both the outline of the melody and the harmonic frame are quite audibly related.[12] Still, as a standard device this seems to have been a development that gathered its momentum after the mid-sixteenth century.

Much of the dance repertory in the early sixteenth century was created by adapting vocal pieces. As described above, borrowing the soprano of a preexistent piece was a norm, but in some fascinating cases a more complex structure acted as a model. An example is the well known *Pavane* based on Josquin's *Mille regretz* (Example 5) which illustrates the combinations of tradition and innovation so characteristic of Renaissance instrumental music.[13] Dance tunes for generations had been borrowed from vocal chansons, and here the process of adapting a vocal model to function as a dance is especi-

EXAMPLE 3

Ronde VIII: Mille ducas en vostre bource

Ronde VIII: Mille ducas en vostre bource, from Susato, *Danserye*, 20–21; used by permission.

EXAMPLE 4
Galliard X: Mille Ducas

Galliard X: Mille ducas, from Susato, *Danserye*, 43; used by permission.

ally clear. In *Mille regretz*, however, Josquin's subtly irregular phrase structures have been regularized into symmetrically repeated units, and beautifully calculated contrasts of high and low voices have been altered to a texture in which soprano and bass predominate. At first sight this represents the kind of thing one might expect of a publisher's hack arranger. Yet on closer examination one sees that the *Pavane* is of itself a sophisticated piece. Whoever was responsible, probably Tielman Susato himself (the arranger or arrangers are not identified in his collection), this is an impressive example of a paraphrase in which true four-part counterpoint has been radically and successfully transformed. Most important for our consideration is that these kinds of changes could not have been manipulated by ensemble musicians in improvisation. In the fifteenth century, in contrast, adaptations could apparently take place on the spot. A body of international pieces was well known, and if a particular melody was desired, a competent group of players, with perhaps a bit of negotiation among themselves, could produce a new version then and there. With the kind of adaptations involved with the *Pavane Mille regretz*, however, someone would have had to set out at least the outlines of the adaptation ahead of time.

In the soprano-dominated dance repertory of the early sixteenth century, musicians performing in three parts (which according to iconography was still frequently the case) may have continued to improvise. The traditional rules of improvisation would have served them reasonably well. However, when they performed in four or more parts, either with imitative textures or with those based on a soprano tune, the performers more likely depended on prearranged versions. In other words, the dance repertory published by Attaingnant and Susato may indeed reflect the kind of adaptations that would have taken place. The *Pavane Mille regretz* quite likely was the kind of dance piece that Susato and his colleagues in Antwerp would have performed in the city hall during his tenure with the civic ensemble there. It should be noted that this was the time when quantities of music were available in relatively inexpensive form through the new processes of printing. It is also from precisely this time that contemporary records begin to note the use of written music by professional instrumentalists.[14]

Of even greater significance was the increasing involvement of instrumentalists in both the new trade of publishing and in composition. Before about 1500 few instrumentalists were known as

EXAMPLE 5
Pavane I: Mille regretz

Pavane I: Mille regretz, from Susato, *Danserye*, 32; used by permission.

composers, but the situation changed rapidly after that date. This was a phenomenon that was international. In Italy one of the significant contributors to a Siena *frottola* print of 1515 was Niccolò Brandini, a leading member of the Siena civic ensemble.[15] Bartolomeo Tromboncino (c.1470–c.1535) had been a trombonist early in his career in Mantua but by about 1500 was known primarily as a composer. In Germany, Augustein Schubinger was renowned for his improvisational skills, but he too apparently composed music, in his case specifically for dancing.[16] A little later Paul and Bartholomeus Hessen added to this dance repertory with two substantial published volumes.[17] In Paris, Jean d'Estrée, "oboist to the king," published four volumes of dances between 1559 and 1564. England was not insulated from this phenomenon, as Philip van Wilder (c.1500–53), a highly paid instrumentalist at the royal court, produced secular songs, motets, and instrumental pieces, many of which were published both in England and abroad. The most striking example from the Low Countries is that of Tielman Susato, who began his musical career about 1530 in Antwerp and subsequently published quantities of music, including the volume of dances to which reference has been made above. He also composed music in a variety of genres, including chansons, motets, and dance pieces. Susato's move to arranging, composing, and publication was not simply taking advantage of new economic opportunities. His activities and those of his publisher/composer/ instrumentalist colleagues throughout Europe reflected fundamental shifts in the way they made music.

For instrumentalists the innovations in dance music in the early sixteenth century would have been far reaching. Their craft, however, was one that was also deeply conservative since they remained tied to unwritten performance practices (contemporary illustrations of dancing which show musicians continued invariably to depict them performing without music). Innovation was balanced against tradition. The three basic skills demanded of musicians in the fifteenth century (reading, decoration, and improvisation) were still assumed to be fundamental for professional performers. After 1500 more emphasis was placed on working from composed texts and on embellishment. The increased importance of composed dances was quickly reflected by a concomitant shift in the career focus of instrumentalists as they themselves became composers to meet the new demand. Still, improvisation continued, especially in dance music. Here too old and new fought for balance; new textures demanded innovative approaches as players had to deal with the new emphasis on the soprano—and with the taste for repeated bass patterns which called for extemporaneous elaboration. Contemporary sources show, however, that the traditional improvisation on tenor structures continued to be taught and to be put to use—an approach which was undoubtedly useful in the long hours of providing the background for dancing. For musicians, the halls used for dancing remained places of dynamic, creative music making.

NOTES

[1]For an extensive discussion see Keith Polk, *German Instrumental Music in the Late Middle Ages* (Cambridge: Cambridge University Press, 1992), 83–86.

[2]For Philip the Fair, see Georges van Doorslaer, "La chapelle musicale de Philippe le Beau," *Revue Belge d'Archéologie et d'Histoire de l'Art* 4 (1934): 21–57, 139–65, but more complete information will be available in the forthcoming dissertation by David Fiala at the University of Tours. For Ferrara see

Lewis Lockwood, *Music in Renaissance Ferrara 1400–1505* (Cambridge: Harvard University Press, 1980), 315 (shawmists from Italy, Avignon, and Germany, 1437), 317 (harpist from England, 1450). On the court of Henry VIII, see Andrew Ashbee, *Records of English Court Music*, 9 vols. (Aldershot: Scolar Press, 1986–96), 7:267. Concerning musicians in Florence, see Timothy J. McGee, "In the Service of the Commune: The Changing Role of Civic Musicians, 1450–1532," *Sixteenth Century Journal* 30 (1999): 731–32; for Siena, see Frank D'Accone, *The Civic Muse: Music and Musicians in Siena during the Middle Ages and Renaissance* (Chicago: University of Chicago Press, 1997), 516–41.

[3]Keith Polk, "The Schubingers of Augsburg: Innovation in Renaissance Instrumental Music," in *Quaestiones in musica: Festschrift für Franz Krautwurst* (Tutzing: Hans Schneider, 1989), 495–503.

[4]Such dances reflected the circles for which they were designed—i.e., only the nobility or the very highest stratum of wealthy urban elites would have had the time, leisure, and resources to master the intricacies posed by these choreographies.

[5]This is a highly simplified description of a complex phenomenon. For an account of the development of dancing, see Daniel Heartz, "The Basse Dance, Its Evolution circa 1450 to 1550," *Annales Musicologiques* 6 (1958–63): 287–340.

[6]For a discussion of the adaptation of chansons for dancing, see Daniel Heartz, *Preludes, Chansons and Dances for Lute* (Neuilly-sur-Seine: Société de Musique d'Autrefois, 1964), xxl–liv.

[7]The modern edition is Tielman Susato, *Danserye (Het derde musyck boexken) 1551*, ed. Bernard Thomas (London: London Pro Musica, 1993).

[8]See Sylvestro Ganassi, *Opera intitulata Fontegara* (Venice, 1535); trans. Dorothy Swainson, *A Treatise on the Art of Playing the Recorder and of Free Ornamentation* (Berlin-Lichterfelde: Robert Lienau, 1959).

[9]The *passamezzo*, an Italian dance of the sixteenth and seventeenth centuries, was similar to the pavane and usually in duple meter. For a discussion of the *passamezzo* with its basses, see Howard Mayer Brown and Louise K. Stein, *Music in the Renaissance*, 2nd ed. (Upper Saddle River, N.J.: Prentice-Hall, 1999), 260.

[10]On the dance piece in the *Augsburg Liederbuch* (D–As 142a), see Polk, *German Instrumental Music*, 141.

[11]See Heartz, *Preludes, Chansons and Dances*, xxxii–xxxiv, 56–57 (first version of *Basse dance La brosse*), 68–69 (second version); these are examples of pieces in which the harmonic frameworks are not closely related (see ibid., lxxv). However, as Heartz observes, with the *Sauterelle* that follows the *Pavane* [*Regina*] (ibid., 100–01), the harmonic structures are quite close. See also the *Bal* (ibid., 109–10).

[12]Susato, *Danserye*, 22.

[13]Recent scholarship has questioned the attribution of *Mille regretz* to Josquin; see Louise Litterick, "Chansons for Three and Four Voices," in *The Josquin Companion*, ed. Richard Sherr (Oxford: Oxford University Press, 2000), 374–75.

[14]Polk, *German Instrumental Music*, 163–66.

[15]See D'Accone, *The Civic Muse*, 699–701.

[16]Polk, *German Instrumental Music*, 141–42.

[17]The two volumes were titled *Viel Feiner Lieblicher Stucklein* and *Etticher gutter Teutscher und Polischer Tentz*, both published in 1555; see Howard Mayer Brown, *Instrumental Music Printed Before 1600: A Bibliography* (Cambridge: Harvard University Press, 1967), 164–67.

DANCE

Improvisation and Embellishment in Popular and Art Dances in Fifteenth- & Sixteenth-Century Italy

Barbara Sparti

Despite the growing interest in the popular culture of early modern Europe on the part of social and cultural historians, musicologists, and art historians,[1] popular—or traditional—dance has been completely ignored by specialists in Renaissance choreography.[2] The first part of this essay will deal with an important group of traditional couple dances which were performed first in country villages and then in both town and court: the *saltarello*, *piva*, *gagliarda*, *corrente*, and *nizzarda*, all of which were characterized by improvisation.[3] Like much secular music of the fifteenth century, these dances belonged to an important and rich "unwritten tradition."[4] Even though little is known about how they were actually performed, it would distort history to ignore them in a study concerning Renaissance dance, and particularly one on improvisation.

In the early 1990s, musicologists F. Alberto Gallo and Iain Fenlon, in an attempt to get a more complete and all-embracing picture of their fields, began to look at medieval and Renaissance music from anthropological and ethnomusicological points of view precisely because of the lack of documents and written music from otherwise important centers.[5] Similarly motivated, I recently listened with great interest to a group of dance ethnologists discussing improvisation in folk dancing who based their findings on field work observations and oral interviews (in particular with an outstanding sixty-five year-old dancer from a village in Romania).[6] Improvisation, it was agreed, is a kind of spontaneous movement based on traditional motifs or models—the building blocks of improvisation (see Appendix 1).[7] The dancer needs to know how to build on a particular motif by repeating it and varying it, and making it his own. The results can be "small flowerings," or, if the dancer is creative and there are, for example, thirty-five movement patterns in a dance, he could come up with hundreds of combinations. These are planned consciously and rapidly, and they are selected and executed by the legs (technique is a pre-requisite for any improvisation)—a combination of mind and body. "I never repeat the same figures" says the village dancer, "I always change. . . . When it becomes very interesting I try and 'fix' it. . . . A bad dancer is one who dances the same as he did when he was sixteen and first danced in his village." Music is a stimulus for improvisation. It provides rhythmic and melodic clues for dancing, for phrasing, and for changes of tempo. "You shape your own dance according to the music. . . . When the music is 'asking,' I dance the figure which answers." There is great interaction—leading and following in turn, though not necessarily through eye contact. The dancer who dances well makes the fiddler play with more drive "rather than trying to play for those people who jump about like popcorn." The audience participates, and its enthusiasm influences the dancer, as does his partner.

I will address some of these points again, but I now wish to return to those "hits" of the Quattro- and Cinquecento, the *saltarello*, *piva*, *gagliarda*, *corrente*, and *nizzarda*. As we know from contemporary chronicles, literary sources, extant music, and dance treatises, these were all couple dances, though the number of couples dancing at the same time was not fixed, and there could be solo variations as well as different sorts of improvisations for the man and for the woman. None of the dances required a particular music nor had a specific choreography.

The earliest extant musical source to include dances labeled *saltarello* is from the late 1300s or early 1400s.[8] A Quattrocento festival poem describes a dance, accompanied by the ever-present *pifferi e tromboni* (shawms and sackbuts), performed outdoors for hours on end, with couples (and, at times, trios) skipping and promenading around, changing partners, resting, and joining in the fray again.[9]

Many of the images on contemporary wedding-chests and in engravings may well be depicting aspects (or moments) of the *saltarello*.[10] Whether or not these are authentic fifteenth-century productions or reliable representations of performance practices of the period,[11] they show movements and gestures that are still found in the *saltarello* as it is danced in Italy today such as turning under the arm, promenading in closed ("waltz") position, and—for the man—hands on hips, and especially leg thrusts and kicks. Even in the nineteenth century, the hop (*saltetto*) and under-arm turn were typical of the *saltarello*.[12] It is possible, however, that the lifted leg and the arm-turn, rather than indicating a specific dance, were Quattrocento symbols for the representation of dance in general.

The *saltarello* was also used by the fifteenth-century dancing-masters, for the most part as an *entrata* with which their composed *balli* initiated.[13] The treatises give us the only specific step description we have to date. Danced to music notated primarily in what corresponds to a modern 6/8,[14] the *saltarello* consisted of only *passi doppi* ("double" steps)—performed long-short-long, with a hop, probably on the up-beat, and a rise on the second—short—step. It could initiate with a *movimento*, possibly a foot *tremolo* or *scosso* (shake), similar to that with which various Balkan and Catalonian dances begin.[15]

For part of the sixteenth century and even in the early seventeenth century, the *saltarello* and the *gagliarda* shared the same music and at times became synonymous. Thomas Morley pointed out in 1597 that "The Italians make their Galliards (which they term Saltarelli) plain, and frame ditties to them which in their masquerades they sing and dance. . . ."[16] Criminal records, a new source and perspective for dance historians, reveal, furthermore, that in 1606 a prostitute, who had been dancing with a group of men in the streets of Rome, claimed that the accompanying bagpiper had played a *gagliarda*, while he asserted that it was a *saltarella*.[17] With the growing popularity of the *gagliarda*, the "art" and "court" *saltarello* seem to disappear entirely. Around 1620, Giulio Mancini —art collector, connoisseur, and physician to Pope Urban VIII— wrote a small theoretical treatise, *Del Origin et Nobiltà del Ballo* (*On the Origin and Nobility of Dancing*), in which he mentions a number of dances, probably learned or seen in his youth in Siena.[18] Among these is the *Matriciana*, performed, he tells us, holding handkerchiefs between the dancers,[19] but we do not know if what he had in mind has anything to do with the *saltarello all'amatriciana* (that is, from Amatrice), which continues to be danced today, along with other distinctive *saltarelli* from different parts of central Italy.[20]

Another traditional dance that was a favorite in the fifteenth century was the *piva* (the name also meant bagpipe).[21] Contemporary writers confirm that it was performed in village and town festivities. Gaugello Gaugelli's poem describes a fête in Pergola, near Pesaro—"Danzare . . . a doi a doi con l'altre damigelle, Quale alla piva e quale a saltarello" ("Dancing two by two with other damsels, who the *piva*, who the *saltarello*").[22] The setting of one of Antonio Cornazano's *Proverbi in facetie* (*Proverbs in Jest*) is a private Carnival party in the city of Piacenza.[23] After dinner a squire and a provincial lass, the hero and heroine of this risqué ballad, take part in the dancing, together with a great crowd of people. The music (at least in Cornazano's poetic rendering) seems to have been supplied by a single player, and the only dances mentioned are the *saltarello* and the *piva*. This same Cornazano, poet, courtier, and author of a dance treatise, was anxious to distance himself from the common folk, and, despite the fact that the *piva* was often included (as a rapid finale made up only of very fast *doppi* steps) in the dancing-masters' *balli*, he looked with condescension on the dance's low pastoral origins. At the same time, he instructed good (male) dancers to ornament their *piva* with turns, jumps, and caprioles.[24]

Because of the rapidity of the *piva*, the music, notated in the dance treatises in both duple (4/8) and compound duple (6/8), probably had a kind of *inégalité* or "ambivalence," often found in traditional dance-music in Italy (as in the *tarantella* and *saltarello*) and elsewhere.[25] The last traces of the *piva* appear in early sixteenth-century dance suites for lute, such as those by Dalza, in which the *piva* follows the *Padovana* (or *pavane*) and the *saltarello*.[26]

Recent research has shown that the *gagliarda*, the most popular dance in Europe from the mid-sixteenth century through the early seventeenth, was already known in Italy at the end of the fifteenth century.[27] The basic step was called *cinque passi* (five steps, or "sink-a-pace," by Shakespeare), and was performed to six beats, or two three-beat bars.[28] However, the dance manuals from 1560 to 1607 by Compasso, Caroso, Arbeau, Lutij, Lupi, and Negri[29] contain hundreds of variations intended as suggestions for individual improvisations (see Appendix 2). These were aimed almost exclusively at male dancers and are vigorous, intricate, virtuosic, and frequently "polyrhythmic"— that is, variations often contained more (or fewer) movements than the beats in the musical phrase.[30] Not only was the *gagliarda* an independent dance type, but it also was often a section of the late sixteenth-century *balletto*. (Caroso occasionally gives the solo dancer a choice of doing his own *gagliarda* variation or one invented by the dancing master himself.)[31] Mancini, in his *Del Origin et Nobiltà del Ballo* that has been cited above, affirms that "nella gagliarda . . . vi è immitatione, immitando l'attioni d'un giovan gagliardo, che con varij gesti, moti, e salti, vada demostrando la sua robustezza, e gagliardia" ("the *gagliarda* imitates the actions of a young 'lustie gallant' who, with various gestures, movements, and jumps, demonstrates his strength and bravura").[32] It is a "simple movement" dance, he explains, in which the hands, arms, and body are quiet and only the legs move, and it is danced without holding one's partner's hands, the variation performed as a solo facing one's partner and the onlookers. The *gagliarda* also inspired instrumental variations well into the seventeenth century when, however, they were often meant "for the ear" (or "*per camera*") rather than "for the feet" ("*per ballare*").[33]

Two other improvisatory dances, the *corrente* and the *nizzarda*, are included in Cesare Negri's 1602 treatise but are so briefly and enigmatically described that they are almost impossible to reconstruct. These were undoubtedly traditional dances that everyone knew, and Negri may have felt obliged to include them in his treatise because they were so much in fashion. Clear instructions (for the *nizzarda*, at least) were superfluous inasmuch as it was "un ballo allegro, alquale se non si può dar regola certa . . . perche ogn'uno nel suo paese la balla à suo modo" ("a merry dance, *with no fixed rules* . . . because every village has its own fashion").[34] Probably born in Nice (part of Piedmont, Italy, until 1860), the *nizzarda* was almost certainly related to the *volta*, danced also by Queen Elizabeth, banned for a period of time in France and Italy, and described in detail in 1588 by Thoinot Arbeau in his treatise *Orchésographie*.[35] In both the *nizzarda* and the *volta*, which show a clear kinship with traditional turning dances found in Northern Europe, the couple alternates promenading freely (as regards direction, duration, and steps) in open position, with the man lifting and turning the lady, in closed position, "hora à un modo, & hora ad un altro" ("now in one way, and now in another"). In the mid-sixteenth century, the *nizzarda* was considered a kind of "national" dance from Piedmont: "chi non sa fare la Nizzarda, non è . . . Piemontese vero" ("the man who cannot dance the nizzarda is not really Piedmontese");[36] and it was performed at the wedding banquet of Henri IV and Maria de' Medici in Lyons in 1600.[37]

As for the rapid ("*quasi correndo*"—almost running),[38] triple-meter, relatively simple, largely improvisatory early Italian *corrente*, it is its inclusion in musical spectacles and the great body of notated music for this dance that confirm its popularity (second only to that of the *gagliarda*).[39] As in other improvisatory dances, promenading as a couple alternates with "un passaggio tantosto" ("a variation every so often"), which in the *corrente* could be made up of small, fast, and hopped steps like *sottopiedi* or *ricacciate* and *passi in fuga in saltino*, done to the sides, forward and backwards, turning round, and changing places with one's partner.[40] The couple, having "danced its pleasure," chose new partners, and the dance continued.[41]

In summary, improvisation in these traditional or tradition-based couple dances is characterized as follows:

1. promenading freely in terms of direction, duration, and steps;
2. alternating promenading with improvised variations;
3. improvisation or variations based on some fixed steps or patterns;
4. differentiation (though not always) between men's and women's variations;
5. improvisation understood both as variation and as embellishment;
6. no fixed length for any dance, each of which could be performed—with changing partners (and probably a variety of tunes)—for hours. Dancers did not necessarily have to start when the music began, or end with the music.

In contrast to the popular (or traditional) "recreational" dances, fifteenth-century Italian dance-masters composed *bassedanze* and *balli*, which, for the first time, were based on a series of aesthetic principles such as *misura*, *maniera*, *aiere* (measure, manner, air).[42] Each of these "art" dances was for a specific number of dancers, had a precise form and organization, its own steps, technique, and music, all of which had to be learned, practiced, and faithfully reproduced. These "composed" dances (often incorrectly dubbed "court" or "social" dances)[43] were performed by nobles as well as by the urban bourgeiosie and, as Otto Gombosi has pointed out, differed in the freedom of their style and in the uniqueness of each dance from the contemporary French *basse danse*, which was "characterized by an utterly strict formalizing of sequences of steps."[44]

Included in the theoretical sections of the dance treatises are many references to ornamentation: adornment, favor, accidentals, grace, alteration, and *fioretti* (flourishings, small flowerings).[45] Just as for Renaissance music, ornamentation was considered essential for good performance.[46] But since ornamentation was not, in most instances, included in the written choreographic descriptions, it was expected that the dancer, like the Quattrocento *suonatore* or band player, would improvise in various and specific ways, thus enhancing the dance. In some cases particular embellishments were obligatory, in others the dancer was free to choose both the step he wished to decorate and the particular ornament. Some embellishments, such as the virtuosic jumps and turns, were only for men. Certain ornaments were for the feet only, some implied body gesture, and still others were spatial alterations. There were also embellishments which involved a play of the feet against the music. All required skill and provided variety. As the sixteenth century drew to a close, many ornaments were written out in full in the choreographies and integrated into specific steps (see Appendix 3), and variations on a theme abounded.

According to Giovanni Ambrosio (né Guglielmo Ebreo da Pesaro), good male dancers would sprinkle their performances with jumps, turns, and other "flowerings" (*fioreggiare*) that necessitated wearing short (rather than long) garments and using one or both hands to hold their capes in place.[47]

Domenico da Piacenza[48] was the first to list and describe "accidental" steps—steps which, for Antonio Cornazano, once again were the man's domain.[49] (It is worth noting the similarity in nomenclature of both "runs" and "shakes" to that of musical accidentals.)[50] For the most part these foot embellishments were to last a quarter of one *tempo* (a *tempo* being the equivalent of both a modern musical bar and the duration of the basic *passo doppio* or "double" step), although for Cornazano the duration of each ornament was *ad bene placitum* (left to each dancer to decide). Domenico affirms that the dancer was to use only one accidental per *tempo*, although some dancers might be capable of inserting two (each lasting 1/8 of a bar), always performing them during up-beats or "off-beats."[51]

Body graces for both men and women consisted of performing

steps *ombreggiando* (with "shading") by turning the upper body or trunk slightly to the left or right with each step. There was also a wave-like motion—called *ondeggiare* by Cornazano and *aiere* by Guglielmo Ebreo—which consisted of rising onto the half-toe and then lowering the body at every step. Domenico counsels that this *maniera corporea* (body manner) should never be taken to extremes, neither too much nor too little. This is still good counsel for all ornamentation.[52]

Dancing was also supposed to include the enigmatic *fantasmata*, which consisted of occasionally freezing one's movement for a *tempo*. This may have entailed the holding and releasing of breath or energy, similar to a fermata, or to rubato or phrasing in music, but the quality meant "molte cose" ("many things") which for Cornazano, unfortunately for us today, "non si sanno dire" ("were too difficult to explain in words").[53]

When steps were performed to one side and repeated to the other, they were to be *differentiate* (diversified), particularly in terms of size (and, I wonder, also in dynamic?).[54] The choreographies occasionally include altering the direction of steps—that is, taking a side step diagonally forward or backward.[55]

Contrapassi were a favorite ornament and were performed by dancing three *passi doppi* (each in turn composed of three steps, with or without a final close) in two bars of music. They occur in various *balli*, particularly in *bassadanza* sections, and in the more challenging *quadernaria misura*.

Finally, both Domenico and Cornazano dedicate several pages of their treatises to explaining how each one of the four *misure* (*bassadanza* in 6/4; *quadernaria*: one-sixth faster and in 4/4; *saltarello*: one third faster than *bassadanza* and in 6/8; and *piva*: twice as fast) could be danced not only in its own "natural" tempo but also in an "artificial" way by performing the steps of one *misura* to the music of another. This required great ability, and not every student of the dance had this skill.[56] Specifically it meant that one could, for example, insert two *piva doppi* in one *tempo* of *bassadanza*, dance a slower *saltarello doppio* to a bar of *quadernaria* music, or embellish the basic *saltarello* by inserting three *contrapassi* in two bars.

While the choreographic descriptions in the treatises do occasionally specify *contrapassi*, moving in diagonal, and dancing the steps of one *misura* to the music of another, there is no mention of other ornaments. Today, most performers of fifteenth-century dance add *ondeggiamenti* and *ombreggiamenti* to their steps. Few, if any, experiment with *fantasmata*, with varying or "differentiating" repeated steps, with improvising their own *contrapassi* or mixing of *misure*, or with adding jumps, turns, and "accidentals."

The written choreographies seem so complete that it has been difficult to imagine how one could embellish them—or so it was thought until the recent discovery, among the papers of a notary from the small city-state of Montefiascone, of highly ornamented versions of three fifteenth-century dance hits.[57] The *fiorito* versions of *Rostiboli gioioso*, *Leoncello*, and a late fifteenth-century favorite, *Tan geloso*, seem to indicate that the practice of embellishing dances was indeed widespread.[58] It is particularly interesting that these examples should be found in an urban bourgeois setting, far removed from dancing-masters, from courts, and from Lombardy, deemed by modern scholars the center of "noble" and "courtly" dancing.[59]

There are actually four distinct descriptions of the three dances. Undated, they are today haphazardly bound together with miscellaneous letters, notes, drafts of notarial deeds, prayers, accounts, verses, all jotted down by the notary Lancilotto Ricciarelli between 1486 and 1505, though more than half the dates fall prior to 1490. Two of the four descriptions are of *El gioioso fiorito*, one having been abruptly abandoned a little more than half-way through. The two versions have similarities and differences, and it is clear that Ricciarelli was either "composing" as he wrote or was recording an ornamented version that he had either performed or seen performed (his own or someone else's).

By comparing the three *fiorito* dances with their "simple" versions, we find that the ornamentations consist of the following:

1. introducing different steps, particularly when a sequence or a step is repeated—such as a *doppio* and a *meza-volta* instead of the second *ripresa*;[60]
2. introducing *piva* steps in *bassadanza misura*;
3. introducing *contrapassi* (even just one or two!);
4. *salti* (jumps, hops, or leaps); and
5. *volte*: half-turns and turns—backwards, inwards, reverse and straight,[61] both the jumps and turns decorating the ends of many steps,[62] the turns presumably performed in the air or pirouetting on the ground.

These *fioriti* choreographies are a concrete example of what Domenico, Guglielmo, and Cornazano expounded in the theoretical parts of their treatises. They give an idea of the complex technique and the high level of performance required of "amateur" dancers from the nobility and the bourgeoisie. Several questions, however, come to mind. Do these ornamented versions imply that the choreographic descriptions in the dance treatises were mere "skeletons" which the better male dancers were expected to ornament in much the same way as the contemporary dance-band players improvised around the stark tenors and dance tunes notated in the same treatises?[63] Is, for example, the *gioioso fiorito* a true and typical example of an ornamented dance that was actually performed? Or is it a kind of exercise in ornamentation, similar to certain settings of *La Spagna* and the improvisation studies in Diego Ortiz's *Tratado de glosas*?[64] Where, amidst all the turns and "flowerings," is the original *Rostiboli*? What of the quality, and the choreographic sense, of the original *ballo*? (On the other hand, if we look at the bare choreographic description and music that have come down to us, it is difficult, particularly at our cultural distance and five hundred years later, to understand what made the unornamented *Rostiboli gioioso* so outstandingly fashionable and worthy of esteem for at least seventy years.) What is the role of the lady in these flowered versions? What steps does she do? In the incomplete rendering of *El gioioso fiorito* there is the phrase "and let the lady go away and then return and then do the *riprese* together." This may well be an indication that the lady was limited to the unornamented version.[65] Last, but not least, how did such an advanced and cultivated kind of dancing find its way to small and independent Montefiascone, with no court or ruling nobility?

I would like to conclude with some considerations regarding improvisation in the performance of fifteenth-century dances today.

The first concerns the Romanian village dancer's statement that good music provokes dance improvisation, and that one shapes one's own dance according to the music. This is precisely what Giovanni Ambrosio had in mind in his "Exercise for Recognizing a Good Dancer" in which he expects the dancer to shape his performance to the style and character ("air") of different instruments, each of which was to play the same piece of music in turn.[66]

That good music provokes dance improvisation is obvious for

anyone who has been "swept off his feet" by a jazz band, a Latin American combo, or a folk dance ensemble. However, most Renaissance dance specialists continue to insist that the musicians playing for dancers must *follow* the dancers. Aside from this not being a contemporary performance practice (the *pifferi* and *tromboni* would not have kept their eyes fixed on the dancers to keep up with them), it stimulates neither players nor dancers to improvise. As the harpist Andrew Lawrence King stated in a presentation entitled "How Many Times Do I Have to Play This Tune?" though improvisation is "a risky business . . . it is thoroughly authentic in its freedom and spontaneity. . . . Playing for dance music must not be bland . . . or controlled to the point where rigor mortis sets in—strong colours and bold brush-strokes are more typical of the dance-music palette [which must] have that indefinable 'swing'."[67] Thirteen years later, King is still somewhat of an exception among "early" musicians who rarely react as one double bass jazz player did when he heard that Quattrocento dance music consisted of improvising on a tenor melody (a sort of "middle" bass line): "A tenor," he shouted ecstatically, "give me a tenor!" Nonetheless, valid advances have been made by a few players of fifteenth-century dance music.[68] I for one find it an absolute delight and inspiration to dance to a totally new arrangement of an old favorite, where the somewhat hidden tenor is "dressed" in enchantingly different apparel.

If musicians specialized in medieval and Renaissance music are making slow but steady progress in improvisation of dance music, "early" dancers have not even begun.[69] Resistance to experimentation—adding embellishments to "art" dances and improvising with "popular" dances—is strong on the part of both specialists and students who prefer to reconstruct, learn, practice, and perform the codified repertoire. What are possible options?

The Quattrocento treatises do not give any specific step descriptions. We know the durations (which makes it possible to match choreography and music), and we have various clues for how to perform the different steps. There are often several contrasting clues for the same step, but, rather than a cause for confusion, I think these can serve as the kind of "motifs" or "stepping stones" to which I referred at the very beginning of this essay when discussing improvisation in folk dancing. These "alterations" can actually help make a choreography come more alive and help satisfy the dance-treatises' pleas for variation and embellishment. "Early dance" performers, furthermore, have rarely thought about "interpretation," though they would agree that to play a piece of music (or act a part in a play) "straight" would be unthinkable. The fact, for example, that we do not know if *sempio* and *doppio* steps ended with feet together in a closed position or were left open (as when we walk), can give the modern performer a chance to choose one or the other possibility according to the particular moment in a dance and the particular quality desired (such as *legato, marcato*). By the same token, the treatises furnish different indications of how to perform a *meza-volta* (half-turn): slowly, perhaps, and while turning into a sideways *ripresa* step; more sudden and shorter, and then *followed* by a *ripresa*; with a hop (done with or without *gagliardia*, exactly in time with the music, or at the last moment).

For Domenico and Cornazano, all of the dance steps were to be accompanied by a slow rise and a rapid lowering of the body, performed "cum tanta suavitade che pari una gondola che da dui rimi spinta sia per quelle undicelle quando el mare fa quieta segondo sua natura alçando le dicte undicelle cum tardeza e abasandosse cum presteza" ("with such smoothness that the movement [or dancer] resembles a gondola driven by two oars through those little waves that the sea makes when it is naturally calm, which rise slowly and lower themselves quickly").[70] This style of *ondeggiare* is, as I have mentioned, practiced by most performers of Quattrocento dance. However, Guglielmo says that Air, another *favore* to make the art of dancing more accomplished, consists of "un dolce & humanissimo rilevamento" ("a sweet and most gentle rising movement"). Thus, anyone dancing a *sempio* or a *doppio*, a *ripresa* or *continenza*, *scosso* or *saltarello* must "fare alchuno aieroso relevamento & sorgere destremente nel battere di tempi" ("make an airy rise and surge up nimbly *on the downbeat*").[71] Guglielmo's words, totally ignored today, were interpreted many years ago by "early dancers" in England as dancing mincingly on the toes. I am now experimenting and improvising with students, and am alternating Guglielmo's instructions with Domenico's, or combining the two, as we find in the late sixteenth century where some steps start high and finish low, and others are flat but end in a small rising and lowering of the heels.[72]

Taking different step explanations or clues and mixing them in performance is certainly not "authentic reconstruction," but to ignore embellishment, improvisation, and interpretation is also not "authentic." We do not know if these variants in step descriptions are geographic, chronological, due to a dancing-master's personal style or to how the amanuensis has expressed the performative concept, or if they are truly "innovations."[73] Once written down, is the brief description of a step the exception or the rule?[74] I am suggesting that choosing particular step variants and performing them with appropriate dynamics is one way of working towards a personal interpretation of various moments in a dance.

Just as the music for a specific dance would rarely have sounded exactly the same because different players would have, in diverse ways, enriched the dance tunes and improvised upon the tenors, so, probably, would the performances of the same *ballo* by two experienced dancers have been quite different. If the notated dance tunes are merely "skeletal indications," the same may be true of the dance descriptions which are jotted down in the treatises bereft of their requisite ornamentation or "small flowerings." If we today keep just to the written choreographies, we may, in Robert Donington's words, be "austerely understating" the spirit of the dances.[75] Attempts by dancers to incorporate the different sorts of ornamentation described in the treatises into their performances need, however, to be accompanied by a notion of what is suitable (in terms of the contemporary aesthetic) and "dance-like." Thus, these early dances, rather than "old" and "preserved," will without doubt be closer to the original spirit and style, so aptly expressed by old Andronico—racked with love for the young Bilora in Ruzante's comedy:

> E digo, che son sì in sù la gamba, che me basteràue l'anemo de ballàr quattro tempi del Zoioso, e farlo strapassaò ancora, e anche la rosina, a farla tutta in fioretti, che no saràue minga puoco.[76]
>
> (I tell you that my legs are still so good that I have the spirit to dance four *tempi* of the *Gioioso* and perform it scrambled besides; and also the whole of *Rosina* with flourishes—which indeed would be no small thing.)

Appendix 1

Improvisation and Composition

Ideas expressed by László Felföldi
based on individual improvisations in Eastern European
village dances and presented here with his permission

Improvisation	Composition
otherness	sameness
freedom	regulations
variability	invariability
temporality	permanence
openness	closedness
unexpectedness	expectedness
unaccountability	accountability
accidentality	intentionality
subjectivity	objectivity
embeddedness in context	independence from context

In *folk dance improvisation*, creation and performance (process and product) are simultaneous. The village dancer is both the choreographer and the performer and has to rely (more than the "professional" choreographer) on the current dance tradition rules. (The dancer who strays far from traditional forms will not be accepted.) Preparation is short and not separate from the performance. Hence, well-known (built-in, i.e., learned and remembered reflexes) stereotypes are used. Improvisation is based on a given ("old") topic and concentrates on its elaboration. Improvisations will always vary due to oral tradition (slips of memory), to different circumstances—time, place, partner, audience, and the demands for novelty by the audience and the dancer him/herself. Therefore, the improvisation attempts to be both the same and different, regulated and free within the framework of a given tradition (a set of rules and "freedoms," known and shared by the entire community).

In *art pieces*, the moment of creation and the event of the performance are distinct, as are the creator and performer. When the *choreographer* creates his "new" composition, he is close to freedom, variability, etc. (the first column), though he is limited by historic style, creative traditions, audience expectations, etc.

Nevertheless, *he is more autonomous than a dancer in a traditional community or village* [italics mine]. In the stage performance of this choreography, the *dancer* is closer to the sameness, regulations, etc. of the second column.

Appendix 2

Principal Italian Dance Sources—c.1455–1630

Fifteenth-Century Treatises with Music
(in chronological order)

Domenico da Piacenza, *De arte saltandi*, c.1455, Paris, Bibl. Nat., fonds ital 972

Antonio Cornazano, *Libro dell'arte del danzare*, 1455/1465, Bibl. Apost. Vat., Cappon 203

Guglielmo Ebreo, *De pratica seu arte tripudii*, 1463, Paris, Bibl. Nat., fonds ital 973

Giovanni Ambrosio [a.k.a. Guglielmo Ebreo], c.1471–74, *De pratica seu arte tripudii*, Paris, Bibl. Nat., fonds ital 476

Other Versions of Guglielmo Ebreo's Treatise
(without music)

c.1477, Florence, Biblioteca Nazionale Centrale: Magliabecchiano XIX. 88†

c.1477, Modena, Biblioteca Estense: Ital. 82.A.J.94†

c.1474, Siena, Biblioteca Comunale: L.V.29

c.1480, New York Public Library of the Performing Arts, Dance Collection: "Giorgio" MS., *MGZMB–Res. 72–254

1510, Florence, Biblioteca Medicea Laurenziana: Antinori 13†

Where the dates of the above MSS. are unknown, I have followed F. Alberto Gallo's suggested datings included in his "Il 'ballare lombardo' (circa 1435–1475)," *Studi musicali* 8 (1979).

"Transition Sources"—Early Sixteenth Century†

1517, Turin, Archivi Biscaretti, Mazzo 4, no. 4 ("Stribaldi roll," 54 *basse-danses*)

1510, Florence, Biblioteca Medicea Laurenziana, Antinori 13 (four "new" *balli*)

c.1515–20, New York Public Library of the Performing Arts, Dance Collection: "Il Papa" MS., *MGZMB–Res. 72–255

1517, Nuremberg, Germanisches Nationalmuseum, MS. 8842 (15th-century Italian *balli*)

Fundamental Sources of the "New Italian Style" c.1540–1630

c.1540–50	MS. "Tuscan balli" (published by Gino Corti)†
1560	Lutio Compasso, *Ballo della Gagliarda*
1581	Fabritio Caroso, *Il Ballarino*
1588	Thoinot Arbeau, *Orchésographie*††
1589	Prospero Lutij, *Opera bellissima . . . Partite, et Passeggi di Gagliarda*
1589	Emilio de' Cavalieri, final *ballo* of the intermedi for *La Pellegrina*
1600	Fabritio Caroso, *Nobiltà di dame*
1600	Livio Lupi, *Mutanze di gagliarda, tordiglione, passo e mezzo, canari,* etc.
1602	Cesare Negri, *Le gratie d'amore*
1604	Cesare Negri, re-editing of *Le gratie d'amore* with new title: *Nuove inventioni di balli*
1605	Fabritio Caroso, re-edition of *Nobiltà di dame*
1607	Livio Lupi, new edition of *Mutanze* (1600) entitled *Libro di gagliarda, tordiglione*, etc.
c.1615–20	Ludovico Jacobilli, *Modo di ballare* (MS.)†
1620	Filippo degli Alessandri, *Discorso sopra il ballo*†
c.1620	Giulio Mancini, *Del Origin et Nobiltà del Ballo*
1630	Fabritio Caroso, re-edition of *Nobiltà di dame*, with the title *Raccolta di varij balli*

†These sources are not cited in this essay.

††A French treatise but cited in this essay.

Appendix 3

Pavoneggiare

The late sixteenth-century choreographies included in the treatises of Fabritio Caroso and Cesare Negri tend to have built-in steps embellishments. This is particularly clear in Caroso's second treatise, *Nobiltà di dame* (1600), where he adds a great many ornamented steps of his own invention. However, in both of Caroso's manuals the grace that seems to dominate style and steps is referred to as *pavoneggiare*, a term which has given rise to some misconceptions. John Florio, in his dictionary *A Worlde of Wordes* (1598), says that a "pavoneggiatore" is "a wanton fellow that will court and fondly gaze upon himself [strutting] up and down . . . as a peacock doth." But Caroso uses the term simply to mean *ornamentation*.

In his Rule for the *Continenza Grave* (in *Nobiltà di dame*), Caroso says that this step "ci si contiene tutta la gratia, e tutto il decoro" ("contains all grace and decorum") and that one must accompany it by bending one's left side a little, giving one's shoulder "un cenno di grazia" (a touch of grace), *pavoneggiando* and containing oneself, and at the end of the step one must *pavoneggiare* with the grace of rising up just a little and lowering one's heels. The "bending" of the upper body may well be a kind of *ombreggiare* (sideways shading), and the rise and fall at the end of the step is similar to the fifteenth-century wave-like *ondeggiare*.

In his first treatise, *Il Ballarino* (1581), Caroso uses the term *pavoneggiare* in describing both the *Seguito ordinario* step and the *Seguiti scorsi*. Cesare Negri in his *Le gratie d'amore* (1600) uses exactly the same words that Caroso does but substitutes the word *habilirse* (to adorn oneself) for *pavoneggiare*, and in his almost identical version of *Il Ballarino*'s rule for *seguiti scorsi* (running steps) Negri says to move the body "con agilità, & gratia" (with agility and grace) instead of Caroso's *pavoneggiandola*.

In *Il Ballarino*, Caroso, in his Rule for the basic *cinque passi* of the *gagliarda*, explains that the arms are lowered but "*pavoneggiandosi* alle volte il destro; poiche brutta vista sarebbe tenendolo sempre disteso" ("*pavoneggiando* the right arm occasionally, since keeping it straight all the time would be unattractive"). However, in *Nobiltà di dame*, he changes this to keeping the right arm straight down, "movendo secondo che à te parrà in maniera più gratiosa" ("moving it as you like in a most gracious manner").

In conclusion, *pavoneggiare* was used to mean: bending or inclining the side of the upper body, giving the shoulder "a touch of grace"; a rising and lowering of the heels; "flourishing" or "adorning" oneself (or the body); carrying oneself with agility and grace; and moving a part of the body as one pleased, in a gracious manner.

NOTES

[1]See, for example, Peter Burke, *Popular Culture in Early Modern Europe* (1978; reprint Aldershot: Scolar Press, 1996). That dance historians have shown interest in contemporary pop-dance culture and in twentieth-century popular dance in general is revealed in their writings and in conference themes—e.g., the Dance Critics Association's 1998 conference entitled "What's Popular about Popular Culture?"

[2]In this article, I use the terms 'popular' and 'traditional' dance instead of 'folk' dance in the same way as the International Council of Traditional Music, which officially replaced the ambiguous term 'folk' with 'traditional.'

[3]There were many other traditional dances that were great favorites, some of which—e.g., the *Spagnoletta* and the *Chiaranzana*—were included in dance treatises (see Appendix 2). Moreover, the period 1480–1530 abounds in dance-music and in references to dances in literary sources, the titles of which are (or sound like) the names of songs. See, for example, Cesare Nappi's "Egloga villereccia" (Biblioteca Universitaria, Bologna), which mentions almost thirty dances, many of which can be found in contemporary musical sources. Musical sources from the fifteenth and sixteenth centuries supply the names of literally hundreds of anonymous (and often local) dances, about most of which little or nothing is known. See, for example, Victor Coehlo, *The Manuscript Sources of 17th Century Italian Lute Music* (New York: Garland, 1995); Knud Jeppesen, *La Frottola*, 2 vols. (Copenhagen: Århus Universitetslaget, 1970); and Ottaviano Petrucci, *Odhecaton* (Venice, 1501); as well as Petrucci's many volumes of *Frottole* published in the first decade of the sixteenth century.

[4]See, in particular, Nino Pirrotta, "The Oral and Written Traditions of Music," in *Music and Culture in Italy from the Middle Ages to the Baroque* (Cambridge: Harvard University Press, 1984), 72–79.

[5]*Antropologia della Musica e Culture Mediterranee*, ed. Tullia Magrini (Venice: Il Molino, 1993), 67–71. Gallo (69) cites Peter Jeffery, *Re-Envisioning Past Musical Cultures: Ethnomusicology in the Study of Gregorian Chant*

(Chicago: University of Chicago Press, 1992), 120, who proposes an "act of historical imagination" to allow a "re-envisioning of the past."

[6]The occasion was a meeting in August 1998 of the Study Group on Ethnochoreology of the ICTM (see n. 2 above). The interview, by Anca Giurchescu, is in her essay, "Interpreting a Dancer's Discourse on Improvisation," in *ICTM 20th Ethnochoreology Symposium Proceedings* (Istanbul: Dans Müzik Kültür Folklora Dogru, 2000), 259–74.

[7]The other paper on which I have drawn is László Felfödi's "Improvisation—An attempt at Defining the Term" (not included in the above *Proceedings*), and on subsequent correspondence with him. All ideas drawn from his work in my article appear with his permission.

[8]British Library, MS. Add. 29987; facsimile: *The Manuscript: London, British Museum Additional 29987*, introd. Gilbert Reaney, Musicological Studies and Documents 13 ([Dallas]: American Institute of Musicology, 1965).

[9]Florence, Biblioteca Nazionale Centrale, MS. Magl. VII, 1121, fols. 66–69^{v}, published in *Un ballo a Firenze nel 1459*, ed. Vittorio Rossi (Milan: Istituto Italiano d'Arti Grafiche, 1885). "In questo tempo i pifferi e 'l tronbone cominciaro a sonare un salterello fondato d'arte d'intera ragione. Allora ongni scudier gentile e snello, che piglia maritata e chi pulzella et a danzar comincia or questo or quello; chi passeggia d'intorno e chi saltella, chi scanbia mano e chi lascia e chi 'nvita e chi in due parti o 'n tre fa danza bella" ("In this time shawms and sackbuts began to play a *saltarello* based on art and reason. Then every courteous and nimble squire took wives and damsels and began to dance this or that; some promenading around, others skipping, others changing hands, some stopping and some inviting, some in twos or in threes doing lovely dancing").

[10]See, for example, the anonymous engraving *The Planet Venus* (London, British Museum), the *cassoni* by Matteo di Giovanni, *The Marriage of Antiochus and Stratonice* (San Marino, Calif., Huntington Library); by Apollonio di Giovanni (The Art Institute of Chicago); the anonymous *Magnanimity of Scipio* (London, Victoria and Albert Museum); and an anonymous wedding scene (St. Petersburg, The Hermitage), reproduced in *Guglielmo Ebreo da Pesaro e la danza nelle corti italiane del XV secolo*, ed. Patrizia Castelli, Maurizio Mingardi, and Maurizio Padovan (Pesaro: Gualtieri, 1987), figs. 35–37, 39–40 (*cassoni*), and 45–46 (engravings). Another "*saltarello*-type" image appears in an anonymous miniature depicting a Purim scene in a *Mishne Torah* (Rome, Biblioteca Apostolica Vaticana), reproduced and discussed in my article "Dancing Couples Behind the Scenes: Recently Discovered Italian Illustrations, 1470–1550," *Imago Musicae* 13 (1996): 9–38, esp. 23, 25.

[11]I discussed this problem in "What Can Pictures Tell Us (and not tell us) About Dance? Reading Italian Renaissance Dance Iconography," an unpublished slide presentation given at the Society for Dance History Scholars' conference in

New York in 1997. The *Proceedings* (Riverside, Calif.: SDHS, 1997) contain a Summary and Bibliography, the latter including Timothy J. McGee's inspiring article, "Misleading Iconography: The Case of the 'Adimari Wedding Cassone'," *Imago Musicae* 11–12 (1992–95): 139–57.

[12]Bartolomeo Pinelli has various etchings, such as "Couple from Rivisondoli dancing the *saltarello*" (1814), and watercolors, including a scene with "briganti che assistono al saltarello" (1828), in *Inediti di Bartolomeo Pinelli (1781–1835) Raccolta di 50 costumi . . . del Regno di Napoli incisi 1814* [catalogue], ed. Pier Andrea de Rosa and Paolo Emilio Trastuelli (Rome: Museo del Folklore, 1984).

[13]See Appendix 2 for a list of the principal dance treatises c.1455–1630. The *ballo* was a dance type created and perfected by the Quattrocento dance-masters and characterized by changes of meter and tempo (*misura,* see below). A few *balli* were pantomimic. Most were for a couple or trio. All had their own specially composed music. See Barbara Sparti, *Guglielmo Ebreo: De pratica seu arte tripudii* (1993; reprint Oxford: Clarendon Press, 1995), esp. chap. 4.

[14]Ibid., 68 (and n. 19), 72, 225. In two *balli*, there is a shift back and forth between 3/4 and 6/8.

[15]The fifteenth-century dancing-masters called this gesture *movimento* and later *scosso*. Descriptions for a "*movimento de piedi*" and a "*tremare dei piedi*" are provided by Cesare Negri in his *Le gratie d'amore* (Milan, 1602; facs. reprint New York: Broude, 1969, and Bologna: Forni, 1969), 32–33.

[16]Thomas Morley, *A Plain and Easy Introduction to Practical Music,* ed. R. A. Harman (1952; reprint New York: W.W. Norton, 1963), 297.

[17]Archivio di Stato, Rome, Tribunale criminale del Governatore, Costituti 573 (1606–07), fols. 80–81, 24 Dec. 1606. I am indebted to Elizabeth Cohen (York University, Toronto) who generously shared this information with me.

[18]*Del Origin et Nobiltà del Ballo*, Rome, Biblioteca Apostolica Vaticana, MS. Barberiniano Latino 4315, fols. 157^r–86^v. Mancini is well-known to art historians for his essays, bound in the same manuscript (but available in modern editions), on the lives and works of artists, the most important being his *Viaggio per Roma per vedere le pitture che si ritrovan in essa* (*Travels through Rome to Look at the Paintings Found There*), considered the first "critical guide" to works of art, and his treatise, *Alcune Considerationi Appartenenti alla Pittura come di Diletto di un Gentilhuomo* (*Certain Considerations About Painting as a Pastime for a Gentleman*), an important source for early Seicento aesthetic ideas and taste in painting, particularly in Rome. I am preparing a critical edition of *Del Origin et Nobiltà del Ballo*.

[19] Mancini, *Del Origin*, fol. 175^v.

[20]This was confirmed to me by ethnochoreologist Pino Gallo. See also Giancarlo Palombini, "La saltarella di Amatrice" [description and transcription of the music], *Choreola* 1, no. 1 (1991): 59–61. Other dances also used handkerchief hand-holds.

[21]See Sparti, *Guglielmo Ebreo*, chap. 4 and pp. 223–24, for more information about the *piva*. The anonymous woodcut on the frontispiece of "La Nencia da Barberino," reproduced in Sparti, "Dancing Couples," 18, may be depicting a *piva*.

[22]Cod. Vatic. Urbin.692 (c.1454), reprinted in Daniel Heartz, "A 15th-Century Ballo: *Rôti Bouilli Joyeux*," in *Aspects of Medieval and Renaissance Music: A Birthday Offering to Gustave Reese*, ed. Jan La Rue *et al.* (New York: W. W. Norton, 1966), 372–73. Here and elsewhere, English translations are mine unless otherwise noted.

[23]*Proverbi di messer Antonio Cornazano in facetie* (1865; facs. reprint Bologna: Forni, 1968).

[24]See Cornazano, *Libro dell'arte del danzare*, 1455 (1465), fols. 5^r, 6^r, 7^v, and 11^v; for an edition, see Curzio Mazzi, *La Bibliofilia* 17 (1915): 1–30; and for translations, Antonio Cornazano, *The Book on the Art of Dancing*, trans. Madeleine Inglehearn and Peggy Forsyth (London: Dance Books, 1981), and A. William Smith, ed. and trans., *Fifteenth-Century Dance and Music* (Stuyvesant, N.Y.: Pendragon Press, 1995), vol. 1. Caprioles were "capers," similar to the *entrechat* in ballet.

[25]See Sparti, *Guglielmo Ebreo*, 70–71.

[26]Joan Ambrosio Dalza, *Intabolatura de lauto libro quarto*, ed. Ottaviano dei Petrucci (Venice, 1508).

[27]See Frank A. D'Accone, *The Civic Muse: Music and Musicians in Siena during the Middle Ages and the Renaissance* (Chicago: University of Chicago Press, 1997), 653–54, 662–63, for a dancing school in Siena (c.1493) which advertised lessons in the *gagliarda*. Also discussed is a contract for another dancing-school (in 1505) in which a dancing master from Brescia, together with his sons, was to teach "calate and gagliarde. . . ."

[28]The *cinque passi* (five steps) consisted in four alternating leg kicks (corresponding to the first four beats of music), the last of which was more vigorous and accompanied by the dancer's jumping into the air on the fifth beat, and a final cadence, when he landed with both feet together on the ground for the fifth "step" and sixth beat.

[29]Lutio Compasso, *Ballo della Gagliarda* (Florence, 1560; facs. reprint [introd. Barbara Sparti] Freiburg: "fa-gisis" Musik- und Tanzedition, 1995); Fabritio Caroso, *Il Ballarino* (Venice: Ziletti, 1581; facs. reprint New York:

Broude, 1967), and *Nobiltà di dame* (Venice: il Muschio, 1600; reissue 1605; facs. reprint Bologna: Forni, 1970), and, for a translation, see *Courtly Dance of the Renaissance*, trans. Julia Sutton with musical transcriptions by F. Marian Walker (Oxford: Oxford University Press, 1986); Thoinot Arbeau (pseud. for Jehan Tabourot), *Orchésographie* (Langres, 1588, followed by many editions; facs. reprints: Geneva: Minkoff, 1972; Bologna: Forni, 1969, facs. of Paris: Laure Fonta, 1888 [music and steps misaligned]; Langres: Dominque Guéniot, 1988); for translations, see Mary Stewart Evans, trans. (1948), and new ed., ed. Julia Sutton (New York: Dover, 1967); Prospero Lutij of Sulmona, *Opera bellissima nella quale si contengono molte partite et passeggi di gagliarda* (Perugia: Orlando, 1589); Livio Lupi, *Mutanze di Gagliarda, Tordiglione, Passo è Mezzo, Canari* (Palermo: Carrara, 1600, and the 2nd ed., *Libro di Gagliarda, Tordiglione* (Palermo, 1607); Negri, *Le gratie d'amore.*

[30]Two examples as given by Negri in his *Le gratie d'amore* will suffice: "Questa mutanza è di 13 botte, & quattro tempi di suono" ("This variation is composed of 13 'beats' and four bars of music" [*Leggiadra Marina*, 238]), and "questa mutanza e de botte 29 & di quattro tempi di suono" ("this variation is composed of 29 'beats' and four bars of music" [*Tordiglione Nuovo*, 195]). The number of *cinque passi* that would perfectly fit four six-beat bars of music would be 20.

[31]See *Laura Suave* and *Nido d'amore* in *Nobiltà di dame.*

[32]*Del Origin*, fol. 164^r. The translation of *gagliardo* is from John Florio, *A Worlde of Wordes* (London, 1598; facs. reprint Hildesheim: Georg Olms Verlag, 1972).

[33]The *Gagliarda* appears in Johann Schein's instrumental dance suites in his *Banchetto musicale* (1617), where he explains that these dances were not for practical use ("Tänze für die Füsse") but were art music and hence "Tänze für die Ohren." It is the Modenese Giuseppe Colombi who composes, in the 1670s, Italian and French dances both "per ballare" (for dancing) and "per camera" (for the chamber). See also (among others), Girolamo Frescobaldi's *Secondo Libro di toccate . . . gagliarde* [5], *correnti* [6] *et altre partite d'intavolatura di cimbalo et organo* (Rome, 1627), and the sixteenth-century *Fitzwilliam Virginal Book*, ed. J. A. Fuller Maitland and W. Barclay Squire, 2 vols. (1899; reprint New York: Dover, 1963).

[34]Negri, *Le gratie d'amore*, 268 (italics mine).

[35]See Appendix 2 and n. 29, above. There is a contemporary anonymous painting (as well as a woodcut) which depicts Queen Elizabeth dancing the *volta*; reproduced in Mabel Dolmetsch, *Dances of England and France from 1450 to 1600* (1949; reprint New York: Da Capo Press, 1975), 129. The woodcut is reproduced in Belinda Quirey, *May I have the Pleasure?* (London: British Broadcasting Corporation, 1976), 6. What is clear from Arbeau's directions and

these images is that the *volta* was danced with the man and woman in "closed" (waltz-like) position. The man held the bottom of the lady's busk, and as she jumped he helped her turn by pushing her gently with his raised knee and bent leg.

[36]The quote is from a long description made in 1606 by the painter Federico Zuccaro in his *Il Passaggio per l'Italia*, ed. Vincenzo Lanciarini (Rome: Tipografia della Mantellate, 1893), 40–41. See also Federica C. Prina, "Nizarda! Ché danza es esa?" in *L'Arte della Danza ai Tempi di Claudio Monteverdi* (Turin: Istituto per i Beni Musicali in Piemonte, 1996), 17–32.

[37]Here it appears as a *branle* or popular circle dance. Other dances performed on this occasion were the *corrente* (see below), the "Gran Ballo" or *Chiaranzana*, and the *volta*. See Anton Giulio Bragaglia, *Danze popolari italiane* (Rome: ENAL, 1960), 34.

[38]The description of the *corrente* at Maria de' Medici's wedding (see n. 37) has the man leading the lady "quasi correndo indietro" ("almost running behind/backwards") and includes changing partners.

[39]See, for example, Emilio de' Cavalieri's *Rappresentazione dell'Anima e del Corpo* (1600), Sigismondo d'India's *Balletti* for the Prince of Savoy (1621), and Luigi Rossi's *Il Palazzo Incantato* (Rome, 1642). See also the *correnti* in Lorenzo Allegri's *balletti* (1608); in the De Bellis MS., San Francisco (c.1611); in Salomone Rossi's *Terzo* and *Quarto Libro de' varie sonate, sinfonie, gagliarde, brandi e correnti* (1613, 1622); in Alessandro Piccinnini's *balletti* (1600–1620s); in Girolamo Fantini's *balletti* for trumpet (1638); in Gasparo Zannetti's *Lo Scolaro* (1645); and in Frescobaldi's *Libro primo di Toccate*, rev. ed. (Rome, 1637); and in his *Secondo libro*.

[40]*Sottopiede* means, literally, "foot under," similar to the *ricacciata* or "chased" step in which a foot is placed behind the other foot, "kicking" it forward. The *passi in fuga in saltino*, "fleeing hopped steps," are not clearly explained but are performed with runs.

[41]Negri, *Le gratie d'amore*, 265.

[42]For definitions of these humanistic terms, see below in the text and in Sparti, *Guglielmo Ebreo* (Glossary and chap. 1). *Ballo* is briefly discussed above in n. 13. The *bassadanza* ("low" dance because it has no hops, such as in the *saltarello*) is both an independent dance type and one of the possible sections of a *ballo*. It is the slowest of the four *misure* and is (in modern terms) in 6/4 or compound duple time.

[43]The terms 'social' (as opposed to 'theatrical') and 'court' dance are discussed in Barbara Sparti, "Breaking Down Barriers in the Study of Renaissance and Baroque Dance," *Dance Chronicle* 19, no. 3 (1996): 255–76, esp. 266–67. Dances for court spectacles were, for the most part, costumed and allegorical

moresche. Many city states in fifteenth-century Italy were republics and had no court.

[44]Otto Gombosi, "About Dance and Dance Music in the Late Middle Ages," *Musical Quarterly* 27 (1941): 303.

[45]I have limited myself to giving only one reference for each term: *adornamento* (Guglielmo, fol. 8^{v}), *favore* (Guglielmo, fol. 8^{r}), *accidentali* (Cornazano, fol. 7^{v}), *gratia* (Caroso, *Nobiltà di dame*, 16), *alteratione* and *fioreggiare* (Giovanni Ambrosio, fol. 24^{v}). Note that the fifteenth-century term *fioretti* (small flowerings) is the same as that used today for improvisations in folk dancing. See the beginning of this essay.

[46]This section of my essay is based, in part, on my paper "Style and Performance in the Social Dances of the Italian Renaissance: Ornamentation, Improvisation, Variation, and Virtuosity," in *Proceedings of the 9th Annual Conference of the Society of Dance History Scholars* (Riverside, Calif.: SDHS, 1986), 31–52. While some of the terminology used there is superseded, the various kinds of ornamentation are discussed in greater depth than here, and the original Italian descriptions are included in the notes. The final part of the article (38–40) deals with the late sixteenth-century concept of *pavoneggiare* and its meaning in the contemporary treatises as a synonym for ornamentation. See Appendix 3 to the present essay.

[47]Sparti, *Guglielmo Ebreo*, 232–33.

[48]See Appendix 2. Domenico da Piacenza, *De arte saltandi et choreas ducendi*; D. R. Wilson, ed., *Domenico of Piacenza*, revised ed. (Cambridge: Early Dance Circle, 1995); ed. and trans. Smith, *Fifteenth-Century Dance.*

[49]As a courtier, Cornazano tends to be more conservative and concerned about who should do what than the dancing-masters. Moreover, his treatise, which was dedicated to Ippolita Sforza, specifies what was appropriate, and not, for a lady to perform.

[50]For Domenico, the *scorsa* (run) was a *moto accidentale* (fol. 2^{v}) which could substitute a *doppio* step. Other "accidentals" included the *frappamento* and the *piçigamento* (Cornazano, fol. 7^{v}). Guglielmo introduced the term *scosso* (shake) for the *movimento*, a "natural" step-unit which, however, was often used as an ornament. See fig. 1 ("Natural and Accidental Steps") in Jennifer Nevile's essay in this volume.

[51]Domenico, fol. 3^{r}; Cornazano, fol. 9^{v}.

[52]Domenico, fol. 1^{v}: "È nota che questa agilitade e mainera [sic] per niuno modo vole essere adoperata per li estremi. Ma tenire el mezo del tuo movimento che non sia ni tropo ni poco . . ." ("And note that this agility and grace must for no

reason be taken to extremes. But keep your movement to the mean so that it is neither too much nor too little").

[53]Domenico refers to the body's breathing through *fantasmata* ("spirando el corpo per fantasmate," fol. 1v). Cornazano (fol. 7r) says, "In questo Misser Domenichino . . . ha avuto evidentissimo giudicio dicendo che'l dançare specialmente di misura larga vole essere simile ad ombra phantasmatica; nella quale similtudine, ad explicarla se intendono molte cose che non si sanno dire" ("In this Messer Domenichino . . . was extremely wise saying that dancing especially in a slow measure should be similar to a phantasmic shade; there are many meanings to explain this comparison which cannot be said in words").

[54]For Cornazano, "*Diversità di cose*" (fols. 4r and 7r) applied more to the man than the woman. "Nella bassadança . . . non è bello senno fare le riprese et le continentie differentiate l'una dall'altra, cioè grandi e piccole, e detro l'una grande non si faccia mai l'altra tale; e cosi e converso" ("In the *bassadanza* . . . it is not lovely unless the *riprese* and the *continenze* are different from each other, that is big or small, and after a big one never do another [the next one] the same; and the opposite is true").

[55]These are called "Portuguese" *riprese* or *doppi*, or *riprese in galone*, and are similar to the fashionable sixteenth-century practice of taking steps *fiancheggati* forwards or backwards.

[56]See Sparti, *Guglielmo Ebreo*, chap. 4, for a discussion of the different *misure*. "[C]he tu sapi e revolvi tutte le mexure a tuo modo cum ragione per natura o per accidentia . . ."; "li altri tri per acidentia lo intelecto li po spartirli e danzarli" ("that you know and re-elaborate all the *misure* in your own way according to what is natural or devised by the intellect . . ."; "the other three accidental ones can be partitioned and danced by using the intellect" [Domenico, fol. 5r]). "Tutte le dicte misure si altarano e si fan l'una su l'altra . . . et è cosa di perfecto magistero, non da ogni scolaro" ("All the said *misure* can be altered and performed on each other's music . . . and it is something which takes real mastery, not for all students" [Cornazano, fol. 13r]). See fig. 2 ("Summary of Steps Danced Outside their Natural Order") in Jennifer Nevile's essay in this collection. *Accidentale*, like *artificioso*, meant the opposite of natural—that is, artful, artificial, man-made, skillful.

[57]For a complete study of these dances, as well as transcriptions and translations, see Barbara Sparti, "*Rôti Bouilli*: Take Two 'El Gioioso Fiorito'," *Studi Musicali* 24, no. 2 (1995): 231–61.

[58]Unfortunately, the *lioncello fiorito* folios are in very poor condition, and any transcription will be approximate.

[59]See, for example, Ingrid G. Brainard, *The Art of Courtly Dancing in the Early Renaissance* (West Newton, Mass.: I. G. Brainard, 1981); F. Alberto Gallo, "Il 'ballare lombardo' (circa 1435–1475)," *Studi Musicali* 8 (1979): 61–84; and

Alessandro Pontremoli and Patrizia La Rocca, *Il ballare lombardo* (Milan: Vita e Pensiero, 1987).

[60]Other examples are: two *tempi* of *piva* "*in cambio de*" the two *sempi* ("simple" steps) with which a second sequence begins, and a *riverenza* (bow) plus a *volta* (turn) instead of a second *doppio*.

[61]The *volte* are problematic. It is not at all clear what exactly is meant by the four terms (used also by Cornazano)—*volta indereto* (backwards turn), *in dentro* (inwards), *reversa* (reverse), and *dritta* (straight)—or how they are performed. *Dentro* appears in *El gioioso* as a "backwards" turn and then as a "reverse" turn. Elsewhere the turn is both *roversa* and *in dereto*. Are these definitions of *dentro*, or are they really different turns? And while *meza volta dritta* appears first as *una volta col pe dritto*, suggesting that a *volta dritta* is not a "straight turn" but a turn with the right foot, further on we have a *volta dritta col pe dritto* (a straight turn with the right foot). Cornazano, fol. 6^r (discussing the *piva*), also gives *volte* "dritti e riversi e dentro e fuori" ("straight and reverse, inwards and *outwards*" [my emphasis]). Further, while *meza volta* (*half*-turn) is specified, does *volta* always mean *full*-turn [my emphases]?

[62]Performed in the *vuodo* (literally, "emptiness") or upbeat.

[63]For examples of how this would have been done, and for suggestions for how to improvise on a tenor melody today, see, among others, Timothy J. McGee, *Medieval and Renaissance Music: A Performer's Guide* (Toronto: University of Toronto Press, 1985), esp. 191–200; Lewis Renee Baratz, "Improvising on the Spagna Tune," *The American Recorder* 29 (1988): 141–46, and its sequel, "Fifteenth Century Improvisation, Take Two: Building a Vocabulary of Embellishments," *The American Recorder* 31 (1990): 7–11; Bonnie J. Blackburn, "On Compositional Process in the Fifteenth Century," *Journal of the American Musicological Society* 40 (1987): 210–84; and Sparti, *Guglielmo Ebreo*, chap. 4. Robert Mullaley, "The Polyphonic Theory of the Bassa Danza and the Ballo," *Music Review* 41 (1980): 1–10, argues for a monophonic (rather than polyphonic) interpretation of the dance tunes.

[64]See Heartz, "A 15th-Century Ballo," 370, and John M. Ward, "The maner of dauncying," *Early Music* 4, no. 2 (1976): 136.

[65] A group of advanced students and I tried to reconstruct and dance the *fiorito* version of *tan geloso*. Though technically challenging, even to expert dancers, both reconstruction and performance proved feasible after some practice, even when the lady danced the "simple" version at the same time. *El gioioso fiorito* continues to be more elusive and problematic.

[66]"Fate sonare de quactro o cinque ragione stromenti . . . uno per uno . . . et soneno un ballo, ongnuno sonara con l'aira sua. . . . Sappiate che cului che dança gli e bisognia de ballare con quell'aira & con quella misura & con quel tempo che

sonaranno li dicti sonatori" ("Get four or five kinds of instruments to play . . . one by one . . . the same *ballo*, each with his own air [style] . . . and remember that the dancer must dance with that air and measure and rhythm that the said players are playing"). Complete citation in Italian and English in Sparti, *Guglielmo Ebreo*, 234–35.

[67]King's lecture-demonstration was given at a Colloquium on Renaissance Dance in Ghent, Belgium, April 1985.

[68]I am thinking in particular of the Basle-based "Ferrara Ensemble," directed by Crawford Young; of Maurizio Mingardi ("Accademia Viscontea i Musicanti") in Milan; and Ian Harrison's "Les Haulz et les Bas" (Freiburg).

[69]I have just learned of a dance group directed by Lieven Baert which performed in Holland in January 1999 and experimented, together with their Amsterdam-based musicians, with phrasing *saltarello* repetitions and "underscoring" changes of *misura*, as well as with "Balkan-type" rhythms (i.e., doing *saltarello* in 7/8). Unfortunately no video exists of this performance, and therefore I cannot express any judgment on this welcome experimentation. My concern is, however, that if the performance purports to be a reproposal (reconstruction) of fifteenth-century dance, then the experimentation-interpretation-ornamentation should be based on the theory or practice in the dance treatises or in the contemporary aesthetic.

[70]Domenico, fol. 1^{v}; Cornazano, fol. 10^{r}.

[71]Sparti, *Guglielmo Ebreo*, 96 (italics mine). It is worth noting that Cornazano gives yet another explanation in his discussion of *Maniera*; he tells (fols. 3^{v}–4^{r}) the dancer performing a *doppio* step to "ondeggiare nel sicondo passo curto levandovi soavemente . . . e con tal suavità abassarvi al terço che compisse el doppio" ("rise gently like a wave during the second short step, . . . and with the same gentleness lower yourself at the third [step] which completes the *doppio*").

[72]The *seguito ordinario* (which is a sixteenth-century equivalent of the basic Quattrocento *passo doppio*) has two steps on half-toe and the final one flat, while *passi puntati* and *seguiti spezzati* (equivalents of *passi sempi* or "simple" steps) and *continenze* are done flat with ornamented rises in the second half of the step.

[73]See David R. Wilson, *The Steps Used in Court Dancing in Fifteenth-Century Italy*, 2nd ed. (Cambridge: D. R. Wilson, 1998).

[74]See, for example, the *riverenza* or bow "*fino in terra*" (down to the ground) cited by Giovanni Ambrosio (in *Voltati in ça Rosina*), by "Giorgio" in the New York copy and also in the Siena redaction (see Appendix 2).

[75]Robert Donington, *Baroque Music: Style and Performance* (London: Faber and Faber, 1982), chap. 1.

[76]Angelo Beolco (Ruzante), *Bilora*, comic dialogue, c.1525, in *Tutte le opere*

del famosissimo Ruzante (Vicenza, 1617). For *Zoioso*, see Heartz, "A 15th-century Ballo," and Sparti, "*Rôti Boulli*"; for [*Voltati in ça*] *Rosina*, see Sparti, *Guglielmo Ebreo*, 234–37, 240–41.

Disorder in Order: Improvisation in Italian Choreographed Dances of the Fifteenth and Sixteenth Centuries

Jennifer Nevile

The surviving dance treatises and manuscripts from Italy provide the richest source of choreographed dances of any country in Europe in the fifteenth and sixteenth centuries. These dances were devised or created by dance masters, each one being a unique combination of steps, floor patterns, and music and therefore required to be learned, memorized, and rehearsed (at least to some degree) before being performed. The nature of improvisation within such a structured activity is the focus of this essay, and the attitude of both the choreographer and performers of these dances towards improvisation was a significant determining factor in how the improvisation was manifest in the dance. In addition, I argue that the presence of improvisatory elements was an indicator of a national choreographic style—that is, improvisation was a fundamental and distinguishing characteristic of Italian dance practices as opposed to the styles performed in other European countries.

In order to examine these issues one must first ask what elements of the choreographed dances were altered, and whether or not this constituted "improvisation." Thus I propose to examine the elements which were altered in fifteenth-century Italian dance practice—that is, the individual steps, with embellishments, additions to, and substitution of entire steps, as well as gestures with the hand and arms. From this examination of improvised elements it is clear that not every aspect of a choreographed dance was open to improvisation. Some elements were rarely or never altered. Thus a set of "rules" or a framework existed in fifteenth-century Italian dance practice that determined which elements of a dance could be varied and which could not. It is clear that there were some characteristics of a choreographed dance which were viewed as so essential to that dance that if any of them were removed or altered, then the dance would be seen as a totally new and different dance.

Improvisation in Choreographed Dances: Diversità di cose *and* Varietà. In the fifteenth (and preceding) centuries there was a flexible attitude to musical composition as illustrated by the many alterations, such as varied rhythms or added notes, that occurred in the different notated versions of the same piece.[1] A similar attitude existed with regard to choreographic composition. The surviving fifteenth-century sources contain many variant readings of the "same" dance: steps were altered, either by substituting one step for another or by changing the step in some way; and the rhythm of the steps was varied, with steps normally performed at one speed and meter (*misura*) being changed to a different *misura*. The important question is whether the elements of the dance which were altered to produce these variant readings were recorded examples of spontaneous actions on behalf of the performers, or whether they were re-compositions by a dance master when he wanted to produce an "up-dated" version of an older or popular dance. In addition, it would be important to know if there was a group of recognized characteristics of the choreographies which were allowed to be spontaneously altered in performance.

Antonio Cornazano, gentleman, member of the Sforza court, author, and accomplished dancer, provides a clue to the flexible attitude to performance of choreographed dances in the fifteenth century when he writes that one of the essential qualities of a good dancer was *diversità di cose* (a diversity of matter),[2] which required dancers to alter each performance of a dance. In Cornazano's opinion, good dancers were supposed to be capable of subtly altering how they executed each step. It was the responsibility of each dancer to add her or his own changes to each step and to make sure that the same variant or variation was not repeated immediately. In order to do this, dancers would have to be completely at ease with the general style in which they were performing, to have each particular dance firmly committed to memory, and to be well aware of the aesthetic limits of "good taste" pertaining to the dance

TABLE 1

Natural and Accidental Steps as given by Domenico and Cornazano in the Theoretical Sections of Their Treatises

	Domenico	Cornazano
Natural Steps	sempi, doppi	sempi, doppi
	riprese, continentie	riprese, continentie
	volte tonde, meze volte	volte tonde, meze volte
	movimenti	movimenti
	riverentie	
	salti	
		contrapassi
		scambii
Accidental Steps	frappamenti	frappamenti
	scorse	trascorse
	cambiamento	
		pizigamenti

style. Later on in his treatise, Cornazano advises that a *bassadanza*, one of the two genres of dances recorded in the treatises, will not be considered beautiful unless the *ripresa* and *continenza* steps are different in size, and, importantly, two successive *riprese* were not to be performed in an identical manner.[3] Clearly, the performer was required to improvise upon the framework provided by the choreographer.

Evidence that the dance masters had a flexible attitude toward improvisation in their creations can also be found in the lists of the steps given in the theoretical section of their dance treatises. Both Domenico da Piacenza and Cornazano list nine steps which they label as "natural steps" and three as "accidental steps." While the number of steps in each category remains the same, the contents of each group differs slightly between Domenico and Cornazano (see Table 1). The "accidental" steps, Domenico reminds us, are made to add variety to the "natural" movements and especially to the *sempio, doppio, represa*, and *volta tonda* steps.[4]

Thus there were a number of "accidental" steps which could be used to embellish or add variety to the longer "natural" steps. The "natural" steps themselves also existed in shorter forms—for example, the *meza ripresa* and the *passetti* (little steps), a shorter version of *sempi*.[5] When one also takes into account the shorter versions of the "natural" steps which are found only in the choreographic descriptions, one can see that performers had considerable discretion in the size of the repertoire of movements they could add to these steps.[6] The decisions which had to be made by the performer included not only what "accidental" step to use at which particular point, but also how many to add at one time and the length of time each embellishment would take. As Cornazano remarked, "gli accidentali sono ad bene placitum" ("the accidental movements were to be performed as one pleases").[7] Domenico, on the other hand, insisted that "accidental" steps were to be performed only one to a *tempo* (or breve) and that they took one-quarter of a *tempo*.[8] Only exceptional dancers could perform two "accidental" movements per *tempo* by doubling the speed at which they were executed.[9]

The importance of *varietà* (variety) or *diversità di cose* to the dance masters can also be seen in the large number of variations on the *quaternaria doppio* step, which in its standard form was a *doppio* followed by a *frapamento*.[10] In the variant *quaternaria doppi*, however, the *frapamento* could be replaced by either a *botta*, *movimento*, *posada*, *salto*, or a *trapasso*.[11] The concepts of *varietà* and *diversità di cose,* the presence of the "accidental" steps, and the variant readings of individual dances all point to the fact that in fifteenth-century Italy both choreographers and performers had a flexible attitude to choreographic composition. Improvisation was more than just an added grace or ornament to the creation of a dance master since it was an essential part of fifteenth- and sixteenth-century choreographed dances. There were a number of ways in which the principle of *varietà* was put into practice by the performers' improvisation for the purpose of adding beauty and grace to their performance.

Modifying Individual Steps: Altering the Rhythm. A commonly used method of modifying a step was to alter its rhythm—that is, to change the total time it took to perform the step and/or to alter the temporal relationship between the individual movements in the step. In the fifteenth-century *balli*, one of the two genres of choreographed dances recorded in the dance treatises, the dance masters choreographed steps out of their natural order—that is, steps belonging to one *misura* were performed to the music of another in a different speed and meter. In the theoretical part of their treatises they outlined all the possible combinations of steps and *misure*, with Domenico and Cornazano both commenting on the degree of difficulty and seemliness of each combination[12] (see Table 2 for Domenico's combinations of steps and *misure*).

This comprehensive exposition is not carried over into the choreographies; as, in the *balli*, most steps appear in their own *misura* (for example, *bassadanza* steps in *bassadanza misura*), and some step/*misura* combinations never occur in the choreographies. The combinations which actually occur in the choreographies are shown in bold in Table 2. The only combination that occurs in any significant amount is *saltarello doppi* in *quaternaria misura,* often used for the opening section of a *ballo*. The others are found in only one, two, or three dances at the most.

Several salient points emerge from an examination of all the occurrences of steps out of their natural order. The *doppi* outside of their natural order do not appear consistently before or after any other particular step and do not appear consistently in any particular position in the choreography. They are used in the opening sequence of a *ballo* and at the end of a dance, and they are also interspersed throughout the middle sections of a dance. Also, these steps are performed by both men and women. Even though the execution of *doppi* in a speed and meter other than their own was considered by the dance masters to be difficult, the degree of difficulty was not so great that it barred women from performing them; it was an improvisatory option appropriate for both men and women. (Other improvisatory practices, such as adding extra or high jumps to steps, were thought to be more fitting for male dancers.)

An aesthetic requirement of the dance practice recorded in the treatises was that *doppi* performed outside of their natural order should not be danced at a speed faster than they normally would be. The dance masters felt that a speedier execution of the *doppi* would result in the appearance of being rushed and hurried, thereby lacking in grace. In order to avoid such a loss of grace in performance while still adhering to the principle of *varietà*, the dance masters choreographed steps of one *misura* in two *tempi* of a faster *misura*.[13] The extra time provided by the second *tempo* resulted in the steps being performed at a slower speed when the new *misura* was not twice as fast as the original one. Instances in which *bassadanza, quaternaria*, and *saltarello doppi* are performed in two *tempi* of *piva misura* (the fastest *misura*), not in one *tempo* are indicated

TABLE 2
Summary of Steps Danced Outside Their Natural Order, as Detailed by Domenico

Bassadanza Misura
(1) bassadanza steps in bassadanza misura
(2) 2 tempi of piva steps in one tempo of bassadanza misura
(3) 1 tempo of quaternaria steps in one tempo of bassadanza misura
(4) 1 tempo of saltarello steps in one tempo of bassadanza misura
(5) 2 tempi of saltarello steps in one tempo of bassadanza misura

Quaternaria Misura
(1) quaternaria steps in quaternaria misura
(2) 1 tempo of bassadanza steps in one tempo of quaternaria misura
(3) 1 tempo of saltarello steps in one tempo of quaternaria misura
(4) 2 tempi of piva steps in one tempo of quaternaria misura

Saltarello Misura
(1) saltarello steps in saltarello misura
(2) 1 tempo of bassandanza steps in two tempi of saltarello misura
(3) 1 tempo of bassadanza steps in one tempo of saltarello misura
(4) 1 tempo of quaternaria steps in one tempo of saltarello misura
(5) 2 tempi of piva steps in one tempo of saltarello misura

Piva Misura
(1) piva steps in piva misura
(2) 1 tempo of bassadanza steps in two tempi of piva misura
(3) 1 tempo of quaternaria steps in two tempi of piva misura
(4) 1 tempo of saltarello steps in two tempi of piva misura

in Table 2. As *piva misura* is exactly double the speed of *bassadanza misura*, in this case the *bassadanza doppi* would be performed at their normal speed. But *piva misura* is less than twice as fast as *quaternaria* and *saltarello misura*, and therefore the *quaternaria* and *saltarello doppi* performed in two *tempi* of *piva misura* would be slower than normal. It is interesting to note that the dance masters also avoided choreographing *piva doppi* in *bassadanza* and *saltarello misure*, even though these two *misure* are slower than *piva misura*. This may have been due to the rustic associations of the *piva* steps which the dance masters did not want to emphasize in their choreographies.

Another characteristic of the dance masters' use of steps out of their natural order is their avoidance of the situation where *doppi* of two different *misure* are performed at the same time, although the reason is not clear. Perhaps it was considered too difficult for common performance. On the other hand, one could surmise that the practice may have occurred more frequently but that the dances in which it appeared were not recorded. It is more likely, however, that the lack of this practice in the surviving recorded choreographies points to the fact that the simultaneous performance of *doppi* from two different *misure* was an improvisatory practice—an example of one element of the dance which was expected to be varied freely in performance and over which the performer had control. The one exception to this occurs in the dance *Belreguardo novo*, a dance for two men and a woman. At one point in this dance the woman does a *bassadanza doppio*, while the men execute a *saltarello doppio* in *bassadanza misura*. Here the use of *doppi* in two different *misure* performed at the same time is a choreographic device which Domenico has employed in order to create a particular dramatic situation. Up to this point, the dancers have been moving in a file, with the woman in between the two men. At the time the steps occur the two men move towards the woman with a *saltarello doppio*, in order to be level with her. Simultaneously the woman moves forward with a *bassadanza doppio* away from the spot for which the men are aiming. The slowness and tranquillity of her step emphasizes the teasing nature of her departure, while the men's *saltarello doppio,* a step performed with a hop and leap, emphasizes their eagerness to return close to the woman.

As an additional modification the rhythm of a step could have been altered by shortening the total time it took to perform the step. This was possible even when it was performed in its own *misura*, as, for example, when the normal length of a *doppio* was curtailed when three *doppi* were performed on the same foot in the time of only two breves rather than the usual three.[14]

Modifying Individual Steps: Additional Movements and Named Variants. A second but far more uncommon way a step was altered or modified was by adding extra movements. Sometimes these extra movements were discrete additions such as a turn or a beat, but at other times they were incorporated into a step as a whole, such as a *doppio* or a *ripresa*. The *ripresa* step was the most frequently varied step with twelve *balli* from six different manuscripts, and thirty-eight *bassedanze* from every manuscript except one having modified *riprese*.[15] The *doppi*, however, have far fewer variants. Only two dances have any named variants—that is, four occurrences of the term *doppio ghaloparto* and eight occurrences of the term *doppio portogallese*. A similar small number of variant *doppi* occur in the *bassedanze*, with only five dances recording named variants of *doppi*. Setting aside the question of precisely how a *doppio ghaloparto* or a *doppio portogallese* was performed, it seems safe to assume that these terms signified a different manner of performance than a plain *doppio* step. The performance of the *doppio* step quite clearly was altered in some way.[16]

If an additional movement such as a leap or turn was added to a *doppio*, it usually occurred either at the beginning or end of the step. In the *bassadanza Zoglioxa* from Domenico's treatise, for example, there is a sequence of three *continenze* and a *saltarello doppio*. Domenico has choreographed a *posada* at the end of the third *continenza* and a *salto* at the beginning of the *saltarello doppio*.[17] On other occasions the dance masters choreographed a half turn at the end of a series of *doppi* or *riprese*, especially in their *bassedanze*.[18]

The modification of individual steps by the addition of extra movements was definitely a part of the choreographies of Domenico, Guglielmo Ebreo da Pesaro, and Cornazano, as was the performance of variant *doppio* and *ripresa* steps. It is interesting to speculate whether the relative scarcity of this type of variation in the notated choreographies was a true reflection of the actual performance practice—that is, whether improvising variants in this manner was an expected and assumed part of a performer's responsibilities rather than a matter for the choreographer. An indication that steps altered in this manner were part of the improvised elements in fifteenth-century Italian dance practice is found in the dance descriptions of a notary in Montefiascone.[19] These dances are the same as those found in the treatises of Domenico and Guglielmo but are full of *doppi* and *riprese* with extra jumps (*salti*) with or without a beat (*botta*) or turns (either 180 or 360 degrees) added to the end of each step. The turns are variously described as *dentro* (inwards), *indereto* (backwards), and *reversa* (reverse), while the *salti* sometimes appear as *salti galanti* (gallant and gracious jumps). While one does not find the same intensity of steps with additional movements in the choreographies of the three dance masters as in the Montefiascone descriptions, the practice is still present, and it therefore seems reasonable to assume that such modifications were part of the improvisatory practices of Italian dance.[20]

Modifying Individual Steps: Step Substitution. Another element that was open to improvisation was the substitution or replacement of one step by another. Within the corpus of more than three hundred notated *balli* and *bassedanze* there are many dances bearing the same name which are found in two or more sources. In some cases these dances are deliberate re-workings by a dance master to create a new version of a dance, but other dances which exist in multiple versions resemble each other far more closely, with differences that are on a much smaller scale and which often involve little more than the substitution of one step for another. One example is the *ballo Prexonera* by Domenico, found in seven manuscripts,[21] in which his original *movimenti* are indicated in four manuscripts while in the remaining three these are replaced with *schoseti* (another type of "accidental" step).[22] Further step substitution is also found between the different versions of this dance. In Domenico's original work he choreographed four *passetti* between the *movimenti* steps. These four *passetti* have been reduced to three in four manuscripts, while in the other two versions of the dance a *ripresa* step has been substituted for the four *passetti*.[23]

Gestures with Hands and Arms. The choice of which gestures are appropriate to each dance, and indeed, to each section of the choreography, seems to have been entirely the responsibility of the individual performer. In their treatises, the dance masters mention how a dancer's gestures should be adapted to fit the circumstances of the dance, the garments worn, and the gender and age of each dancer. Guglielmo notes that just as there were movements and steps which were appropriate to the wearing of short tunics by men, so too was there a different manner of dancing when wearing long garments.[24] In the latter situation a man's movements and gestures had to be solemn and courteous, and he had to have great dexterity and a great understanding of the harmony between the music and the steps.[25] The jumps, turns, and flourishes that were appropriate—and indeed necessary—when dancing in a short tunic would be a sign of incomprehension and gracelessness if performed while wearing a long garment. For Guglielmo it was especially important for young ladies to be light on their feet when dancing and to have appropriate gestures.[26] Guglielmo clearly differentiated between male and female courtiers when discussing the quality of movement, or deportment, and the gestures and manner of executing the steps. Gestures with the hands and arms and movements of a dancer's body were an important part in any polished and graceful performance of these dances. Unfortunately, what these gestures are is not described in the treatises, neither in the choreographic descriptions themselves nor in the theoretical sections of the treatises.[27] However, it is clear that decisions on how to execute such movements, all of which were subtle, would have been ultimately up to each performer and thus could legitimately be included in those elements which were improvised.

The importance of moving and gesturing in a manner appropriate to the dancer's age and gender is underlined by Leon Battista Alberti in his treatise on painting. Here Alberti makes a distinction very similar to Guglielmo as to the quality of movement found among men and women.

> The movements and poses of virgins are airy, full of simplicity with sweetness of quiet rather than strength. . . . The movements of youths are light, gay, with a certain demonstration of great soul and good force. In men, the movements are more adorned with firmness, with beautiful and artful poses. In the old the movements and poses are fatigued; the feet no longer support the body, and they even cling with their hands. Thus each one with dignity has his own movements to express whatever movements of the soul he wishes.[28]

In this extract Alberti is describing the different movement styles of young men, young women and older men—distinctions which should be observed by artists when painting scenes containing people of different ages. In *quattrocento* society one's mode of deportment was dependent upon a person's age, gender, and position in society. Consequently it was also a crucial part of the dance style and could not be omitted without debasing a performance and rendering it totally without grace. This aspect of the dance style was improvised in that it was not written down in great detail in the treatises, but even an improvised element was of such importance that its absence could ruin a dancer's performance.

Rules for What Parts of Choreographed Dances Could be Improvised. Any improvisation by the performers would have to have conformed to limits, constrained by stylistic, aesthetic, and even moral considerations.[29] Furthermore, in order for a dance to retain its identification as the particular creation of a dance master, those elements that were essential to its identity as a unique work of art had to be retained. Dancers, therefore, did not have total freedom to vary, add, or subtract as they might wish. Indications of which elements were considered essential can be found in the choreographies themselves, many of which bear the same name and are found in two or more sources. From an examination of these dances it is clear that the dance masters did not hesitate to alter both choreographies of their own devising and those of others. The changes which occur in dances that still retain the same name range from the simple substitution of one step for another to complex changes in the number of performers (and in the gender of those performers) as well as in the floor tracks of the dances. These complex changes often combined to cause a complete change in the mood of the dance because the altered choreography causes a change in the interaction among the performers.

Some elements of the choreographies, however, were not likely to be altered by the dance masters. Dances with the same name often retain the same important structural markers such as the position in the dance of the *tempi* of *misura*, repetitions of choreographic sections, and step sequences. Repetitions of choreographic sections would normally be continued in the new variant of a dance, as would the step sequences. Of all the different versions of a *ballo* from the different manuscripts which carry the same name, in only one (and its variants), Domenico's *L'altra fia guielmina*,[30] is the starting position changed. Steps may be substituted for one other, the order of steps changed, and the floor track altered, but not the starting position of the dancers.

The invariability of these choreographic elements is illustrated by two versions of *Rostiboli Gioioso* recorded in the New York Public Library manuscript (NY), one for two performers attributed to Domenico, and one for three performers to Guglielmo.[31] In both versions the dance is still the same dance as the structure has not been changed. The steps are hardly varied, and the sections of the choreography which are repeated in the dance for two are repeated in the dance for three. The important structural markers are also to be found in the same place—that is, the tempo of *saltarello* and all the occurrences of the *riprese*. Within the constraints of keeping an identical structure, however, Guglielmo has exploited the extra resources gained from the additional person. He has changed the focus of the dance so that there is a great deal more interaction between the three participants: circling around each other, the two men crossing in front of the woman in the middle, instead of most of the movement being in a forward direction. Even when he does not vary the steps, Guglielmo does change aspects of the choreography. In *Gioioso a due*, for example, the opening sequence of steps is repeated, with the woman imitating exactly the path that the man has just traversed. In the dance for three, the steps of the opening sequence are repeated, but on the second occasion an entirely new floor pattern is performed with the two men changing places in front of the woman.

Thus for the dance masters the important determining features of a choreography which gave it its unique character were the actual step sequences and their repetitions, the position in the choreography of individual steps which act as structural markers, and the starting position of the dancers. Conversely, the actual path traced out by the dancers was not of such crucial importance, and neither were changes in the gender and number of the performers.[32]

In terms of improvisation, performers were free to substitute one step for another, but not those important steps which acted as structural markers such as the *riprese* in the two versions of *Rostiboli Gioioso* recorded in the New York Public Library (NY) manuscript. For these steps, ornamentation by additional, accidental movements rather than step substitution would have been required, since that form of improvisation would not alter the essential characteristics of a choreographed dance.

In the theoretical parts of their treatises the dance masters imply that a step of one *misura* could be danced in any other *misura*. But, as noted previously, this comprehensive exposition is not carried over into their choreographies. From the surviving choreographic evidence it appears that one of the "rules" for performing a step out of its natural order is that it must be danced at a speed slower than normal. A second rule is that in *bassadanza* and *saltarello misura* there was to be an avoidance of *piva doppi*. Two *tempi* of *piva doppi* could be performed in one *tempo* of *quaternaria misura,* but, because the resultant steps would be faster than normal, this combination was mostly used in public entries or triumphs rather than at private entertainments.[33]

The use of "accidental" steps was also restricted in the number which could be added to each "natural" step and also in the type of accidental step that could ornament each specific "natural" step. Domenico states that the *sempio*, *doppio*, *represa*, and *volta tonda* steps are especially suitable to be ornamented with the three "accidental" steps, and especially with the *frappamento* because this step is used with all these four "natural" steps. The use of the *scorsa*, however, differed from that of the *frappamento*, inasmuch as it was especially suitable when one made a half turn with a single *doppio* step. The *cambiamento* movement, according to Domenico, is only to be used in *bassedanze*, and certainly the only explicit reference to that step in his choreographies is in the *bassadanza Corona.*[34] Thus it is clear that in Domenico's mind there were appropriate and inappropriate situations during a performance when a dancer could improvise by adding extra movements to certain steps.

The Sixteenth Century. The tradition of improvisation continued in the later sixteenth-century Italian dance tradition of Fabritio Caroso and Cesare Negri, even in choreographed dances, but the form it took had changed from that of the preceding century. By the second half of the sixteenth century the step vocabulary described in the treatises and utilized in the choreographies had increased in comparison with the time of Domenico and Guglielmo. Whereas the number of steps and their variants described in the fifteenth-century treatises and found in the choreographies was approximately two dozen, by the time Caroso had published *Il Ballarino* in 1581 fifty-eight different steps were described in his treatise, while nineteen years later in *Nobiltà di Dame* that number had increased to seventy-four steps.[35] Negri, in his treatise *Le Gratie d'Amore* published in 1602, described fifty-one widely used steps as well as forty-two different ways of doing the *cinque passi,* twenty-seven types of *salti*, thirty different types of *capriole*, ten types of *zurlo*, and thirty-four different *mutanze* of *gagliarda.*[36] Not only did the size of the step vocabulary increase in these printed treatises, but so too did the length of the description of each individual step. Far more detail simply is given concerning the mechanics and timing of each step than in the manuscripts of the fifteenth-century Italian dance masters. It would appear that, by the second half of the sixteenth century, the freedom enjoyed in performance during the previous century to embellish, modify, or substitute *individual* steps had been codified by the choreographers, who, with a far larger pool of possible steps, specified exactly what type of step was required.

If *individual* steps were not so freely improvised in the choreographed dances of late *cinquecento* Italy, *sequences of steps* were. Throughout the choreographies we find passages of *mutanze* (sequences of steps in one particular meter and tempo) that are left up to the performer. In the dance *Cortesia*, for example, Caroso asks the man to do a *mutanza* in the time of four *tempi* of *gagliarda* and indicates that he is to perform whatever pleases him.[37] Sometimes the choreographies suggest a step sequence, as in *Cortesia*, but at other times this does not happen: in the final dance of the sixth *intermedio* for the 1589 Florentine production of *La Pellegrina,* Cavalieri does not elucidate the steps he required for the men's *mutanze* of *gagliarda* and *canario*, nor does he offer any suggestions for these step sequences.[38] From this one has to assume that the precise steps performed depended upon the skill and inventiveness of the individual dancer.

Another change which occurred in the Italian dance practice was in the gestures of the performers while dancing. In contrast to the previous century, this is not a topic which is mentioned a great deal in the treatises of Caroso and Negri. Caroso's description of the correct behavior of a lady when dancing indicates that neither excessive arm movements nor hand gestures were part of the style.[39] While a lady was allowed gracefully to move her right arm, these movements were small and started from a position where both arms were held low and close to the sides of the body.

One should also note here that the sleeves of ladies' dresses from the second half of the sixteenth century were set differently from today and hence it was much more difficult even to raise their arms above shoulder height.[40] The gentlemen's costume also restricted arm movements or gestures while dancing. It was considered a sign of ill-breeding in a man to dance without wearing a cape,[41] and so his left arm was used to pin down his cloak in order to keep it from flapping about, while often his opposite hand would be fully occupied in controlling his sword. Movements of the body for both men and women (for example, a strutting movement with the hips) were usually included as part of the description of individual steps[42] or occur in specific situations, such as the subtle movements ladies were required to make when dancing backwards if they wished to avoid stepping on the train of their dresses.[43]

By the second half of the sixteenth century gestures of the hands and arms had assumed a lesser importance in the dance style than in the previous century. Step variants had been codified and were specified in the choreographies, and therefore individual steps were no longer freely embellished or modified by the performers to the same extent as in the previous century. Sequences of steps, however, were often left to the discretion of the performer. There were probably many reasons for the changes in improvisatory practices during the sixteenth century, due to both alterations in societal mores and choreographic practices. Examples of the former could include changes in costume; in society's concept of beauty;[44] and in what constituted the appropriate style of movement or movement patterns for different groups in society, including changes in the permissible level of virtuosity,[45] while choreographic practices could include changes in the structure of choreographed dances, in the function of the dances (that is, from a communal activity to a more ritualistic activity, or vice-versa), and in the characteristics of the dance practice that were important to choreographers and/or performers. It is likely that changes in the improvisatory practices over a period of one hundred years were a result of a combination of factors, but more research is needed to establish the patterns of interaction and the influence each factor had on the dance practices in Italy during the sixteenth century.

Improvisatory Elements and an Italian Style. As the preceding discussion makes clear, improvisation was an important part of choreographed dances in both fifteenth- and sixteenth-century Italy. Indeed the presence of improvisation in fifteenth-century Italian choreographed dances is a distinguishing feature of the style, whereas, by contrast, the fifteenth-century French dance practice had no such improvisatory elements.[46] The presence of a such a large number of improvisatory elements in the choreographed dance was, I argue, a characteristic fundamental to *Italian* practices, and this was not unique to the dance. Improvisation was also found in music, painting, architecture and sculpture, and in the horticultural art of the design and planting of gardens. The principle on which improvisation in the art of dance was based was the same as that which operated in the other artistic practices: the imitation of nature both in its outward appearance and its underlying basic order. The specific interaction between art and nature and the way it was manifested varied from one artistic practice to another, but in all cases ornamentation and improvisation were essential features of this interaction.

In architecture and garden design human skill and knowledge transformed the matter of nature into an artificial human order, but this is still an order that reflects the numerical order of the cosmos. Human ingenuity shaped and proportioned the raw materials of building—stone, wood, marble—into beautiful ordered forms, just as the skills and craftsmanship of human artistic endeavor shaped, re-created, and ornamented the existing natural landscape.[47] For a building to be perfect it had to have both beauty and ornament. Beauty, according to Alberti, is innate, all-pervasive, as it is the "reasoned harmony of all the parts within a body, so that nothing may be added, taken away, or altered, but for the worse."[48] Ornament is not inherent in a building, because it is an embellishment of beauty and thus has the "character of something attached or additional."[49] Beauty is the intellectual framework of a building, its essential idea, while ornament is the "individual expression and embellishment of the framework."[50] That it is ornament in architecture which encompasses improvisation is made clear by Alberti in his treatise *De re aedificatoria* when commenting on the necessity of ornament in the construction of private houses, villas, and gardens. In these private buildings the ornamentation must be more restrained than that permitted in public buildings, yet Alberti admits that in the former "a certain license is often possible."[51] The license in the ornament of private houses springs from the inventiveness of the architect, who in his unexpected improvisations can charm and entertain those who view his work.

> How charming was the practice of those more fanciful architects of stationing huge statues of slaves at the door jambs of a dining room, so that they support the lintel with their heads; and of

> making columns, especially for garden porticoes, that resembled tree trunks, their knots removed and their branches tied into bundles, and the shaft scrolled and plaited with palms and carved with leaves, birds, and channels. . . . In doing this, the artist must, as far as he is able, guard each part in its noble form by skilfully maintaining the lines and angles . . . yet seeming to entertain the viewer with a charming trick—or, better still, to please him by the wit of his invention.[52]

Ornament and improvisatory practices in architecture were a result of human inventiveness and therefore lay on the art side of the art *versus* nature competition. Ornament was far more than just the imitation of nature since it went beyond the bounds of nature "by means of its artificial inventions"[53]—inventions (or improvisations) which if absent would debase the work of art.[54]

A similar line of reasoning operated in the theory of painting, where improvisatory practices were covered by the concept called *ornato*. Following the rhetorical theory of Roman authors such as Quintillian, fifteenth-century writers on the art of painting equated *ornato* with that which was something extra, something beyond a clear and correct imitation of the natural world. When painters such as Filippo Lippi and Fra Angelico were praised for possessing the quality of *ornato* in their paintings, they were being praised for the piquancy, polish, richness, liveliness, charm, and finish of their work.[55] In painting, as in architecture, it is the embellishment of the work by human skill and ingenuity, the added elements, that gracefully enhance a correct representation of nature. In the context of our discussion on the art of dance, it is interesting to note that *ornato* was often applied to the movements, poses, or gestures of human figures in a painting in which the work was full of figures with curved and varied poses. People depicted in the act of moving would be said to possess *ornato*.[56]

The new concept of a garden in which the skills and craftsmanship of human artistic endeavour shaped, re-created, and ornamented the existing landscape first appeared in Italy in the second half of the fifteenth century at the same time as the three dance masters were writing their treatises. Garden design and construction shared the fundamental principle of order and proportion and geometrical forms found in the other artistic practices. Similarly, improvisation was found in the skill and ingenuity in which the gardens were planted and ornamented. I have argued elsewhere that there were close similarities between the static choreography of the formal gardens of the nobility and the moving choreographies performed by members of the court, so I do not need to repeat the details here.[57] Rather, I would like to extend the similarities between garden design and the art of dance to the improvised ornamentation provided by the performers of the Italian dances. When describing the steps used in fifteenth-century Italian dance practice, Domenico divided the steps into "natural" and "accidental" steps. For Domenico the "natural" steps performed in their own order were the choreographic equivalent of the building blocks of nature present in an uncultivated garden: flowers, streams, crags, caves. They were the "nature" side of the art/nature competition for the art of dance. The "art" half of the equation was represented by the "accidental" steps, the use of a step outside of its natural order, and all of the other improvisatory practices previously discussed. These improvisatory practices were the way in which the garden of dance was ornamented, skilfully cultivated, controlled, and ordered, both by the choreographer and by the performers, in order that the most perfect fruit would be the result—a fruit which would surpass anything achieved through the actions of one part alone.

Conclusion. As outlined above, the presence of improvised elements was a fundamental characteristic of Italian artistic practices in fifteenth and sixteenth Italy. It is found in dance just as it was a part of music, architecture, painting, and the design and planting of formal gardens. Ornamentation and improvisation by both the composer and performer(s) of a dance were seen as essential to Italian practice because it was the way in which artistic theory in Italy in general—and in particular the understanding of the relationship between art and nature within that theory—was expressed in the art of dance. The dances recorded in the fifteenth- and sixteenth-century treatises were all individual works of art, each a unique combination of steps, floor patterns, and music. Improvisation during performances did occur, but it operated within an agreed framework of rules. In the fifteenth-century Italian practice there existed a group of recognized characteristics which were allowed to be spontaneously altered in performance. Individual dance steps were changed, either by substituting one step for another, adding extra movements, altering the rhythm of the step, or modifying the step in some way. Steps which acted as structural markers were embellished by the addition of extra movements rather than by step substitution. There were also restrictions as to the number and type of accidental steps which were allowed to be added to each "natural" step. Gestures of the hands and arms were also included in the group of elements that were permitted to be improvised. By the second half of the sixteenth century, however, gestures of the hands and arms had assumed far lesser importance. Step variants had been codified and were specified in the choreographies, and therefore individual steps were no longer freely embellished or modified by the performers. Sequences of steps, however, were often left to the discretion of the performer.

In Italy, in the grand gardens of the nobility, human artistic endeavor controlled, ornamented, varied, and re-shaped the material provided by nature. Similarly, in the danced "gardens" of Renaissance Italy performers through their improvisatory practices ordered, ornamented, and cultivated the "natural" choreographic material so that the resulting fruit was more perfect, graceful, and full of beauty—an exquisite reflection in the movements of the dance of the virtuous and of the honorable state of the performers' souls.

NOTES

[1]Timothy J. McGee, *The Sound of Medieval Song: Ornamentation and Vocal Style according to the Treatises* (Oxford: Clarendon Press, 1998), 2.

[2] Biblioteca Apostolica Vaticana, Codex Capponiano 203, fol. 3ʳbis. The fifteenth-century Italian dance manuscripts, with the abbreviations used hereafter in this essay, are as follows: Domenico da Piacenza, *De arte saltandj & choreas ducendj De la arte di ballare et danzare,* Paris, Bibliothèque Nationale, MS. fonds it. 972 (Pd); Antonio Cornazano, *Libro dell'arte del danzare,* Rome, Biblioteca Apostolica Vaticana, Codex Capponiano 203 (V); Guglielmo Ebreo da Pesaro, *Guilielmi Hebraei pisauriensis de practica seu arte tripudii vulgare opusculum, incipit,* Paris, Bibliothèque Nationale, MS. fonds it. 973 (Pg); Giovanni Ambrosio, *Domini Iohannis Ambrosii pisauriensis de pratica seu arte tripudii vulgare opusculum faeliciter incipit*, Paris, Bibliothèque Nationale, MS. fonds it. 476 (Pa); Guglielmo Ebreo, *Ghuglieimi hebrei pisauriensis De Practicha seu arte tripudij vulghare opusculum feliciter incipit,* Florence, Biblioteca Nazionale Centrale, Codex Magliabecchiano-Strozziano XIX 88 (FN); Guglielmo Ebreo, *Qui chominca elibro Ghulielmus ebreis pisauriensis de praticha seu arte tripudii volghare opusculum*, Florence, Biblioteca Medicea-Laurenziana, Codex Antinori, A13 (FL);

Guglielmo Ebreo, *Ghuglielmi ebrej pisauriensis de praticha seu arte tripudi vulghare opusculum, feliciter incipit,* New York, New York Public Library, Dance Collection, *MGZMB-Res. 72–254 (NY); (Guglielmo Ebreo), Siena, Biblioteca Comunale, Codex L.V. 29 (S); (Guglielmo Ebreo), Modena, Biblioteca Estense, Codex Ital. 82. a. J. 94 (M). Several ways of paginating these manuscripts have appeared in print, depending on whether the author has decided to count the first folio of the manuscript as folio 1 or has deemed folio 1 to start with the commencement of the main text of the treatise. In this essay I have followed the pagination as given by F. Alberto Gallo in "Il 'ballare lombardo' (circa 1435–1475)," *Studi Musicali* 8 (1979): 61–84, where the first folio of the manuscript is folio 1, and the numbers follow consecutively to the end.

[3]V, fol. 6^{r}.

[4]Pd, fol. 3^{r}.

[5]*Passetti* are found in Domenico's *ballo*, *Prexonera*, where each step takes half the time of a *sempio* (Pd, fols. 14^{v}–15^{r}).

[6]See David Wilson, *The Steps Used in Courtly Dancing in Fifteenth-Century Italy* (Cambridge: D. R. Wilson, 1992), for a discussion of all the natural and accidental steps and how they were used in the choreographies.

[7]V, fol. 8^{v}. The statement that the timing of the "accidental" steps was left to the performer's discretion is based on the assumption that when teaching a new dance to a pupil a dance master did not decide on the timing himself.

[8]In fifteenth-century Italian dance theory, the word *tempo* was often used as a synonym for a breve. A breve was the name given to a note of a specific duration, which in many modern transcriptions is equal to a bar.

[9]Pd, fol. 3^{r}.

[10]Ibid., fol. 5^{v}.

[11] Wilson, *Steps Used in Courtly Dancing*, 34.

[12]Pd, fols. 5^{r}–7^{r}, and V, fols. 10^{v}–12^{r}.

[13]One example is the dance *Anello*, which opens with eight *saltarello doppi* in sixteen *tempi* of *piva misura*.

[14]Since this subject has been discussed elsewhere, I will not repeat the material here. For arguments concerning why three *doppi* on the same foot take two

tempi rather than three, see Mauro Lo Monaco and Sergio Vinciguerra, "Il passo doppio in Guglielmo e Domenico: Problemi di mensurazione," in *Guglielmo Ebreo da Pesaro e la danza nelle corti italiane del xv secolo*, ed. Maurizio Padovan (Pisa: Pacini, 1990), 127–36. For discussion of how one could perform three *doppi* all on the same foot in only two *tempi*, see Diana Cruickshank, "Doppij suxo uno piede or contrapassi in quadernaria misura," *Historical Dance* 3, no. 1 (1992): 11–13; and additionally Wilson, *Steps Used in Courtly Dancing*; as well as Barbara Sparti, "The tale of three contrapassi in quadernaria," in *The Marriage of Music and Dance: Proceedings of a Conference of the National Early Music Association* (London, 1991).

[15]In the *balli* there are five different modifiers of a *ripresa* (*françese, gallone, ghaloparto, meza,* and *portogallese*), while the *bassedanze* have four different modifiers of the *ripresa* step (*françese, gallone, ghaloparto,* and *portogallese*).

[16]For example, in the *ballo Fioretto* from NY, the plain *doppi* which occur in other versions of this dance from S and M are replaced by *doppi ghaloparti*.

[17]Pd, fol. 28^{r}.

[18]That the *meza volta* occurred at the end of the step is stated explicitly in the version of Guglielmo's treatise in the NY manuscript. The instructions for the *bassadanza Cupido* (fol. 9^{v}) are typical in this regard: "Imprima dua pasi sempi e dua doppi chominciando chol pie mancho e nela fine del sechondo dopio gluomini dieno meza volta in sul pie rito" ("First they do two *sempi* and two *doppi* starting with the left foot, and at the end of the second *doppio* the men make a *meza volta* on the right foot"). By contrast, in the instructions for *Cupido* in Pg the positioning of the *meza volta* at the end of the second *doppio* is not clear: "In prima doi sempi & doi doppi cominciando col pie sinistro et poi gli huomini diano meza volta in sul pie dritto" (fol. 27^{v}).

[19]Quirino Galli, "Una danzografia in un protocollo notarile a Montefiascone nella seconda metà del XV secolo," *Arte e Accademia (Accademia di Belle Arti 'Lorenzo da Viterbo')* (1989): 121–43.

[20]There is some question, however, as to how representative were these choreographic descriptions from Montefiascone—that is, whether they were a study or exercise in improvisation rather than an actual performance record. The number of choreographies is not large, and they are not associated with any major center of dance, so one cannot state with certainty how widely applicable were the practices recorded in these descriptions. For an extended discussion of these dances, see Barbara Sparti, "Rôti bouilli: take two. *El gioioso fiorito*," *Studi Musicali* 24, no. 2 (1995): 231–61.

[21]Recorded in Domenico's treatise (Pd) as well as in Pg, Pa, S, FN, FL, and NY.

[22]The manuscripts which retain the original *movimenti* are the version Guglielmo recorded in his 1463 treatise (Pg) and in Pa and S, while the manuscripts with the *schoseti* are NY, FN, and FL.

[23]The manuscripts with three *passetti* are Pg, Pa, FN, and FL, while those with one *ripresa* are NY and S.

[24]Pa, fol. 31^r–31^v.

[25]Ibid., fol. 31^r.

[26]Pg, fol. 17^r.

[27]In their treatises dance masters provide terms that refer to the movements of dancer's body (*ondeggiare* and *campeggiare*), but exactly how these movements were performed is not explained in any detail and hence debate continues concerning their meaning; see, for example, Sharon Fermor, "Studies in the Depiction of the Moving Figure in Italian Renaissance Art, Art Criticism, and Dance Theory" (Ph.D. diss., Warburg Institute, University of London, 1990); Mark Franko, *The Dancing Body in Renaissance Choreography (c.1416–1589)* (Birmingham, Alabama: Summa Publications, 1986); Jennifer Nevile, "'Certain Sweet Movements': The Development of the Concept of Grace in 15th-Century Italian Dance and Painting," *Dance Research* 9, no. 1 (1991): 3–12, and "The Platonic Theory of Ethos in Fifteenth-Century Italian Court Dance," *Literature and Aesthetics* 3 (Spring 1993); 42–54; Diana Cruickshank, "The Passo Doppio in 15th-Century Balli and Basse Danze: Some Possibilities of Interpretation," *Dance and Research* (Louvain: Peeters Press, 1989), 29–39; Alessandro Pontremoli, "Estetica dell'ondeggiare estetica dell'aeroso: da Domenico a Guglielmo, evoluzione di uno stile coreutico," in *Guglielmo Ebreo da Pesaro e la danza nelle corti italiane del xv secolo*, ed. Maurizio Padovan (Pisa: Pacini, 1990), 159–68; and Barbara Sparti, "Style and Performance in the Social Dances of the Italian Renaissance: Ornamentation, Improvisation, Variation and Virtuosity," *Proceedings of the 9th Annual Conference of the Society of Dance History Scholars* (1986), 31–52.

[28]Leon Battista Alberti, *Della Pittura*, trans. John Spencer (London: Routledge and Kegan Paul, 1956), 80.

[29]In addition to aesthetic limits on the dance style there were also moral limits, since in the Renaissance it was believed that a person's bodily movement was the outward manifestation of the state of his or her soul.

[30]The versions of *L'altra fia guielmina* found in S and M, also for two performers, both start the same way as the one from Domenico's treatise. Cornazano's version, *Befiglie guilielmin*, is for two couples, and it is this version which has a different starting position from the other three.

[31]The dance for two performers appears on fol. 25^r, while Guglielmo's version for three is found on fols. 25^v–26^v.

[32]It must be emphasized, however, that dances with the same name but different numbers of performers did not always designate the same dance. For example, the *ballo Amoroso in tre* from S is totally different from the version for two recorded in Pa, and *La Grazzosa nove a tre* from NY is also an entirely different dance from *Gratiosa a due* from the same manuscript.

[33]Pd, fol. 6^v.

[34]Ibid., fol. 3^r. In the dance *Corona*, the *cambiamenti* are choreographed at the end of *doppio, represa,* and *sempio* steps, and always immediately preceding a *doppio* step (Pd, fol. 27^v). For more details concerning the precise use of the *cambiamento* and *frappamento* in the choreographies, see Wilson, *Steps Used in Courtly Dancing*, 38–42.

[35]Fabritio Caroso, *Il Ballarino* (1581; facs. reprint New York: Broude, 1967), and *Nobiltà di Dame* (1600; facs. reprint Bologna: Forni, 1980).

[36]Cesare Negri, *Le Gratie d'Amore* (1602; facs. reprint New York: Broude, 1969).

[37]Caroso, *Nobiltà,* 338.

[38]Cristofano Malvezzi, *Intermedii et concerti fatti per la commedia rappresentata in Firenze nelle nozze del serenissimo don Ferdinando Medici, e madama Christina de Loreno, gran duchi di Toscana* (Venice: G. Vincenti, 1591), ninth partbook.

[39]Caroso, *Nobiltà*, 86.

[40]Naomi Tarrant, *The Development of Costume* (Edinburgh: National Museums of Scotland; London: Routledge, 1994), 59; and Janet Arnold, *A Handbook of Costume* (London: Macmillan, 1973), 136.

[41]Caroso, *Nobiltà*, 65–66.

[42]For example, in ibid., 19–21 and 18–19, Caroso's description of the *passo*

puntato semigrave and the *continenze.*

[43]Ibid., 79–80.

[44]For a discussion of the sixteenth-century Italian concept of *bellezza*, see Sharon Fermor, "Poetry in Motion: Beauty in Movement and the Renaissance Conception of Leggiadria," in *Concepts of Beauty in Renaissance Art*, ed. Francis Ames-Lewis and Mary Rogers (Aldershot: Ashgate, 1998), 124–33.

[45]See Fermor, "Studies in the Depiction of the Moving Figure," 197–250.

[46]The fifteenth- and early sixteenth-century French dance practice is known only through collections of *basse danses.* These have always been assumed to be processional couple dances, and unlike the fifteenth-century Italian dances had no complicated floor plan or patterns of interactions between the performers. The step sequences were highly structured into a system of measures, and only four different steps and a reverence were used. It is difficult to believe that the fifteenth-century French *basse danse* practice would have included a strong improvised element of added movements or steps or the substitution of one step for another, because if one were to substitute one of its four steps for another, the system of step-sequences or measures—such an integral part of a *basse danse*—would be entirely destroyed. It is true that by the 1530s and 1540s the rules for combining the step-sequences into measures as well as the measures into a whole dance were changing. See David Wilson, "Theory and Practice in 15th-Century French basse danse," *Historical Dance* 2, no. 3 (1983): 1–2, and the same author's "The Development of the French basse danse," *Historical Dance* 2, no. 4 (1984–85): 5–12; and also D. Heartz, "The basse dance: Its Evolution circa 1450 to 1550," *Annales Musicologiques* 6 (1958–63): 287–340. However, even in this time of flux, the number of different steps in the *basse danse* did not increase, nor did the dance ever approach the flexibility in step combinations to be found in the Italian *basse-danze.*

[47]The relationship between art and nature in the design of gardens was recognized at the time and was much commented upon by contemporary writers. See Claudia Lazzaro, *The Italian Renaissance Garden* (New Haven: Yale University Press, 1990), 2, 8–10.

[48]Leon Battista Alberti, *On the Art of Building in Ten Books*, trans. Joseph Rykwert, Neil Leach, and Robert Tavernor (Cambridge, Mass.: MIT Press, 1988), 156.

[49]Ibid., 156. In architecture one of the main forms of ornament was sculpture. For further discussion of Alberti's views on sculpture in architecture and as an art in its own right, see Kathleen Weil-Garris Brandt, "The Relation of Sculpture and

Architecture in the Renaissance," in *Italian Renaissance Architecture from Brunelleschi to Michelangelo*, ed. Henry A. Millon (London: Thames and Hudson, 1996), 75–99.

[50]Joseph Rykwert *et al.*, "Glossary," in Alberti, *On the Art of Building*, 420.

[51]Alberti, *On the Art of Building*, 293.

[52]Ibid., 293–94.

[53]Brandt, "The Relation of Sculpture and Architecture," 98. See also Alberti, *On the Art of Building*, 25, for his explanation of how architects go beyond the shapes and forms found in nature when they are ornamenting buildings with columns.

[54]The point is made by Alberti, *De re aedificatoria*, book 9, chap. 8, where he is discussing the faults of ornament, one of which is its absence. "It will also be a fault if . . . those who think the sole business of the wall is to support the roof, and there is no need to embellish it, in an appropriate and distinctive manner, with noble columns, magnificent statues, graceful paintings, and splendid revetment" (*On the Art of Building*, 311–12).

[55]Michael Baxandall, *Painting and Experience in Fifteenth-Century Italy* (Oxford: Oxford University Press, 1985), 131–33.

[56]In general terms it is in these added qualities of *ornato* that improvisation is found in the art of painting, for which see especially the essay by Leslie Korrick in the present volume. Similarly, since improvisation in the art of music is the focus of essays elsewhere in this volume, the subject will not be addressed here.

[57]Jennifer Nevile, "Dance and the Garden: Moving and Static Choreography in Renaissance Europe," *Renaissance Quarterly* 52 (1999): 805–36.

Ornamentation and Improvisation in Sixteenth-Century Dance

G. Yvonne Kendall

Throughout the sixteenth century several treatises chronicle the performance practice history of music and dance in the life of the amateur. Not only were complex solo pieces available in both arts, but teaching pieces and simple dances also became accessible through the increased use of the printing press. These sources, including several treatises referring to the arts of ornamentation and improvisation, were produced in this era.[1]

In his book on improvisation in music, Pellegrino Santucci asserts "i vari movimenti di Danza sono legati indissolubilmente a quelli della Musica" ("the various movements of dance are inextricably linked to those of music").[2] While there is, of necessity, a close relationship between dance and music, the question of ornamentation and improvisation in sixteenth-century dance has never been addressed in any degree of detail. The crucial questions would not disgrace an Agatha Christie mystery. Was it done? If so, who did it? When? What did they do? How?

Although the music treatises on ornamentation are relatively well known, instruction sources concerning dance ornamentation are relatively unknown; such is the case even when dance ornamentation is found in well-known dance treatises. This article will identify the sources of information on ornamentation and improvisation in dance, discuss and interpret the practices these sources explain, compare the subject presentation methodology of dance master and musician, and, finally, offer some thoughts on the importance of these findings for scholars in both disciplines.

On the subject of ornamentation, the music sources, among them music treatises by Diego Ortiz, Sylvestro Ganassi, and others, systematically leading the reader through intervals of increasing size, give several examples of possible elaborations for each interval as they move from the simplest to the most virtuosic. These possibilities are intended to become part of a vocabulary of musical

TABLE 1 — CHOREOGRAPHIC SOURCES

Author	Title	Publication Information
Anon.	*The Practise of Dauncinge*	London, ca. 1606 (Bodleian Library, MS. Douce 280)
Arbeau, Thoinot	*Orchésographie*	Langres, France, 1589
Caroso, Fabritio	*Ballarino*	Venice, 1581
Caroso, Fabritio	*Nobiltà di Dame*	Venice, 1600
Compasso, Lucio	*Ballo della Gagliarda . . . Sopra le mutanzie della gagliarda . . .*	Florence, 1560
Lupi, Livio	*Libro di gagliarda, tordiglione, passo è mezzo, canari e passeggi*	Palermo, 1607
Lutij, Prospero	*Opera bellissima nella quale si contengono molte partite et passeggi di gagliarda*	Perugia, 1589
Negri, Cesare	*Le Gratie d'Amore*	Milan, 1602

gestures that can be inserted into an actual performance at the will of the musician. Treatises such as Ganassi's also include extremely elaborate cadential figures that can be chosen in a similar manner. Some of these treatises provide actual musical examples showing how the figures could be used, although examples from actual musical works were most frequently used for the lengthier elaborations on popular melodies. In Ortiz these elaborations, known as *recercadas*, follow the original version of the melody and appear to be improvised versions of famous melodies that have been notated.

Similar to the music ornamentation treatises, dance treatises list ornaments of various types that the dancer can insert into an actual choreography. The treatises include fundamental volumes by Arbeau, Caroso, and Negri as well as works by lesser known dance masters (see Table 1).[3] Among their contents are ornaments that garnish steps using gestures with the foot, the upper body, the hands and head in addition to instructions for steps that can be subdivided in order to make them more ornate. Dance sources differ from music sources, however, in containing elaborate dance variations that can be substituted for the simpler ones normally found in most basic choreographies. Some of these choreographers even indicate places in their dances where the dancer may choose to make such a substitution.

Fabritio Caroso, author of two major dance treatises, furnishes instructions for a number of movements from which a lady should choose in order to garnish the strolling passages (*passegi*) she does while her partner is performing elaborate feats of terpsichorean daring. Caroso does include *passeggi* for men, but they are not as ornate as those for women. In addition to *passeggi*, he cites instances where a performer's favorite variation may be exchanged for one Caroso has written.

Creating diminutions or subdivisions for steps is discussed in Arbeau's famous dance manual *Orchésographie.* During a lesson on the art of substituting small quick steps for a longer slower step, termed *mignardez*, French dancemaster Thoinot Arbeau teaches his mythical student Capriol steps that can be enlivened in this manner at the dancer's discretion. He provides examples for *branles*, easy group dances that can be done in lines or circles, and for the basic *gagliarda* step. Cesare Negri has lists of step patterns of varying levels of difficulty which thus offer the skilled dancer options to the simple dance steps, particularly in dances like the *gagliarda* which are widely known as vehicles for virtuosity in both dance and music. All three of these dance masters refer to certain steps and performance practices as ornamental while emphasizing their vital importance for issues of style and grace in the dancing of professionals and amateurs alike.

Part of the understanding of improvisation comes from extrapolation from the existing evidence. Although there are formally-notated versions for all types of choreographies, it is clear from Negri and others that the ability to improvise, especially in variation choreographies, was a necessary skill for dancemasters. Important evidence comes from Treatise I of Cesare Negri's tripartite dance manual *Le Gratie d'Amore* in which he gives recognition to those dancemasters who were adept at the performance of these dances and to those who actually notated them. Almost all of the dancemasters he cites as having "written" or "composed" dances have left extant choreographies.

In the first part of Treatise I, for example, Negri provides an annotated list of thirty-nine dancemasters whose careers were worthy of notice. He praises Caroso, whose book (most likely referring to *Il Ballarino*) he calls, "very beautiful, a clear and illustrious testimony of his valor"; Lucio Compasso, whose volume has only recently been discovered; and Ernandes (also spelled Arnandes), one of whose choreographies appears in Caroso's *Il Ballarino*.[4] For many of these colleagues he indicates a professional specialty—for example, vaulting on horseback, playing the lute, or dancing the *gagliarda*. Virtuoso performance of variation dances, among them the *gagliarda, canary*, etc., was a skill he frequently praises. Concerning Ludovico Palvello he says, "il cui valore su infinito, e meraviglioso nella prestezza della gamba" ("the valor and marvel in the speed of his legs was endless"); Cesare Agosto Parmegiano is said to be "molto leggiero, disposto e garbato nel ballare la gagliarda" ("most graceful, adept, and pleasing in dancing the *gagliarda*").[5] Negri even relates the story of his pupil, young Clara Tettone, a nine-year-old prodigy who danced solo before the Duke of Mantua in 1592. On 10 July of that year, when the Duke of Mantua visited Milan, Clara, daughter of Sig. Rinaldo Tettone, was brought before the duke with Negri, her teacher, who describes the apparent prodigy as "miracolosa in ballare, in la musica de sonare, e cantare" ("miraculous in dancing, in playing music, and in singing").[6] Under his direction she performed the *gagliarda, pavaniglia*, and *canaries*, all virtuoso variation dances that provide an excellent arena for improvisation. Seven years later, in 1599, she is cited as having danced in a quadrille before Isabella, Archduchess of Austria.[7]

Similarities in the organization of music and dance sources are seen in a Neapolitan music treatise that was a contemporary of *Le Gratie*. This source, *Della Prattica Musica* by Scipione Cerreto, lists musicians by their particular expertise for much the same purpose as Negri lists dancemasters.[8] Another interesting connection between the two volumes is the 1611 edition of *Le Gratie* that was published in Naples.

Baldassar Castiglione contributes a negative reference in his renowned courtesy book, *Il Libro del Cortegiano*, when he gives the following advice concerning the courtier dancing in public:

> Even though he may feel himself to be the very lightest on his feet and a master of time and movement, he should not attempt

> those virtuosities of the feet and double spins with beats which serve our Barletta so very well. . . . On the other hand, when he is performing in a private room . . . then I think he should be allowed to try them . . . but not in public unless he is at a masked ball.[9]

Because it indicates choices among dance movements that are available to the dancer depending on skill level, this statement can be interpreted to imply accepted spontaneity in dancing as well as a distinction between the performance expectations of professionals and amateurs, especially as it relates to virtuosity. The mention of Barletta, who was a professional dancer, helps in marking the distinction between professional and amateur, but the issue of a public *gravitas* seems uppermost in Castiglione's mind.

An anonymous English manuscript, *The Practise of Dauncinge*, contains some choreographies that have no specific steps, implying a certain impromptu nature in their performance. The instructions for the Spanish Pavan are a perfect example of this type because "[i]t must be learnd by practise & demonstration, beinge performd with boundes & capers & in the end honour."[10] The sole concordance among the formal choreographies in every major dance manual is the Spanish Pavan (It. *Pavaniglia*, Sp. *Pavana Italiana*, Fr. *Pavane d'Espagne* or *Espagnolle*), which bears the same form in each of these dance manuals—that is, a series of variations. Each variation has a ternary form (ABC), beginning and ending with a set pattern (A and C). The middle section (B) is the actual variation, changing with each repeat of the music. Although Italian and Spanish sources have choreographies for this complex dance that are quite specific and yet different from one another, both the complexity and the numerous possibilities may be reasons why the author of *The Practise of Dauncinge* gave such sketchy instructions.

An additional (and better known) English source by Thomas Morley in 1597 describes the *volta* (a *gagliarda* variant) and the *courante* as dances that can be done in groups, but unlike the customary sets of *branles* these are "danced after sundrie fashions."[11] Arbeau describes the basic *branles* (double, simple, gay, and bourgogne) as group dances with simple steps performed in sets, each dance of the set having a tempo faster than the preceding one. The *volta*, however, is a dance that requires couples because the lady leaps toward the gentleman who then uses centrifugal force (supplied by her momentum aided by his thigh placed at her hip) to lift her into the air and to twirl her around. A picture of Elizabeth I in mid-air showed the scandalous nature of this dance as the vigor of its movements gave observers a glimpse of her ankle! Arbeau instructs the lady to hold her dress so that the glimpse does not become more explicit.[12] Couples could easily extemporize additional spins to this dance, since their movements would not necessarily interfere with the other couples on the dance floor. One connection of the *volta* to its progenitor, the *gagliarda*, is that they both use the same musical rhythms. In fact, the *gagliarda* (with its leaps), the *volta* (with its spins), and the *tourdion* (a kinder, gentler *gagliarda* performed faster, yet closer to the ground with kicks instead of leaps) all use the same music and the same basic step rhythms but with different tempos depending on the situation. Since the *gagliarda* and the *tourdion* are both well known as variation dances, there is no reason to believe the *volta* would be omitted from this important family characteristic.

As for the *courante*, Arbeau's description identifies it as a light duple-meter dance quite different from the vigorous triple-meter *volta*, which he had discussed in the preceding section of his treatise.[13] What they have in common is their playful and suggestive natures, exhibited in the *courante* by light flirtatious steps used in a game of changing partners. Arbeau gives specific steps for the *courante*, while at the same time he admits that most dancers just do what they please and only aim to land on the cadence at the appropriate time.

Caroso, too, gives examples of situations in which a gentleman may do as he wishes, being careful to limit himself to a specific amount of time. An example occurs in *Alta Vittoria* when, instructing the man to do whichever four-pattern *gagliarda* variation seems best, he advises him to use capers if he knows how to do them.[14] This evidence makes it clear that both ornamentation and improvisation did occur and also indicates that both professionals and amateurs were expected to and actually did practice both these skills.

A wide variety of sources furnish evidence concerning the contexts in which these movements would have been appropriate. Professional command performances were one opportunity for virtuoso improvisation; *passeggi* in couple dances presented another. *Passeggi* were stylish strolling passages that one partner danced while the other executed an intricate variation. They provide the dance equivalent of a musical bass line supporting the ornate melody of the partner's variation (also called *mutanza* in Italian sources). Caroso admonishes the stroller to do various gestures in order to avoid standing "paia una statua" ("like a statue").[15]

The variations themselves presented yet another improvisation opportunity. In both *passeggi* and variations, step patterns of the dancer's choice could be substituted for those of the dancemaster, these patterns being relatively brief sets of organized steps. For example, *Laura Suave*, a balletto by Caroso, is constructed of an entry section (A), *gagliarda* variations for the man and for the woman (B), a *saltarello* section (C), followed by a *canary* (D).[16] In the *gagliarda* section of this choreography he allows the man the choice of doing a variation of his own, or he may use the one provided in the manual: "If the man knows how to do the *gagliarda*, he can do a solo variation . . . of four patterns." However, "if he wishes to do my variation," he can do the steps Caroso has set specified.[17]

Another context for improvisation would be a generic dancing occasion such as a *festa*, when the musicians begin to play *gagliarda* music and the dancers, taking to the floor, dance with no specific planned choreography. This may have been the case in 1574 when onboard ship Don Juan, half brother of King Philip II of Spain, danced the *gagliarda* en route to Spain from the battle of Lepanto.[18] Given Castiglione's remarks on the amateurs and their desire to attempt difficult dance movements, and Negri's inclusion of the complex leaps known as tassel jumps which were used as the basis of competition among men, it is not difficult to imagine improvisation as part of a scenario of men glorying in the physicality of these movements as they go off to war.[19]

Having determined that improvisation was indeed performed and the circumstances under which it occurred, it would seem important to determine the specifics of what the dancer actually did. Having examined the available data, I have created three designations for ornamentation and improvisation in sixteenth-century dance: (1) ornamental gestures; (2) ornamental steps; and (3) improvisation.

1. Ornamental gestures include the *tremare*, hand gestures, and those of the upper body. The *tremare* as Negri calls it, or *tremolante* as Caroso calls it, is the only true ornamental gesture specifically described as such. Negri says, "Knowing that the major grace of

dance comes from shaking the feet [*tremare*], I would fault myself if I did not mention it."[20] He gives three ways of doing this: *da tutte due le bande* (moving the foot from side to side) four times; *in sù, & in giù* (moving it up and down); and *inanzi, & indietro à dritta linea* (moving it forward and backwards). Caroso describes this gesture:

> Questi tremolanti ponno usarsi in ogni sorte di passi, & si fanno nel tempo istesso che si fa un passo grave, in questo modo cioè; alzando il piè sinistro si muove tre volte con presteza grandissima, sguizzando alla sinistra, & alla destra: & all' ultima volta si cala esso piede in terra; poi levandosi col destro, si tiene il medesimo ordine con esso, che s'è tenuto col sinistro. Et da questo essetto di tremolar' il piede, hanno preso il nome di tremolanti.[21]
>
> (These *tremolanti* can be used in every kind of step and are done in the same time as a *passo grave*, in the following manner. Raising the left foot, move it three times with the greatest speed, flying briskly to the left and to the right, and for the last time, this foot is lowered to the ground. Then, raising the right, the same order is maintained as for the left. From this effect of shaking the foot has come the name of the *tremolanti*.)

The hand gestures found in Caroso's volumes include faux hand-kissing and delicately touching the brow with a handkerchief; he considers these graceful movements especially appropriate for a woman to do while performing a *passeggio* so as not to stand like the aforementioned statue. She may also adjust her train, sway gracefully, don a glove, and fan prettily. As a result, "quei vaghi & honesti moti farà una vista gratiosissima" ("these pretty and charming movements will make a most gracious sight").[22]

The final designation in the category of ornamental gestures includes a gesture found in many dances with Spanish designations: the *pavonneggiare* or "peacocking" movement, a seductive flanking movement of the shoulders and head so that the dancer can bestow a sidelong glance on his or her partner.[23] In this movement the dancer moves toward the partner with the side turned toward him or her, a movement Negri incorporates into his choreography *Lo Spagnoletto.* The Spanish association may come from what Caroso calls the swagger or strutting, a type of movement for which Spanish gentlemen were alternately praised and criticized during the Renaissance.[24] The praise seems related to the grace of the movement; criticism came from the arrogance that might be implied by such strutting.

2. The most ubiquitous of the ornamental steps is the *fioretto* (Eng. *flourish*; Fr. *fleuret*), found in all the major treatises. As with many common steps, there are several versions. Negri, for example, proposes five different versions, Caroso gives four, while Arbeau, the most succinct of the major authors, gives only the most basic: a rapid alternation of three kicks in the time of a note of short duration (a *minim*).[25] Because it is often used as any other step might be, the *fioretto*'s ornamental function may seem a bit obscure, but there are valid reasons for considering it in this category. One indication comes in Rule 31 of *Nobiltà* where Caroso encourages the dancer to use this step in any dance because, "without intermingling *fioretti* in your dancing, your movements seem dead."[26] This is the similar to his instructions to dancers in which he advises them to enliven their *passeggi* with improvised gestures. Caroso's other *fioretti* (Rules 32–34) are the *fiancheggiato* (moving sideways with a movement where one foot kicks behind the other), *a piè pari per fianco* (keeping feet parallel while scooting sideways), and *battuto al canario* (rapidly stamping feet "in the style of" the dance called the *canary* instead of the usual kicking).[27]

Negri's four interchangeable versions of the *fioretto* (Treatise II, Rule 8) underscore its function as ornamental since each can be incorporated into other steps.[28] His basic *fioretto* is accompanied by a picture of the dancer performing the first movement of the step and has instructions for doing this step moving forward (Caroso's *fioretto ordinario*), backward, in a circle, and, with a slight adjustment of step action, sideways (Caroso's *per fianco*). The remaining three *fioretti* are more intricate although they each take the same amount of time—one *minim*. The second has four actions including a subdivided hop; the third has five tiny steps that must be done *con grande prestezza* (with great speed); and the fourth is much like skipping. Later (Treatise III, Rule 25), Negri furnishes his version of the *fioretto battuto al canario*.[29]

Arbeau discusses the *fleuret* as a method by which "vous serez les pas mignardez" ("you will do the steps *mignardez*").[30] He says, "Vous notterez que ces cinq pas augmenteront leur grace, si vous les faictes mignardez" ("You will note that the grace of the five-step will be augmented if you do them *mignardez* [=in dainty fashion]").[31] However, he then proceeds with a description of *mignardez* as the substitution of small quick steps for a longer step. A hop performed in the time of one *minim*, for example, might be divided into the even smaller *semiminim* steps. In this section of his instructions to Capriol he supports improvised ornamentation in adding small steps or divisions, which he refers to generically as *decoupements* to the basic *gagliarda* step. Arbeau also uses a *decoupement*—in this case a variant of the *fleuret*—in the *branle double* in a response to Capriol's question "Feray je point de decoupements en dançant ces branles?" ("May I add some *decoupements* while dancing these *branles*?").[32]

The identification of the *fioretto* as both a step in its own right and one that can be used to ornament other steps leads to the consideration of "step families," a term I have coined to describe a set of related steps where each member is similar to the parent step. One such is the *seguito* family, a walking step similar to the French double step, common in Renaissance choreographies. Negri describes eight specific versions of the *seguito*, some more involved than others, but frequently neglects to specify which is desired in a particular choreography.[33] This is not a problem, however, if there exists the expectation that the dancer could use whichever version he or she wished in an improvisatory manner. Since all eight can be executed in the same period of time, the actual choice would not pose difficulties.

Another family of steps is headed by the *ripresa*.[34] These sideways steps are given in four versions, although I contend that an additional step, the *continenzia*, a sideways step with a flanking motion added, is a close relative of the family because of the similarity of movement.[35] This contention is supported by evidence found in choreographies where the *ripresa* substitutes for the *continenzia* in its position immediately following the bow as part of the opening sequence of many dances.[36]

3. Since many of the numerous spins, jumps, *capriols*, and turns cited in Negri, Caroso, and Arbeau take similar amounts of time, they can easily be substituted for one another. This would provide the dancer with the tools for improvising by substituting more impressive step patterns for simpler ones or by subdividing basic steps to add to their complexity. Castiglione's warning, however, comes to mind; the possibility of appearing foolish—a horrible fate against

which more than one Renaissance courtesy book warns—is still a consideration. In Giovanni Della Casa's *Galateo*, for example, the author uses a dance metaphor in criticizing foolish behavior when he says it is like "someone very fat with an enormous *derrière* . . . dancing . . . in his shirt-sleeves."[37]

Step elaboration or substitution could be used in any genre of choreography, whether *balletto*, *bassa*, *brando*, *cascarda*, or variation. While these genres differ in basic form, they each offer opportunities for brief ornaments at the level of the step. *Balletti*, found in all Italian dance manuals of this period, are generally composed for one or two couples and can contain two or more dance types, including some of those that are typically variation form dances. In some *balletti* the women imitate the men or vice versa. In such a situation, individuals could alter a step without interfering with the other dancers, much as musicians who are repeating a passage can ornament the repeated phrase. This would be easier, of course, in a couple dance with alternating actions. Examples from Caroso include *Alta Vittoria*, where "Il Cavaliere farà una Mutanza la più bella che saprà" ("The gentleman does the most beautiful variation he knows"),[38] and *Il Piantone*, "s'il Cavaliere vorrà far detto Passeggio in Gagliarda, con le Mutanze, & Capriole, stará à suo arbitrio" ("if the gentleman would like to do said passage as a *gagliarda* with variations and *capriol*s, it will be at his discretion").[39] Caroso generally writes out the lady's variation in *gagliarda* and *tordiglione* sections, but only occasionally offers her the option of doing her own variation. In *Cortesia*, for example, the lady may do any *tordiglione* that she knows if she likes, but if she does not know one she may do the simple pattern Caroso provided for a man who does not know a pattern that he might do.[40]

Treatises such as Lutii and Lupi, not to mention Negri, have long lists of variations for dances like the *gagliarda* that can simply be learned and plugged into whatever choreography the amateur is performing. These serve the same function as the "plug-ins" found in the music ornamentation treatises in which the author gives a set interval between two notes for which several increasingly virtuosic possibilities are then given for moving from one note to another (see Example 1).

EXAMPLE 1

Ortiz, *Tratado de glosas*, 21. Excerpts from "*para subir la segunda de semibreve*." Ganassi, *Opera intitulata Fontegara*, 20. Excerpt from "*moto de seconda assendente.*"

The *bassa* and *cascarda*, normally choreographed for one couple, tend to keep the couple together, and therefore ornamentation without disturbing the dancing of the partner might be more difficult. The *brando,* with four to eight dancers, would provide less scope for individuality because of the number of dancers involved and the intricacy of their choreographic interactions. This concern is also found in music where more complex pieces with several lines are less likely to present a context for improvisation since they are already sufficiently involved. For larger-scale improvisations, the variation dances represent the widest scope for dancers aside from solo dances. No known solo choreographies exist from this period.

All of the variation dances (*canary*, *gagliarda*, *passamezzo*, *pavaniglia*, *tordiglione*) with extant choreographies generally fall into a basic formal structure with an *entrata* (a stylized processional) followed by alternating variations for each partner of the couple, with the other dancer performing a *passeggio*.[41] After several variations, the couple performs a recessional. This is the form that easily lends itself to improvisation because in most cases the dancers do their variations solo, and in fact these choreographies are among the most difficult in the dance manuals.

Similar examples are found in Treatise II of Negri's manual. Allowing for the difference in presentation style required for dance instructions, Negri names a particular step and then supplies a rule under which all the versions of that step are explained. Rule 10, concerning the basic *gagliarda* step (five-step), is a good example.[42] I have placed numbers in parenthesis to mark the actions—which Negri calls "beats"—for each version.

On the five-step passing and turning a half turn . . .
RULE 10

Do a hop on the left foot raising the right (1). Raise the left backwards (2) and, putting the toe of this foot to the right heel, raise the right (3). Lowering it, raise the left (4). Then do the cadence (5). Afterwards do it on the right foot in the same way, going around. Said five-step is done in five ways. The first is done as said.

For the second do a syncopated *fioretto* with the right foot (1), jumping on the left (2). Afterwards do three more steps (3–5) and the cadence (6). Because they begin before the beat there are six beats.

The third way is done in the same way as the first, but in doing the first hop do a *capriol* passing both feet four times (1–2). Afterwards do the other three steps (3–5) and the cadence (6). With the two beats of the *capriol* there are six beats.

In the fourth way, do the same as the first, but in doing the first hop throw the right leg behind the left in a half *capriol* (1). Do the three steps (2–4) and a *capriol* passing four times (5–6), doing the cadence with this. There are six beats.

In the fifth way, do a syncopated *fioretto* with the right foot (1) and a beaten *capriol* with the left (2). Do the three steps (3–5), with the *capriol* passing four times (6–7), and do the cadence (8). All this is done with the greatest speed. There are eight beats.

Each version of this five-step is a bit more elaborate than the one before. The five-beat first version has hops raising the feet forwards or backwards, the six-beat second version adds a *fioretto*, the third a *capriol*, and the fourth a half *capriol*. By the fifth version a beaten *capriol* has been added and the number of beats has risen to eight. Despite the change in numbers of beats, all these steps are intended to be performed in the same amount of time. This is very much like the added notes or changes of rhythm that produce the diminutions in music ornamentation treatises where the music figures given must be performed in the same period of time. In both cases it seems clear that professionals or extremely skilled amateurs created their passages of dance or music, while published passages were more likely intended for the less experienced who were seriously interested in advancing their skill.

In *Nobiltà*, Caroso presents an interesting improvisational possibility when he defines the *pedalogue* as a dialogue or "call and response" between the feet of the two dancers. *Pedalogue* may well be a play on words combining teacher (*pedagogue*), foot (*pedes*), and dialogue. In fact, the final paragraph of *Laura Suave* describes the pedalogue as a dialogue where the correspondence takes place between the feet.[43] In the *balletto Nido d'amore*, the choreographic form has four distinct sections.[44] It begins with a complex entry passage in duple meter for the dancing couple (A), followed by a *gagliarda* variation for each of the dancers (B), then a *saltarello* section done together (C), and finally a *canary* section (D) performed as a pedalogue. The gentleman, serving as the teacher, does steps that become ever more difficult, each time imitated by his student, the lady. At the end of the section they come together and bow as equals, and the music is then repeated so that the lesson can continue once more. Each of the sections of this choreography is accompanied by a distinctive change of music and meter. Another pedalogue appears in *Altezza d'amore*; again, a couple dance with four-part form similar to *Nido*, with different music for each part: an *entrata* (A); two *gagliarda* variations (B); a *saltarello* (C); and the final *canary* (D) danced as a pedalogue.[45]

A fourth dance containing a pedalogue in *Nobiltà* is *Le Bellezze d'Olimpia*.[46] It differs from the other two in having music that remains the same throughout this choreography, the five subsequent repeats of that music supplying canvasses on which Caroso paints differing choreographic pictures. For the first two playings of the music, the couple dances together; the pedalogue occurs the third time. As in *Nido*, the gentleman is the teacher, and the lady is the student. The pedalogue is followed by three sections of dancing together, ending with the usual reverence. *Bellezze* is the only one of Caroso's pedalogue dances that appears in his earlier volume *Il Ballarino*.[47] The choreographies that are concordant to both volumes are edited in *Nobiltà* in order to produce more symmetry, and *Bellezze* is no exception. In *Ballarino* the choreography is in five sections, not six, and, although the word *pedalogue* is not used, there is an alternation of steps between the gentleman and the lady in the third section of the dance.

Even though Caroso makes it clear in all of these dances that the responding feet must repeat the steps of the calling feet, this dialogue looks very much like the choreographic version of what in jazz is called "trading four," a practice in which two soloists alternate solos of exactly the same length, often incorporating each others' improvisations into their own. It would seem most likely that the student would be encouraged to try to elaborate on what was being taught by adding ornamental gestures to the teacher's steps.

A final point connecting ornamentation in dance and music treatises concerns terminology held in common by both music and dance. In dance, *passeggi* have been explained as strolling passages, but this term also is used for the diminution passages found in the works of Lupi and Lutij—passages which seem to be much more elaborate examples of the simple strolling ones found in Caroso. A similar term, *passaggi*, is used for similar passages found in some music sources. In fact, a volume published in Negri's own Milan, the work of Duomo musician Giovanni Battista Bovicelli, uses the words *salti* (leaps), *tremolo* (shakes), and *groppetti* (knots), all terms related to concepts of similar meaning found in dance sources. The *passeggi* in music sources serve the purpose of replacing a simple passage of notes (like standing or walking in dance sources) with one that is more ornate; the *salti* in Bovicelli's 1594 treatise are leaps in music intervals and the *tremolos* are shakes in the voice (*tremar di voce*). The *groppetti* are vocal or instrumental ornaments winding around a note, similar to the *groppo* in Caroso and Negri where the dancer leaps to the side onto one foot and winds the other foot around the ankle of the standing foot. Bovicelli even uses language that mirrors Negri when he describes a passage that "can be done in two ways."[48] This evidence combines further to confirm the identification of *passeggi* and *passaggi* as patterns intended to be improvisatory and for which the published versions supply ideas. It also serves to confirm a close relationship between the music sources and the practice of dance. Given this connectedness, perhaps the advice in the ornamentation treatise written by Roman musician Luca Conforto could apply to dancers as well as musicians. He recommends that the musician should memorize several *passaggi*, practice them well, and then use them improvisationally when playing or singing in ensemble.[49]

Additional study and interpretation are required to discover the full role of ornamentation and improvisation in dance of the sixteenth century, but the rewards already achieved are a deeper understanding of the structure of late Renaissance dance and of its relationship to the music of that period. Both these skills did exist and were clearly an important part of the *virtù* of dancing for both amateur and professional. Dance was closely connected to several of the other arts. Literary elements are expressed both in the writings that celebrate this art and the description of dance as poetry in motion. The aural aspects are expressed through the musical accompaniment and the rhythm of the steps themselves. The visual aspects of dance are underscored by the concerns of dance and courtesy manual authors encouraging the dancers to be alert to how they appear to public observers. Simply stated by Rinaldo Corso in his *Dialogo del Ballo*, "Nell' arte del ballare sono tutte le altre arti unite" ("In the art of dancing, all the other arts unite").[50]

NOTES

[1]Pellegrino Santucci, *L'Improvvisazione nella musica* (Bologna: Cappella musicale S. Maria dei Servi, 1982), 197. While Santucci subsequently treats the relationship of dance to texted and untexted music as well as the evidence for improvisation in dance music, he provides no discussion, however, of improvisation for the dancers.

[2]Ornamentation and improvisation for musicians are discussed in the following: Giovanni Bassano, *Ricercate, passaggi et cadentie* [Venice, 1585], ed. Richard Erig (Zurich: Musikverlag zum Pelikan,1976); Gio. Battista Bovicelli, *Regole, passaggi di musica* (Venice, 1594; facs. reprint Rome: Società Italiana del Flauto Dolce, 1986); Scipione Cerreto, *Della prattica musica vocale et strumentale* (Naples, 1601; facs. reprint Bologna: Forni, 1969); Gio. Luca Conforto, *Breve et facile maniera* (Rome, 1593; facs. reprint Società Italiana del Fauto Dolce, 1986); Giovanni Dalla Casa, *Il vero modo di diminuir con tutte le sorti di stromenti* (Venice, 1584; facs. reprint Bologna: Forni, 1970); Sylvestro Ganassi, *Opera intitulata Fontegara* (Venice, 1535; facs. reprint 1934), ed. Hildemarie Peter, with English trans. by Dorothy Swainson (Berlin: Robert Lienau, 1959); Diego Ortiz, *Tratado de glosas sobre clausulas y otros generos de puntos en la musica de violones* [Rome, 1553], ed. Max Schneider (Kassel: Bärenreiter, 1936); Ricardo Rogniono, *Passaggi per petersi essercitare nel diminuire terminatamente con ogni sorti d'instromenti, et anco diversi passaggi per la semplice voce humana* (Milan, 1592); Tomas de Sancta Maria, *Libro llamado el arte de tañer fantasia* (Valladolid, 1565; facs. reprint Geneva: Minkoff, 1973), and for an English translation, see Almonte C. Howell and Warren Hultberg, *The Art of Playing the Fantasia* (Pittsburgh: Latin American Literary Press, 1991); Aurelio Virgiliano, *Il Dolcimelo* (Venice, c.1590; facs. reprint Florence: Studio per Edizioni scelte, 1986); Lodo-

vico Zacconi, *Prattica di musica utile* (Venice, 1596; facs. reprint Bologna: Forni, 1967). Useful secondary source materials include: Howard Mayer Brown, *Embellishing Sixteenth-Century Music* (London: Oxford University Press, 1976); Nelly van Ree Bernard, *Interpretation of Sixteenth-century Iberian Music on the Clavicord* (Buren, Netherlands: Frits Knuf, 1989); Richard Erig, *Italian diminutions* (Zurich: Amadeus, 1979); María A. Ester Sala, *La ornamentacion en la musica de tecla iberica del siglo XVI* (Madrid: Sociedad Española de Musicologia, 1980).

[3]Facsimile editions of these manuals include Thoinot Arbeau, *Orchésographie* (Hildesheim: Georg Olms Verlag, 1989; also published earlier at Geneva by Minkoff in 1972); Fabritio Caroso, *Ballarino* (New York: Broude, 1967), and *Nobiltà* (Bologna: Forni, 1980); and Cesare Negri, *Le Gratie d'Amore* (New York: Broude, 1969). English translations include: Arbeau, *Orchésographie*, trans. Mary Stewart Evans (New York: Dover, 1967); Fabrito Caroso, *Nobiltà*: *Courtly Dance of the Renaissance*, trans. Franco Iachello and Julia Sutton (New York: Dover, 1995); and Cesare Negri, *Le Gratie d'Amore*, trans. Gustavia Yvonne Kendall (DMA Final Project, Stanford University, 1985). Citations for published translations will be cited in parentheses following the page numbers in the original language edition; for Arbeau the folio numbers will be cited from the Minkoff facsimile with the Dover translation pages thereafter in parentheses. The English translation citations are given for the reader's convenience, but all translated passages in this paper are my own.

[4] "Fabricio Caroso da Sermoneta, di cui habbiamo di sopra fatto mentione non solo è stato di molte belle cose in questa virtù inventore, mà come dicemmo, hà mandato in luce un bellissimo libro, testimonio del suo valore ben chiaro, & illustre" ("Fabritio Caroso of Sermoneta, of whom we have made mention above, was not only the creator of many beautiful things in this art, but, as stated, he brought to light a most beautiful book, a quite clear and illustrious testimony of his valor") (Negri, *Le Gratie d'Amore,* 4).

"Lucio Compasso Romano, è stato valenthuomo nella professione del ballare alla gagliarda; hà scritto diverse mutanze della gagliarda, ha fatto scuola in Roma, & in Napoli fioritissima" ("Lutio Compasso, Roman, was a valiant man in the profession of dancing the *gagliarda*; he has written diverse variations of the *gagliarda*, has a school in Rome and flourished greatly in Naples") (ibid., 3). "Gio. Paolo Ernandes romano ha fatto scuola di ballare in Napoli, & in Roma, & è stato in Francia per la sua rara virtù stipendiato dal gran Priore fratello del Rè di Francia Enrico terzo, dapoi hà sempre fatto scuola in Roma molto honorata, & è sempre stato nella virtù agile, & garbato nel ballare la gagliarda, & il canario, & altre sorti di balli, & è stato inventore di molte belle mutanze del detto canario" ("Gio[vanni] Paolo Ernandes, Roman, has a school of dance in Naples and in Rome, and in France, because of his rare skill, he received a stipend from the great Prior, brother of King Henry III. Since then he has always kept a very honored school in Rome. And in this art he has always been agile and pleasing in dancing the *gagliarda*, the *canario* and other sorts of dances. He also was the creator of many beautiful variations for said canary") (ibid., 4). One of Ernandes's creations (his only known extant choreography), *Amor mio*, is found in *Ballarino*. The music for this dance is played nine times, the first three having varied *passeggi* for both dancers. The next two times are variations for the man with the woman instructed to make various modest, charming movements; the woman then repeats the man's variation, and both do two sections that lead to the end of the dance (Caroso, *Ballarino*, 106–07).

[5]Negri, *Le Gratie d'Amore,* 2, 6. It is quite intriguing that there are others—Pietro Martire, Giovanni Pietro Fabianino, and Martino da Asso—who are cited as having composed or invented choreographies (ibid., 2, 4), but whose works have not yet come to light. There are, however: Bastiano (*Se pensando al partire*), Battistino (*Alta Ragonia*, *Barriera*, *Contentezza d'Amore*, *Coppia Matthei*, *Lucretia Favorita*, *Pavana Matthei*, *Rustica Palina*, *Torneo Amoroso*, *Bassa Honorata*, *Bassa Romana*, and *Bassa Toscana*), Andrea da Gaeta (*Bassa Colonna*), Ippolito Ghidotti da Crema (*Felice Vittoria*), and Oratio Martire (*Allegrezza d'Amore*, *Alta Vittoria*), all of whom were responsible for choreographies in *Ballarino* but were not mentioned in Negri's list. Also curious is the lack of identification for the M. Stefano, who created some of the choreographies found in *Le Gratie d'Amore*.

[6]Negri, *Le Gratie d'Amore*, 12.

[7]Ibid., 14.

[8]Cerreto, *Dalla Prattica*, 158. Further evidence of connections between ornamentation sources is Cerreto's mention of Ortiz as a Spanish composer who lived in Rome.

[9]"e benché si senta leggerissimo e che abbia tempo e misura assai, non entri in quelle prestezze de' piedi e duplicati rebattimenti, i quali veggiamo che nel nostro Barletta stanno benissimo . . . benché in camera privatamente, come or noi ci troviamo . . . ma in publico non così, fuor che travestito" (Baldassar Castiglione, *Il Libro del Cortegiano*, ed. Amedeo Quondam and Nicola Longa [Garzanti, 1998], 134).

[10]Anon., "The Practise of Dauncinge," Bodleian Library MS. Douce 280, fol. 203.

[11]Thomas Morley, *A Plain and Easy Introduction to Practical Music,* ed. R. A. Harman (1952; reprint New York: W. W. Norton, 1963), 297.

[12]Arbeau, *Orchésographie*, fol. 64^v [121].

[13]Ibid., fols. 65^v–66^v [123–24].

[14]Caroso, *Nobiltà*, 296 [270].

[15]Ibid.

[16]Ibid., 111–20 [162–72].

[17]Ibid., 113 [163].

[18]"Lettere di D. Giovanni d'Austria a D. Giovanni Andrea Doria," British Library MS. Add. 10,909, m.18.

[19]Negri, *Le Gratie d'Amore,* 65–72. In Negri's second treatise, Rules 19–33 are devoted to tassel jumps. The instructions include illustrations of the opening positions with the tassels.

[20]"Mancherei à me stesso, sapendo io che la maggior gratia del ballare viene dal tremare de i piedi, quando io no ne facessi la dovuta mentione" (ibid., 33). This is the seventh of Negri's nine basic admonitions on dancing. All nine deal with details of comportment and ornaments.

[21]Caroso, *Ballarino*, fols. 14^{v}–15^{r}. This is step Rule 46, listed on fol. 2^{v} among *diciasette altri movimenti* (seventeen other movements).

[22]These instructions feature most prominently in the dance *Laura Suave* (ibid., 113 [163]).

[23]While there is some discussion in the dance history community concerning the finer points of this movement's definition, it seems clear that it includes a type of swaggering strut with the chest proudly forward. In Negri's *Spagnoletto*, it is combined with a motion that moves backwards while alternately turning each side of the body toward the partner.

[24]Caroso, *Nobiltà*, 16 (100). Caroso considers that doing this movement (*si pavoneggia*) is one of the subtle but important graces of dancing.

[25]Arbeau, *Orchésographie*, fol. 57^{r} (107).

[26]Caroso, *Nobiltà*, 38 (115): "perche non facendovisi fioretti tramischiati in essa, pare un'attione morte."

[27]Ibid., 39–40 (114–16).

[28]Negri, *Le Gratie d'Amore,* 51.

[29]Ibid., 113.

[30]Arbeau, *Orchésographie,* fol. 57^{v} (108). The translation of *mignardez* as "mincing," as in the Evans translation, is misleading to my mind since the use of the term as designating a practice of step subdivision is never clarified.

[31]Ibid., fol. 57v (108).

[32]Ibid., fol. 70v (131).

[33]Negri's seguitos include *seguito grave finto*, *s. grave*, *s. ordinario*, *s.col piede alto alla battuta*, *s.spezzato*, *s. scorso*, *s. battuto al canario*, and *s. spezzato al canario* (*Le Gratie d'Amore*, 107–10).

[34]*Ripresa grave*, *r. in sottopiede*, *r. minima*, *r. minuita* (ibid., 111).

[35]Ibid., 105. Treatise III, Rule 3 describes the *continenze*.

[36]See ibid., *Gratioso* (137), *Brando di Cales* (152), *So Ben* (222), *Fedeltà* (242), *Bizzarria* (254r *in sottopiede*). In just over ten percent of dances, *saltini* (hops) take the place of these steps. One unusual dance, the *Pavaniglia all'uso di Milano* (157), has both: *riverenza,* two *continenzie*, and two *riprese*. Nearly eighty percent of dances open with one *riverenza* and two *continenzie*.

[37]Giovanni Della Casa, *Galateo*, trans. Konrad Eisenbichler and Kenneth R. Bartlett (Toronto: CRRS, 1994), 70.

[38]Caroso, *Nobiltà*, 299 [272]. This instruction occurs in the first *canary* variation. Instructions for substitution also occur in the *gagliarda* section (296).

[39]Ibid., 334 [292].

[40]Ibid., 339 [295]: "La Dama farà una Mutanza di Tordiglione; & se non la saprà, faccia . . . come harà fatto il Cavaliere" ("The lady does a *tordiglione* variation; and if she doesn't know one, she does . . . as the gentleman has done").

[41]In progress is an article on variation form in sixteenth-century choreographies which is an extended version of the paper I presented at the Twentieth Annual Conference of the Society of Dance History Scholars (Barnard College, 19–22 June 1997).

[42]In order to clarify the example for those who are not Renaissance dance specialists, I have edited Negri's instructions. For the full text in translation, see my translation of *Le Gratie d'Amore* (revision of this work for publication in progress).

[43]Caroso, *Nobiltà*, 115 (164).

[44] Ibid., 289–93 (266–69).

[45] Ibid., 172–76 (206–10).

[46] Ibid., 236–39 (239–41).

[47]Caroso, *Ballarino*, fols. 65^{r}–66^{r}.

[48]Bovicelli, *Regole*, 22.

[49]Conforto, *Breve et facile maniera*, 35.

[50]Rinaldo Corso, *Dialogo del Ballo* [Venice, 1555] (Verona: AMIS, 1987), 48.

DRAMA

Improvisation in Medieval Drama

Clifford Davidson

Since drama when presented on stage is both verbal and visual, improvisation may involve one or the other or both of these together. When playscripts are studied as literature the implications of this fact are obscured, and the same may be the inadvertent effect of modern editing methods applied to drama texts with their meticulousness in preserving and attempting to restore them as much as possible to the state originally written by the playwright.[1] The documentation presented by recent research, including work done under the aegis of the Records of Early English Drama project, has demonstrated, however, that the idea of fixed authorship and definitive texts must be put aside for a theater that was more fluid and more open to changes as anonymous scripts were revised and copied and as players transformed these into performances.[2] The extent to which medieval plays were seen as performance art, not as literature, may be gauged by the slowness with which they would be taken up by the newly invented medium of print. Unlike sixteenth-century France, where many playbooks containing medieval plays became available to a reading public,[3] early British playtexts containing religious drama were generally not set up in type and, when not destroyed by chance, carelessness, or the vicissitudes of the Reformation, were retained in manuscript. Those which did survive only found their way into general circulation in the nineteenth and twentieth centuries, though, as in the case of the Chester plays, it might be necessary for editors to work from late manuscript copies prepared by antiquarians wishing to preserve the textual tradition of the plays.[4]

In spite of the existence of playtexts as well as surviving dramatic records and iconographic evidence, on the whole our understanding of many of the specifics of production, especially improvisation, has been meager, and this comes from the under-representation of gesture, movement, and other performance aspects in the scholarship.[5] Attempts at physical re-creation of conditions of performance such as the staging of play cycles on pageant wagons at Toronto, Leeds, and other locations have been very useful,[6] but these sorts of endeavors require being joined to scholarly examination, which to be sure cannot answer all our questions. Much difficulty arises from the problems attending the interpretation of the rubrics or stage directions (sometimes very ambiguous or sketchy) in the playscripts, and we have so far as I know no detailed contemporary reports of performances that may be consulted, for even so rare a description as that of R. Willis concerning *The Cradle of Security* at Gloucester in the 1570s gives little useful detail.[7] Improvisation is the most ephemeral aspect of performances from half a millennium ago and also perhaps the most vexed scholarly question. Any attempt to arrive at specifics in our discussion of improvisation under these circumstances can only involve speculation if our aim is to determine the full dimensions of the sights and sounds of a medieval play at a specific time and place. Yet the available evidence will allow us to ascertain much about the *possibilities* for improvisation even when we cannot achieve the kind of certainty that we would wish to have. We can determine the range of the performance options, from formulaic ceremony with dialogue to plays which make available very considerable space for improvisation.

Shakespeare's Hamlet suggests the limit on one side—or a point that is *beyond* the limit endurable by scripted drama if it is to retain its coherence: "And let those that play your clowns speak no more than is set down for them, for there be of them that will themselves laugh to set on some quantity of barren spectators to laugh too, though in the meantime some necessary question of the play be then to be consider'd" (3.2.38–43).[8] Improvised speeches (and presumably gestures) were the object of the playwright's displeasure, which was directed against those licenced fools who would entertain an audience at the expense of the action of the play. This has, however, larger ramifications for the "medieval" drama that was still alive in Shakespeare's boyhood—and which he almost certainly witnessed personally at nearby Coventry, a city that retained its biblical play cycle until 1579.[9] It also may reflect the professional playwright's antipathy toward even more loosely organized popular entertainments such as those described by Sandra Billington—entertainments which, she argues, paradoxically informed plays such as *King Lear*, whose hero echoed the "mistake" of one playing royalty in a summer game in valuing "the appearance of royalty without its substance."[10] Improvised entertainments of this kind seem to have been common up to the seventeenth century, as in the case of an event recorded on a Sunday in 1620 at Bunbury in the Diocese of Chester. On this occasion, Elizabeth Symme presented herself "as Ladye of the game," while one Richard Coddingtoun was dressed up "in womans apparell" and sent forth "with a great trayne of rude people tumultuously gaddinge after him from thence to the Church hill to bringe a present of Cheryes to the sayd Elizabeth where shee sate . . . readie to receive them."[11] The low-born player in such a game was required to engage in improvised speeches and gestures, which represented his or her fantasizing about how a king or queen would act. Other improvised identities might also have been acted out: one might have pretended that he was an inebriated pontiff, another that he was a particularly arrogant nobleman, and yet another that he had taken on the authority of the actual king of England himself.[12] A Lord of Misrule playing the role of winter king such as George Ferrers in 1553 would enter the city of London in great ceremony with his retainers like a monarch in "purprelle welvet" and a "robe braded with spangulls of selver," dine with the Lord Mayor, and perform a ceremony in which he created a knight.[13] Even an improvised "play of execution" was part of the entertainment.[14] And real violence might be promised, as on 25 January 1443 when a crowned Christmas king, John Gladman, led an insurrection at Norwich in which a rabble threatened to burn the cathedral priory and murder the monks—a threat that, in spite of an attack on the priory gates, would be abandoned a week later.[15]

A summer king might preside at summer festivities at which Robin Hood plays were performed. Very few texts for such dramas are extant, and it may be surmised from the evidence that they may have been worked up from Robin Hood ballads, the earliest of which have been recorded as early as the end of the thirteenth century,[16] and that they were mainly improvised. In the first reference to a Robin Hood play, the account rolls for the city of Exeter reported 20*d* paid out to players in 1427, though, as the Records of Early English Drama editor warns, this and other references to Robin Hood in the Devon records are not necessarily unambiguous.[17] The earliest scripts have been dated nearly fifty years later, in East Anglia, found among the Paston papers; these two short combat dramas, including (1) the execution of a knight and (2) a prison escape and further fighting, demonstrate a need for extensive improvisation—archery, stone throwing, wrestling, and swordplay—to become theatrically viable.[18] David Wiles's plausible attempt at reconstruction of ascription of the speeches to individual characters and stage directions includes descriptions of the action—e.g., "Having loosened their bonds inside the prison, Robin and his men catch the Sheriff unawares. After a fight, they bind the Sheriff and his men."[19] The players could of course also have engaged in further improvisation although it is not indicated in the playscripts. Then, changes in the location of the playing place or the positioning of the audience would likewise affect the action and possibly also the speeches, so skepticism is in order concerning the value of these texts in reporting the early performances that they document. The texts instead appear to survive as imperfect reflections of the action of the Robin Hood plays, since circumstances might carry the drama in somewhat different directions though not to different conclusions at its ending. Perhaps most importantly, it is impossible to imagine the combat or the displays of archery to have been done in complete silence and without any improvised sounds and words.

The extant dramatic records naturally attend to physical matters such as costumes rather than improvisation, as in accounts dated 1525–26 at Bristol, where expenses for hose for Robin and Little John are listed.[20] More extensive records such as the churchwardens' accounts at Kingston-upon-Thames, Surrey, from 1507 to 1538 nevertheless yield some clues. These report five days of Whitsun week entertainments "fro whet sonday wn to seyer [?fair] day at nythe" in 1507 that were presided over by a summer king.[21] The main attraction seems to have been the Robin Hood play but involving much more, in some years including a lute player, taborer, and morris dancers, the latter perhaps new in 1507.[22] The event, a church ale, was highly popular and attracted as many as, if not more than, two thousand people in a single year.[23] For example, in 1507 payments were made "to jhon payntar for M*i*lle of leveres," "to Wyl*ia*m skott [bloge] for xjj C leveres & xl gret [liveries]," and to an unspecified person for a hundred more liveries.[24] While the "great" liveries were articles of clothing assigned to major players, the other (small) "leveres" have been identified by reference to Philip Stubbes's jaundiced description of a generic king game.[25] These (costing the churchwardens at Kingston-upon-Thames in 1507 only 8*s* 3*d* and in addition an amount for painting certain of these) were small colored paper badges to be attached to the purchasers' clothes with the 2,500 pins ("ij M*i*lle & a d*imidium* of pynnys") for which 10*d* had been paid out.[26] Since the pedlars who sold them were Robin Hood and his "company" in their Kendal green—their purpose was the support of the Kingston-upon-Thames parish church[27]—the principals, interacting with the crowd, were blended into the fabric of the event even when they were not performing their play.[28] The very elaborateness of the entertainments would have precluded fully scripted performance and hence must have required improvisation, which may well have been at the heart of the Robin Hood play. Some of Robin's men (and Maid Marian, who may have been a woman and not a male impersonator) danced as well, but this would not have detracted from the dramatic scenes in which traditional Robin Hood stories were dramatized.[29]

The greatest scope for dramatic improvisation would thus have been found not in carefully controlled civic drama such as the Corpus Christi or Whitsun plays of Coventry, York, or Chester but in forms of drama that involved non-scripted playing in whole or in part. These might involve a considerable spectrum, all under the term *game* as it was then understood. If Lawrence Clopper were to be found correct in his interpretation of the English term 'somergame,'[30] many references which seem to indicate medieval drama actually would be indicative of some form of these unscripted or partially scripted performances. The attempt to identify such entertainments in ambiguous dramatic records is, to be sure, highly theoretical, and one must be quite skeptical concerning the lack of a text simply because vague records are joined with the non-survival of a playscript.[31] It would seem that such a formulaic drama, if it existed in specific instances which Clopper has proposed in the dramatic records, might well have been flexible, allowing adaptation to each audience situation within the bounds of a set of rules as in a game. The possibilities for irreverent treatment of saints' legends, if these were involved in such plays, would have been considerable but would have depended on the reception by those watching and listening to the play. Even scurrilous improvisation could have occurred, for devotion to individual saints involved fierce partisanship which did not necessarily extend to the whole company of saints. Unfortunately for such theorizing, the saints that are noted in the dramatic records in the pre-Reformation period tended to be those for whom there was very strong local devotion which would militate against their mistreatment by improvising players; further, connections between entertainments identified with saints and, for example, the midsummer entertainment identified as a "somyr play" at Wistow in Yorkshire in 1469 seem extremely problematic.[32] Nevertheless, Clopper's argument for attention to a tradition of unscripted playing more akin to game reminds us that consideration of the terminology for playing will show the distance from *drama* to *game* (even as we interpret these words today) to have been a matter of degree, not a difference of kind. We need to keep in mind the fact that *playing* even nowadays is an ambiguous term, for it can designate both acting and making instrumental music as well as participation in a game, which might be anything from poker to baseball or a children's game such as London Bridge.

At the end of *The Castle of Perseverance*, the God of Judgment appears and begins the final speech of the play by announcing: "Þus endyth oure gamys."[33] But *game* also had wide currency denoting gambling, sport, and other kinds of entertainment.[34] In the fifteenth century, the term *game* or *games* could as easily mean the kind of activity that nowadays would be identified as a game as what we would call a play. John Coldewey places the terminology in perspective when he remarks that "the word 'play' is historically and conceptually a philological subset of the word 'game,' not the other way around."[35] This distinction is important for understanding the significance of "pley" and "game" in the most extensive (though hostile) contemporary discussion of drama in medieval England. Playing, as in theatrical presentations and especially in religious theater, is an activity that was understood by the authors of *A Tretise of Miraclis Pleyinge* to be inauthentic in its adoption of illusion when imagining sacred scenes such as the Passion, but they also seem to have a puritanical antipathy to any form of play, for even children's games are regarded with suspicion. The standard is the literal truth, which cannot according to these writers be achieved by improvising movement and gestures or speaking the imagined dialogue of sacred persons and events. They completely reject the mnemonic and devotional functions of religious drama, which as a genre seems to them to be a reversal rather than an affirmation of the works of Christ.[36] All play acting is "in pley and bourde" whether improvised or fixed by tradition,[37] and falls in their view within the category of prohibited behavior.

The *Tretise* thus argues for the extension of the category that had been designated in the *Constitutions* of Walter Cantilupe under the term *ludi inhonesti*[38] and by Alexander Carpenter under *perverse illusionis*[39] to include all playing without exception. Few late medieval writers seem to have shared the extremely antitheatrical view of the authors of the *Tretise* who collapsed distinctions between edifying plays, valid recreation, and scurrilous entertainment. The actors in these types of drama required differing amounts of imaginative freedom to move about, to make gestures, and to speak—and to seem spontaneous even if little improvisation were involved. Our task, then, must be to distinguish certain nearly invisible aspects of performance which exist between different types of medieval plays and the games related to such plays in form and content. Though complicated by the ephemeral nature of playing and the silence of playscripts, the parameters for understanding the range of improvisation that existed in medieval drama and its closest relatives, ranging from dramatic ceremonies to unscripted games, need to be sorted out.

In this regard, the most stylized forms to be found in the European Middle Ages with regard to movement, gesture, and musical intonation were the Latin liturgical dramas and quasi-dramatic ceremonies such as the *Depositio*, *Elevatio*, and *Visitatio Sepulchri* for Holy Week and Easter as they appeared in the *Regularis Concordia* from tenth century Winchester.[40] These appear in the manuscript without musical notation, and are less well known than the more elaborate Continental types of the Visit to the Sepulcher, Herod, or St. Nicholas plays in the Fleury Playbook (Orléans, Bibliothèque Municipale MS. 201) or even the Benediktbeuern Passion Play.[41] The early examples, sometimes marginalized in modern commentary as *paraliturgical* or *extraliturgical*, were developed as ceremonies that reinforced the liturgy and made the presentation of events at the center of sacred history more vivid, especially for the unlearned and for neophytes.[42] The movements and gestures of the participants in them would need to have been worked out initially by very rudimentary improvisation prior to the actual performance, but the extant records suggest a crystallized set of motions that represent events (not in the mode of realism, and in the case of the *Depositio* and *Elevatio* only symbolically) in imitation of the historical persons in sacred time at the Entombment, Resurrection, and visit of the three Marys to the empty sepulcher. In the text in the *Regularis Concordia*, the monks (*fratres*) were told to vest themselves, and those taking the roles of the holy women were to proceed "haltingly, in the manner of seeking for something"—a stage direction that suggests some cautious improvisation. The entire scene was to be "done in imitation of the angel seated on the tomb and the women coming with spices to anoint the body of Jesus" ("ad imitationem Angeli sedentis in monumento, atque Mulierum cum aromatibus uenientium, ut ungerent corpus Ihesu"). So far as we can tell, the manner in which the actors such as those impersonating angels or the Marys took their places and processed was almost imperceptibly differentiated from the traditional Easter rituals themselves, and the *Visitatio* concluded with the singing of the antiphon *Surrexit Dominus de sepulchro*, which was a direct link back to the liturgy.[43] No special coaching in acting would have been required for the participants, for they would have been expected to fall back on their training in ceremony and ritual.

By way of comparison, even the *Depositio* and *Elevatio* would have been less stylized than a non-European form, the South Indian sacred dance drama known as *Bharata Natyam*, which appears to provide an example of a genre in which *only* conventional movements were used in performance.[44] Reputed to have its origins more than two millennia ago, *Bharata Natyam* relies on traditions which were believed to have been taught by the god Indra and which are so codified that even the eyes must come under perfect control. The techniques involved in this dance drama were passed down by dance teachers to their disciples as carefully guarded secrets which specified exact foot, leg, arm, and body movements as well as facial expressions to the complex rhythms of traditional Carnatic music. Performances present an exact iconography, of which an example may usefully be cited: one hand placed over the other with the thumbs extended will always signify fish.[45] The dance, which experienced a revival in the twentieth century through the efforts of the great Madras dancer Balasaraswati and others, provides narration of stories from sacred Hindu scriptures.[46]

Similarly stylized is *Kathakali*, the traditional Hindu dance drama of Kerala that is characterized by elaborate masks and lengthy all-night performances.[47] *Kathakali* was one of the direct Indian influences that helped to shape a form of religious drama from Kerala that is derived from European liturgical drama brought to the region by Portuguese missionaries in the sixteenth century. *Chavittunātakam*, designating plays which emphasize foot stamping and which range in subject matter from David and Goliath to the Coming of the Magi (*Muvaraśunātakam*), saints' lives, and Charlemagne (*Kāralmān)* vs. the Moors, may well have involved improvisation in the earliest stages of their development, but these now are fully rehearsed over a long period, sometimes up to one year, under the direction of an *Āśān* (Master) to codify every movement.[48] Neverthless, they necessarily fall back on some improvisation in battle scenes, as in the dramatizations of Charlemagne's alleged role in sacred history—scenes which are descended ultimately from the battle of Christians and Moors acted out on the Iberian peninsula.[49] *Chavittunātakam* was designed for Church festivals among the Roman Catholic community of the Malabar coast, probably with the immediate goal of presenting shows that would keep its members away from competing Hindu dance dramas and at the same time would prove enticing to potential converts. Joining music and spectacle as had been the practice in *Kathakali*, they provided complex presentations of the Christian stories. They represent a significant blending of cultures in which other traditional dramatic practices foreign to the European liturgical drama were absorbed and served to transform the imported liturgical plays.

I have mentioned *Chavittunātakam* because it is an almost unknown variant of a medieval European genre, but also because a comparison may be made, I believe, with the developments in twelfth- and thirteenth-century Europe which brought forth the most complex forms of medieval music-drama. In these cases in Europe other influences must have come to bear to transform the liturgical drama into something different from forms that were neatly inserted into a particular place in the liturgy on a feast day. Scholars no longer give support to the evolutionary theory of the development of drama from lower to higher forms[50] or to the suggestions of Oscar Cargill that at this time the Church incorporated secular entertainers who helped to enliven and "contaminate" the formerly stately liturgical dramas and ceremonies.[51] But when a play such as the Beauvais *Daniel* is identified in the unique manuscript (British Library, Egerton MS. 2615) which contains it as *Ludus Danielis*,[52] the term *ludus* must indicate that here is a form that differs in very significant ways from the dramatic ceremonies described in the *Regularis Concordia*. The differences must come from seeing the performance as *play*, as an imaginative re-creation in which a stylized drama was joined with the freedom of a *game* in the high

Middle Ages in Europe. The extravagant feast using sacred vessels at the Babylonian court, Balthasar's reaction to the handwriting on the wall, and the movements required for his deposition by Darius as well as the acting of the roles of the lions could hardly have been fixed by tradition. Margot Fassler has argued that the Beauvais *Daniel* was produced as part of a deliberate effort to replace the disrespectful playing and fooling that characterized the *festum stultorum*, or Feast of Fools, associated with the festival of the Circumcision on 1 January.[53] She quotes William of Auxerre, who compared such reform to the displacement of pagan custom: "In the same way, ludi, which are against the faith [the church], changed into ludi which are not against the faith."[54] Blasphemous playing at ritual—for example, using shoe leather instead of incense in processions and at Mass, even for "censing" the altar—by the lower clerical orders is replaced by playing which internalizes blaspheming behavior and other elements of the Feast of Fools within the drama in a context which is actually a corrective to blasphemy. The resulting play is one which is unimaginable without some room for improvisation by the actors.

The *Daniel* was written for performance at the cathedral at Beauvais rather than for a monastery. Monasteries nevertheless remained an important venue for liturgical drama, for records point especially to monastic churches, very frequently associated with the Benedictine order, where liturgical drama was performed. These music-dramas incorporated chant melodies, sometimes ones that were very familiar to members of the community, and, depending on the location of the performance, vocal improvisation would have been expected as part of the performance technique. Improvisation was reported in the day-to-day chanting during the Office and Mass not only in singing technique but also utilizing histrionic gestures and movement, and hence these performance practices would easily have been transferred to the Latin music-drama. Aelred of Rievaulx, the abbot of the Cistercian abbey at Rievaulx and no friend of Benedictine practices, wrote a strong denunciation of such practices:

> Types and figures, aside, whence, I ask, all these organs, all these cymbals in the church? To what purpose, I ask, that horrible inflating of bellows, expressing the crash of thunder rather than the smoothness of human voice? To what end that contracting and weakening of the voice? This singer harmonizes,

> that expresses dissonance; another divides and breaks off notes in the middle. Now the voice is strained, now it is shattered, now it swells louder, now it is broadened into a fuller sound. At one time (shame to say) it is forced into horse-like neighing; at another with its masculine vigor ignored, it is sharpened into the slenderness of the female voice; sometimes it is twisted and twisted again with a certain kind of artificial convolution. Sometimes you may see a man with his mouth open as if he were expiring, with his wind cut off, not singing, and with a kind of ridiculous suspension of sound as if to threaten total silence; now imitating the agonies of the dying or the terror of the suffering. Meanwhile, his whole body is busy with various histrionic gestures, the lips are contorted, the arms whirl about and play wantonly; and a flexing of the fingers responds to each particular note. And this ridiculous dissoluteness is called religion; and where such things are done the more often, there the clamor is that God is the more honorably served. Meanwhile the common folk, trembling and astonished, marvel at the sounding of bellows, the clashing of cymbals, the harmony of pipes; but the lascivious gesticulations of the singers, the meretricious quavering and breaking of their voices, ought to be regarded not without merriment and laughter, as you ought to consider them suitable not to the house of prayer, but to the theater, not to praying, but to viewing.[55]

The Cistercian reform had aimed at liturgical simplicity and in its service books had attempted to return chant to simpler, less rhythmic, and less ornamented forms that were imagined to reflect the original performance practice of the Church's liturgy in antiquity. There was no more sympathy in these quarters for liturgical or theatrical improvisation than there was for the artistically ornamented interiors and elaborate painted glass of Benedictine churches. Ornaments, neither of stone, wood, or glass nor of melody, found favor with the monks associated with the order of which Bernard of Clairvaux was the intellectual head. While improvements in the late twelfth and early thirteenth centuries in notating music also affected Benedictine and cathedral choirs in paradoxically reducing improvisation—a trend which would continue over the following centuries—the earlier conventions of singing complex and ornamented melodies with their use of vibrato, trills, pulsation, and indefinite pitch as well as the later trend toward the use of polyphony were more definitively rejected by the Cistercians along with the entire corpus of Latin liturgical drama. The latter indeed was repudiated as thoroughly as the vernacular drama would be denounced by the authors of the *Tretise of Miraclis Pleyinge*.[56]

None of the liturgical music-dramas, even the *Daniel* from Beauvais Cathedral, actually allows for *subversive* improvisation either in speech and singing or movement and gesture that might act to undermine the meaning of the play—that is, the kind of improvisation that Shakespeare later would identify as an offensive diversion from "some necessary question of the play." The liturgical Visit to the Sepulcher, which in its various forms was to be officially abandoned by both the Reformation and the Counter-Reformation, was essentially mnemonic and devotional, and was one of the dramatic ceremonies organized by the fourteenth-century abbess Katherine of Sutton at Barking, Essex, to stimulate deeper faith and piety among her nuns.[57] Yet Martin Walsh has called attention to an account among the merry pranks of Till Eulenspiegel of subversion in a *Visitatio Sepulchri*, undoubtedly apocryphal.[58] As told in the thirteenth episode in *Ein Kurtzweilig lesen von Dyl Ulenspiegel* (Strassburg, 1515), Eulenspiegel was serving as a sacristan in a rural parish when the priest announced that an Easter play, a Visit to the Sepulcher drama, was planned for Easter. Assisted by the priest's maid who would be the angel at the tomb, Eulenspiegel recruited two farmers to join him in the role of the Marys, while the priest was to impersonate the Risen Lord. But when the maid recited the line "Quem queritis [in sepulchro]," the first farmer spoke the line he had been taught by Eulenspiegel: "Wir suchen ein alte einäugige Pfaffenhur" ("We're looking for a priest's old, one-eyed whore").[59] This resulted, as might be expected in an Eulenspiegel story, in a pitched battle as the maid attempted to attack him but instead struck one of the farmers with consequent mayhem (fig. 1). Congregations in a real-life situation may well have been scandalized by the blasphemy of the scene (though we might imagine some nervous laughter), but in the context of Eulenspiegel stories the event is unambiguously turned to humor. Yet this tall tale is a reminder that the possibility of subversive improvisation or simply a humorous mistake in the course of a play is not to be ruled out.

At York, the subverting of the text, either by the means described above or by a weak and incompetent actor, and hence the

1. *How our Lord rose from the tomb. Ein Kurtzweilig lesen von Dyl Ulenspiegel geboren uss den Land zu Brunsswick* (Strassburg, 1515), Episode 13. Courtesy of Harlan Hatcher Graduate Library, University of Michigan, and Martin Walsh.

stimulating of inappropriate audience response, was a concern of the city corporation, which controlled the city's Creation to Doom cycle. In 1476 the corporation appointed four men to inspect the plays, pageant stages, and players in the York Creation to Doom cycle prior to their performance on the feast of Corpus Christi,[60] and in 1542 the civic records note that the city clerk positioned himself at the gates of Holy Trinity Priory, the first station at which the plays were to be performed, with the Register (now British Library MS. Add. 35,290) in hand.[61] While some have insisted on the carnivalesque as central to such plays as those in the York cycle, the evidence is on the other side.[62] Though the plays were far less predetermined in speeches, movement, and gesture than the liturgical plays, the corporation's great concerns were that they should serve as a devotional aid appropriate to the occasion and for the suppression of vice[63] and, perhaps more importantly, that they should enhance the honor of the city and its crafts and should be presented to the glory of God.[64] This does not mean that the members of the audience were always complaisant or that they conformed with the standards of behavior desired by the Corporation—indeed, there is some evidence to the contrary. But that the performers and their sponsoring guilds were in agreement with the corporation with regard to the purpose of the plays seems clear enough, and when one of the playtexts produced the wrong effect—laughter and derision rather than devotion and respect—it was apparently seldom performed and was not transcribed into the Register. Complaints indicate that the play of *Fergus*, dramatizing the funeral procession of the Virgin Mary which was attacked by the Jew Fergus, drew the audience into the action—an instance of improvised participation on the part of members of the audience,[65] particularly unpleasant on account of the anti-Semitic overtones of their actions.

Opportunities for improvisation nevertheless were clearly available to the actors in the York plays. The stage directions in the York Register are scanty,[66] and the actions demanded in the plays were more often either specified by the dialogue or passed on from year to year by the actors themselves if not by the pageant master. There was no regimen of extensive rehearsals such as we find in the Kerala *Chavittunātakam,* but the retention of actors from year to year and the number of times (potentially twelve or more) that a particular pageant was performed along the York pageant route would be factors suggesting stability and uniformity. On the other hand, different stations for playing along the pageant route would have meant necessary adaptation of the performance to different audiences and spaces.[67] Also, when the playtexts are closely examined it is clear that a minimalist approach to movement and gesture could not have resulted in the kind of spectacle that would be repeated (with revisions and variations, to be sure) over more than a century and a half at least and perhaps longer.

In defining some parameters here, knowledge of codes of behavior is useful in indicating rules for the persons of the deity and upright human characters, both static by current standards since quick and frequent motion was thought to be in bad form.[68] Others, such as devils and, for example, the executioners at the Crucifixion, would have been characterized by nervousness and inappropriate movements of hands, limbs, and body. These effects would all need to have been performed by the actors to fit the circumstances of the individual performance. If no actual words were added to the York texts, I would still be most surprised if improvised non-verbal sounds were not an important part of the repertoire of such characters—e.g., grunts at the weight of the cross being lifted into place at the Crucifixion, screaming in terror by the devils at the Fall of the Angels as they tumbled into hellmouth. It is hard to believe that any two performances, even any two done in succession along the pageant route, would have been identical. Over the course of the performance of the cycle in any particular year the greatest amount of space for improvisation would have been made available not to God, the angels, or humans destined eventually to inhabit bliss. The extent of actual improvisation would depend on the individual character being portrayed, especially whether presented as good or evil, serious or comic, and on the actor's abilities to represent that character fully in performance.

The liveliness often noted in certain of the plays in the Towneley manuscript would potentially have provided more space for improvisation than in the York cycle, but here we have no assistance from West Riding dramatic records concerning the location or conditions of performance. Some of the plays are adapted from York pageants, others are written or adapted by a playwright we know as the Wakefield Master; yet no connection with staging as a cycle at a particular town has yet been established now that it has been revealed that these dramas do not make up the Corpus Christi cycle once believed to have been mounted at Wakefield.[69] As J. W. Robinson remarked in an endnote in his *Studies in Fifteenth-Century Stagecraft*, "the only good evidence that the Wakefield Master's plays were in fact ever presented is their eminent playability."[70] This playwright created an array of lively evil characters, especially notable in his depictions of the Cain and Abel story, Passion events, and the Last Judgment. In the latter we encounter the devil Tutivillis, the demon who conventionally gathers up words misspoken or missed at Mass—and who also appears elsewhere in a scene that would undoubtedly have involved improvised movement and gesture, including whatever a left-hand blessing would have involved, in the East Anglian morality *Mankind*.[71] In the Towneley *Iudicium*, Tutivillus's cohorts would especially have been expected to engage in jerky gestures and unpredictable movement, both of necessity improvised, that parallel their speeches as they gather up their documents, "tolys," and other "gere" in preparation for their appearance as prosecutors at the final Judgment Day.[72] And when Tutivillus himself enters he speaks of blowing his horn (30.364), an item that appears in iconography, most famously in a wall painting in the Guild Chapel at Stratford-upon-Avon but also in Continental examples such as a depiction painted on the ceiling of the parish church at Östra Vemmerlöv in Skåne in Sweden.[73] There was a strong convention that the devil lacked musical skill, so we would expect Tutivillus to have made only improvised and unmusical (perhaps scatological) sounds on his instrument.[74]

The movements of the tormentors—ungraceful, jerky, and hostile—in the Wakefield Master's *Coliphizacio* are choreographed according to a "game" here called "Kyng Copyn" (21.241), which is similar to the modern blind man's buff.[75] Each of these characters would have had ample space to invent his own variations on the movements specified in the text—and indeed would have been given licence to engage in such improvisation since the aesthetic of this play is consistent with the *Meditations on the Life of Christ* and the popular vernacular redaction produced by Nicholas Love.[76] Imagining the Passion with great sympathy for the victim was, according to these texts, obligatory for salvation. Hence here and in other plays of the Passion, if Christ's body is violated and even, from the point of view of the tormentors, made into the object of cruel games or competitions,[77] or even in one scholar's view into a commodity,[78] audience reaction would probably have responded to the acting "in pley and bourde" with apprehension and horror at seeing the Savior of the world so treated. One needs to keep in mind the intensely personal devotion to Christ, his mother, and the saints in late medieval England; these are sacred persons to whom many (probably the great majority) of the spectators would have felt kinship ties as if they were members of their own families. The grotesquerie of the tormentors, often approaching caricature, in the Passion therefore would have become obligatory in the service of audience response—response that would be very difficult if not impossible to achieve among Anglo-American audiences today.[79] But in bringing such scenes to life, the role of improvisation, applied within careful limits, would have been as essential as maintaining the integrity of the scene's iconography.

The example of an evil character whose improvising in the medieval English drama was most notorious was Herod in the

Coventry Shearmen and Taylors' pageant to whom Shakespeare seems to have alluded in Hamlet's famous speech: "I would have such a fellow whipt for o'erdoing Termagant, it out Herods Herod, pray you avoid it" (*Hamlet* 3.2.12–14). The Coventry rubrics "Here Erode ragis in the pagont and in þe strete also" and "There Erode ragis ageyne"[80] are indicative of improvisation involving gesture, bodily movement, and voice. In iconography this king may sit on a throne rather off-balance, often with his chin thrust out and his legs crossed in the regal posture. His sword is his emblem, as in painted glass at Fairford where the tyrant reaches out to stab an infant as a sign of his unstable viciousness.[81] As Peter Meredith once remarked, in no case is there sufficient iconographic evidence in any of the British plays in which Herod appears to guide an actor through his appearances, and in fact his very unpredictability would have been a factor in stimulating the desired audience response to his erratic actions.[82] Innovative and irascible actions would have been expected, just as consistency and patience would have been expected of the Savior Christ, the silent sufferer who would thus have had very little if any scope for inventive acting, certainly not screams of pain when he appears to be beaten until he is bloody during his Passion.[83]

The Smiths' play of the Passion at Coventry is lost, but the dramatic records over a long period indicate the usual severe threats and tortures, for these documents list the accouterments of violence—e.g., in an inventory of 1490, a falcion for Herod and "iiij scourges and a piller"[84] for the Flagellation. That the demon present at the Coventry Passion had a (hairy) leather coat is indicated by another set of accounts[85]—a role that would presumably have been unconstrained by the demands incorporated in a text and hence would have been free to do as the actor liked so long as his acts were consistent with his evil character. Here or elsewhere this might even have involved threatening children in the audience or attempting to incite inappropriate laughter designed to make viewers ashamed of themselves for their lack of control in the presence of the central event of salvation history.

Improvisation in plays on religious or moral themes would have been associated with evil characters, with tyrants and devils, with Lucifer, Cain, and Judas rather than Abel, Abraham, or the apostles, and with Mischief rather than Mercy. Fools and comic characters also were allowed scope for improvisation, at least in matters of movement and gesture. Even Joseph as a comic (but good) character in the Coventry Shearmen and Taylors' play would have required some freedom within the limits of a tightly organized script. But how much more open to improvised action or speech and out-of-tune singing would have been the scene at the pagan temple in the Digby *Mary Magdalene* with its scurrilous boy acolyte-deacon and priest who represent the world-upside-down of an anti-Christian worship service where the effect would have been to fracture the Office and Mass in dizzying parody?[86] The movements and gestures, joined to a text which gives a hint of what these should be, would need to have been an improvised mimicry of Christian worship—mimicry which subverted for the purpose of affirming. The distance here is not far from the scatological Christmas song that is taught to the audience by the fool Nought in *Mankind* (333–43)—a profane hymn ultimately designed, however, to make the members of the audience uncomfortable for joining in the singing.

In plays such as *The Castle of Perseverance* and more especially the Cornish *Ordinalia*, the layout of the playing area itself with the necessity of moving between scaffolds or stations[87] would argue for considerably more space for improvisation than pageants on wagons as at Coventry, York, or Chester. In the stage directions in the Resurrection play in the *Ordinalia*, for example, Jesus is to rise "from the dead, and he shall go wherever he likes [ubicunque voluerit]" while the angels intone *Christus resurgens*.[88] A horse is mounted and ridden out of the playing area by King David (*s.d.* after 1.2210). But even a term such as *pompabit* in a rubric could have been interpreted in different ways, depending on the character directed to parade down into the acting area, if that is what the term means in examples such as "hic pompabit abraham et postea dicit" (1:1259) and "Hic pompabit rex pharo et postea dicit moyses" (1.1479).[89] Opportunities for improvisation would have been especially present when the character doing the parading was Pharaoh or, especially, Lucifer.

That improvisation also affected the spoken text in the *Ordinalia* is perhaps made less likely if the mode of acting involved the use of a prompter in the manner reported by Richard Carew, who nevertheless told a story about misunderstanding that is perhaps of a piece with the Till Eulenspiegel account cited above:

> [T]he players conne not their parts withoute booke, but are prompted by one called the Ordinary, who followeth at their back with the booke in his hand, and telleth them softly what they must pronounce aloud. Which maner once gave occasion to a pleasant conceyted gentleman, of practising a mery pranke: for he vndertaking (perhaps of set purpose) an Actors roome, was accordingly lessoned (before-hand) by the Ordinary that he must say after him. His turne came: quoth the Ordinary, Goe forth man and shew thy selfe. The gentleman steps out vpon the stage, and like a bad Clarke in scripture matters, cleauing more to the letter then the sense, pronounced those words aloud. Oh (sayes the fellowe softly in his eare) you marre all the play. And with this his passion, the Actor makes the audience in like sort acquainted. Hereon the prompter falles to flat rayling and cursing in the bitterest termes he could deuise: which the Gentleman with a set gesture and countenance still soberly related, vntill the Ordinary driuen at last into a madde rage, was faine to giue ouer all. Which trousse . . . brake off the Enterlude. . . .[90]

While this story too has all the marks of an apocryphal account—it is unlikely that the audience would have found the termination of the performance as entertaining as twenty similar plays (Carew's claim).[91] It does, however, give us pause also concerning the recitation of texts elsewhere on the medieval stage; if, as some records imply, only a very few rehearsals for a performance were scheduled, then the possibility of forgetting would be quite great, necessitating improvisation by the forgetful actor and perhaps also in turn by his fellow performers.

The present excursus into the question of opportunities for improvisation will serve as a reminder that not only speeches but also movement and gesture were involved. Conventional gestures of the type that can be studied in the visual arts, iconography, and rhetorical treatises were unquestionably dominant and formed an essential core in the medieval English religious plays, but this does not mean that there was no room even there for the improvised gesture. And physical movement, especially in less confined spaces or in cases in which the actor was not familiar with the stage area, of necessity must have been flexible enough to be convincing to audiences even though television-style verisimilitude was hardly expected or desired. Other occasions also would lead to the need for improvisation. Peter Happé has called attention to a stage direction in a sixteenth-century play, Ulpian Fulwell's *Like Will to Like*, in which Nichol Newfangle, the devil Lucifer, and a black-faced collier sing a song and dance: "Nichol Newfangle must have a gittern or some other Instrument, if he may, but if they have none they must daunce about the place all three, and sing this song that followeth, which must be doon though [i.e., as if] they have an instrument."[92] Here the choice, if Nichol does not have a gittern or is unable to play it, is to improvise playing one.

In considering the matter of improvisation, it has been necessary to be speculative, but I think not off the mark even in considering especially the religious stage, which was designed to stimulate the cultural memory and devotion of those who listened and looked on. And for the less restrictive demands of the secular shows such as Robin Hood plays and the King Game, we can hardly go wrong in assuming that improvisation was as integral to them—indeed, even more so than scripted or formulaic verse, gesture, and physical movement.

NOTES

[1]See Ronald B. McKerrow, *Prolegomena for the Oxford Shakespeare: A Study in Editorial Method* (Oxford: Clarendon Press, 1939), xv.

[2]For important discussions of editing applied to early drama, see Ian Lancashire, "Medieval Drama," in *Editing Medieval Texts English, French, and Latin Written in England*, ed. A. G. Rigg (New York: Garland, 1977), 58–85, and A. F. Johnston, ed., *Editing Early English Drama: Special Problems and New Directions* (New York: AMS Press, 1987). That the playtexts were designed to be used as theater pieces and hence were intended "for performing" is stressed by Meg Twycross, "The Theatricality of Medieval English Plays," in *The Cambridge Companion to Medieval English Theatre*, ed. Richard Beadle (Cambridge: Cambridge University Press, 1994), 37ff.

[3]See Graham A. Runnalls, "Medieval Actors and the Invention of Printing in Late Medieval France," *Early Drama, Art, and Music Review* 22 (2000): 59–80, and, for English slowness to print drama, Greg Walker, *The Politics of Performance in Early Renaissance Drama* (Cambridge: Cambridge University Press, 1998), 6–50.

[4]The manuscripts are discussed by R. M. Lumiansky and David Mills, *The Chester Mystery Cycle: Essays and Documents* (Chapel Hill: University of North Carolina Press, 1983), 3–86.

[5]For a recent collection of studies, however, see Clifford Davidson, ed., *Gesture in Medieval Drama and Art*, Early Drama, Art, and Music Monograph Series 28 (Kalamazoo: Medieval Institute Publications, 2001). The present essay, which should be seen as complementing this book, treats aspects that are more intractable than those which can be verified through reference to the visual arts.

[6]Reviews of these productions have appeared in *Research Opportunities in Renaissance Drama* and *Medieval English Theatre*; see also the special issue *The York Cycle Then and Now*, published as *Early Theatre* 3 (2000).

[7]Peter Meredith, "Stage Directions and the Editing of Early English Drama," in *Editing Early English Drama*, ed. Johnston, 65–90; Audrey Douglas and Peter Greenfield, *Records of Early English Drama: Cumberland, Westmorland, Gloucestershire* (Toronto: University of Toronto Press, 1986), 363.

[8]Quotations, cited by act, scene, and line numbers, are from *The Riverside Shakespeare*, ed. G. Blakemore Evans, 2nd ed. (Boston: Houghton Mifflin, 1997).

[9]For Shakespeare's probable knowledge of the Coventry plays, see Clifford Davidson, *On Tradition: Essays on the Use and Valuation of the Past* (New York: AMS Press, 1992), chap. 4. The Coventry records are edited by R. W. Ingram, *Records of Early English Drama: Coventry* (Toronto: University of Toronto Press, 1981), and the extant Coventry plays, with critical discussion, are presented in Pamela M. King and Clifford Davidson, eds., *The Coventry Corpus Christi Plays*, Early Drama, Art, and Music Monograph Series 27 (Kalamazoo: Medieval Institute Publications, 2000).

[10]Sandra Billington, *Mock Kings in Medieval Society and Renaissance Drama* (Oxford: Clarendon Press, 1991), 206.

[11]Public Record Office: CHES 24/115/4, as quoted by Elizabeth Baldwin, "Rushbearings and Maygames in the Diocese of Chester before 1642," in *English Parish Drama*, ed. Alexandra F. Johnston and Wim Hüsken (Amsterdam: Rodopi, 1996), 37.

[12]Billington, *Mock Kings*, 85.

[13]Billington, *Mock Kings*, 40, 42–43; Henry Machyn, *Diary of a Resident in London from 1550 to 1563*, ed. John Gough Nichols, Camden Society 42 (London: J. B. Nichols and Son, 1848), 28–29.

[14]*The Loseley Manuscripts*, ed. A. J. Kempe (London, 1836), 54, as quoted in Billington, *Mock Kings*, 42.

[15]*The Records of the City of Norwich*, ed. William Hudson and John Cottingham Tingey, 2 vols. (Norwich: Jarrold and Sons, 1906–10), 1:340–41, and, for a brief mention, see Nicholas M. Davis, "'His Majesty shall have tribute of me':

The King Game in England," in *Between Folk and Liturgy*, ed. Alan J. Fletcher and Wim Hüsken (Amsterdam: Rodopi, 1997), 101. The episode, taking place on the feast of the Conversion of St. Paul, still fell within the extended Christmas season.

[16]For a useful recent compilation, see *Robin Hood and Other Outlaw Tales*, ed. Stephen Knight and Thomas Ohlgren (Kalamazoo: Medieval Institute Publications, 1997).

[17]John M. Wasson, *Records of Early English Drama: Devon* (Toronto: University of Toronto Press, 1986), xxv, 89; see also the survey by Alexandra F. Johnston, "The Robin Hood of the Records," in *Playing Robin Hood: The Legend in Performance in Five Centuries*, ed. Lois Potter (Newark: University of Delaware Press, 1998), 27–40.

[18]For the texts of these and of the *Gest of Robin Hood* printed by William Copland sometime between 1548 and 1569, see the editions prepared by W. W. Greg for the Malone Society *Collections*, 1, pt. 2 (Oxford, 1908), 117–42; these texts appear along with introductions and notes by Paul Whitfield White, in *Robin Hood and Other Outlaw Tales*, ed. Knight and Ohlgren, 269–95. The East Anglian fragments seem anomalous, but the connection of Robin Hood plays with the Paston family is verified by a letter written by John Paston II and dated 16 April 1473; see *Paston Letters and Papers of the Fifteenth Century*, ed. Norman Davis (Oxford: Clarendon Press, 1971), 461. For a useful performing edition, see Mary Blackstone, *Robin Hood and the Friar* (Toronto: Poculi Ludique Societas, 1981).

[19]David Wiles, *The Early Plays of Robin Hood* (Cambridge: D. S. Brewer, 1981), 35.

[20]Mark C. Pilkinton, *Records of Early English Drama: Bristol* (Toronto: University of Toronto Press, 1997), 37.

[21]Kingston Museum and Heritage Centre, Local History Room, KG2/2/1, p. 51 (Kingston-upon-Thames churchwardens' accounts). I am grateful to Sally-Beth MacLean for making available to me her transcriptions of these records and to Emma Rummins, Local History Officer at the Kingston Museum and Heritage Centre, for permission to use them in this article. See also Sally-Beth MacLean, "King Games and Robin Hood: Play and Profit at Kingston-upon-Thames," *Research Opportunities in Renaissance Drama* 29 (1986–87): 85–94. A partial transcription of some of the records is published by Wiles, *The Early Plays of Robin Hood*, 68–70.

[22]John Forrest, *The History of Morris Dancing, 1458–1750* (Toronto: University of Toronto Press, 1999), 161.

[23]MacLean, "King Games and Robin Hood," 86; Kingston Museum and Heritage Centre, Local History Room, KG2/2/1, p. 54.

[24]Kingston Museum and Heritage Centre, Local History Room, KG2/2/1, p. 51.

[25]Philip Stubbes refers satirically to "certain papers, wherin is painted some babblerie or other, of Imagery woork, and these they call my Lord of mis-rules badges, these they giue to euery one, that wil giue money for them. . . . And who will not be buxom to them, and giue them money for these their deuilish cognizances, they are mocked, and shouted at, not a little" (*Anatomie of Abuses* [London, 1583], sigs. M2^{v}–M3^{r}). See also William Kelly, *Notices Illustrative of the Drama, and Other Popular Entertainments, Chiefly in the Sixteenth and Seventeenth Centuries* (London: John Russell Smith, 1865), 67; also, for brief discussion, Wiles, *The Early Plays*, 9–10, and Davis, "His Majesty shall have tribute of me," 101.

[26]Kingston Museum and Heritage Service, Local History Room, KG2/2/1, p. 54.

[27]Johnston, "The Robin Hood of the Records," 29, 39–40. For the description of a Robin Hood play as "a civic mimesis-*cum*-fund raiser," see James Stokes, "Robin Hood and the Churchwardens in Yeovil," *Medieval and Renaissance Drama in England* 3 (1986): 8.

[28]The necessity of improvisation may be surmised from the following: On an occasion when two colleagues and I were on the program at a drama conference at the University of California at Irvine, we were taken to an "Elizabethan" restaurant where the waitresses had been given phrases in "Shakespearean" English to use with customers. However, when they were asked a question they could not answer with one of their memorized phrases, they were speechless. If Robin Hood and his company were able to improvise speeches imaginatively, they would have had no trouble with their roles as they mingled with the crowd and very likely also as they participated in their play.

[29]Forrest, *The History of Morris Dancing*, 163.

[30]See Lawrence M. Clopper, *Drama, Play, and Game: English Festive Culture in the Medieval and Early Modern Period* (Chicago: University of Chicago Press, 2001), chap. 2 *passim*. Clopper's use of the term 'somergame' seems dependent to a considerable degree on a sermon exemplum published by Siegfried Wenzel, "*Somer Game* and Sermon References to a Corpus Christi Play," *Modern Philology* 74 (1977): 279–80, which purports to be about a Crucifixion play but does not fit the biblical narrative in that it introduces Peter and Andrew on the crosses on each side of Jesus instead of the thieves. But is a 'summergame,' whatever it is, more likely to be a play performed at midsummer than on a saint's day?

[31]See my "British Saint Play Records: Coping with Ambiguity," *Early Theatre* 2 (1999): 97–106, and 113 ("Response"), and Alan Somerset's review of Clopper's book in *The Early Drama, Art, and Music Review* 24, no. 2 (2002).

[32]J. S. Purvis, ed., *Tudor Parish Documents of the Diocese of York* (Cambridge: Cambridge University Press, 1948), 160–61, n. 1; Roscoe E. Parker, "Some Records of the 'Somyr Play'," *Studies in Honor of John C. Hodges and Alvin Thaler* (Knoxville: University of Tennessee Press, 1961), 20–22.

[33]*The Castle of Perseverance*, l. 3645; quotations from this play and *Mankind* are from Mark Eccles, ed., *The Macro Plays*, EETS, 262 (London: Oxford University Press, 1969).

[34]See John C. Coldewey, "Plays and 'Play' in Early English Drama," *Research Opportunities in Renaissance Drama* 28 (1985): 181–88. 'Game' is related to Latin *ludus*, for which see Abigail Ann Young, "Plays and Players: The Latin Terms for Performance," *Records of Early English Drama Newsletter* 9, no. 2 (1984): 58–59.

[35]Coldewey, "Plays and 'Play' in Early English Drama," 182. For the connection between 'play' and 'drama,' see V. A. Kolve, *The Play Called Corpus Christi* (Stanford: Stanford University Press, 1966), esp. 8–32.

[36]*A Tretise of Miraclis Pleyinge*, ed. Clifford Davidson, Early Drama, Art, and Music Monograph Series 19 (Kalamazoo: Medieval Institute Publications, 1993), 105.

[37]Ibid., 93.

[38]David N. Klausner, *Records of Early English Drama: Herefordshire, Worcestershire* (Toronto: University of Toronto Press, 1990), 347–48.

[39]Marianne G. Briscoe, "Some Clerical Notions of Dramatic Decorum in Late Medieval England," *Comparative Drama* 19 (1985): 4–5. See, however, the justifications for recreation, including theater, discussed by Glending Olson, *Literature as Recreation in the Later Middle Ages* (Ithaca: Cornell University Press, 1982).

[40]Karl Young, *The Drama of the Medieval Church*, 2 vols. (Oxford: Clarendon Press, 1933), 1:133–34, 249–50; Pamela Sheingorn, *The Easter Sepulchre in England*, Early Drama, Art, and Music Reference Series 5 (Kalamazoo: Medieval Institute Publications, 1987), 19–22, figs. 1–4 (facsimiles); I quote translations below from David Bevington, *Medieval Drama* (Boston: Houghton Mifflin, 1974), with original texts from Young's edition. My interest in such plays has been as a dramatic director, not as a Latinist; see Audrey Ekdahl Davidson and Clifford Davidson, *Performing Medieval Music Drama* (Kalamazoo: Medieval Institute Publications [for the Society for Old Music], 1998).

[41]Young, *The Drama of the Medieval Church*, 2:316–51 (texts of the Nicholas plays and discussion), 518–32 (Greater Passion Play, labeled *Ludus de Passione* by Young). For a facsimile of pages containing the Nicholas plays, see *The Fleury*

Playbook: Essays and Studies, ed. Thomas C. Campbell and Clifford Davidson, Early Drama, Art, and Music Monograph Series 7 (Kalamazoo: Medieval Institute Publications, 1985), figs. 8–37.

[42]Young, *The Drama of the Medieval Church*, 1:133, 2:410.

[43]Later versions of the *Visitatio Sepulchri* commonly conclude with the *Te Deum*, a connection to the Matins liturgy; see the texts collected by Walther Lipphardt, *Lateinische Osterfeiern und Osterspiel*, 10 vols. (Berlin: Walter de Gruyter, 1975–90).

[44]See Rina Singha and Reginald Massey, *Indian Dances: Their History and Growth* (New York: George Braziller, 1967), 20–22, 39–50.

[45]Ibid., pl. facing p. 33.

[46]Ibid., 20–21. For my remarks in this paragraph I am also indebted to discussions many years ago with Balasaraswati's brother, the late T. Ranganathan.

[47]Ibid., 79–113, and Phillip B. Zarrilli, *Kathakali Dance Drama: Where Gods and Demons Come to Play* (London: Routledge, 2000).

[48]Joly Puthussery, "Chavittunātakam: A Music-Drama of Kerala Christians," *Early Drama, Art, and Music Review* 19 (1997): 93–104, and "Chavittunātakam: An Appendix," *Early Drama, Art, and Music* 20 (1997): 27–33 (photographs). I am grateful to Joly Puthussery for reviewing my comments on Chavittunātakam in the present article.

[49]See Max Harris, *Aztecs, Moors, and Christians: Festivals of Reconquest in Mexico and Spain* (Austin: University of Texas Press, 2000), 31–42.

[50]See O. B. Hardison, Jr., *Christian Rite and Christian Drama in the Middle Ages* (Baltimore: Johns Hopkins Press, 1965), 1–34.

[51]Oscar Cargill, *Drama and Liturgy* (New York: Columbia University Press, 1930).

[52]Text in Young, *The Drama of the Medieval Church*, 2:290–301; facsimile and music transcription by Marcel Zijlstra in Dunbar H. Ogden, *The Play of Daniel: Critical Essays*, Early Drama, Art, and Music Monograph Series 24 (Kalamazoo: Medieval Institute Publications, 1997).

[53]Margot Fassler, "The Feast of Fools and *Danielis Ludus*: Popular Tradition in a Medieval Cathedral Play," in *Plainsong in the Age of Polyphony*, ed. Thomas Forrest Kelly (Cambridge: Cambridge University Press, 1992), 65–99.

[54]Henri Villetard, *Office de Pierre de Corbeil* (Paris, 1907), as quoted by

Fassler, "The Feast of Fools and *Danielis Ludus*," 77.

[55]Aelred of Rievaulx, *Speculum Charitatis* 2:33, as quoted in translation by Herbert M. Schueller, *The Idea of Music: An Introduction to Musical Aesthetics in Antiquity and the Middle Ages* (Kalamazoo: Medieval Institute Publications, 1988), 354–55; for the Latin text of this passage, see Young, *The Drama of the Medieval Church*, 1:548.

[56]See Timothy McGee's conclusions concerning medieval singing in his *The Sound of Medieval Song: Ornamentation and Vocal Style According to the Treatises* (Oxford: Clarendon Press, 1998), 117–52. McGee emphasizes the difference between medieval singing styles and modern practice and notes "the wide range of choices in type, placement, and quantity of ornament" (134). The ornaments described by McGee must have required singing that was not dominated by the vibrato so common in trained singers today; see also Audrey Ekdahl Davidson, "High, Clear, and Sweet: Singing Early Music," in *Sacra/Profana: Studies in Sacred and Secular Music for Johannes Riedel*, ed. Audrey Ekdahl Davidson and Clifford Davidson (Minneapolis: Friends of Minnesota Music, 1985), 217–26. For my observations on Cistercian reform in music I am indebted to Chrysogonus Waddell, O.C.S.O.

[57]Young, *The Drama of the Medieval Church*, 1:381–85; Sheingorn, *The Easter Sepulchre in England*, 134–37.

[58]Martin W. Walsh, "Eulenspiegel (Episode 13) as a Theater-Historical Document," *Early Drama, Art, and Music Review* 14 (1992): 43–53.

[59]Ibid., 43–44.

[60]Alexandra F. Johnston, *Records of Early English Drama: York*, 2 vols. (Toronto: University of Toronto Press, 1979), 1:109.

[61]Ibid., 1:278.

[62]See Clifford Davidson, "Carnival, Lent, and Early English Drama," *Research Opportunities in Renaissance Drama* 36 (1997): 123–42.

[63]Johnston, *Records of Early English Drama: York*, 1:37.

[64]Ibid., 1:37, 65, 109; cf. 1:283.

[65]See ibid., 1:43, for Friar William Melton's complaints concerning rowdiness and inappropriate behavior in 1426, and, for *Fergus*, see Mark R. Sullivan, "The Missing York Funeral of the Virgin," *EDAM Newsletter* 1, no. 2 (1979): 5–7. I am grateful to Lynette Muir for reporting an even more extreme reaction to stage action in a "very apocryphal" account that has, however, been "widely quoted": "Longinus . . . thrust his spear into the side of Christ and killed him; as he fell off

the Cross he landed on and killed St John at which the King [of Hungary] leapt up and killed Christ [sic] and the people rebelled and killed the king" (personal communication).

[66]See Richard Beadle, ed., *The York Plays* (London: Edward Arnold, 1982), and for useful commentary, see Peter Meredith, "Stage Directions and the Editing of Early English Drama," 65–94.

[67]See especially Eileen White, "Places to Hear the Play: The Performance of the Corpus Christi Play at York," *Early Theatre* 3 (2000): 49–78.

[68]See Natalie Crohn Schmitt, "The Body in Motion in the York *Adam and Eve in Eden*," in *Gesture in Medieval Drama and Art*, ed. Davidson, 161.

[69]Barbara D. Palmer, "'Towneley Plays' or 'Wakefield Cycle' Revisited," *Comparative Drama* 21 (1987–88), 318–48, and "Corpus Christi 'Cycles' in Yorkshire: The Surviving Records," *Comparative Drama* 27 (1993): 218–31. Citations to the plays are to *The Towneley Plays*, ed. Martin Stevens and A. C. Cawley, EETS, s.s. 23–24 (Oxford: Oxford University Press, 1994).

[70]J. W. Robinson, *Studies in Fifteenth-Century Stagecraft*, Early Drama, Art, and Music Monograph Series 14 (Kalamazoo: Medieval Institute Publications, 1991), 207, n. 21.

[71]*Mankind*, l. 522. For an extended study but one that does not take full account of the iconography, see Margaret Jennings, *The Literary Career of the Recording Demon*, Studies in Philology, 74, no. 5 (1977).

[72]Play 30; see especially ll. 166, 196, 207–08, 210, 238, 257, etc.

[73]Clifford Davidson, *The Guild Chapel Wall Paintings at Stratford-upon-Avon* (New York: AMS Press, 1988), pl. 17; Siegrun Fernlund, *Kyrkor i Skåne: En kulturhistoria* (Lund: Signum, 1980), 86–87 (before and after restoration); for other examples and the comment that "the musical instruments . . . are shrill and screeching, raucous and rough," see Dorthe Falcon Møller, *Music Aloft: Musical Symbolism in the Mural Paintings of Danish Medieval Churches* (Copenhagen: Forlaget Falcon, 1996), 46–48.

[74]Richard Rastall, *The Heaven Singing*, Music in Early English Religious Drama 1 (Woodbridge: D. S. Brewer, 1996), 208.

[75]See Kolve, *The Play Called Corpus Christi*, 180–82, 185–86.

[76] Nicholas Love, *Mirror of the Blessed Life of Jesus Christ*, ed. Michael G. Sargent (New York: Garland, 1992).

[77]See Kolve, *The Play Called Corpus Christi*, 175–205; Hans-Jürgen Diller,

"The Torturers in the English Mystery Plays," in *Evil on the Medieval State*, ed. Meg Twycross [special issue of *Medieval English Theatre*] (Lancaster, 1992), 63.

[78]Claire Sponsler, *Drama and Resistance: Bodies, Goods, and Theatricality in Late Medieval England* (Minneapolis: University of Minnesota Press, 1997), 158.

[79]See my "Sacred Blood and the Medieval Stage," *Comparative Drama* 31 (1997): 437.

[80]Shearmen and Taylors' Pageant, ll. 722 *s.d.*, 747 *s.d.*; quotations are from *The Coventry Corpus Christi Plays*, ed. Pamela M. King and Clifford Davidson, Early Drama, Art, and Music Monograph Series 27 (Kalamazoo: Medieval Institute Publications, 2000).

[81]Hilary Wayment, *The Stained Glass of the Church of St. Mary, Fairford, Gloucestershire* (London: Society of Antiquaries, 1984), 80, pl. XXXIX. See also the useful survey by Miriam Anne Skey, "The Iconography of Herod the Great in Medieval Art," *EDAM Newsletter* 3, no. 1 (1980): 4–10.

[82]Comment during discussion following Meredith's paper "Herod and the Megalomaniac Acting Style," at the International Congress on Medieval Studies, Western Michigan University, May 1987.

[83]Iconographic conventions are crucial here in the presentation of Christ; especially significant is Isaiah 53:7: "he opened not his mouth: he shall be led as a sheep to the slaughter, and shall be dumb as a lamb before his shearer, and he shall not open his mouth" (Douay). See also James H. Marrow, *Passion Iconography in Northern European Art of the Late Middle Ages and Early Renaissance* (Kortrijk: Van Ghemmert, 1979), 96–99.

[84]Ingram, *Records of Early English Drama: Coventry*, 73–74.

[85]Ibid., 60.

[86]*Mary Magdalene*, ll. 1143–1248; citation to *The Late Medieval Religious Plays of Bodleian MSS Digby 133 and E Museo 160*, EETS, 283 (Oxford: Oxford University Press, 1982).

[87]See my *Illustrations of the Stage and Acting in England to 1580*, Early Drama, Art, and Music Monograph Series 16 (Kalamazoo: Medieval Institute Publications, 1991), 41–49.

[88]*The Ancient Cornish Drama*, ed. and trans. Edwin Norris, 2 vols. (1859; reprint New York and London: Benjamin Blom, 1968), 2:34–35 (*s.d.* following l. 422) and 1:166 (*s.d.* following l. 2210).

[89]Ibid., 1:96 (l. 1259 *s.d.*) and 112 (l. 1479 *s.d.*).

[90]Richard Carew, *Survey of Cornwall* (London, 1602), 71. That the prompting indicated by Carew has credibility is argued by Philip Butterworth; see especially his article "Richard Carew's 'Ordinary': Theatre by Different Rules," *Medieval English Theatre*, forthcoming.

[92]Ibid., 72.

[93]Ulpian Fulwell, *Like Will to Like*, l. 178 *s.d.*; quotation from Peter Happé, ed., *Tudor Interludes* (Harmondsworth: Penguin, 1972). Attention is called to this stage direction in Peter Happé, "The Devil in the Interludes, 1550–1577," in *Evil on the Medieval Stage*, ed. Twycross, 47.

Medieval and Modern Deletions of Repellent Passages

Linda Marie Zaerr

The Middle English popular romances provide some of the most intriguing variants among medieval texts. Deletions in the Middle English manuscripts of *Sir Beues of Hamtoun* evince characteristics that cannot be entirely explained by scribal activity. The most significant omissions follow two patterns, both of which operate to diminish Princess Josian's active role in the plot. My personal performance experience with another Middle English text may provide insight into the purpose and motivation for these changes and the process which may have engendered them.

The Middle English *Sir Beues of Hamtoun* is particularly suited to a study of variants. The thirteenth-century Anglo-Norman *chanson de geste*, the earliest and oldest form of the poem, was probably the source for the English accounts. It survives in two mutilated manuscripts, Bibliothèque Nationale fr. nouv. acq. 4532, which contains the first section, and MS. Didot, which contains the second.[1] The English form is extant, at least in fragmentary form, in seven manuscripts in Middle English as well as in fourteen early printed editions. It is thus possible to trace transformations of narrative elements through numerous redactions across several centuries.

The tale begins with Beves, as a child, sold into slavery by his wicked mother. He is bought by the King of Armenia, whose daughter, Josian, falls in love with him and converts to Christianity. After many trials and adventures, Beves and Josian are married, and Beves regains his rightful position as Earl in England. But, to save his horse from death, Beves goes into exile with Josian, who is captured as she gives birth to twin boys. Eventually the family of four is reunited. Several battles ensue in which the family holdings are expanded dramatically, and, finally, when everything is settled, the horse Arundel, Josian, and Beves all die on the same day and are buried together.

The popularity of the romance is attested by the numerous and varied redactions in English and also by the number of versions in other languages: several in Continental French and Italian, several in various Germanic languages, two in Celtic languages, and several in Slavic languages.[2] Despite its popularity in earlier times, however, this tale has not been studied much in this century.[3] It is remarkable that variants among the Middle English redactions have not previously received sufficient scholarly attention.

These variants are, however, of very great interest for their depiction of decreasing initiative on the part of the ideal woman. Harriet Hudson observes that "the later romances are less subversive than the earlier,"[4] and Rosamund Allen develops the concept in different terms: "As the Middle Ages advances towards the so-called Renaissance, so did women's always vestigial authority diminish. The growing awareness of the importance of the individual from the twelfth century, an awareness which is the mainspring of the chivalric romance, in practice deprived women of status and authority as public power shifted from the family viewed collectively to the male who acted as its head and representative."[5] While this principle has been amply demonstrated by looking at a range of romances across time, it is intriguing to find such shifts in attitude even within the variants of a single romance. Exploration of two instances of deletion centering around Princess Josian reveals increasingly rigorous principles of decorum applied to this romance heroine and a diminishing tolerance for any hint of initiative or masculinity.

Since most of the text is surprisingly stable from the Anglo-Norman text through the Middle English redactions, it thus seems worthwhile to examine passages that have attracted alternative versions and to consider the nature of those variants. The locus of the greatest change within the lengthy aggregate of adventures that comprise the romance is Josian's second encounter with King Yvor. In this episode, the structure of the plot changes substantively in translation to English, and then it is transformed again, primarily by two deletions, in subsequent redactions.

The situation is complicated, however, because the relationship between manuscripts is not linear. Later manuscripts are not directly derivative of the earliest extant Middle English manuscript. Eugen Kölbing, the editor of the standard edition of the poem, divides the manuscripts into two groups and, postulating intermediary forms, admits some unexpected connections between classes.[6] His classification is based entirely on internal evidence.

While Kölbing's purely textual approach is helpful in indicating patterns, it is worth considering another way of explaining variation between manuscripts: some differences may most reasonably be accounted for as ossification of improvisational modifications. Murray McGillivray has discussed some of the ways variants between manuscripts of four Middle English romances may indicate memorial transmission. He claims that "[i]t seems certain that omissions would occur if a poetic text were imperfectly memorized," and further characterizes the process: "Omissions which disfigure a text are probably scribal, though, since someone reconstructing a text from memory would try to come up with something sensible. The suspicion must always exist, on the other hand, that omissions which do not disfigure a text, but leave it legible, sensible, and poetically well formed, whether or not these involve the introduction of newly composed material, are the result of intentional editing."[7] A possibility he does not discuss is that the "intentional editing" may be done improvisationally.

Josian's second encounter in *Sir Beues* provides opportunity to explore two different types of deletion, both directed to the same end of reducing Josian's active role in the plot. In all redactions this episode begins when Josian, Beves, and their squire Terry travel into exile. As they pass through a forest, Josian goes into labor and sends away the two men. She gives birth to twin boys and is immediately captured by Saracens and taken back to King Yvor. In all versions she is rescued by Beves's uncle Saber, and the two of them search for Beves for seven years, the point at which the family is reunited. The circumstances of the rescue, however, vary substantially.

In the Anglo-Norman version represented by the thirteenth-century MS. Didot, Sabaoth and his band of knights, disguised as pilgrims, overtake Josian while she is being led captive to King Yvor. When he asks what has happened to Beves and his son Terry, she explains the situation. Sabaoth immediately kills Ascopard, whereupon he and his companions slaughter all of the Saracens and thus rescue Josian. When she asks how she can now travel through that land, Sabaoth suggests that she be disguised as a man. He has her dressed in a man's clothing, and they buy an herb that dyes her face and body dark. They travel as far as Abreford, where Sabaoth comes down with a virulent disease. One day Josian begins singing about Beves, and noblemen from many lands give them rich gifts. Thus she sustains herself and Sabaoth for seven years and three months, when Sabaoth finally recovers. Shortly thereafter, Sabaoth finds Beves and presents him a Josian with the ointment rubbed off.

There is some evidence for a powerful saracen princess motif in thirteenth-century France. In *Aucassin et Nicolete*, which survives in a thirteenth-century manuscript, a saracen princess disguises herself as a male jongleur using an herb that turns her face dark.[8] Like Josian, Nicolete is a saracen princess who has become a Christian and who loves a Christian man. Like Josian, she dresses as a man and puts on an ointment that dyes her face dark so she can travel without being molested. Like Josian, she plays the vielle. Unlike Josian, however, Nicolete exerts power to effect reunion with her beloved, whereas Sabaoth leads Josian in her quest for her husband.

The Auchinleck manuscript version of *Beues* (1330–40) seems to be drawing on this broader notion of the Christianized saracen princess. By way of extension of the Anglo-Norman version, the Auchinleck manuscript gives Josian an independence and initiative that go well beyond known sources. In this earliest English redaction, Josian, like Nicolete, plays the vielle and thinks of herbal solutions to her problems independently. This section of the romance is much expanded from the original, and the redactor presents a substantially more effective heroine.

In this version, Josian is not rescued until after she has been taken to Mombrant and incarcerated. She is thus again thrown on her own resources in finding a way to maintain her sexual fidelity to Beves. The Auchinleck manuscript includes a lengthy interpolation, which does not appear in any other version and which discusses her adventures on the way to Mombrant as well as her reception there.[9] In this interpolation, Josian tricks Ascopard into letting her go off the road by telling him that women need privacy to relieve themselves:

> & in here wei ase thai go*n*ne wende
> she seide ascopard freli frende
> for bou*n*te ich dede the while
> and sauede the fro perile
> tho beues the wolde ha*n* slawe
> and ibrought of the lif dawe
> ich was the bourgh the schost be trewe

thar fore ipraie on me the rewe
and yeue me space alite wight
for wende out of this folkes sight
te do me nedes in priuite
for kende hit is wi*m*ma*n* te be
scham faste and ful of corteisie
& hate dedes of fileinie
(fol. 195^{v}, ll. 3651–64)

(And as they went along on their way, she said, "Ascopard, noble friend, return the favor I did you earlier when I saved you from danger when Beues would have slain you and brought you to the end of your life days. I was your surety; you should be true. Therefore I beseech you to have pity on me and give me a little room to go out of these people's sight to take care of my needs in private. For it is known that women are shamefast and full of courtesy and hate deeds of villainy.")[10]

She thus develops an elaborate rhetorical presentation of a mundane request, and Ascopard responds that she can go where she likes as long as she does not go out of sight.

She takes the opportunity to employ a stratagem that is clever and unexpected—and one which is only possible because of her extensive training in medicine. While she is squatting down, she eats an herb that makes her look like a leper.

While she was in ermonie
bothe fysik and sirgirie
she hadde lerned of meisters grete
of boloyne the gras and of tulete
that she knew erbes mani & fale
to make bothe boute and bale
on she tok vp of the grou*n*de
that was an erbe of meche mou*n*de
to make aman i*n* semlaunt there
a foule mesel alse yif awere
whan she hadde ete that erbe ano*n*
to the sarasines she gan go*n*
and wente he*m* forth with oute targing
to ward yuore the riche king
thai nadde ride in here way
boute fif mile of that contray

she was in semlaunt & in ble
a foule mesel on to se
(fol. 195^{v}, ll. 3671–88)

(While she was in Armenia, she had learned both medicine and surgery from great masters of Bologna the great and of Toledo, so she knew many herbs, many that would cause both benefit and harm. She took up one from the ground that was an herb of great value that could make a person appear as if he were a foul leper. When she had eaten that herb, at once she returned to the Saracens and went on with them without tarrying toward Yvore, the rich king. They had only ridden about five miles on their way through that country when she became in appearance and complexion a foul leper to look at.)

As a result, when she is brought before King Yvor, he does not recognize her and is repelled by her. He sends her to a distant castle to be guarded by Ascopard, and thus she has effectively taken the initiative to evade sexual disloyalty to Beves.

This lengthy and complex passage (ll. 3647–3710) in the earliest Middle English version of the poem is deleted by all subsequent manuscripts in Middle English. But this deletion is one which must be textual rather than improvisational, since the subsequent versions, which follow the Auchinleck manuscript in many details, revert to the Anglo-Norman plot in substance and in some specific wording. Revision is accomplished in part by simple deletion of the lengthy passage discussed above, but an additional modification becomes necessary at a slightly later point in the story.

While all manuscripts agree that it is Beues's uncle Saber who rescues Josian by fighting Ascopard, the Auchinleck manuscript sets that rescue in Mombrant, after the events described above.

whan þai come to þe londe
faste þai gonne fraine & fonde
in what londe were the quene
and men tolde he*m* al be dene
how the geaunt ascopard
in a castel hire hadde to ward
in wildernesse al be selue
þo Saber and is fere*n* twelue
þourȝ help of god þat ilche stou*n*de
sone þai han þe castel founde

þe castel ase ȝhe ȝede aboute
for to diuise the toures stoute
iosian lay in atour an hiȝ
saber and felawes ȝhe siȝ
and to him ȝhe gan to crie
help saber for loue of marie
þo ascopard herde that steuene
how ȝhe gan saber to neuene
he wente him out wiþ hertte wroþ
& be mahoun aswor his oþ
to deþe ascholde saber diȝte
his sclauin ech palmer of twiȝte
þo schon here armur wel clere
þo saber and his felawes ifere
aboute ascopard þai þringe
and harde on him þai go*n*ne dinge
and hew h[im] alle to pices smale
and brouȝte iosian out of bale
(fols. 196ᵛ–197ʳ; ll. 3860–88)

(When they landed, they quickly inquired and discovered in what region the queen was, and people told them also how the giant Ascopard was her warden in an isolated castle in the wilderness. Then Saber and his twelve companions at that time, through the help of God, soon found the castle. As they walked around the castle scoping out the sturdy towers, Josian, reposing in a high tower, saw Saber and his group, and she began to cry out to him: "Help, Saber, for the love of Mary!" Then Ascopard heard that cry, how she began to call out to Saber. He went out, angry at heart, and he swore an oath by Mohammed that he would do Saber to death. Each pilgrim threw off his cloak. Then their armor shone very brightly. Then Saber and his group of companions thronged around Ascopard and began to strike him hard and hew him into small pieces, and they brought Josian out of misery.)

The presumed Anglo-Norman source of the poem, represented by the Didot manuscript from the thirteenth century, has Josian recount her adventures to Saber; she mentions that she is now being led captive to King Yvor. The rescue scene is recounted as follows:

Ja encontrerent Jos*ian* o le cler vis,

Sab*aoth* la veit se est m*u*lt joiz.
"Dame, ou est B*oves e* Terri, mu*n* fiz?"
"Sire," dist ele, "entendez me diz,
en une boys m'en avai *deus* fiz;
q*u*ant fu deliv*eré* p*ar* la deu m*er*ciz,
a loins alerent misires *e* Terriz;
lors vindrent tuz ses Sarzins,
ore me amenent al fort roi Yroviz."
"di moi, dame," dist Sab*aoth*, "sont il Sarzins?"
"Oyl, bel sire, veez le pautoner,
Ke B*oves* fist baptiser *e* lever."
Sabaoth p*re*nt le burdon, le t*r*aitor feri
just le oy, mort li abati
a haute voice crie: "Ferés, mi pelerins!"[11]

(At once they came upon Josian of the radiant face. Sabaoth saw her there with much joy. "Lady, where are Beues and Terry, my son?" "Sir," she said, "Listen to me. In a wood I gave birth to two sons. When I had been delivered, by God's grace, my lord and Terry had gone far away. Then all the Saracens came. Now they are leading me to the strong King Yvor." "Tell me, Lady," said Sabaoth, "are these the Saracens?" "Yes, Fair Sir. There is the villain that Beues had baptized and brought up." Sabaoth took up his pilgrim's staff. He struck the traitor (Hear this), and beat him mortally. In a loud voice he cried, "Strike, my pilgrims!")

This version emphasizes the treacherous behavior of Ascopard and downplays Josian's fear and Saber's heroism.

British Library MS. Egerton 2862, probably from the end of the fourteenth century, follows the plot in the Anglo-Norman version but eliminates Josian's plot summary and the focus on Ascopard's treachery:

as she com toward vmbraunt *[Mombrant*
saber agayn him gan wynde *[came upon them*
gentyl kny3t she seide and hende *[noble*
do me now som socoure and reed *[advice*
but thou me help y am but deed *[dead*
dame he seide with out ȝelpe *[boasting*
I am com þe to helpe
smyte he seide eche palmere *[pilgrim*

sir saber smot ascopart þere *[smote*
with his burdon in to the brest *[pilgrim's staff*
þat no lenger his lyf leest *[lasted*
(fol. 89v)

Caius College Library MS. 175, from the early fifteenth century, follows roughly the same pattern but returns to something closer to the Anglo-Norman version in underscoring the treachery of Ascopard ("þat wylked traytour") and his companions ("Traytours ȝe schole dye echon"). Naples, Biblioteca Nazionale MS. XIII.B.29, dated 1457, reverts to something like the Egerton manuscript, and Cambridge University Library MS. Ff.II.38, from the middle of the fifteenth century, also follows this pattern with little variation. Chetham Library MS. 8009, from the late fifteenth century, likewise adheres roughly to the same approach but considerably elaborates the passage, thereby explaining the significance of what happens in keeping with the strategy adopted in the rest of this redaction:

For ass she went toward Vmbraunt
To the place there as she lend
Sabere and his meyne *[troop*
Mett with Ascaparte sodenly
With hym and all his felowhede *[companions*
God send them evyll spede
For by Ascaparte that fals man
Begyled was good Iosyan
And yf she had to courte com
Her liffe had be but litull and som *[very short*
And she dyd by the way went
Anon she spyed Sabere her ffrend
Sabere agayn her can wend *[was coming toward her*
And met Iosyan that was hend *[noble*
She said do me some good reed *[advice*
But thou helpe me y am but deed
Dame be god said sabere *[by God*
I am come to helpe the here
Hym selfe slew Ascaparte there
With that wepyn that he bare *[was carrying*
(fol. 177v)

The pilgrim disguise is not significant here, and both Ascopard's companions and Saber's companions almost disappear. The fight itself is reduced to a simple statement.

Cambridge, Trinity College Library MS. O.2.13/IV, from the late fifteenth century, moves in the opposite direction. It presents the most simplified version of the passage, focusing on action and nearly eliminating Josian's role:

Saber aftur her gon wende [*journeyed after her*
As a knyght curtes and hende [*courteous and noble*
A non [as gu*n*] sche hy*m* sye [*as soon as she saw him*
Vnto hym sche gon to cry [*began*
helpe me s*er* thorowe þy rede [*through your advice*
or well I wott I am but dede [*know*
Dame he sayd to here well sone
the to help I am I cum
Sabir smote at ascopart ther*e*
At all to pecis brak his spere
he smote hym so vppon the brest
That his life myth no lenger[*e*] lest [*could no longer last*
(fols. 151^{v}–152^{r})

In again elaborating the passage, Rycharde Pynson's early printed edition, dated around 1503, further increases Saber's heroism:

Whan Iosian was nere at Mambraunt
Iesu Cryst he hyr warrant
She met wyth sabere in the vylage
And sayde palmer in hyr langage
I pray you of socour and rede [*advice*
But ye me helpe I am but dede
Certys Iosyan sayde Sabere
Me lyketh wel that ye be here
For of you madame verament [*in truth*
I shal make beuys a present
Than agreued was ascaparde [*aggrieved*
For they assayled hym ful harde
They hym beset on euery syde
But there wolde none his dynt abyde [*abide his blow*
Fro his stroke away they dyd shone [*shy*
And start agayne as knyghtes anone
And gaue hym great strokes and sore

For anger he fomed lyke a bore [*boar*
Than as he smote after a knyght
Syr sabere ran to hym ful ryght
And wyth his swerde wythout dout
He bare ascaparde thoroughout [*ran Ascopard through*
That he fel dede to the grounde
(fols. 60v–61r)

While the exact relationship among the manuscripts has not been determined, examination of the different redactions of this passage underscores the complexity of the revisions. Josian's role is altered in keeping with tendencies documented in other passages ranging from the early fourteenth-century Auchinleck manuscript through the early sixteenth-century printed edition. While there is considerable variation among the versions, they nevertheless consistently and progressively reduce the role of the Princess Josian. This pattern of variation does not seem improvisational since it requires systematic revision of a subsequent passage as well as simple deletion.

The second major deletion associated with this episode, however, exhibits a very different character. After the passage discussed above, the various manuscripts converge again in describing Josian and Saber/Sabaoth setting out together to look for Beves. In the Anglo-Norman version, Sabaoth falls ill. At this point this text provides a rather sketchy suggestion that while Sabaoth is sick Josian earns their support by her music. Here she starts to sing about Beves because he is in her thoughts. She attracts noblemen, who give her rich gifts, enough for her to take care of Sabaoth. There is no indication of the location where she might be singing that would facilitate attracting such an audience; the issue of professionalism is cautiously skirted by avoiding specifying a context.

Jeskes a Abreford ne volent arest*er*.
Dunc se p*r*ist Sab*aoth* forement a malader.
Un jur se comence Jos*ian* purpenser
e de B*oun* comence a chant*er*.
E venent li barons p*ar* ample contrez,
chivals *e* robes donent assez pur achat*er*.
M*u*lt garda bie*n* Sab*aoth* li guerrer
jeskes a *set* ans *e trois* mois pleners.
(ed. Stimming, p. 97)

> (They did not stop until they came to Abreford, where Sabaoth came down with a virulent disease. One day, Josian began to think through things, and she began to sing about Beves. And barons, coming from many countries, gave enough horses and robes to purchase things. Thus she took good care of Sabaoth, to cure him, for fully seven years and three months.)

The Auchinleck version clarifies the situation, and the writer may be drawing on a romance tradition that has not survived in developing Josian's character at this point. He states that she is a musician, like Nicolete in the thirteenth-century *Aucassin et Nicolete*. Like Nicolete, she is clearly functioning as a professional performer in this situation. Unlike Nicolette, however, she was very well trained in music when she was growing up, so her level of competence is high.

> Seue ȝer to gedres þai hi*m* souȝt
> er þan hii him finde mouȝte
> In grete grese so saith the bok
> saber gret sikenesse tok
> that other half yer in none wise
> ne miȝte he out of is bed arise
> and tresor he nadde namore
> than half amark of olde store
> while iosian was in ermonie
> she hadde lerned of minstralcie
> vpon a fithele for to play
> staumpes notes garibles gay
> tho she kouthe no beter red
> boute in to the bourgh ano[n] she yed
> and boughte afithele so saith the tale
> for fourti panes of one me[n]strale
> and alle the while that saber lay
> iosian eueriche aday
> yede aboute the cite with inne
> here sostenaunse for to winne
> thus iosian was in swiche destresse
> while saber lai in is siknesse
> at þat oþer half ȝer is ende
> swiche grace god hi*m* gan sende
> and heled him of his maladie
> and forþ þai wente hastelie

beues and terry for to seche
wheder þat god he*m* wolde teche
so þourȝ a toun þai com þringe
þar Beues was in also a kinge
(fol. 197r, ll. 3897–3926)

(Together they sought him for seven years before they could find him. In great Greece, as the book says, Saber became very sick so that for half a year he could in no way rise out of his bed, and he had no more treasure than half a mark from his former cache. While Josian was in Armenia, she had learned music, to play estampies, melodies, cheerful tunes (?) on a vielle. When she had no better idea, she went at once into the city and bought a vielle, as the tale tells, for forty pence from a minstrel. And all the while that Saber lay sick, Josian, every day, went about in the city to win their sustenance. Thus Josian was in such distress while Saber lay in his sickness. At the end of half a year, God sent him such grace that he healed him of his malady, and they went forth hastily to seek Beues and Terry wherever God would show them. So they passed through a town where Beues was king.)

This goes well beyond clarifying the rather vague Anglo-Norman reference. There is a playful quality to the treatment of Josian. She does not sing love songs, and Beves is not even mentioned. Instead she plays dances on a vielle which she has purchased from a minstrel. She wanders through the city earning "here sostenaunse." Again, as with the earlier Auchinleck passage from this episode, she meets an urgent problem with a solution that draws on her rich collection of skills.

All subsequent manuscripts, while following Auchinleck fairly closely in plot and form if not wording, simply omit this passage except for the first two lines by skipping ahead to 3925, where Saber and Josian meet Beues and Terry. A fourteenth-century example, from MS. Egerton 2862, will suffice to illustrate the principle:

Seuen ȝere sir beues he souȝt
or þat he him fynde mouȝt [*might*
þrouȝ a toun he gan spryng
þere was sir beues woonyng [*where . . . dwelling*
(fol. 89v)

Here, then, is a simple deletion of a repellent passage. The passage included in the Auchinleck manuscript and omitted in all subsequent redactions portrays the heroine as a professional musician —a role evidently repugnant to subsequent redactors, who progressively and increasingly over time revise Josian into a more decorous princess. This pattern fits with the tendency over this period to limit the activity of romance heroines.

What is intriguing about this entire complex incident in the *Beues* manuscripts is that we find evidence of two types of deletion of repellent material: the first, which seems more textual, returns to an earlier form of the poem, and the second, which seems more improvisational, simply leaves out a block of text. This is typical of Middle English romance manuscripts, poised as they are on the brink between orality and textuality.

As different as these two deletions are, both reflect an increasing insistence on the passive heroine. In the early fourteenth century, Princess Josian is free to squat down off the road to relieve herself, eat an herb to make herself look like a leper, and earn her living by playing the vielle, all to accomplish the goal she has established for herself of union with Sir Beves. By the late fifteenth century she will take no action on her own behalf. Someone else initiates all strategies of protection, and the text is modified to eliminate episodes where she exhibits indecorous behavior or takes on the appearance of a man. These two deletions, then, following two very different processes, both illustrate the strength of attitudes that deprived romance heroines, representing the ideal woman, of an active role in shaping and interacting with the world they inhabit.

The Middle English romance is ideally suited to exploring changing attitudes through the Middle Ages. The oral dimension[12] gives the texts flexibility to reflect the views of individual redactors, while the textual dimension provides a coherent structure within which that change can be tracked. Certainly, the variants within the manuscript tradition of one romance may represent any number of accidents of circumstance or individual whim, but, nonetheless, transformations do occur. In this instance, the transformations seem consistently aligned with what critics have described as one of the shifts within the genre—a shift to an increasingly conservative perspective. Combined with other similar studies, these changes may prove indicative of a movement in thought.

A modern performance of another medieval romance can further help us to understand the nature of the *Beues* manuscript modifications and to indicate the extent to which improvisation may have played a role in the transformation of the Middle English romances. Modern performance demonstrates that such deletions can be made on an improvisatory basis and that live performance provides powerful impetus to eliminate passages the performer feels might be repellant to the audience. By examining the manuscript deletions in the light of modern performance deletions, we find evidence that some of the *Beues* modifications may have been motivated not by a scribe's careful consideration but by a performer's response to the urgent and concrete expectations of the audience.

Two deletions were introduced into my first two memorized performances of *The Weddynge of Sir Gawen and Dame Ragnell* in May 1996: I planned in advance to eliminate the pious ending, and I spontaneously omitted forty-five lines of recapitulation. As carefully as I transcribed *The Weddynge of Sir Gawen and Dame Ragnell* from the original manuscript and checked it for accuracy time and again, as painstakingly as I memorized each preposition, as thoughtfully as I worked through each character and each theme in the poem, I nonetheless glibly left out the ending as I prepared a memorized performance.[13] The entire romance takes fifty minutes to perform; this passage takes less than a minute. Time was not an issue.

The Weddynge of Sir Gawen and Dame Ragnell tells how Arthur is given a year to find out what women most desire. If his answer is wrong, he will be slain. The hideous Dame Ragnell offers to tell him the answer if he will let her marry Sir Gawain. Gawain agrees to marry her, and she tells Arthur that women most desire sovereignty. Gawain marries the loathly lady, and on their wedding night she turns beautiful. She offers him a choice: to have her beautiful during the day or during the night. Gawain leaves the choice in her hands, and that frees her from a spell, allowing her to be beautiful both day and night.

In the passage I eliminated at the end of the poem, there is a shift in the narration when the speaker prays to God to protect the listeners from hell and to help the person "that this tale dyd devyne" (l. 842) who has long been imprisoned in torment. The poem concludes with the speaker yielding "body and soull" into God's hand. I did not find the passage personally repellent, but I thought it would be perceived as naïve and intrusive by my audience. My decision was thus shaped by my perception of my audience more than by my own views. As a performer, I submerged my scholarly quest to reproduce a text as accurately as possible to the more urgent demand to produce a compelling and acceptable performance. I was reluctant to introduce an *Angst*-ridden persona for the "devyner" of the tale at the last minute. In terms of the structure of the poem, though, and in terms of themes that are developed throughout, the passage at the end is integral. It presents the creator of the story as a person who lacks control in society. Yielding sovereignty into God's hands, he looks to God for relief from "daunger." In designating God as "veray kyng ryoall," he contrasts God with the political figure of the king. Carl Lindahl sees this passage suggesting a challenge to the power structure: "[T]he narrator, who in closing describes himself as one 'be-sette with gaylours many' (844), reinforces the fact that this poem is a plea for liberation as well as a charter for undermining the authoritarian world. With the elevation of Ragnell comes at least the implication that others—including the jailed knight himself—can rise."[14] It is not clear whether the story maker's torment is a physical imprisonment or a deep depression which keeps him from living freely. In either case, the issue of who holds sovereignty is developed in this passage and brought into the audience/storyteller context. The narrator asks the deity to protect the listeners/readers from torment, and then he describes his own suffering and, because of his pain, yields himself to God. The phrase "For body and soull I yeld into thyne hand" resonates with Gawain's yielding to Ragnell earlier in the poem:

> The choyse I putt in your fyst
> Euyn as ye woll I putt itt in your hand
> (ll. 679–80)

The manuscript ending thus suggests an ongoing issue. In the face of suffering, who has control? Who has power to fulfill desires? What is the role of the king? of God? In the complex power structure, when is it appropriate to yield sovereignty and when to maintain it? What are appropriate uses of sovereignty? All of these dimensions were significantly diminished by my glib omission. The reasons for my choice were nonetheless reasonable and accurate. They reflect an attitude that has changed since the time the text was written, as the omissions in the *Beues* manuscripts represent an attitude that had changed since the time that earlier version was written.

What made me conscious of the motivations behind that fundamental choice was a second omission I developed in the process of performance. The first public performance of the text was for a general audience in Boise, Idaho. I was very aware of the audience throughout the performance. I knew exactly which parts they enjoyed and understood—and which parts pushed the limits of their Middle English tolerance. As I neared the end of the poem, I approached the passage where all the characters tell each other their perspectives concerning the adventure.[15] On the spur of the moment and impelled by a fear of losing the audience's attention, I cut that entire passage. A glance at the remarkably flexible harpist cued her in to what I had done, and the performance was seamless—and the audience enjoyed it.

We were so pleased with the omission that we decided to cut the "he said/she said" passage, as I scornfully titled it, for our performance at Kalamazoo.[16] We performed the work with both cuts, and the audience of about eighty medievalists accepted the choices. No one mentioned the two omissions, and I assumed that they were acknowledging the performer's right to make cuts. It was only later that I wondered if those choices might give insight into the original fifteenth-century text by drawing attention to features I preferred to ignore or deride and had trouble presenting sympathetically. Improvisations in performance can thus highlight cultural disjunction and perhaps therefore allow us to examine more accurately the cultural context we bring to the texts.

The motives for my omission of the "he said/she said" passage were compelling. The action stops while each character delivers his or her perspective on what has happened. Clearly there is a place for serial contextualizing in our popular entertainment,[17] but it works only because we respond within that culture. The passage I omitted does not play well to a modern audience because the contextualizing happens within another culture. It was not the lull in the action that motivated my cut, but the fact that the culture into which the adventure is being grounded in the text is not our own. The passage begins with King Arthur telling the entire court how Ragnell has saved him from death. Then he tells the Queen specifically what the danger was and that Ragnell has saved him because she loves

Gawain. Thereupon Gawain tells the King the nature of Ragnell's enchantment, and Ragnell tells the king how Gawain released her by giving her the sovereignty. She turns to Gawain and promises to obey him as long as she lives. He thanks her and announces to everyone that she need never crave his love. The queen promises to love Ragnell. I left out an additional six lines in which Gawain begets Gyngolyn and Ragnell is the most beautiful lady at court feasts.

I had difficulty reading, much less memorizing or performing, the six lines in which Ragnell promises to obey Gawain for the rest of her life and never argue with him.

> Therfore curteys knyght and hend gawen [*gracious Gawain*
> Shall I neu*er* wrath the s*er*teyn [*anger thee certainly*
> That p*ro*myse nowe here I make
> Whill*is* that I lyve I shalbe obaysaunt [*obedient*
> To god aboue I shall itt warraunt
> And neu*er* with you to debate
> (ll. 781–86)

I found such a promise repellent and dramatically in contrast to Ragnell's bold assurance in her dealings with King Arthur. In terms of the structure of the story, however, there is a very definite balance. Gawain has already given Ragnell "the souereynte euery dell" (l. 776). In nine lines when they are alone in bed, he moves from leaving the current choice in her fist to making his body and goods hers:

> I ne wott in this world what I shall say [*I do not know*
> Butt do as ye lyst nowe my lady gaye [*do as you like*
> The choyse I putt in your fyst
> Euyn as ye woll I putt itt in your hand
> Lose me when ye lyst for I am bond [*Loose … desire … bound*
> I putt the choyse in you
> Both body and goodis hartt and euery dele [*every bit*
> Ys alle your oun for to by and sell [*buy*
> That make I god avowe [*of that I make a good vow*
> (ll. 676–84)

He has not retracted that vow in the "he said/she said" passage. On the contrary, he gives her sovereignty in private, and she makes that act public before Arthur and, also publicly before Arthur, gives Gawain sovereignty over her. This vow is important, since Arthur is at the center of the whole sovereignty issue. Ragnell bargains with him, not Gawain; and Gawain marries Ragnell for Arthur's sake, not her own.

When I look beyond my immediate aversion to the passage, I find an interesting interplay of power. It is for Arthur's sake that Gawain has married Ragnell; it is for Gawain's sake that Ragnell has saved the king's life. So in this passage, Arthur acknowledges to all and to the queen what Ragnell has done for him and that it was for Gawain's love. Ragnell has publicly declared her love for Gawain, and never until this point has he responded to that. Now, publicly and freely, without being coerced in any way, he gives her his love, the thing she has sought from the outset. Gawain and Ragnell give each other sovereignty, but Arthur is their sovereign. Together they have saved his life, and the process of how that has happened must be publicly announced in the court context.

Like the ending of the poem, the "he said/she said" passage emphasizes ambiguous elements in the story. Even as the power structures of the court are acknowledged, they are questioned. If Ragnell and Gawain have power to save the king's life, has he lost sovereignty? What does it mean when the queen swears to love Ragnell because she has saved Arthur's life? The queen's acceptance of Ragnell seems vital in the court context, but what does it say about her previous derision of the loathly lady? The answer to the riddle of what women desire is "sovereignty," but in this passage love is introduced. Ragnell saves Arthur for Gawain's love, and here, publicly acknowledging his love for her, he reassures the court that she need never again crave his love. What is her deepest desire? What motivates Gawain's love for her?

From a performance standpoint, the omission of the "he said/she said" passage was well justified. A modern audience, however steeped in medieval culture, is not likely to respond to a long culturally-specific passage toward the end of a lengthy text in a challenging language. I am not suggesting that historical performance become stultified and unresponsive to modern contexts. Performers can challenge the limits of audience tolerance of the other, but there are some boundaries over which we cannot step and continue to communicate effectively. As scholars, we are free to examine which elements fall beyond the pale of modern performance, which elements must be excluded or transformed in which settings. Exploration of what is behind those performance-motivated transformations can guide us in reconsidering our understanding of the culture that shaped and received the medieval texts.

Recent performance theory has emphasized the importance of cultural context. John Miles Foley, for example, argues for a dual approach to works with elements of orality: "To the extent that an audience is able to co-create the work by enriching its textual integers and bridging its gaps of indeterminacy according to the rules of the idiom, that audience can recover its traditional, performance-centered resonance. And since such works, which emerge from oral tradition and yet involve textuality in various ways, clearly lay claim to a double heritage, it seems indefensible to eliminate either dimension from our own reading strategy, our role in the making of the work of art."[18] The difficulty of recovering "the rules of the idiom," however, has always been a problem in historical performance. However careful we might be with original texts—seemingly endlessly poring over the documents—and musical instruments, nonetheless our cultural context is fundamentally different in ways we may not always understand. Some aspects of performance stay the same and survive transfer to another culture, but other aspects are transformed out of recognition or disappear in a successful modern performance. The fact is that, even in a context where the audience is seeking historical realities, the realities of cultural context for performance remain the same. A responsible performer will not move outside of her culture and the culture of her audience.

Yet this very limitation of historical performance can also provide an intriguing tool for assessing our responses to medieval texts. As a performer, I am sensitive to what will play well to medievalists as a group. Like the *Beues* redactor, my choices are based not only on my own tastes but on amorphous information I gather from our community in a variety of ways. If I intentionally leave out passages from a text I generally adhere to fairly carefully, that might provide significant information about which parts I—and perhaps the community—find uncomfortable, the parts we want to explain away, change, omit, or denounce. In other words, the degree of *mouvance* in a modern performance may provide warning signs about where our culture may run counter to the original cultural context.[19]

An intriguing corollary to this premise is that the variation tends to disappear in a recorded performance or under the influence of a sustained determination to revert to the original. The video I made in 1999 included every line without significant deviation from the manuscript,[20] and subsequent performances were much more accurately aligned with the original. In such cases, I had become aware of my cultural responses and was consciously working to efface them. Improvisation seemed to occur most fluidly and revealingly when the text was flexibly memorized and when I was exploring audience responses. Only in live memorized performance did cultural anomalies come out in improvisations.

These principles deriving from my performance experience illuminate the omissions in the manuscripts of *Sir Beues*. The later *Beues* manuscripts that so urgently eliminate Josian's "indecorous" behavior can be understood in terms of the compelling force I felt to expunge elements of the text I felt would be repellent to my audience. In the *Beues* manuscripts, the removal of Josian's herbal solution to her problem is highly textual and requires several manipulations to maintain consistency. On the other hand, the simple omission of the vielle passage has a more improvisatory flavor. The transformations exhibited in my performance include both types of elimination. The removal of the ending of *The Weddynge of Sir Gawen and Dame Ragnell* is textual in that it was planned in advance and constituted a premeditated adaptation of the text. The omission of the lengthy recapitulation passage, however, constitutes a genuinely improvisational adaptation. The characteristics of that change are quite similar to the elimination of the vielle passage in the *Beues* manuscript in that it is a simple deletion of lines which can be accomplished without jarring the continuity of the text, and the omission is motivated by ideological considerations. The modern performance illuminates the variants in *Sir Beues* and similar variants in other Middle English romances by demonstrating that genuinely improvisational deletions are possible in a memorized performance of narrative verse, that such changes follow characteristics evinced in variants of Middle English romances, and that the urgency to eliminate perceived repellent passages can be astonishingly powerful in a performance context.

NOTES

[1]Both manuscripts include ll. 915–1268; line numbers are from Albert Stimming, ed., *Der Anglonormannisches Boeve de Haumtone* (Halle: Max Niemeyer, 1899).

[2]Eugen Kölbing, ed., *The Romance of Sir Beues of Hamtoun*, EETS, e.s. 46, 48, 65 (London: Kegan Paul, Trench, and Trübner, 1885–94), 1:xxxiv–xxxv.

[3]The Anglo-Norman version of the tale was explored nearly a century ago by John E. Matzke ("The Oldest Form of the Beves Legend," *Modern Philology* 10 [1912–13]: 19–54), and more recently Judith Weiss has compared the English text and its Anglo-Norman source with respect to two interpolations ("The Major Interpolations in Sir Beues of Hamtoun," *Medium Ævum* 48 [1979]: 71–76). Working with the French text, François Suard has examined the expression of amorous sentiment in the French text ("Le *Beuves de Hantonne* en prose: importance et expression du sentiment amoureux," *Actes du 5e colloque international sur le Moyen Français* [Milan, 1986], 73–88), while Stephen Hunt has discussed cruces in the Icelandic translation ("Further Translation Errors in *Bevers Saga*," *Notes and Queries* 32 [1985]: 455–56) and Herbert Schendl has explicated the term "randon" in the text ("ME *Randon* in *Sir Bevis of Hampton*," *Anglia* 102 [1984]: 101–07). Working more directly with the Middle English text, Linda Brownrigg has convincingly demonstrated that several illustrations in the Taymouth Hours portray episodes in the romance of *Sir Beves* ("The Taymouth Hours and the Romance of *Beves of Hampton*," *English Manuscript Studies* 1 [1989]: 222–41), Maldwyn Mills has discussed the structure of the poem in connection with *Guy of Warwick* ("Structure and Meaning in *Guy of Warwick*," in *From Medieval to Medievalism*, ed. John Simmons [New York: St. Martin's Press, 1992], 54–68), and Jennifer Fellows has looked at elements in Johnson's treatment of the St. George legend borrowed from *Sir Beves* ("St. George as Romance Hero," *Reading Medieval Studies* 19 [1993]: 27–54).

[4]Harriet Hudson, "Construction of Class, Family, and Gender in some Middle English Popular Romances," in *Class and Gender in Early English Literature: Intersections*, ed. Britton J. Harwood and Gillian R. Overing (Bloomington: Indiana University Press, 1994), 76–94.

[5]Rosamund Allen, "Female Perspectives in Romance and History," in *Romance in Medieval England*, ed. Maldwyn Mills, Jennifer Fellows, and Carol M. Meale (Cambridge: D. S. Brewer, 1991), 133–47.

[6]Kölbing, ed., *The Romance of Sir Beues of Hamtoun*, 1:xxxvii–xli.

[7]Murray McGillivray, *Memorization in the Transmission of the Middle English Romances* (New York: Garland, 1990), 40.

[8]The full passage follows: "Ele se porpensa par quel engien ele porroit

Aucassin querre; ele quist une viele, s'aprist a vieler, tant c'on le vaut marier un jor a un roi rice paiien. Et ele s'enbla la nuit, si vint au port de mer, si se herbega ciés une povre fenme sor le rivage; si prist une herbe, si en oinst son cief et son visage, si qu'ele fu tote noire et tainte. Et ele fist faire cote et mantel et cemisse et braies, si s'atorna a guise de jogleor; si prist se viele, si vint a un marounier, se fist tant vers lui qu'il le mist en se nef. Il drecierent lor voile, si nagierent tant par haute mer qu'il ariverent en le terre de Provence. Et Nicolete issi fors, si prist se viele, si ala vielant par le païs tant qu'ele vint au castel de Biaucaire, la u Aucassins estoit" (*Aucassin et Nicolette*, ed. Mario Roques [Paris: Librairie Honoré Champion, 1982], 36) ("She considered by what means she might seek Aucassin. She bought a vielle and learned to play vielle, until the day came when she would have to marry a powerful pagan king. She avoided that fate by sneaking away at night. She went to the seaport and found lodging with a poor woman on the shore. There she took an herb and smeared it on her face so that she was completely black, and she arranged for a coat and mantle and shirt and breeches, and thus she took on the appearance of a jongleur. She took her vielle, went to a mariner, and arranged with him to take her in his boat. He dressed the sail and navigated the high sea until they arrived in the land of Provence. Nicolette disembarked. She took her vielle and went through the country playing her vielle until she came to the castle of Beaucaire, the place where Aucassin was living.")

[9]Weiss fails to give attention to this passage in her article "The Major Interpolations in *Sir Beues of Hamtoun*."

[10]Unless otherwise indicated, translations are my own, as are the glosses throughout. Except where otherwise noted, quotations from Middle English texts are my own transcriptions from the manuscripts. I am grateful to the National Library of Scotland; the British Library; Trinity College Library, Cambridge; and Chetham's Library, Manchester, for permission to use these texts in my paper.

[11]*Der Anglonormanisches Boeve de Haumtone*, ed. Stimming, 96–97.

[12]In the last decade, building on the work of Milman Parry, *The Making of Homeric Verse* (London: Oxford University Press, 1971), Albert Lord, *The Singer of Tales* (Cambridge: Harvard University Press, 1960), and William Quinn and Audley Hall, *Jongleur: A Modified Theory of Oral Improvisation and its Effects on the Performance and Transmission of Middle English Romance* (Washington, D.C.: University Press of America, 1982), scholars have increasingly explored elements of orality in the Middle English romances and have come to see romance texts as a blend in varying degrees of oral and written traditions. McGillivray has posited a theory of memorial transmission based on variants within certain romances. Karl Reichl ("The Middle English Popular Romance: Minstrel versus Hack Writer," in *The Ballad and Oral Literature*, ed. Joseph Harris [Cambridge: Harvard University Press, 1991], 243–68), and Andrew Taylor ("Fragmentation, Corruption, and Minstrel Narration: The Question of the Middle English Romances," *The Yearbook of English Studies* 22 [1992]: 38–62) have looked at variants to assess the role of the minstrel. Carl Lindahl ("The Oral Undertones of

Late Medieval Romance," in *Oral Tradition in the Middle Ages*, ed. W. F. H. Nicolaisen [Binghamton, N.Y.: Medieval and Renaissance Texts and Studies, 1995], 59), has seen oral undertones indicating a social and cultural range—a tradition having "roots and branches in both the most popular and the most refined segments of medieval society."

[13]The passage deleted from the end of the poem is as follows:

Nowe god as thou were in Bethleme born
Suffer neu*er* her soules be forlorne
In the brynnyng fyre of hell
And Jh*es*u as thou were borne of a virgyn
Help hym oute of sorowe that this tale dyd devyne
And that nowe in alle hast
For he is be sett with gaylours many
That kepen hym full sewerly
With wiles wrong and wraste
Nowe god as thou art veray kyng ryoall
Help hym oute of daunger that made this tale
For therin he hath bene long
And of greatt pety help thy seru*au*nt
For body and soull I yeld into thyne hand
For paynes he hath strong
(ll. 838–52)

[14]Lindahl, "The Oral Undertones of Late Medieval Romance," 73.

[15]The recapitulation passage follows:

Than the kyng them alle gan tell
How did hel[p] hym att nede dame Ragnell
or my deth had bene dyght
Ther the kyng told the queen by the rood
Howe he was bestad in Ingleswod
With s*yr* Grom*er*som*er* Joure
And whate othe the knyght made hym swere
Or ell*is* he had slayn me ryght there
W*ith*oute m*er*cy or mesure
This same lady dame Ragnell
From my deth she dyd help me ryght well
Alle for the love of gawen
Then gawen told the kyng alle to geder
Howe forshapen she was with her stepmoder
Tyll a knyght had holpen her agayn
Ther she told the kyng fayre and well
Howe gawen gave her the sou*er*eynte eu*er*y dell
And whate choyse she gave to hym
God thank hym of his curtesye
He savid me from chaunce and vilany

That was full foull and grym
Therfore curteys knyght and hend gawen
Shall I neu*er* wrath the s*er*teyn
That p*ro*myse nowe here I make
Whill*is* that I lyve I shalbe obaysaunt
To god aboue I shall itt warraunt
And neu*er* with you to debate
Garam*er*cy lady then sayd gawen
W*ith* you I hold me full well content
And that I trust to fynde
He sayd my loue shall she haue
Therafter nede she neu*er*more craue
For she hath bene to me so kynde
The queen sayd and the ladyes alle
She is the fayrest nowe in this halle
I swere by Seynt J[o]hn
My loue lady ye shall haue eu*er*
For that ye savid my lord Arthoure
As I am a gentilwoman
Syr gawen gatt on her gyngolyn
That was a good knyght of strength and [kynn]
And of the Table Round
Att eu*er*y greatt fest that lady shold be
Of fayrnesse she bare away the Bewtye
Wher she yed on the ground
(ll. 760–804)

[16]Presentation at the Thirty-first International Congress on Medieval Studies, Western Michigan University, 9 May 1996.

[17]In both *Deep Impact* and *Armageddon*, for example, all the astronauts say goodbye to their loved ones at interminable length and describe their particular views on the dangerous comet adventure.

[18]John Miles Foley, *The Singer of Tales in Performance* (Bloomington: Indiana University Press, 1995), 137.

[19]Paul Zumthor's theory of *mouvance* describes a grid on which the vertical axis is the model and the horizontal axis the variations ("Intertextualité et mouvance," *Littérature* 41 [1981]: 9). He elsewhere notes the importance of the poetic voice emanating from a particular mouth, expressions on a specific face, punctuated by gestures of a particular hand ("Jongleurs et diseurs: interprétation et création poétique au moyen âge," *Medioevo Romanzo* 11 [1986]: 26). The theory of *mouvance* can include these modern performances, my variations from the textual norm.

[20]*The Weddynge of Sir Gawen and Dame Ragnell*, TEAMS and the Chaucer Studio, December 1999.

Shakespeare's Rhetorical Riffs

Jane Freeman

In play after play, Shakespeare's characters demonstrate their wit through various forms of rhetorical improvisation, and their improvisational skill is often highly admired and explicitly evaluated by characters who witness it. Clearly these characters are fictional creations who have no independent reality, but through the use of very specific rhetorical strategies, Shakespeare creates characters who seem to improvise through metarhetorical wordplay. In "The Improvising Vice in Renaissance England," which appears later in this volume, David N. Klausner divides "the modes of improvisation in Renaissance theater into two: those planned by the playwright and those unplanned." In this paper, I shall suggest a third mode: scripted improvisation.

Scripted improvisation may seem to be an *oxymoron*, but Elizabethan audience members who never saw a script, and who might have been unable to read one even if they had seen it, might not always have been able to distinguish between spontaneous improvisation and rehearsed improvisation that was sufficiently well written and well performed to seem spontaneous. Instead of regarding scripted drama and improvisation as two completely discrete categories, I suggest they function as parts of a continuum, for Shakespeare's scripted improvisation is both modeled on and a model of the extemporaneous dialogue of actual improvisation. By examining the specific rhetorical devices Shakespeare uses to create scenes of seemingly spontaneous wordplay, we learn certain structures useful both to improvisers and to Shakespearean actors.

In order to embody the characters whom Shakespeare has invested with improvisational skill, actors must understand the rules of the rhetorical games which characters are playing. These games are characterized by a heavy reliance on two specific types of rhetorical figures: puns and figures of repetition. While these figures account for only about twenty of the almost two hundred rhetorical devices listed in sixteenth-century style manuals, these particular figures appear again and again in scenes of rhetorical improvisation, and thus it is on puns and figures of repetition that I wish to focus attention. I call these devices "rhetorical riffs" because there is a significant similarity between Shakespeare's techniques of rhetorical improvisation and those of jazz improvisation—a similarity that helps to clarify the potential benefits, even today, of training in classical rhetoric.

There are almost two hundred rhetorical figures, and for centuries they were considered an essential part of an elementary education.[1] The curriculum in Elizabethan grammar schools was based on the trivium of grammar, logic, and rhetoric. According to Cicero, whose works were widely studied in Renaissance England, there are five stages of rhetorical composition, including invention (the discovery of ideas), disposition (the arrangement of ideas), elocution (style), memory, and delivery (voice and gesture), and "each one is in its own right a great art."[2] Although training in elocution covers the differences in high, middle, and low styles as well as stylistic features such as decorum, clarity, and purity of utterance, in most Renaissance style manuals the section on elocution is heavily, if not entirely, dominated by an examination of rhetorical figures.

While there was disagreement among rhetoricians regarding the best methods for naming or categorizing the figures, there was not much controversy as to the usefulness of these devices. As William Kempe's treatise on education illustrates, rhetorical training was a fundamental component of the Elizabethan grammar school curriculum:

> First the scholler shal learne the precepts concerning the divers sorts of arguments in the first part of Logike, (for that without them Rhetorike cannot be well understood) then shall followe the tropes and figures in the first part of Rhetorike, wherein he shall employ the sixth part of his studie, and all the rest in learning and handling good authors. . . . [H]e shall observe not only every trope, every figure, as well of words as of sentences; but also the Rhetoricall pronounciation and gesture fit for every word, sentence, and affection.[3]

Elizabethan schoolchildren, including the young William Shakespeare, studied between 130 and 200 rhetorical devices. The pedagogical strategy used had three stages: children were to memorize the figures, identify them in what they read, and then use them in what they wrote.[4] The word "figure" is used to denote both the genus of rhetorical devices and one of the species. While almost two hundred devices are loosely referred to as rhetorical figures, these devices are divided into categories. As Kempe's words demonstrate, the three most common categories in Renaissance style manuals were tropes, figures of words, and figures of thought (which Kempe calls figures of sentences). Tropes, such as *metaphor* or *metonymy*, involve a transference of meaning; figures of words, such as *alliteration*, work at the level "of words, diction, expression, language or style"; and figures of thought, such as *personification*, express movements "of the mind, feeling or conceptions."[5] We tend to learn only twenty or thirty rhetorical devices now, but to an Elizabethan schoolchild figures like *anaphora* (beginning a series of clauses with the same word: AB, AC, AD), *antistrophe* (ending a series of clauses with the same word: AB, CB, DB), and *antimetabole* (akin to logical conversion in that it repeats words in converse order: AB, BA) [6] were taught side by side with *metaphor*, *simile*, and *alliteration*.

Learning the figures of classical rhetoric is like learning the scales of music. A music student might be told "Learn the scales. Practice them, practice them, practice them, and then forget about them and play music." In Elizabethan classrooms, a similar approach was taken to rhetorical figures; children were to learn the figures, practice them, practice them, practice them, and then forget about them and be eloquent. I am not the first, of course, to draw a parallel between musical and rhetorical figures. Henry Peacham drew parallels between specific figures and music in the 1593 edition of *The Garden of Eloquence.* As Gregory Butler notes, three of the four figures Peacham links closely with music are "figures of repetition, in which a word or words are repeated in various ways to produce certain effects."[7] In *The Compleat Gentleman* (1622), Peacham's son emphasizes the relationship between rhetoric and music even more forcefully. He refers to music as "a sister to Poetry" and writes:

> Yea, in my opinion no Rhetoric more persuadeth or hath greater power over the mind [than music]; nay, hath not music her figures, the same which Rhetoric? What is a revert but her *Antistrophe* [AB, CB, DB]? her reports, but sweet *Anaphoras* [AB, AC, AD]? her counterchange of points, *Antimetaboles* [AB, BA]? her passionate airs, but *Prosopopoeias* [*personification*]? with infinite other of the same nature.[8]

In tracing the relationship between Peacham's musical and rhetorical terms, Butler notes that "revert, report, and counterchange, are not only highly technical fugal procedures but, what is not generally realized, are renderings into English of the Greek rhetorical figures with which they are here linked. . . . Peacham the Younger had probably studied George Puttenham's *The Arte of English Poesie* (1589), the only treatise on rhetoric of the period in which Greek and Latin rhetorical terms are given specific English translations."[9]

Although Puttenham was the only rhetorician of his time to translate the figure names, he was not the only one to write an English rhetoric manual. In translating Greek and Latin figure names into English, Puttenham was participating in a late sixteenth-century trend to make rhetorical study accessible to a wider audience. Until the middle of the sixteenth century, the study of rhetoric had been limited to those who could read Greek or Latin, which usually meant those who had the opportunity to receive some formal education. By 1589 when *The Arte of English Poesie* was written, however, seven books on rhetoric had been published in English, and thus a new group of readers was gaining access to rhetorical training.[10]

Whether the figures were learned in English or in Latin, in school or at home, there is no doubt that these devices were extensively studied and highly valued in Elizabethan England. In an engaging portrait of *homo rhetoricus*, Richard Lanham considers both the pedagogical strategies used to teach rhetoric in sixteenth-century England and the societal effects of the Renaissance preoccupation with rhetoric:

> Start your student young. Teach him a minute concentration on the word, how to write it, speak it, remember it. . . . Let words come first as objects and sounds long before they can, for a child, take on full meaning. . . . From the beginning, stress behavior as performance, reading aloud, speaking with gesture. . . . Stress, too, the need for improvisation, ad-lib quickness, the coaxing of chance. Hold always before the student rhetoric's practical purpose: to win, to persuade. But train for this purpose with continual verbal play, rehearsal for the sake of rehearsal. . . . The aim is scoring. Urge the student to go into the world and observe its doings from this perspective. And urge him to continue this rehearsal method all his life, forever rehearsing a spontaneous real life. Fill public life, agora, forum, court, with

> men similarly trained. Make this intense training in the word, in dramatic incarnation, union-card to public life. . . . Whatever sins [*homo rhetoricus*] might enregister, stylistic naivete would not be one.[11]

As we shall see, many of Shakespeare's characters exhibit exactly the sort of rhetorical self-consciousness that Lanham describes. Sometimes characters engage in lengthy metarhetorical jousting matches, but more often they demonstrate their eloquence by adeptly twisting the words of others to suit their own purposes or by recognizing, and creatively imitating, the speech patterns of others. As mentioned above, two types of figures are particularly useful to Shakespeare's improvisers: puns and figures of repetition. There is some overlap between these two categories, for some puns are figures of repetition while others involve the transference of meaning that characterizes tropes.[12]

Shakespeare's clever wordplay in the form of puns is widely recognized. Less widely recognized, however, are the specific structures of different types of puns. To rhetorically trained Elizabethans, a pun was not merely a pun. Sister Miriam Joseph explains: "Rightly to appreciate Shakespeare's puns, one should regard them as examples of four highly esteemed figures of Renaissance rhetoric—*antanaclasis*, *syllepsis*, *paronomasia* and *asteismus*—which have their roots in the logical distinction between the various meanings of a word, and depend for their effect on the intellectual alertness necessary to perceive the ambiguity."[13] The pleasure of punning lies not only in the speaker's ability to invent but also in the listener's ability to respond quickly and in kind. As M. M. Mahood notes, "the prosperity of a pun, like that of all poetic devices, lies in the ear of him that hears it."[14] A speaker makes a clever pun, and a listener responds with some cleverness of his own by returning the pun with a twist. Similar to call and response sessions between jazz musicians, punning sessions require both participants to listen carefully and to respond precisely.

The one-upmanship that often characterizes punning is clearly evident in the initial meeting of Kate and Petruchio in *The Taming of the Shrew*. Petruchio, who is known to be a bully, and Kate, who is known to be a shrew, are both accustomed to winning their rhetorical jousting matches. Shakespeare creates them as tough competition for each other, and he begins their courtship with an exchange full of competitive punning. The four punning figures are *antanaclasis* (in which a repeated word shifts from one of its meanings to another); *paronomasia* (which differs from *antanaclasis* in that the words repeated are nearly but not precisely alike in sound); *syllepsis* (the use of a word having simultaneously two different meanings, although it is not repeated); and *asteismus* (a figure of reply in which the answerer catches a certain word and throws it back to the first speaker with an unexpected twist, an unlooked-for meaning). Kate's facility with these figures is clearly evident even in her opening lines:

Pet. Hearing thy mildness prais'd in every town,
Thy virtues spoke of, and thy beauty *sounded*, (*syllepsis*)
Yet not so deeply as to thee belongs,
Myself am *mov'd* to woo thee for my wife.
Kath. *Mov'd!* in good time! Let him that *mov'd* you hither (*antanaclasis*)
Remove you hence. I knew you at the first (*paronomasia*)
You were a *moveable*. (*syllepsis*, *asteismus*)
Pet. Why, what's a *movable*?
Kath. A join'd-stool.
Pet. Thou hast hit it. Come, sit on me.
Kath. *Asses* are made to *bear*, and so are you. (*syllepsis*)
Pet. Women are made to *bear*, and so are you. (*antanaclasis*, *isocolon*) (2.1.191–200)

Their exchange continues in this vein for over fifty lines. Petruchio begins his speech to this unknown woman with his characteristic bluntness: "Myself am mov'd to woo thee for my wife." Kate picks up his word "moved," and in three lines of speech which include all four of the punning figures, she unceremoniously dumps the word back in his lap—and thus begins the rhetorical contest between them.

Kate and Petruchio's exchange combines elements of both sociablility and competition as they try to outdo each other in the witty inventiveness of their insults.[15] In several of Shakespeare's plays, couples engage in lengthy rhetorical rallies as a form of courtship, and such matches are characterized by a heavy use of the four types of puns mentioned above. *Asteismus* is especially in evidence in Kate and Petruchio's exchange (2.1.194–278), as it is in the competitive punning of Benedick and Beatrice in *Much Ado About Nothing* (1.1.113–45) and in the numerous rhetorical games between pairs of lovers in *Love's Labor's Lost* (2.1.90–112, 113–27, 179–93; 5.2.203–29, 230–37, 242–55, 339–88).

The call and response of punning matches often serve as a form of rhetorical flirtation, as we have seen in the exchanges just mentioned, but it is not only would-be lovers who engage in this kind of rhetorical improvisation. In *Romeo and Juliet*, to take one of many possible examples, we hear the very same sort of verbal dueling among gang members who vie for supremacy, as in the following playful exchange between Romeo and Mercutio:

> *Mer.* . . . You gave us the counterfeit fairly last night.
> . . .
> *Rom.* Pardon, good Mercutio, my business was great, and in such a case as mine a man may *strain courtesy*.
> *Mer.* That's as much as to say, such a case as yours *constrains* a man to bow in the hams. (*paronomasia*, *asteismus*)
> *Rom.* Meaning to *cur'sy*. (*paronomasia*, *asteismus*)
> *Mer.* Thou hast most kindly hit it.
> *Rom.* A most *courteous* exposition. (*paronomasia*)
> *Mer.* Nay, I am the very *pink* of *courtesy*.
> *Rom.* *Pink* for *flower*. (*antanaclasis*)
> *Mer.* Right.
> *Rom.* Why, then is my *pump* well *flower'd*. (*antanaclasis*)
> *Mer.* Sure wit! Follow me this jest now, till thou hast worn out thy *pump*, that when the *single sole* of it is worn, the jest may remain, after the wearing, *soly singular*. (*antanaclasis*, *paronomasia*)
> *Rom.* O *single-sol'd* jest, *soly singular* for the *singleness*. (*asteismus*, *paronomasia*, *antanaclasis*)
> *Mer* Come between us, good Benvolio, my wits faints.
> *Rom.* Swits and spurs, swits and spurs, or I'll cry a match.
> . . .
> *Mer.* Why, is not this better now than groaning for love? Now *art* thou sociable, now *art* thou Romeo; now *art* thou what thou *art*, by *art* as well as by nature. . . . (*antanaclasis*) (2.4.45, 49–70, 88–91)

In this exchange, Shakespeare demonstrates Romeo's sociability through his willingness to engage in rhetorical improvisation with his friends. Writing of a similar match of wits in a different context, Ingrid Monson emphasizes "the fundamental sociability of improvisation" as a "creative process" and notes that "[o]ne of the chief functions of such verbal exchanges is to sustain the sociability as long as possible. The challenge of the verbal game, as it were, is to keep the interaction at the highest possible pitch of creative intensity."[16] In the male society of *Romeo and Juliet*, social creative intensity often shifts into anti-social physical intensity: being "sociable" in this play means being ready to fight both verbally and physically. Gang members sharpen their wits through competitive wordplay. The *stichomythia*, or quickly paced thrust and parry of Romeo and Mercutio's exchange, captures the combative tone of their street fights. In asking Benvolio to "come between them" Mercutio makes explicit the connection that exists throughout the play between wordplay and swordplay.

When performing a scene such as this one, actors must be able to enter into the spirit of the rhetorical game the characters are playing. Acting coaches, such as Patsy Rodenburg, John Barton, and Cicely Berry, provide exercises and instructions which help Shakespearean actors to meet the demands of such scenes, and the exercises often begin with some form of verbal improvisation.[17] Patsy Rodenburg offers the following advice to actors on how to approach scenes containing extensive wordplay:

> When doing a sequence [like the one above] you must allow yourself to enter a zany world where words, associations and ideas come together with lightning quickness. Forget the intellect when playing comedy like this but go, instead, for the collision of sounds and images. See if you can find a timing or rhythm that suits this exchange.[18]

John Barton refers to lengthy, swift-flowing passages such as that between Romeo and Mercutio as pieces of "ding-dong dialogue where two actors will get lost if they don't go with the rhythm and pick up the cues as Shakespeare wrote them."[19] Responding to actors who had just performed a similarly structured exchange, he writes:

> The verse works there like a rally at tennis. You both served the text up to each other, which is clearly the way it's written. . . . we should be very conscious of the verse in rehearsal but we shouldn't think about it in performance. If you've got it into your system it should then work on your subconscious.[20]

Ian McKellen, one of the actors who worked with Barton in the *Playing Shakespeare* series, agrees with Barton that the goal of extensive textual work in rehearsal is to make the work invisible: "We don't want [the audience], as they're sitting through a play, to be aware of all this work that we've done. We must have absorbed it so that what we are saying is easy to listen to and more understandable and more beautiful and precise."[21] In other words, scripted dialogue should seem to be spontaneous, or, as Barton puts it: "The words must be *found* or *coined* or *fresh-minted* at the moment you utter them. They are not to be thought of as something which pre-exists in a printed text. In the theatre they must seem to find their life for the first time at the moment the actor speaks them."[22]

As noted above, the two types of figures that Shakespeare uses most often to create scenes of seemingly spontaneous improvisation are puns and the figures of repetition. The figures of repetition are among the easiest rhetorical devices to identify, for they involve the repetition of a sound, a word, or a group of words. Among the most common of these devices are *alliteration*, *anaphora* (AB, AC, AD), and *antistrophe* (AB, CB, DB). An improviser whose ear is attuned to these rhetorical riffs can imitate and modulate them at will. An unusually lengthy example of such imitation is found in *The Merchant of Venice* in Portia's response to her new husband's excuse for giving away his wedding ring:

Bass. Sweet Portia,
If you did know to whom I gave the ring,
If you did know for whom I gave the ring,
And would conceive for what I gave the ring,
And how unwillingly I left the ring,
When naught would be accepted but the ring,
You would abate the strength of your displeasure.
Portia. If you had known the virtue of the ring,
Or half her worthiness that gave the ring,
Or your own honor to contain the ring,
You would not then have parted with the ring.
(5.1.192–202)

By stretching Bassanio's *antistrophe* to such a ridiculous length, Portia insures he will never forget the importance of the ring. It is very uncommon for Shakespeare to extend a figure of repetition in this way. In most cases, the echoing of a figure is either much shorter or much more interactive. Cicely Berry helps actors to understand the sort of game being played by Bassanio and Portia when she writes that "[t]he humour and delight we get from the games in there is huge—not sophisticated but very real, like the pleasure children get from nursery rhymes, when the rhyme and the rhythm is part of the satisfaction, and the delight in seeing whether the sense can be made to fit into the scheme"; however, "it is deadly serious, because it is to do with a passion for both."[23]

Another example of metarhetorical echoing is found in *Love's Labor's Lost* as Don Armado gives the boy Moth an impromptu rhetoric lesson. When Moth calls Armado "my tough signior" in response to being called "my tender juvenal," Armado asks him to explain his choice:

Arm. Why tough signior? Why tough signior?
Moth. Why tender juvenal? Why tender juvenal?
Arm. I spoke it tender juvenal as a congreuent *epitheton* appertaining to thy young days, which we may nomiate tender.
Moth. And I tough signior as an appertinent title to your old time, which we may name tough.
Arm. Pretty and apt. (1.2.11–18)

Here we witness a rhetoric lesson of the very sort that Elizabethan schoolchildren experienced daily. Moth demonstrates his skill not only by explaining his choice of *epithet* but also by perfectly imitating the structure of Armado's words through the figure known as *isocolon* (the use of phrases of equal length and corresponding structure).[24] Armado notes Moth's precise imitation and praises him for it.

Countless examples of rhetorical echoing could be given, especially from the early comedies which tend to make heavy use of the figures of repetition. In most cases, however, the echoing is far less self-conscious than it is in the examples just given. In *Comedy of Errors*, for example, Antipholus of Syracuse attempts to comfort his alarmed servant by responding in rhetorical kind to Dromio's series of questions:

S. Dro. Do you know me sir? Am I Dromio?
Am I your man? Am I myself?
S. Ant. Thou art Dromio, thou art my man, thou art thyself.

S. Dro. I am an ass, I am a woman's man, and besides myself.
S. Ant. What woman's man, and how besides thyself?
S. Dro. Marry, sir, besides myself I am due to a woman: one that claims me, one that haunts me, one that will have me.
(3.2.73–83)

The adoption of each other's figures is extreme in this passage for it continues through several lines. More common is the echoing of a figure in a single-lined response, as heard in Dromio of Syracuse's sarcastic mimicry of his twin's calling of the servants:

E. Dro. Maud, Bridget, Marian, Cic'ly, Gillian, Ginn!
S. Dro. Mome, malt-horse, capon, coxcomb, idiot, patch!
(3.1.31–32)

This exchange combines *isocolon* with *meiosis* (which belittles through a trope of a single word). Dromio of Syracuse ridicules his brother here by imitating the rhythms of his speech syllable for syllable. Such rhetorical echoing is not mentioned in the rhetoric manuals, for they treat oration as monologue. In dramatic dialogue, however, one of the noteworthy rhetorical skills of certain speakers is the ability to respond immediately to the rhetoric of others: an ability which should seem spontaneous on stage, but which has clearly been carefully scripted by Shakespeare.

Later in this volume, in "The Improvising Vice in Renaissance England," Klausner considers two anecdotes from *Tarlton's Jests* as possible evidence of Richard Tarlton's "manner and style of unplanned theatrical improvisation." In the context of our examination of Shakespeare's use of puns and figures of repetition, it is worth noting that Tarlton uses those very figures in his response to an audience member who threw an apple at him:

Pip in, or *nose in*, chuse you whether,
Put yours *in*, ere I *put in* the other.
Pippin you have *put in*: then for my grace,
Would I might *put* your *nose in* another place.

In this response, Tarlton relies on the puns *paronomasia* (in which the words repeated are nearly but not precisely alike in sound) and *antanaclasis* (in which a repeated word shifts from one of its meanings to another) to provide the structure for his growing response. In the second of Tarlton's jests quoted by Klausner, Tarlton employs the pun *syllepsis* (the use of a word having simultaneously two meanings, although it is not repeated) on the word "crab," and two figures of repetition: *anadiplosis* (the repetition of a word at the end of one clause and at the beginning of the next) and antithesis (which sets contraries in opposition to give greater perspicuity by contrast).[25]

> Gentlemen, this fellow, with this face of mapple,
> Instead of a pipin, hath thrown me an *apple*,
> But as for an *apple*, he hath cast a *crab*;
> So *instead of an honest woman, God hath sent him a drab*.

Both of these jests use end rhyme: a rhetorical figure listed in Renaissance rhetoric manuals as *homotioteleuton*. Whether or not Tarlton could name the devices he used is irrelevant to his effective employment of them. As Quintilian explained when writing of the changes in nomenclature used for figures, "it makes no difference by which name [a device] is called, so long as its stylistic value is apparent . . . since [the value of rhetorical devices] lies not in their names, but in their effect. . . . [It] is best therefore in dealing with these topics to adopt the generally accepted terms and to understand the actual thing, by whatever name it is called."[26]

Tarlton certainly seemed to understand the value of puns and figures of repetition as improvisational tools that help to provide a structure for extemporaneous remarks. The value of these devices is evident in the frequency with which Shakespeare uses them in scenes involving scripted improvisation. In some scenes the repetition itself is more important than the meaning of the words repeated. One example of meaningless repetition is found in *All's Well That Ends Well*. In act 4, scene 1, several soldiers play a trick on their colleague Paroles, a braggart soldier who is clearly a coward. In the attempt to force him to reveal his cowardice, these soldiers kidnap and blindfold Paroles and then speak in an improvised gibberish in order to convince him he has been captured by the enemy troops. The figures of repetition provide a structure for their invention of meaningless words, and even in gibberish the figures of *epizeuxis* (the repetition of words with none in between), *diacope* (the repetition of a word with one or more between, usually in exclamation), and *epanalepsis* (the repetition of the same word at the beginning and end of a clause) are easily identifiable:

1 Lord. Throca movousus, *cargo, cargo, cargo*. (*epizeuxis*: AAA)
All. *Cargo, cargo, cargo*, villanda par corbo, *cargo*. (*epizeuxis*, *diacope*: AABA)
Par. O, ransom, ransom! Do not hide mine eyes. (*epizeuxis*)
1 Sold. *Boskos* thromuldo *boskos*. (*epanalepsis*: ABA)
(4.1.65–68)

The soldiers in this scene are playing a metarhetorical game, and they find it easier to repeat words than to create a stream of new words in their invented language. In this scene, Shakespeare uses the figures only for their rhythmic and tonal effects, for the words he is repeating have no meaning. As an example of planned improvisation, Klausner refers to the stage direction in Heywood's *If You Know Not Me You Know Nobody*, which reads: "*Here the Queene entertaines the Ambassadors, and in their seueral languages confers with them*," apparently calling, as Alan Somerset has pointed out, for "improvised gibberish."[27] The dialogue from *All's Well* quoted above may well provide a scripted example of the sort of improvised gibberish called for.

Epizeuxis, which is used extensively in this passage, is one of the four figures Henry Peacham links closely with music in *The Garden of Eloquence*. Butler explains:

> Peacham does compare the rhetorical figure *epizeuxis* . . . with a specific musical procedure, that of the quaver or shake. Not only does he draw a clear parallel between two neighbouring notes as the unit within the shake and single words as the unit within the phrase, but between their function and effect when reiterated repeatedly without a break—namely that of a vehement and powerful stress on that particular unit with its attendant powerful impact on the listener. In so doing, he adds a dimension to the concept of the affective function of the shake or gruppo that was held at this time.[28]

In the above dialogue between the soldiers and the blindfolded Paroles, the figures of repetition are used by Shakespeare both to provide a structure for the soldiers' seemingly extemporaneous word-play and to create an appropriately urgent and intimidating tone.

Not all of the figures of response involve the repetition of specific words. One of the figures Shakespeare uses most often in scenes of scripted improvisation is *isocolon* (the use of phrases of equal length and corresponding structure). A few examples from *The Taming of the Shrew* demonstrate the range of effects Shakespeare achieves by creating characters who seem to imitate consciously the structure of the sentences they hear. In the Induction scene, the Second Servingman frequently picks up on the rhythms in his cohort's lines in a seemingly improvised attempt to create a tone of great formality.

> *1 Serv.* Will't please your lordship drink a cup of sack?
> *2 Serv.* Will't please your honor taste of these conserves?
> (Induction 2.2–3)

He does it again a few lines later:

> *3 Serv.* O, this it is that makes your lady mourn.
> *2 Serv.* O, this is it that makes your servants droop.
> (Induction 2.26–27)

Through *anaphora* and *isocolon*, Shakespeare allows the Second Servingman to maintain the tone of obsequious servitude created by his fellows, and demonstrates that this servant is dependent, rhetorically speaking, on his colleagues. In a later scene, however, *isocolon* is used in combination with *symploce* (a combination of *anaphora* and *antistrophe*: ABC, ADC) to assert another servant's independence: Grumio frequently mocks the statements of others by mimicking them in sarcastic asides, as in his mockery of Gremio:

> *Gre.* *O* this learning, what a thing *it is*!
> *Gru.* *O* this woodcock, what an ass *it is*! (1.2.159–60)

Only a few lines later, Grumio uses *isocolon* and *antistrophe* (AB,CB) in his response to Gremio's comments on the fair Bianca:

> *Gre.* Beloved of me, and that my deeds *shall prove*.
> *Gru.* And that his bags *shall prove*. (1.2.176–77)

Grumio does more than just mimic Gremio's structure here: he further demonstrates his cleverness by adding a bawdy pun on the word "bags."

Kate and Petruchio often repeat each other's words as they vie for verbal supremacy. In this play about taming, the figures of repetition are frequently evident as instruments of both defiance and obedience. The shift from one to the other is best seen in act 4, scene 5, in which Kate finally decides to abide by the idiosyncratic rules of Petruchio's rhetorical game. On the way to Baptista's house, Petruchio, testing Kate's obedience, says, "I say it is the moon that shines so bright," to which she responds with a defiant use of *symploce*: "I know it is the sun that shines so bright" (4.5.4–5). Only a few lines later, however, she realizes such defiance will not serve her own turn, and thus she shifts her rhetorical strategy and uses the same figure to express obedience:

Pet. I say it is the moon.
Kath. I know it is the moon. (4.5.16–17)

As is evident in the above examples, Shakespeare frequently and consciously creates characters who seem to imitate and modulate each other's syntactic structures. This form of rhetorical improvisation is uniquely dramatic. Politicians and lawyers are required to respond to the comments of others, but their responses usually take the form of prepared orations delivered as monologues. Only in dialogue can a speaker develop and use the skill of immediate response. The adoption of another speaker's syntactic structures is more than mere mimicry. When writing of the heavy use of repetition in jazz improvisation, Monson explains that such repetition has a social function: it "emphasizes the face-to-face character of the musical [or, here, rhetorical] interaction." She rejects the disparaging comments sometimes made about repetition in jazz improvisation and underscores "the function of repetition in creating a participatory . . . framework against which highly idiosyncratic and innovative improvisation can take place."[29]

Some of Shakespeare's plays contain extended rhetorical improvisation among groups of speakers—rhetorical jam sessions, as it were. After Falstaff's villainies have been exposed in *The Merry Wives of Windsor*, for example, Ford, Evans, Page, and Mistress Page pummel him with a series of insults in the form of *similes*, and the rhythm of their lines comes from *anaphora* and *polysyndeton* (the use of a conjunction between each phrase):

Ford. What, a hodge-pudding? A bag of flax?
Mrs. Page. A puff'd man?
Page. Old, cold, wither'd, and of intolerable entrails?
Ford. And one that is as slanderous as Sathan?
Page. And as poor as Job?
Ford. And as wicked as his wife?
Evans. And given to fornications, and to taverns, and sack, and wine, and metheglins, and to drinkings and swearings and starings, pribbles and prabbles?
Fal. Well, I am your theme. You have the start of me, I am dejected. I am not able to answer the Welsh flannel; ignorance itself is a plummet o'er me. Use me as you will.
(5.5.151–64)

Strictly speaking, only Evans uses *polysyndeton* in this exchange, for only his line includes a series of conjunctions. Since drama is by nature interactive, however, a playwright can continue a rhetorical figure through the lines of several characters and thereby create a figure in dialogue that does not exist in any single speech. In the above exchange, the characters jointly create the figure *polysyndeton*: they clearly enjoy adding to the ever-growing list of Falstaff's faults, and thus they pick up on the structure of each other's insults. In Evans's enthusiasm for this rhetorical game, he gets carried away with *polysyndeton* and continues to list Falstaff's offences even after he has run out of things to add. He resorts to repetition and rhyme and gibberish in order to keep the list growing. In Falstaff's response to the above series of insults, he acknowledges he is the butt of the characters' rhetorical joke, but not without noting the characteristic linguistic ineptitude of Evans. Falstaff's rhetorical skill is evident even as he admits defeat.

Shakespeare's scripted improvisation is not always funny. In some plays Shakespeare creates characters who use rhetorical skill to threaten or intimidate others. One such character is Shylock in *The Merchant of Venice*. On several occasions in the play, characters make a point and Shylock instantly rearranges the point to serve his own purpose, as he does in his first scene with Bassanio. Bassanio urges him to accept Antonio's bond, to which Shylock responds:

Shy. . . . I *think* I *may* take his bond.
Bass. Be *assured* you *may*.

> *Shy.* I will be *assured* I *may*; and that I *may* be *assur'd*, I will *bethink* me. (*antimetabole*: AB, BA)
> (1.3.26–30)

Shylock turns this exchange into a double example of the figure *antimetabole*. By repeating the words "think" and "assured" in converse order, he effectively ignores Bassanio's assurance and takes the conversation back to its starting-point, which is his acknowledgment that he will think about Antonio's offer. In the courtroom scene, he uses a variation of *antimetabole* again in order to twist the meaning of Bassanio's words:

> *Bass.* Do all men kill the things they do not love?
> *Shy.* Hates any man the thing he would not kill?
> (4.1.66–67)

A few lines later, he picks up both the rhythm and the figure in the Duke's words, and by using *isocolon* and a rhetorical question Shylock throws a question back at the Duke and thereby diminishes the power of the Duke's intended point:

> *Duke.* How shalt thou hope for mercy, rend'ring none?
> *Shy.* What judgment shall I dread, doing no wrong?
> (4.1.88–89)

Like several of the other characters I have mentioned, Shylock uses figures of repetition as an improvisational technique, but his ability to twist the meaning of others' words is far more sophisticated than simple mimicry. Shylock is created not only as a good speaker but also as a good listener. He can quickly turn the comments of others to his own advantage, and this skill makes him a feared and forceful adversary.

When we think of Shakespeare's most eloquent speakers, we may think first of his great orators, like Mark Antony or Henry V or Richard III, but some of Shakespeare's most skilled rhetoricians demonstrate their virtuosity in dialogue rather than in monologue. Two characters whom Shakespeare has endowed with a particular gift for interactive rhetoric are Touchstone in *As You Like It* and Feste in *Twelfth Night*. In their jobs as court jesters, these two are professional wordsmiths. Just as some professional musicians "can imitate consecutive patterns with the ease of 'catching a ball and throwing it back',"[30] these jesters can catch and transform the words of others with an ease that several characters explicitly admire. Touchstone is one of the most verbally challenging of Shakespeare's comic characters, for he is skilled in both rhetoric and logic. He is always able and willing to flaunt his linguistic abilities when called upon to do so. In his rhetorical testing of Corin (3.2.52–85), his imitation of Orlando's bad poetry (3.2.100–14), his coining of new terms (3.2.160–62), his rhetorical domination of William (5.1.16–57), and his apt explanation of "the quarrel on the seventh cause" (5.4.68–103), he reveals his mastery of the arts of language. Several characters in the play comment on his skill. Jaques praises Touchstone for railing "on Lady Fortune in good terms, / In good set terms" (2.7.16–17) and admits his delight at meeting a fellow whose brain "hath strange places cramm'd/ With observation" (2.7.40–41). Duke Senior notes that Touchstone is "very swift and sententious" (5.4.62) and later suggests his motley functions as a kind of Trojan horse preventing listeners from protecting themselves from his jibes: "He uses his folly like a stalking-horse, and under the presentation of that he shoots his wit" (5.4.106–07).

It is not enough for an actor playing Touchstone to understand the meaning of single rhetorical terms such as "places" or "sententious"; Touchstone is a paid entertainer, and his words are his wares. His metarhetorical awareness is evident in almost all his scenes. He is a better rhetorician than anyone else in his circle, and he knows it. Others engage him in rhetorical jousting matches for their own pleasure and practice, but they expect him to win, and he always does. For the actor playing Touchstone, as for Touchstone himself, skill in rhetorical improvisation is part of the job description.

Like Touchstone, Feste is a court entertainer who is paid, in part, for his way with words. Viola contemplates the work of court fools when she responds to Feste:

> This fellow is wise enough to play the fool,
> And to do that well craves a kind of wit.
> He must observe their mood on whom he jests,
> The quality of persons, and the time,
> And like the haggard, check at every feather
> That comes before his eye. This is a practice
> As full of labor as a wise man's art. . . .
> (*Twelfth Night* 3.1.60–66)

Several of the skills Viola lists are skills of rhetorical improvisation: students of rhetoric learn that aspiring rhetoricians must develop a quick and able invention, must pay attention to the specific audience being addressed, and must observe the rules of decorum on all occasions. Feste has mastered these skills and more. Viola's comment that a court fool must "check at every feather/ That comes before his eye" is a wonderful description of Feste's metalinguistic sensibility. Always at the rhetorical ready, he picks up words that others let drop, juggles them for his listeners' entertainment, and then gives the words back to the speaker with a twinkle in his eye and an open palm.

Rhetorical improvisation is part of his job, and when he performs well, he gets paid. Indeed, the direct connection between rhetorical skill and payment is more obvious in this play than in Shakespeare's other plays containing jesters. Touchstone and Lear's Fool obviously make their living as court fools, but they never ask for a coin. Feste, on the other hand, seems to have two jobs: he is Olivia's fool, but he also moonlights as a freelance clown who gets paid by the joke or the song (2.3.31, 2.4.67, 3.1.43, 4.1.19, 5.1.35). He is a free-spirited rhetorical entrepreneur who performs for money at the drop of a word.

Feste seems to understand he must live up to the rhetorical expectations placed upon him in his role as fool. In scene after scene he is required to earn his keep, and he does this by singing, by joking, and by acting as a rhetorical jousting partner for those who seek to hone their skills. In act 1, scene 3, Maria easily defeats Sir Andrew in a match of wits, but two scenes later she meets her rhetorical superior in Feste. She says Olivia will hang him for his long absence, and Feste responds to this threat with the tennis-ball rebound of *antanaclasis*, as he sends the word "hang" back to Maria with a spin: "Let her hang me! He that is well hang'd in this world needs to fear no colors" (1.5.5–6).[31] "Make that good," says Maria, and thus, in a single line, Feste establishes himself as a rhetoric tutor. He later praises his capable student for her clever use of *asteismus*: "Apt, in good faith, very apt" (1.5.26)—a compliment very similar to Don Armado's previously quoted praise of his clever student Moth: "Pretty and apt" (*Love's Labor's Lost* 1.2.18).

Feste meets a worthy rhetorical opponent in Viola. They have only one extended conversation in the play, and it is about the reliability of words. Early in their conversation, Feste, who claims he is "not [Olivia's] fool, but her corrupter of words" (3.1.35–36), displays his verbal wares through a clever use of the figure *antimetabole* (AB, BA). Viola responds by using *antimetabole* herself. It is this exchange that sparks their discussion of rhetorical display:

> *Feste.* . . . I do live by the *church*, for I do live at my *house*, and my *house* doth stand by the *church*.
> *Viola.* So thou mayst say the *king* lies by a *beggar,* if a *beggar* dwells near *him*; or the *church* stands by thy *tabor*, if thy *tabor* stand by the *church*.
> *Feste.* You have said, sir. To see this age! A sentence is but a chev'ril glove to a good wit. How quickly the wrong side may be turn'd outward!
> *Viola.* Nay, that's certain. They that dally with words may quickly make them wanton. (3.1.5–15)

The suggestion that fondness for *antimetabole* is characteristic of "this age" is reinforced in John Hoskins's *Directions for Speech and Style* (1599), a rhetoric manual written at approximately the same time as *Twelfth Night*. After defining *antimetabole*, Hoskins warns against the overuse of this fashionable figure when he writes:

> [N]otwithstanding that this is a sharp and witty figure and shows out of the same words a pithy distinction of meaning, very convenient for schoolmen, yet Mr. P. did wrong to tire this poor figure by using it thirty times in one sermon. For use this, or any other point, unseasonably, it is as ridiculous as it was in the fustian oration: horse-mill, mill-horse, etc. But let discretion be the greatest and general figure of figures.[32]

Through Feste, Shakespeare notes the same late sixteenth-century fashion for *antimetabole* that Hoskins acknowledges, but Hoskins's words draw our attention to issues of more significance than any single figure. While sitting at a sermon, Hoskins is able to hear, identify, and evaluate the rhetoric of a speaker who fails to keep audience attention. His rhetorical training shapes his perceptions even when his mouth is shut, and this is worth remembering. Skillful rhetoricians do more than just speak well: they hear well. Rhetorical training, which requires students to be alert to the figures they read and hear, facilitates an active awareness of the structures of language used by others. Here again we find a similarity between rhetoricians and musicians. Monson notes that "nearly every musician who talked to [her] mentioned the importance of listening in good ensemble playing. Listening in an active sense—being able to respond to musical opportunities or to correct mistakes—is implicit in the way that musicians use this term."[33]

Throughout this paper, I have referred to various similarities between jazz improvisation and rhetorical improvisation, and in closing, I would like to emphasize the significance of these similarities. Clearly jazz and rhetoric function in different media, and they come from different continents and different eras, but these two arts provide beginners with fundamentally similar training, and that training enables students to conceptualize sound sequences (be the sounds words or musical notes) at a far more sophisticated level than that of an untrained listener. As mentioned earlier, Elizabethan schoolchildren spent many hours at the repetitive tasks of memorizing the figures of rhetoric, identifying them in the writing and speaking of great masters, and finally using them in their own writing and speaking. These tasks are also accomplished by students of jazz as they develop "the discrete patterns in their repertory storehouses [known] as vocabulary, ideas, licks, tricks, pet patterns, crips, cliches" or even "figures."[34] In *Thinking In Jazz: The Infinite Art of Improvisation*, Paul F. Berliner describes both the practice and the benefits of figure drills:

> There is no objection to musicians borrowing discrete patterns or phrase fragments from other improvisers . . . indeed, it is expected. Many students begin acquiring an expansive collection of improvisational building blocks by extracting those shapes they perceive as discrete components from the larger solos they have already mastered and practising them as independent figures. They acquire others selectively by studying numerous performances of their idols. For some musicians, this is the entire focus of their early learning programs. . . . Whereas analysis of complete solos teaches students about matters of musical development and design, analysis of discrete patterns and melodic cells elucidates the building blocks of improvisations and reveals commonalities among improvisations that are not necessarily apparent in the context of larger performances.[35]

Through repetitive drills of figure identification and imitation, students improve their memory and their listening sophistication. As Berliner explains:

> Initially, youngsters are satisfied to anticipate the proper sequence of figures and approximate their phrasing, but as they gain greater confidence, they listen more intently to the recording artist, playing and regulating their parts accordingly. With practice, musicians come to penetrate more deeply into the solo, hearing the music as if their ears had developed greater powers. An illusory transformation occurs: the solo seems to ensue more slowly, presenting, paradoxically, ever finer yet enlarged details.[36]

Such training helps students to develop "the strong and flexible aurality that the jazz world expects of its accomplished artists," and gathering a "storehouse" of figures provides improvisers with "options that facilitate fluid thinking under the pressures of performance."[37]

Sixteenth-century rhetorical training has far more in common with twentieth-century musical training than with twentieth-century language training. Rote memory of the sort described above is shunned in most language classrooms, and students no longer learn figures like *isocolon* or *antimetabole*. By becoming aware of these structures, however, we increase our ability to hear. Through his creation of skilled speakers such as Feste, Touchstone, or Shylock, Shakespeare provides us opportunities to witness "strong and flexible aurality" at work in conversation.[38] These characters demonstrate their rhetorical sophistication, in part, by the speed with which they can turn the words of others to their own advantage. As we learn to hear the structures that their creator was able to hear, "an illusory transformation occurs" and his words become music to our ears.

NOTES

[1]As Brian Vickers notes, "The principle of learning the figures is solemnly recorded in a host of school statutes—St. Paul's, Ipswich, Eton, Canterbury (Marlowe's school), Bury St. Edmunds, Aldenham and many more" (*Classical Rhetoric in English Poetry* [London: Macmillan, 1970], 49).

[2]Cicero, *Brutus*, trans. G. L. Hendrickson, Loeb Classical Library (Cam-

bridge: Harvard University Press, 1939), 37.

[3]William Kempe, *The Education of Children in Learning* (London, 1588); as quoted in T. W. Baldwin, *William Shakespeare's Small Latine and Lesse Greeke*, 2 vols. (Urbana: University of Illinois Press, 1944), 2:1.

[4]For the most comprehensive study of Shakespeare's rhetorical education, see ibid., esp. the section entitled "The Rhetorical Training of Shakespeare" (2:69–238).

[5]Quintilian, *Institutio Oratoria*, trans. H. E. Butler, 4 vols., Loeb Classical Library (Cambridge: Harvard University Press, 1920–22), IX.i.17.

[6]All figure definitions in this study are from Sister Miriam Joseph's *Shakespeare's Use of the Arts of Language* (New York: Columbia University Press, 1947); she, in turn, took many of her definitions directly from Peacham or Puttenham. I have added the patterns in letter form (AB, BA) in order to make the essential structures of each device clear and memorable.

[7]Gregory G. Butler, "Music and Rhetoric in Early 17th-Century Sources," *Musical Quarterly* 66 (1980): 53–64.

[8]Henry Peacham, *The Compleat Gentleman* (1622; reprint New York: Da Capo Press, 1968), 103.

[9]Butler ("Music and Rhetoric in Early 17th-Century Sources," 58) concludes that the names of these rhetorical figures were applied to fugal techniques in the second half of the sixteenth century, for they all appear in Thomas Morley's *A Plain and Easy Introduction to Practical Music* (1597).

[10]Rhetoric manuals in English published before Puttenham's *The Arte of English Poesie* (1589) include Leonard Cox's *The Arte or Crafte of Rhethoryke* (c.1530); Richard Sherry's *A Treatise of Schemes and Tropes* (1550); Thomas Wilson's *The Arte of Rhetorique* (1553); Richard Rainolde's *A Booke Called the Foundacion of Rhetorike* (1563); Henry Peacham's *The Garden of Eloquence* (1577, 1593); Dudley Fenner's *The Artes of Logike and Rhetorike* (1584); and Abraham Fraunce's *The Arcadian Rhetorike* (1588).

[11]Richard A. Lanham, *The Motives of Eloquence: Literary Rhetoric in the Renaissance* (New Haven: Yale University Press, 1976), 2–3.

[12]Of all methods used to characterize stylistic devices, the most common is to divide the devices into tropes and figures. The clearest explanation I have read of the difference between a figure/scheme and a trope is Brian Vickers' description: "A trope (or "turn") involves a change or transference of meaning and works on a conceptual level; a figure essentially works on the physical level of the shape or structure of language, and involves the disposition of words in a certain

way. A trope affects the meaning of words; a figure only affects their placing or repetition. (The distinction between trope and figure is analogous to that in music between harmony and rhythm: a trope is like harmony, it exists vertically on various planes, while a figure is like rhythm, it exists horizontally, on one plane only)" (*Classical Rhetoric in English Poetry,* 86).

[13]Joseph, *Shakespeare's Use of the Arts of Language*, 165.

[14]M. M. Mahood, *Shakespeare's Wordplay* (New York: Methuen, 1957), 12. Quotations from Shakespeare's plays are from *The Riverside Shakespeare*, 2nd ed., ed. G. Blakemore Evans (Boston: Houghton Mifflin, 1997). Terms in parentheses that identify the figures and the addition of italics are mine.

[15]Keir Elam, *Shakespeare's Universe of Discourse: Language Games in the Comedies* (Cambridge: Cambridge University Press, 1984), 9.

[16]Ingrid Monson, *Saying Something: Jazz Improvisation and Interaction* (Chicago: University of Chicago Press, 1996), 69, 88.

[17]These three coaches work extensively with Shakespearean actors in the Royal Shakespeare Company and in theater schools. Several of their books are widely used in acting classes: Patsy Rodenburg, *The Need for Words: Voice and the Text* (London: Methuen, 1993); Cicely Berry, *The Actor and his Text* (London: Harrap, 1987); and John Barton, *Playing Shakespeare* (London: Methuen, 1986).

[18]Rodenburg, *The Need for Words*, 133.

[19]Barton, *Playing Shakespeare*, 43.

[20]Ibid., 44.

[21]Ibid., 45.

[22]Ibid., 50.

[23]Berry, *The Actor and his Text*, 126.

[24]*Isocolon* is usually taken to mean "Phrases of equal length and corresponding structure" (Richard A. Lanham, *A Handlist of Rhetorical Terms*, 2nd ed. [Berkeley and Los Angeles: University of California Press, 1991], 93). Some rhetoricians list *isocolon* and parison as two separate figures, while others use the terms *isocolon*, parison, and compar to mean the same thing.

[25]Since antithesis can involve both balanced sentence structure and balanced content, it is sometimes categorized as a figure of repetition and sometimes as a figure of thought. Klausner's source for this quotation is *Tarlton's Jests and News Out of Purgatory*, ed. J. O. Halliwell (London: Shakespeare Society, 1844), 13–14.

[26]Quintilian, *Institutio Oratoria*, IX.i.8–9.

[27]*If You Know Not Me, You Know Nobody*, ed. W. W. Greg, Malone Society Reprints (Oxford: Oxford University Press, 1934/5), l. 1051; as quoted in Klausner's "The Improvising Vice in Renaissance England," below.

[28]Butler, "Music and Rhetoric in Early 17th-Century Sources," 55.

[29]Monson, *Saying Something: Jazz Improvisation and Interaction*, 89.

[30]Paul F. Berliner, *Thinking in Jazz: The Infinite Art of Improvisation* (Chicago: University of Chicago Press, 1994), 96.

[31]The author of *The Arte of English Poesie*, generally believed to be George Puttenham, renamed *antanaclasis* "the Rebound" because a word being bounced back and forth with different meanings is similar to "the tennis-ball which being smitten with the racket rebounds back again" (ed. Gladys Doige Willcock and Alice Walker [Cambridge: Cambridge University Press, 1936], 207). In *Acting Shakespeare* (London: Routledge and Kegan Paul, 1960), Bertram Joseph notes the striking connection between Puttenham's description of *antanaclasis* and the effect of that figure in the repeated use of the word "mock" in Henry V's famous response to the Dauphin's gift of tennis balls (*Henry V* 1.2.259–97). Joseph urges actors playing Henry V to be aware of Puttenham's description, for if an actor clearly understands Henry's rhetorical technique, then this understanding benefits both audience and actor: "while educated members of [an Elizabethan] audience would have an appreciation of technicalities somewhere in their response to a performance, it would not be anything like dominant. And those in the audience who could neither name the figures, not hear them as such, would still respond to the actor's expression through them of the character's emotion and purpose. . . . The superficial details of poetic technique reveal fundamental truths of character, helping the actor to achieve his objective" (*Acting Shakespeare*, 5–6).

[32]John Hoskins, *Directions for Speech and Style*, ed. Hoyt Hudson (Princeton: Princeton University Press, 1935), 15.

[33]Monson, *Saying Something: Jazz Improvisation and Interaction*, 84.

[34]Berliner, *Thinking in Jazz*, 102. Some melodic and rhetorical figures have identical structures. Berliner explains that "some blues pieces comprise a single repeating figure or simple phrases based on AA'B melodic prototype. . . . More elaborate pieces rely on ABAC or AABA melodic prototypes" (66). In rhetoric, ABAC is the figure *anaphora* (*I* came, *I* saw, *I* conquered) while AABA is the figure *diacope* (*A horse! A horse!* My kingdom for *a horse!*).

[35]Ibid., 101.

[36] Ibid., 96.

[37]Ibid., 111, 114.

[38]For a fuller examination of Portia and Shylock's rhetoric, see Jane Freeman, "Fair Terms and a Villain's Mind: Rhetorical Patterns in *The Merchant of Venice*," *Rhetorica* 20 (2002): 149–72.

The Improvising Vice in Renaissance England

David N. Klausner

Any discussion of dramatic improvisation in the theater of sixteenth-century England will normally begin with a citation of the mode's most influential critic and his advice to the players: "let those that play your clowns speak no more than is set down for them" (3.2.38–40). I will want to return to this passage in more detail a bit later, but let us note for the moment that it has elicited a wide range of interpretations. If, for example, we believe that Shakespeare is here voicing his own opinions through Hamlet's mouth, we will read the passage in a manner very different from that to which we would be led by the belief that Hamlet is to be seen here as the overwrought and not very experienced theater director attempting to micro-manage his troupe for a very specific effect which he feels may be lost by the slightest deviation from his script. The only thing we can take from the passage unequivocally is that it would make no sense to the audience unless such improvisation were, in fact, common.

It may also be noticed that in the title of this paper, I use the word "vice," whereas Shakespeare's injunction is directed at the "clown." I will use the two words as if they were virtually the same, distinguished primarily by period. The Vice of the moral interludes was a ubiquitous figure on the English stage from *The Castle of Perseverance* at the beginning of the fifteenth century through at least the 1580s. The clowns in the plays of Shakespeare and his contemporaries are among the immediate progeny of these Vice figures, both of them distinguished by what Bernard Spivack called "[t]his histrionic intimacy of the Vice with his audience," though these later manifestations often lack the Vice's moral ambiguity and his puppet-master control of the action—aspects of the figure which are taken over by such characters as Iago.[1] The comic aspects of the Vice and his kinship with fools, clowns, and jesters were clearly recognized by his contemporaries; Spivack lists a wide variety of such sources, including Phillip Stubbes's dyspeptic comment, "For who wil call him a wiseman, that plaieth the part of a foole and a vice?"[2] So Touchstone, the clown of *Twelfth Night*, invokes his own lineage in the song with which he torments the imprisoned Malvolio, "Like to the old Vice, / Your need to sustain" (4.2.124–25). Though our evidence is often limited, we will also see that both the style of the moral interludes and their characters, including the controlling Vice, appear to have persisted considerably longer in the provinces, outside of the ever-changing theatrical world of London.

Rather than proceeding chronologically, I intend to consider some of the modes of improvisation for which we have clear evidence and to concentrate on the later sixteenth and early seventeenth centuries, though reference will be made to earlier plays. Before turning to forms of improvisation, however, I want to look briefly at the question of direct address to the audience, a characteristic of the plays of both the Middle Ages and Renaissance which has often been misinterpreted. For a previous generation of critics it was common to see direct address as "extradramatic," as "a stepping out of the world of make-believe into that of reality."[3] This can now be seen as a gross over-simplification of a device which both implies and provokes a considerable range of relationships between actor and audience. Consider, for example, Cain's tithing speech in the Towneley *Mactacio Abel*, in which he complains directly to his rural or semi-rural audience about having to give up a tenth of his produce to a God who does not seem to be very interested in the *quid pro quo*, good weather and a bountiful harvest.[4] Cain's address to his audience is in no way a stepping outside the play, but a drawing of the members of the audience into it, a very effective device to elicit their sympathy and thus their complicity in the murder of Abel which follows inexorably from his complaints. Similarly in the Towneley *Processus Noe*, Noah speaks directly to the audience about his marital woes in a passage which draws them into the play rather than stepping out of it.

> Yee men that has wifys,
> Whyls thay ar yong,
> If ye louf youre lifys,
> Chastice thare tong.[5]

Joseph's plaint to the men in the audience in the Coventry Nativity pageant of the Shearmen and Taylors strikes a very similar note.[6]

This mode of direct address, in which the audience is brought further into the world of the play, continues through the period. Later examples might include the repentance of Penitent Brothel in act 4, scene 4 of Thomas Middleton's *A Mad World, My Masters* who asks the audience to bear witness that he'll never embrace his paramour again.[7] I would suggest that direct address to the audience is generally throughout the period a mode of drawing the audience into the action rather than the actor's stepping out of it. The exceptions, of course, are prologues and epilogues, in which the actor steps outside the play to comment on it. Puck's final speech of *A Midsummer Night's Dream* would be a good example. This brief excursus on direct address to the audience has been necessary because, as we will see, direct address and improvisation often overlap.

We can divide the modes of improvisation in Renaissance theater into two: those planned by the playwright, and those unplanned. Planned improvisation was a staple of the period. The *locus classicus* on the continent was, of course, the Italian *commedia dell'arte*, in which actors improvised the whole play around a basic scenario. The evidence for knowledge of *commedia* and use of its techniques in England, however, is very slim. Polonius's description of the players has occasionally been taken as evidence of an understanding of *commedia* techniques: "For the law of writ and the liberty, these are the only men" (*Hamlet* 2.2.401–02), in which "the law of writ" would be taken as scripted plays and "the liberty" as an improvised mode like *commedia*. There are, however, other ways to read the passage, and while Polonius might well be referring to scripted and unscripted playing, there is still little reason to link this with the Italian style. It seems, in fact, unlikely that England, in contrast to France, played host to Italian players in any number.

The English plays are, however, full of planned improvisation. This is most commonly set up in one of two ways. First, the improvisation may be indicated in a stage direction. Thus in John Cooke's play *Greene's Tu Quoque* (1611), a scene between a wooer and his uncooperative lady degenerates into unscripted banter:

W. Rash. When will your tongue be weary?
Joyce. Never.

W. Rash.	How! never? Come, talk, and I'll talk with you: I'll try the nimble footmanship of your tongue; And if you can out-talk me, yours be the victory. *Here they two talk and rail what they list.*[8]

In the Induction to Ben Jonson's *Cynthia's Revels* (1601), the actors are similarly expected to improvise: "*At the breaches in this speech following, the other two interrupt him, still.*"[9] A particularly interesting example of planned improvisation occurs in the second part of Heywood's *If You Know Not Me You Know Nobody* (1605), in which the following stage direction occurs: "*Here the Queene entertaines the Ambassadors, and in their seueral languages confers with them,*" apparently calling, as Alan Somerset has pointed out, for "improvised gibberish."[10] Prepared improvisation by the Vice appears in Thomas Lupton's *All for Money*: "*Here the vyce shal turne the proclamation to some contrary sence everie time all for money hath read it, and here followeth the proclamation.*"[11] The Vice's reversal of the proclamation's meaning also appears in scripted versions in Garcio's parodying of Cain's "crying of the peace" in the Towneley *Mactacio Abel* as well as in Ulpian Fulwell's *Like Will to Like*, as Nichol Newfangle distorts the praise which Lucifer directs him to say:

Luc.	All haile, Oh noble prince of hel.
New.	All my dames cow tailes fel down into the wel.
Luc.	I wil exalt thee above the clowdes.
New.	I wil sault thee, and hang thee in the shrowdes.
Luc.	Thou art the inhauncer of my renowne.
New.	Thou art Haunce, the hangman of Callis town.
Luc.	To thee be honour alone.
New.	To thee shall come our hobling Jone.
Luc.	Amen.
New.	Amen.[12]

More common, however, as an indication that the playwright intends the actors to improvise is the speech which ends with an "etcetera." As Alan Somerset has pointed out, many of the occurrences of "etc." in later plays are in passages of oaths or potential obscenity and may represent a form of censorship for the printed text, in which the actor is expected to have a clear understanding of what he can get away with at a particular time and place.[13] Thus in the anonymous *The Pilgrimage to Parnassus* (1599) Philomusus swears, "I faith &c," while in Robert Armin's *The Two Maids of Moreclacke* (1609) Sir William warns his father of his mother's adultery: ". . . if you wil see my mother & your wife, fellow'd in bed make haste, / *Iames* your man writes on your pillow &c."[14] In *The Fair Maid of the Exchange* (1602), possibly by Thomas Heywood, one of the lovers describes his lady's beauty: ". . . her forehead is pretty, somewhat resembling the forehead of the sign of the maidenhead in &c."[15] It is quite possible that this was intended as an opportunity for the actor to insert an appropriate local reference.

There are, of course, cases in which the actor was actually expected to say "et cetera," but I suspect these are considerably fewer than occur in modern productions. Take, for example, Mercutio's comments to Benvolio on Romeo's new-found love as printed in the first and fourth quartos:

> If love be blind, love cannot hit the mark.
> Now he will sit under a medlar tree
> And wish his mistress were that kind of fruit
> As maids call medlars, when they laugh alone.
> O, Romeo, that she were, O, that she were
> An open et cetera, thou a pop'rin pear!
> (2.1.33–38)

So in the A-text of *Doctor Faustus*, Robin says, "I a goblet *Rafe*, I a goblet? I scorne you: and you are but an &c.,"[16] and in *Wily Beguiled* (1602) the Nurse says, "Out you rogue! you arrant &c.,"[17] or the entry of the devil's in Ben Jonson's *The Devil is an Ass* (1616): "Hoh hoh hoh &c."[18]

Having cited the allegedly "bad" 1604 quarto of *Doctor Faustus*, let me note a potential source for further evidence of improvisation, here most likely unplanned by the playwright. When both a "bad" and a "good" text of a play survive, and the source of the bad text seems to lie in memorial reconstruction, some of its variations from the "good" text may be due to improvisatory aspects of a particular performance. Since "bad" and "good" are often subjective judgments, there are relatively few playtexts which fit these criteria, but *Hamlet* is definitely one of them. The differences between the "bad" quarto of 1603 and the second quarto of a year later are obvious, and although the theory that the earlier printing is a result of memorial reconstruction is still being debated almost sixty years after it was first proposed, it has nonetheless achieved wide acceptance.[19] Many of the differences of a memorial reconstruction may, of course, be attributed to flawed memory, but some may derive from improvisations in a particular performance or production which may well not have been sanctioned by the playwright.

Somerset notes the irony that in the first quarto, which as a whole is just over half the length of the second quarto, Hamlet's directions to the players are over twice as long as in the later text.[20] I would like to look at these two speeches in detail, since I think that the longer one may well represent a not very successful attempt at improvisation. In the "good" quarto, Hamlet says:

> . . . let those that play your clowns speak no more than is set down for them, for there be of them that will themselves laugh to set on some quantity of barren spectators to laugh too, though in the mean time some necessary question of the play be then to be consider'd. That's villainous, and shows a most pitiful ambition in the fool that uses it. Go make you ready. (3.2.38–45)

Now the sense of this speech is crystal clear; the clown is not to insert a joke for the benefit of the audience so as not to interrupt the course of the action of the play. The "bad" quarto elaborates this simple statement with a series of examples inserted between the last two clauses.

> . . . let not your Clowne speake
> More then is set downe, there be of them I can tell you
> That will laugh themselues, to set on some
> Quantitie of barren spectators to laugh with them,
> Albeit there is some necessary point in the Play
> Then to be obserued: O t'is Vile, and shewes
> A pittifull ambition in the foole that vseth it.
> And then you haue some agen, that keepes one sute
> Of ieasts, as a man is knowne by one sute of
> Apparell, and Gentlemen quotes his ieastes downe
> In their tables, before they come to the play, as thus:
> Cannot you stay till I eate my porrige? and, you owe me
> A quarters wages: and, my coate wants a collison:
> And, your beere is sowre: and, blabbering with his lips,
> And thus keeping in his cinkapase of ieasts,

When, God knows, the warme Clowne cannot make a iest
Vnlesse by chance, as the blinde man catcheth a hare:
Maisters tell him of it.

Players: We will my Lord.
Hamlet: Well, goe make you ready.[21]

Here, Hamlet's simple point is buried in exemplification. It could be argued that that was Shakespeare's intention, to provide in this speech an example of what he wanted the players to avoid, but if this is so, the example is overdone and ill-organized, contributing little to the scene and not at all in character with Hamlet's manic preparations for springing his mousetrap. It does in fact provide a striking example of Hamlet's point, but not I think in a way intended by Shakespeare.

Through the period of the great performing companies—that is the thirty years after about 1580—each company's clown developed his own style of improvisation, and it is clear that the techniques of Richard Tarlton, for example, were quite different from those of his successors Will Kemp or Robert Armin. Tarlton in particular has often been cited as a key figure in the transition from Vice to clown; as one critic typically comments, "Tarlton is seen as an innovator, attributed with fusing the Vice with the Clown traditions. . . ."[22] With a few notable exceptions such as Will Summers' part in Thomas Nashe's *Summers Last Will and Testament* (1592), the parts written for (or about) these well-known clowns do not show clear evidence of opportunities provided by the playwrights for improvisation. That is supplied by the elaborate jest-books published by several of them, notably Tarlton and Armin. It is by no means clear that the stories which Tarlton and Armin tell about themselves are fact rather than fiction, nor do all the tales occur in theatrical situations. Nonetheless, for them to have achieved sufficient popularity to run to three editions in less than a decade, as Armin's collection did, they must have reflected the reality of the clown's techniques or at least the audience's perception of them.

Relatively few of the anecdotes in the jest-books give direct illustration of theatrical practice. Armin's *Fool upon Fool* and his *Nest of Ninnies* (as the third printing was called) deal with the variety of fools in the world, and most of them ignore the theater except for several anecdotes which are presented as tales of fools encountered during his tours with Lord Chandos's players. The most relevant to theatrical practice is Armin's story of Jack the clean fool, one of whose turns was to play a fair merchant with a stuttering inability to pronounce the letter 'p' and whose cry could not be more ill-suited to him: "Buy any flawne, pasties, pudding pyes, plumbe pottage, or pescods."[23] Though not part of a formal dramatic presentation, Jack's foolery is called a "play" by Armin and may well show us a possible style of theatrical improvisation.

The vice/clown's penchant for interaction with the members of the audience, for which there is clear evidence in the play-texts, must have created frequent opportunities for improvisatory exchanges with them, and insults to the audience were clearly a common mode. As a scripted example, at his final entrance the cobbler/clown Strumbo in *Locrine* (1591) greets the audience with the following:

> How do you, maisters, how do you? how haue
> you scaped hanging this long time?[24]

This is a none-too-subtle way of noting how long the stage has lacked his presence.[25] It cannot of course be included in the play-text, but it seems to me very likely that upon occasion such a line would elicit a reply from an audience member that would set up an improvisatory exchange.

Tarlton's Jests, first published in 1611, does provide a pair of such anecdotes from the theater among his so-called "sound city jests." Since they involve both unplanned improvisation and direct address to the audience, they are worth examining in some detail. The first is entitled "Tarlton's Jest of a pippin":

> At the Bull in Bishops-gate-street, where the queenes players oftentimes played, Tarlton comming on the stage, one from the gallery threw a pippin at him. Tarlton tooke up the pip, and, looking on it, made this sudden jest: —
>
> Pip in, or nose in, chuse you whether,
> Put yours in, ere I put in the other.
> Pippin you have put in: then, for my grace,
> Would I might put your nose in another place.[26]

Tarlton's improvised quatrain is prompted by heckling from a member of the audience—and in the gallery, we might note, not one of the groundlings. Since Tarlton's jest is about bodily orifices, it would seem to me quite likely that on the third line, "Pippin you have put in," he may well have taken a bite of the pippin.

Tarlton's second anecdote, entitled "A jest of an apple hitting Tarlton on the face," directly follows the first and refers to the same occasion:

> Tarlton having flouted the fellow for his pippin which hee threw, hee thought to be meet with Tarlton at length. So in the play, Tarlton's part was to travell, who, kneeling down to aske his father blessing, the fellow threw an apple at him, which hit him on the cheek. Tarlton taking up the apple, made this jest: —
>
> Gentlemen, this fellow, with this face of mapple,
> Instead of a pipin, hath thrown me an apple,
> But as for an apple, he hath cast a crab;
> So, instead of an honest woman, God hath sent him a drab.
>
> The people laughed heartily, for he had a queene to his wife.[27]

The sense of this improvisation is very much like the first. The only difference is that Tarlton's insult is now directed at the man's wife.

There is, of course, no proof that the anecdotes recorded in these jest-books are fact or fiction, though as examples of the manner and style of unplanned theatrical improvisation that matters little. A strikingly similar story which is unlikely to be fictional is recorded in the commonplace book of Philip Powell, a merchant of Brecon, South Wales.[28] During a trip to Bristol in 1620, Powell attended a play at which the following event took place:

> on Kendal a foole in a stage play in Bristoll being meerie acct-inge the part of the vize, spake extempore as foloweth, in dis-praise of the noble Brittans,
> if thou art a Brittane borne,
> it fitts thee to were ye horne
> Iohn Brittan a prentiz of on Thomas Dean of Bristoll his reply to Kendall:
> twise: as foloweth:
> A Brittans name I truly beare,
> I leaue the horne for thee to were:
> the horne becomes the saxons best
> I kisd thy wife supose the rest:[29]

A marginal note defines the event: "Kendall the Saxon put to silence:" Here the interchange between the audience member and the vice/clown is verbal, not physical. It is words which are thrown, not apples, and the exchange is initiated by the actor, not the audience member. Kendall is called Vice and fool, rather than clown. It is not clear whether this means that the play being performed was a late survival of the moral interlude tradition of the previous century, but it does alert us to be aware that the theatrical situation in London is not at all applicable to the provinces, where earlier traditions persisted for a considerable period of time. It is also important to note that the Vice's improvisation, like Tarlton's, is in verse. In fact, I think the importance of the story for Powell is that the apprentice could beat Kendall at his own game by replying in improvised couplets as good or better than Kendall's. Verse is an almost universal feature of the unplanned improvisations which survive; I have found no clear evidence for improvisation in prose outside of planned situations in which the actors are directed to improvise by the playwright such as the stage direction to Guido in Marston's *The Insaciate Countess* (1610): "*Tell him all the plot*," where Guido is unlikely to summarize the plot in verse.[30]

Such a situation as the Bristol play in which the vice/clown is bested by a member of the audience (assuming that Powell has given us the full story) must have been rare. More common would have been the sort of escalating interchange described in "How Tarlton and one in the gallery fell out":

> It chanced that in the midst of a play, after long expectation for Tarlton, being much desired of the people, at length hee came forth, where, at his entrance, one in the gallerie pointed his finger at him, saying to a friend that had never seene him, that is he. Tarlton to make sport at the least occasion given him, and seeing the man point with the finger, he in love againe held up two fingers. The captious fellow, jealous of his wife, for he was married, and because a player did it, took the matter more hainously, and asked him why he made hornes at him. No, quoth Tarlton, they be fingers:
>
> For there is no man, which in love for me,
> Lends me one finger, but he shall have three.
>
> No, no, sayes the fellow, you gave me the hornes. True, sayes

> Tarlton, for my fingers are tipt with nailes, which are like hornes, and I must make a shew of that which you are sure of. This matter grew so, that the more he meddled the more it was for his disgrace; wherefore the standers by counselled him to depart, both hee and his hornes, lest his cause grew desperate. So the poore fellow, plucking his hat over his eyes, went his wayes.[31]

Though the sample here is necessarily small, it would seem quite likely that improvisatory insults to the audience tended to revolve around generalized accusations of cuckoldry.

Improvisation in the English theater, then, can be divided into two types, improvisation intended by the playwright, which I have called planned improvisation, and improvisation not intended by the playwright, or unplanned improvisation. The evidence for planned improvisation rests entirely in the playtexts, and although in most cases its content is reasonably clear, we cannot by its very nature recover its exact form and style. From the surviving stage directions it seems most likely that such improvised passages were prose rather than verse, and it is also clear that planned improvisation was not influenced in any significant way by the Italian *commedia* tradition. Evidence for unplanned improvisation, the sort to which Hamlet objects, is entirely anecdotal, but fortunately a few examples do survive, and they suggest that, in sharp contrast to planned improvisation, unplanned improvisation was frequently in verse, often involving exchanges with the audience which had nothing to do with the play. Since our anecdotal evidence is very limited, we can only view through a small window what must have been a common and widespread aspect of renaissance English professional theater.

NOTES

Quotations from Shakespeare's plays in this article are from *The Riverside Shakespeare*, 2nd ed., ed. G. Blakemore Evans (Boston: Houghton Mifflin, 1998), unless otherwise stated.

[1]Bernard Spivack, *Shakespeare and the Allegory of Evil* (New York: Columbia University Press, 1958), 192. Robert Weimann notes that the "clown and fool of Renaissance drama" combines "elements of the morality Vice and the outmoded court fool" (*Shakespeare and the Popular Tradition in the Theater* [Baltimore: Johns Hopkins University Press, 1978], 186–87).

[2]Phillip Stubbes, *Anatomie of Abuses*, ed. F. J. Furnivall (London, 1877–79), 146; as quoted in Spivack, *Shakespeare and the Allegory of Evil*, 199–205.

[3]Doris Fenton, *The Extradramatic Moment in Elizabethan Plays before 1616* (Philadelphia: University of Pennsylvania Press, 1930), 8.

[4]*The Towneley Plays*, ed. Martin Stevens and Arthur C. Cawley, EETS s.s.13–14 (Oxford: Oxford University Press, 1994), 1:17–18 (ll. 184–223).

[5]Ibid., 1:41 (ll. 573–76).

[6]*The Coventry Corpus Christi Plays*, ed. Pamela M. King and Clifford Davidson, Early Drama, Art, and Music Monograph Series 27 (Kalamazoo: Medieval Institute Publications, 2000), 87 (ll. 126–28).

[7]Thomas Middleton, *A Mad World, My Masters* (1606), ed. Standish Henning (Lincoln: University of Nebraska Press, 1965), 75–76.

[8]*Select Collection of Old English Plays*, ed. W. C. Hazlitt, 15 vols. (London, 1874–76), 11:255.

[9]Ben Jonson, *Works*, ed. C. H. Herford and Percy Simpson, 11 vols. (Oxford: Clarendon Press, 1925–63), 4:36.

[10]*If You Know Not Me, You Know Nobody*, ed. W. W. Greg, Malone Society Reprints (Oxford: Oxford University Press, 1934/5), l. 1051; J. A. B. Somerset, "The Comic Turn in English Drama, 1470–1616" (Ph.D. diss., University of Birmingham, 1966), 468. I would like to express my gratitude to Professor Somerset for giving me access to the wealth of material in his dissertation.

[11]Thomas Lupton, *All for Money* (London: Tudor Facsimile Texts, 1910), l. 1008.

[12]*Towneley Plays,* 1:23–24 (ll. 418–41); *Tudor Interludes,* ed. Peter Happé (Harmondsworth: Penguin, 1972), 329 (ll. 206–15).

[13]Somerset, "The Comic Turn," 806.

[14]*The Three Parnassus Plays, 1598–1601*, ed. J. B. Leishman (London: Nicholson and Watson, 1949), 116; Robert Armin, *An Old-Spelling Critical Edition of "The History of the Two Maids of More-clacke*," ed. Alexander S. Liddie (New York: Garland, 1979), 159 (ll. 72–74).

[15]*The Fair Maid of the Exchange*, ed. W. W. Greg, Malone Society Reprints (Oxford: Oxford University Press, 1962/3), ll. 491–92.

[16]W. W. Greg, ed., *Marlowe's Doctor Faustus, 1604–1616* (Oxford: Oxford University Press, 1950), 234 (ll. 995–96).

[17]*Wily Beguiled*, ed. W. W. Greg, Malone Society Reprints (Oxford: Oxford University Press, 1912), l. 592.

[18]Jonson, *Works*, ed. Herford and Simpson, 6:164.

[19]G. I. Duthie, *The 'Bad' Quarto of Hamlet* (Cambridge: Cambridge University Press, 1941).

[20]Somerset, "The Comic Turn," 448.

[21]William Shakespeare, *Hamlet*, ed. H. H. Furness, The Variorum Shakespeare, 2 vols. (Philadelphia: Lippincott, 1877), 2:64–65.

[22]David Mann, *The Elizabethan Player* (London: Routledge, 1991), 62; discussing Weimann, *Shakespeare and the Popular Tradition*, 185ff.

[23]*A Shakespeare Jestbook, Robert Armin's "Fool upon Foole" (1600): A Critical, Old-spelling Edition*, ed. H. F. Lippincott (Salzburg: Institut für Englische Sprache und Literatur, 1973), 115–16.

[24]*The Shakespeare Apocrypha*, ed. C. F. T. Brooke (Oxford: Oxford University Press, 1908), 57.

[25] Somerset, "The Comic Turn," 510.

[26]*Tarlton's Jests and News Out of Purgatory*, ed. J. O. Halliwell (London: Shakespeare Society, 1844), 13–14.

[27]Ibid., 14.

[28]Cardiff County Library, MS. 3.42, p. 139.

[29]*Records of Early English Drama: Bristol*, ed. Mark C. Pilkinton (Toronto: University of Toronto Press, 1997), 215.

[30]John Marston, *The Insaciate Countess*, ed. Giorgio Melchiori (Manchester: Manchester University Press, 1984), 162.

[31]*Tarlton's Jests*, 14–15.

ART

Improvisation in the Visual Arts: The View from Sixteenth-Century Italy

Leslie Korrick

In the visual arts, the concept of improvisation is primarily associated with twentieth-century Modernist production. For many, the word itself immediately calls to mind the early experiments toward non-representational painting of Wassily Kandinsky, who used it to title images representing what he called in 1911 a "hauptsächlich unbewußte, größtenteils plötzlich entstandene Ausdrücke der Vorgänge inneren Charakters" ("largely unconscious, spontaneous expression of inner character").[1] As a working method, improvisation was adopted and subsequently exploited by Surrealist image-makers whose "[a]utomatisme psychique" ("psychic automatism") of the later 1920s and 1930s was both inspired and justified by Sigmund Freud's psychoanalytic research at the turn of the century.[2] Within this stream of development, the act of improvisation was preserved and glorified through the now canonical black and white photographs by Hans Namuth of Abstract Expressionist painter Jackson Pollock at work in his East Hampton studio in 1950 and the short color film of Pollock in action released the following year.[3] Improvisatory activity has also informed Modernist performance art, from the stage events of 1916 at the Dada Cabaret Voltaire in Zurich to the Neo-Dada intermedia presentations of Fluxus which began in 1962 chiefly inspired by the chance operations of John Cage.[4] On the basis of these and other projects, Modernist definitions of improvisation are typically characterized by a belief in the simultaneous conception and manifestation of a given work which is rendered quickly, impulsively, and with a concomitant freedom of expression. In addition, they tend to link improvisation to novel working methods and forms which challenge traditional conventions of making, viewing, and evaluation.

Because so many of the positions on art and artistic identity allied with Modernism find their origins in the Renaissance—and, particularly, in sixteenth-century Italy—we might expect to find evidence of a vibrant tradition of artistic improvisation, and even a parallel definition, in the images and texts of the Cinquecento. Certainly the concept and the term were known within contemporary artistic circles, as documented in Giorgio Vasari's *Le vite de' più eccellenti pittori scultori ed architettori* (*Lives of the Most Excellent Painters, Sculptors, and Architects*), a hefty compendium of biographies of selected Italian artists working from the late Middle Ages to the author's own day. First published in Florence in 1550 and again in a revised and expanded version in 1568, the *Vite* established Vasari as a powerful authority on and apologist for central Italian visual culture at mid-century. In its codification of art theory and practice during the first half of the century and its prescience on those matters which would come to be important in the decades which followed, the work serves as a reliable barometer of the dominant artistic ideology in this region across much of the Cinquecento. In his biography of Leonardo da Vinci, for example, Vasari twice relates that this artist was experienced and successful in improvisation. In the first instance, Leonardo's ability to perform extemporaneously is featured with respect to his musical ability and especially his playing of the *lira da braccio* (lyre), an instrument intimately connected to the practice of improvisation during the Renaissance. "Dette alquanto d'opera alla musica," Vasari tells his reader, "ma tosto si risolvé a imparare a sonare la lira, come quello che da la natura aveva spirito elevatissimo e pieno di leggiadria, onde sopra quella cantò divinamente all'improviso" ("He gave some little attention to music, and quickly resolved to learn to play the lyre, as one who had by nature a spirit most lofty and full of refinement: wherefore he sang divinely to that instrument, improvising upon it"). Subsquently, he recounts with even greater enthusiasm that when it came to the recitation of *rime* (rhymes), Leonardo was "il migliore . . . a l'improviso del tempo suo" ("the best improvisor . . . of his day").[5] But Vasari never takes up the theme of improvisation in discussions of Leonardo's practice of the visual arts or, for that matter, the practice of any other artist included in the *Vite*. As he makes clear in his lives of the architect Bramante, the sculptor Silvio Cosini, and the painter Timoteo da Urbino, the ability to improvise is a praiseworthy skill which is virtually exclusive to musical performance. Like Leonardo, Bramante and Timoteo improvised on the *lira da braccio*, while Cosini sung extemporaneously.[6]

What accounts for Vasari's reluctance to extend his remarks on improvisation from the realm of the aural to that of the visual? It is too easy to assume that Leonardo and his contemporaries simply did not improvise images; as I will demonstrate, there is evidence to the contrary. To be sure, the mere absence of evidence would not have deterred Vasari had he thought it profitable to connect it to their endeavor given that the employment of formulaic *topoi* is standard in his biographical writing regardless of their relationship to the facts of the subject's life and work.[7] Besides, the humanist penchant for analogy made the transfer of a specific characteristic or working method from one discipline to the next possible and plausible. Under these circumstances, Vasari's lack of reference to artistic improvisation appears to be meaningful as does the fact that he is not alone in his silence. Among Cinquecento writers of art history and theory, only the priest-painter Giovanni Battista Armenini takes up the problem of improvisation in the visual arts; his exceptional remarks are contained in his treatise *De' veri precetti della pittura* (*On the True Precepts of the Art of Painting*), published in Ravenna in 1586. Oriented toward Rome and written as a practical guidebook for artists as well as a lament on the alleged decline of later sixteenth-century Italian painting, Armenini's text offers a richly layered yet ambivalent review of the improvisatory act for those who painted. It is, moreover, a review which is formulated without reference to music even though Armenini occasionally joins painting and music for other purposes in the treatise.[8] Using *De' veri precetti della pittura* as a guide, I want to explore the definition and implications of improvisation in sixteenth-century Italy, consider its benefits and drawbacks for artists and their audiences, and suggest reasons why it could not be embraced wholeheartedly within artistic circles of the period.

Armenini's consideration of improvisation occurs largely in book 1, chapter 9, of his treatise which is devoted to his exposition on *invenzione* (invention), the process by which an artist researches the subject to be depicted and then begins to conceive of it visually.[9]

With his hallmark pessimism intact, he opens the chapter by proposing to outline those *diffetti* (defects) which keep the artist from becoming a *bello inventore* (fine inventor) and initiates the discussion by highlighting the frequent lack of accord between the *verità* (truth) of a given narrative, contained in what he describes as *buone scritture* (good writings), and the image he renders. According to Armenini, this disjuncture is at least in part the result of improvisation by such artists:

> [I]nvaghitosi d'un suo inusitato capriccio, per farsi tener di primo tratto inventori maravigliosi e prattichevoli maestri, pigliaranno un piombino overo una penna all'improviso, e quivi di molte figure cominciaranno a ingarbugliare insieme. E ciò fanno con molta facilità e prestezza, dove che per diversi modi e con sfoggiate attitudini li pongono diversissime stravaganzie, né restano fin a tanto che tutto lo spazio sia pieno con infinite linee e per fine poi si discopre e comparisce di stranissime forme d'uomini e di cose ripieno, il qual componimento, come poi si trovi essere dalla composizione ch'essi tentano e dal soggetto lontano, non è da pensarvi.
>
> (Driven by some capricious fancy and wishing to be considered marvelous . . . inventors and experienced masters, they suddenly pick up pen or pencil and begin to draw many figures all tangled together. This they do with so much facility and quickness that they put down the most eccentric figures in diverse attitudes and pompous postures. They do not rest until all the space is filled with countless lines. When the work is displayed in the end, it abounds in the strangest forms of men and things, and one cannot imagine how far removed it is from the subject they are treating and from the composition they were striving for.)[10]

In other words, the artist's proclivity for improvisation leads to poor *invenzione* because he is galvanized by his own unlicenced mark-making rather than by an authoritative text, and consequently the improvisatory act inhibits him from keeping the subject of his *invenzione* sharply focused in his mind's eye.[11]

On first reading, Armenini's skeptical view of improvisation might be said to reflect a knowledge of and adherence to the prevailing taste among Catholic reformers for visual intelligibility (that is, a clear, well ordered composition) and historical accuracy (allegiance to Church-authorized texts) during the last years of the Council of Trent, especially as it was codified in the treatise of the theologian Giovanni Andrea Gilio da Fabriano, the *Due dialogi . . . degli errori de'pittori* (*Two Dialogues . . . on the Errors of Painters*), published in Camerino in 1564.[12] But Armenini's skepticism was equally colored by the widespread contemporary alliance of the improvisatory act with *prestezza* (speed of execution)—a skepticism which would be recorded in first edition of the authoritative *Vocabolario degli Accademici della Crusca* (*Dictionary of the Accademia della Crusca*), published in Venice in 1612. Based on an example of usage excerpted from Pietro de' Crescenzio's *Trattato dell'agricoltura* (*Treatise on Argriculture*), a Trecento Italian translation of his *Opus ruralium commodorum* written between 1304 and 1309, improvisation has the connotation of acting "subito, cioè senza pensare, o premeditare" ("quickly, namely without thinking or premeditation").[13] Armenini, subscribing to the spirit of this definition, employs the phrase *all'improvviso* as a synonym for working speedily—both in the passage on wayward inventors and again shortly thereafter when he contrasts working *all'improvviso* with a mode of working which occurs *con tempo* (over time, or slowly).[14] But since working speedily was a highly controversial mode of artistic production during the Cinquecento, it was often perceived in a negative light, and this perception is reflected in Armenini's treatise.[15] As he indicates in this section, there are times when rapid rendering might be tolerated, as when decorating temporary structures built to stage royal entries and weddings, feasts, plays, pageants, and the like, for these must be executed on a tight schedule and are intended to last for only a short period of time. Later in the treatise he advocates working with *prestezza* when drawing from the live model who can hold a pose for only so long or when painting with the quick-drying medium of fresco. However, all of these circumstances relate to the process of completing a work rather than establishing the *invenzione*, which is Armenini's main concern in the chapter encompassing improvisation. More significantly, he maintains that works "far cosí presto et all'improvviso" ("executed quickly and through improvisation") may well lead to artistic impoverishment—or what he calls a demonstration of "la pazzia e goffezza" ("madness and clumsiness")—and cannot bring honor to the artist. In this atmosphere, quantity detrimentally takes precedence over quality, and accordingly Armenini advises the artist to leaven "la pazzia del troppo ardire" ("the folly of too much daring") ordinarily seen in the production of those who work quickly.[16] Yet because improvisation by definition requires *prestezza*, we can only assume that this leavening will preclude improvisatory action.

Having unequivocally rejected improvisation as a means of initiating an *invenzione*, Armenini nonetheless proposes that it is a useful studio technique to generate an appropriate composition through which the *invenzione* will be communicated. In this instance, improvisation provides the artist with a mode of working which compensates for what Armenini describes as his inability to conceive of a fully formed or well ordered *invenzione* since it allows him to transfer a variety of compositional possibilities from his imagination to paper "in un tempo brevissimo" ("in a very short time").[17] From these *primi pensieri* (first thoughts), he develops the final composition which will ultimately be transferred to painting. Here, Armenini justifies the improvisatory act by proposing that it be patterned after the example of the poet. Because poetry shared with the visual arts an ability to imitate nature through the ancient rhetorical device of *ekphrasis*, which functions to create for the listener a mental picture of the poet's narrative through vivid description, it customarily served as a way of clarifying, authorizing, or enlarging upon aspects of Renaissance visual production at a moment when the status and nature of painting relative to the other arts was under scrutiny.[18] Hence, we read in *De' veri precetti della pittura* that just as the poet may begin to compose a verse through improvisatory activity, so too may the painter begin to structure a visual composition in this manner. The *schizzi* or *bozze* (sketches) which the artist executes as a result are understood by Armenini to represent only an intermediate step toward artistic perfection rather than an end in and of themselves. After all, he points out, "a i buoni poeti accade delle sue composizioni improvise, alle quali dipoi, piú volte discorrendovi sopra con diverse mutazioni, o tuttto o parte ne rimovono, e cosí da loro si limano, che come incomparabili restano e di perfezzione e di bellezza insieme" ("good poets consider their first [extemporaneous] attempts at length, will make various changes, will delete either all or part of their efforts, and will polish a composition until it be incomparable in perfection and beauty").[19] Thus rapidly rendered, multifaceted, and suggestive *schizzi* give way to more diligently executed, clean, detailed, and synthetic *disegni* (drawings).[20]

Armenini's analogy connecting the improvisatory techniques of the painter and poet is strongly reminiscent of Leonardo's own statement on the subject contained in what has come to be called the *Trattato della pittura* (*Treatise on Painting*):

> [H]or non ai tu mai considerato li poeti componitori de lor versi alli quali non da noia il fare bella lettera ne si cura di canzellare alcuni d'essi versi riffaccendoli migliori adonque pittore componi grossamente le membra delle tue figure e' attendi prima alli movimenti apropriati alli accidenti mentali de li animali componitori della storia, che alla bellezza e' bonta delle loro membra per che tu hai a' in tendere che se tal componimento inculto ti reussira apropriato alla sua inventione tanto maggior mente sattisfara essendo poi ornato della perfettione apropriata a' tutte le sue parte.
>
> (Now, have you never considered how poets compose their verses? It does not annoy them, just because they have written beautiful letters, to erase some of their verses, then writing them out again better. Therefore, painter, compose the parts of your figures arbitrarily, then attend first to the movements representative of the mental attitudes of the creatures composing your narrative painting, rather than to the beauty and goodness of the parts of their bodies. Because you must understand that if such an unfinished composition turns out to be consistent with your invention, it will satisfy all the more when afterward it is adorned with the perfection appropriate to all its parts.)[21]

Moreover, traces of the improvisatory technique which they both describe as a way of materializing the production of the intellect are evident in such preparatory *schizzi* as Leonardo's *Study of the Virgin and Child with St. Anne and the Infant St. John the Baptist with Studies of Machinery*, which was executed c.1508 (fig. 1). These images were considered innovative for the time in their extensive *pentimenti* (changes or, literally, repentances) made possible and enhanced by Leonardo's adoption of the malleable and fluid drawing media of chalk and pen and ink.[22] But although

1. Leonardo da Vinci, *Study of the Virgin and Child with St. Anne and the Infant St. John the Baptist with Studies of Machinery* (recto), c.1508. Pen and brown ink with gray wash over black chalk; some white heightening. London, British Museum. Alinari/Art Resource, N.Y.

Armenini cites "l'eccellentissimo" ("the most excellent") Leonardo first among the artists he holds in high regard as worthy inventors in this chapter (along with Raphael, Michelangelo, Giulio Romano, Polidoro da Caravaggio, and Perino del Vaga), he avoids any further citation of the term 'improvisation' or its variations even if improvisatory practice is implied in his references to the speed with which some of them initially render their visual ideas: Raphael draws *velocemente* (swiftly), while Michelangelo produces a drawing *in breve tempo* (in a short time). Instead, much of the discussion emphasizes how these artists treat the compositional *schizzi* produced via the improvisatory process in order to ensure that they exhibit what Vasari calls *fine* (finish), a key characteristic unique to his third or modern manner of progressive sixteenth-century artists working in central Italy and one that he calls "la perfezzione et il fiore dell'arte" ("the perfection and bloom of art") in the *Vite*.[23]

For example, Armenini explains how Giulio—described by Vasari as at his conceptual best when in the heat of rendering relatively rapidly[24]—would take a *schizzo* executed in lead or charcoal and then finish it through a laborious and time-consuming process of transferring the initial rendering to clean paper by covering the verso of the *schizzo* with charcoal and tracing over its lines with a stylus, inking up the contours of the transferred image, wiping clean the extraneous charcoal marks, and, finally, modeling the forms in three dimensions through pen and ink cross-hatching or washes. By employing what was known as this *calco* (carbon copy) technique, "li profili poi si vedevano restar netti e senza macchia o segno alcuno sotto di essi" ("the delineations would be left neat and without any spot or mark under them").[25] This is evident in Giulio's *calco* drawing of *Three Angels Carrying the Virgin's Crown*, which still exhibits depressions made by the stylus (fig. 2). At this point in the process, the spontaneity and multiplicity of the ideas encapsulated within an improvised *schizzo* are erased in favor of a controlled and definitive *disegno*—something Armenini underlines by describing how Polidoro and Perino produced such *disegni* using procedures akin to Giulio's. Surely Armenini signifies the central importance of this aspect of the transformative process when he enthusiastically reports that Perino "finiva [il disegno] con tanta grazia, che pochi o niuno lo pareggiò" ("finished the drawing with

2. Giulio Romano, *Three Angels Carrying the Virgin's Crown*, c.1529. Black chalk, pen and brown ink, brown wash, and white highlights; incised contours. Prepared for the vault over the choir, Duomo, Verona; probably painted by Francesco Torbido in 1534. Paris, Musée du Louvre. Réunion des Musées Nationaux/Art Resource, N.Y.

so much grace that few or none ever equaled him").[26] In this context, the conception of *fine* has as much to do with bequeathing to the image a particular aesthetic quality—i.e., that *pulito* (polish) which the poet had sought after improvising—as it does with ensuring that the image is visually complete within the picture frame or through the artist's application of, say, *ultimi finimenti* (finishing touches).[27]

Of the several illustrations which Armenini provides, it is only in the case of Michelangelo that improvised image-making clearly does not require additional finishing techniques to legitimize the work. In Armenini's view, an improvised image might equally be a finished image within this artist's oeuvre, and thus his production provides a potential escape from the tension Armenini otherwise posits between the two in his chapter on *invenzione*. Michelangelo, he informs his reader, was once asked by a Ferrarese youth to whom he was indebted for firing some earthenware to draw for him on the spot a standing Hercules figure in exchange. With Armenini and others also in attendance, Michelangelo soon set to work and produced the image impromptu. After praising its *finito* (finished quality), Armenini concludes his account with the observation that "era un stupor grande a quelli che ciò ave[v]ano veduto fare in cosí poco tempo, che altri vi averebbe giudicato dentro la fatica di un mese" ("[t]hose who had seen him do the work in such a short time, a work which others would have judged could be made only with a month's effort, were completely amazed").[28] Through this statement, Armenini suggests that as long as the fundamental visual characteristics of improvisational rendering are immediately camouflaged under the veneer of *fine*, the act of improvisation itself is still acceptable and even functions as a viable procedure which allows virtuoso artists to demonstrate their extraordinary worth. Armenini's selection of Michelangelo as the artist through whom he could chart a positive relationship between improvisation and *fine* is in retrospect predictable. Michelangelo's legacy as a draftsman whose mark-marking was in every way deemed to be both perfect and effortless was well established when Armenini was compiling his treatise in the 1580s, in part because he had burned many of his *schizzi* shortly before his death in 1564 in an attempt to construct just such a legacy.[29] By then, the posthumous physical evidence of his practice represented an anomalous ideal which few other artists could match. For, as Armenini indicates at the outset of the account, while Michelangelo's demonstration was for him *molto agevole* (very easy), it would be *difficile* (difficult) for others, and, as a result, this artist's ease separates him from the ordinary talents.[30]

Distinctions between improvisation as performance and improvisation as a studio tool for locating the composition of a given invention are drawn through a variety of details which Armenini attaches to Michelangelo's feat. First, the artist is said to have executed the work in a public space, behind the Vatican church of new Saint Peter's rather than in his closely-guarded workshop in the vicinity of Trajan's Forum. Further, it is a space closely tied to the most public of his professional projects during the latter part of his life; Michelangelo served as superintendent of the project to erect the church on the site of the old Early Christian basilica from 1547 until his death. Second, he performed the improvisatory act for an audience which included not only Armenini and the youth but an unspecified number of others. And third, in Armenini's telling, Michelangelo was decidedly aware of his audience and even played to its members to some extent. After moving to a bench sheltered by a small roof, he struck a pose designed to signal that the performance had begun: "[E]ra un scanno da sedervi, sul quali postovi su il piè destro et il gomito sul ginocchio alto, poggiatosi la mano al viso si stette pensoso un poco; dipoi si mise a disegnar quello . . ." ("He put his right foot on the bench, his elbow on his raised knee, and his hand against his face, and remained awhile in thought. Then he began to draw the figure . . .").[31] When he was done, Michelangelo gestured to the youth to come forward out of the audience to accept the image and then left the vicinity alone, a departure from the stage, so to speak.[32]

Armenini's report is likely apocryphal. There is no drawing of Hercules in Michelangelo's extant oeuvre which might be related to it, nor is the incident recorded in any other extant contemporary source.[33] Yet it rings true if only because it fits convincingly with the artist's knowledge of the performative aspect of improvisation in music which might have made him sensitive to the possibility of a counterpart in the visual arts even if he could not necessarily name it. It is now well established that improvisational performance was an integral part of Florentine musical practice by the later Quattrocento and was heavily promoted at the Medici court where Michelangelo lived and studied from 1489 to 1492.[34] According to Ascanio Condivi, Michelangelo's only authorized biographer, the last years of the century saw him establish a friendship with the Medici-sponsored Flemish musician Jean Cordier, who sang *all' improvviso* "maravigliosamente" ("marvelously") while accompanying himself on the *lira da braccio*.[35] By 1515, Michelangelo had joined the Sacra Accademia of the Medici, a Platonic literary group with what appears to have been an active musical program reflecting the Florentine taste for improvisation. In fact, the academy's *perpetuo cytharedo* (lutenist in perpetuity), Atalante Migliorotti, as well as one of its protectors, Bernardo Accolti, were renowned improvisational singers with reputations which extended well beyond the city's borders.[36] With these many opportunities to experience musical improvisation it is no surprise that Michelangelo would have developed an appreciation for it. This is documented in the autobiography of the goldsmith and sculptor Benvenuto Cellini, begun in 1558, who records that Michelangelo's delight in the extemporized (and beautiful) singing of Luigi Pulci in the streets of Florence was so great that he regularly joined those who followed his performances.[37] But all this, I think, would have been of relatively little interest to Armenini, who had a larger point to make about the nature of performed improvisation and its production in recounting the Michelangelo-Hercules story. This point can be ascertained once we acknowledge how readily Michelangelo's alleged execution of a finished image in this manner calls to mind a mode of presentation already codified in Baldessare Castiglione's influential handbook on noble behavior and activity, *Il libro del cortegiano* (*The Book of the Courtier*), completed at the court of Urbino by c.1516 and published in Venice in 1528. As is well known, the handbook is written in the form of a dialogue between various personalities in attendance at the court. In book 1, Count Ludovico Canossa is asked by Cesare Gonzaga to speak on *grazia* (grace), that quality which the courtier was to exhibit in all endeavors. It is also an aesthetic quality which, as we have noted, Armenini explicitly associates with the finish of Perino's drawing, but here the emphasis is on *grazia* as a modifier of action.[38] I quote Canossa's definition at length:

> [A]vendo io già piú volte pensato meco onde nasca questa grazia . . . trovo una regula universalissima, la qual mi par valer circa questo in tutte le cose umane che si facciano o dicano piú che alcuna altra, e ciò è fuggir quanto piú si po, e come un asperissimo e pericoloso scoglio, la affettazione; e, per dir forse una nova parola, usar in ogni cosa una certa sprezzatura, che nasconda l'arte e dimostri ciò che si fa e dice venir fatto senza fatica e quasi senza pensarvi. Da questo credo io che derivi assai la grazia; perché delle cose rare e ben fatte ognun sa la difficultà,

onde in esse la facilità genera grandissima maraviglia; e per lo contrario il sforzare e, come si dice, tirar per i capegli dà somma disgrazia e fa estimar poco ogni cosa, per grande ch'ella si sia. Però si po dir quella esser vera arte che non pare esser arte; né piú in altro si ha da poner studio, che nel nasconderla: perché se è scoperta, leva in tutto il credito e fa l'omo poco estimato.

(Having thought many times about how this grace is acquired . . . I have found quite a universal rule which in this matter seems to me valid above all others, and in all human affairs whether in word or deed: and that is to avoid affectation in every way possible as though it were some very rough and dangerous reef; and (to pronounce a new word perhaps) to practice in all things a certain *sprezzatura* [nonchalance], so as to conceal all art and make whatever is done or said appear to be without effort and almost without any thought about it. And I believe much grace comes of this: because everyone knows the difficulty of things that are rare and well done; wherefore facility in such things causes the greatest wonder; whereas, on the other hand, to labor and, as we say, drag forth by the hair of the head, shows an extreme want of grace, and causes everything, no matter how great it may be, to be held in little account. Therefore we may call that art true art which does not seem to be art; nor must one be more careful of anything than of concealing it, because if it is discovered, this robs a man of all credit and causes him to be held in slight esteem.)[39]

It is evident that Canossa's speech underlining the importance of *grazia* operates as a warning to avoid the *goffezza* that Armenini was fearful would mar improvisatory or, in the hands of less virtuosic talents, what we might call slapdash artistic production. More importantly, it reveals that when performing *all'improvviso*, the conscious mind is hard at work in advance and at the moment of the improvisatory act even if, in the best of circumstances, its production *appears* otherwise. And Canossa reiterates this as he presents a series of concrete illustrations displaying the way in which experts handle weapons, dance, sing, and paint when they know they are being observed. The last two activities—singing and painting—are particularly closely related, and for each of these Canossa stresses the deceptive effortlessness of the expert, the apparently aleatory quality of the performance, and, most crucially, its impact on the audience:

> Un musico, se nel cantar pronunzia una sola voce terminata con suave accento in un groppetto duplicato, con tal facilità che paia che cosí gli venga fatto a caso, con quel punto solo fa conoscere che sa molto piú di quello che fa. Spesso ancor nella pittura una linea sola non stentata, un sol colpo di pennello tirato facilmente, di modo che paia che la mano, senza esser guidata da studio o arte alcuna, vada per se stessa al suo termine secondo la intenzion del pittore, scopre chiaramente la eccellenzia dell' artifice, circa la opinion della quale ognuno poi si estende secondo il suo giudicio.
>
> (A singer who utters a single word ending in a group of four notes with a sweet cadence, and with such facility that he appears to do it quite by chance, shows with that touch alone that he can do much more than he is doing. Often too in painting, a single line which is not labored, a single brush stroke made with ease and in such a manner that the hand seems of itself to complete the line desired by the painter, without being directed by care or skill of any kind, clearly reveals the excellence of craftsmanship, which people will then proceed to judge, each by his own lights.)[40]

From the Cinquecento perspective, then, we may now differentiate between publicly performed improvisation and improvisation as a studio technique employed more or less privately by referring to the former as one which the artist counterfeits. It is conceived as a virtuosic display deliberately feigned for the pleasure of both the performer and his audiences.[41] The discerning audience enjoys the performance precisely because its members realize that it is generally hard won. With this in mind, Armenini's passing remark that Michelangelo put his hand to his head and thought *un poco* (a little) before he began to improvise the Hercules takes on more significance; the pose functions as a sign of the preparation which lies behind the performance for those who are able to read it. In contrast, the audience which accepts the performance at face value will not decipher the signal and will instead simply marvel at the image which the delusively spontaneous and effortless action produces.[42]

That Armenini wished to represent performed improvisation as being to some degree premeditated is supported when considered beside two statements he offers on the artist's training regimen in this same chapter. In each case, he underlines the importance of developing a repertoire of stock mental images which can then be mined and expressed through the hand as required. Referring to Giulio's extemporaneous drawing practice, Armenini reports "che si potea piú presto dire che egli imitasse e che avesse inanzi a gli occhi ciò che faceva, che ch'egli componesse di suo capo, perciò che era la sua maniera tanto conforme e prossimana alle scolture antiche di Roma che, per esservi stato studiosissimo sempre mentre era giovine, che ciò che deponeva e formava pareva esser proprio cavato da quelle" ("one could say that he was copying a subject in front of his eyes rather than composing from his own ideas. His style was so near to, and in conformity with, the ancient sculpture of Rome, to which he had studiously devoted much time while he was a youth, that what he placed and formed on paper seemed to be exactly drawn from those works").[43] In discussing how less mature artists might cultivate the type of repertoire Giulio already had in mind, Armenini writes:

> [I]o vi avertisco bene che abbiate per costume infallibile di far ogni giorno qualche dissegno, acciò che con piú facilità poi si esprimano le cose, che tuttavia si sono da voi imaginate. . . . [S]i svegli la mente tuttavia con diversi schizzi su le carte, i quali si de[v]e fare per piú vie, e quando una e quando un'altra cosa da sé formando e quando con l'imitare l'altrui farle sue, con diverse maniere e modi di fare e con differenti materie ancora, e questo acciò che poi le siano tutti agevoli per ogni suo bisogno.
>
> (I strongly advise you to draw every day without fail so that you will be able to express with great facility what you have imagined. . . . [O]ne stimulates the mind with various sketches on paper, which must be made in several ways—at times drawing something of one's own, and at times something else; at other times imitating someone else's works and making them one's own in different styles and ways, as well as with different materials. This is to be done so that all these methods will be at one's command when the occasion demands.)[44]

As if to convince the novice of the worthiness of this type of training, Armenini notes that Raphael would literally surround himself in the studio with *disegni* he had previously generated on a similar subject—a tactic which "fatta ricca" ("made rich") his rendering of the new *invenzione* he had in mind.[45] Taken together, these remarks on training indicate that in Armenini's world the artist's ability to mount an improvisatory performance depends on his intimacy with a given repertoire of images as well as his ability to produce variations on that repertoire with ease and celerity. Indeed, he writes immediately after this passage that such training ensures manual *spedita* and *pronta*, two synonyms for that very characteristic of quickness he had earlier condemned when it came to completing a painted image. We should recognize, however, that the application of the skills acquired through this training was not limited to public performance. Vasari provides a salient example of their application in the privacy of the studio in his biography of Giuliano Bugiardini. There he relates that when Bugiardini asked Michelangelo to assist him with the soldiers in his altarpiece of the *Martyrdom of St. Catherine*, a painting with which he had been struggling for some twelve years due to his lack of *invenzione*, Michelangelo immediately "accostatosi con un carbone alla tavola, contornò de' primi segni, schizzati solamente, una fila di figure ignude maravigliose, le quali in diversi gesti scortando, variamente cascavano" ("went up to the picture with a piece of charcoal and outlined with a few strokes, lightly sketched in, a line of marvelous nude figures, which, foreshortened in different attitudes, were falling in various ways").[46] But in either context, if we accept the argument that improvisation does not emerge from a *tabula rasa*, it helps us to understand the conditions under which Armenini posited the possibility of achieving *fine* while performing an improvisation.

Let us return once again to Michelangelo by way of example. Of all the subjects Armenini could have assigned to him as he fashioned what I want at this point to call his fictional account of the artist's improvised performance, it is probably no coincidence that he selected Hercules. While still a youth attached to the Florentine court of the Medici toward the close of the fifteenth century, Michelangelo was undoubtedly already aware of the significance of the classical Hercules figure within the city, cast variously since the thirteenth century in terms of political, military, and moral power—and, over time, also in terms of the might of the ruling Medici family. By Michelangelo's day, Florence was replete with images of Hercules, both in the public and private spheres, so he must have had ample opportunity to absorb the physiognomy and iconography of the figure as it was favored in this milieu from the earliest years of his artistic training.[47] Shortly after the death of his early mentor, Lorenzo Il Magnifico de' Medici, in 1492, Michelangelo himself embarked on carving a colossal freestanding marble statue of Hercules, possibly commissioned by Lorenzo's son Piero. Michelangelo addressed the subject again on and off for at least two decades as he vied for the commission to carve a Hercules and Cacus group, finally completed in 1534 by Baccio Bandinelli under the auspices of Pope Clement VII de' Medici, to stand as a pendant to his *David* in the Piazza della Signoria. During his Roman years, he would have had access to a range of antique statues and relief carvings of Hercules then on display. And Vasari records that in 1561 the artist made a wax model of *Hercules and Antaeus* for the goldsmith and sculptor Leoni Leone. Additionally, there is at least one extant Hercules drawing from Michelangelo's hand and perhaps a bronze statuette.[48] Knowing this, we can deduce that were Michelangelo actually asked to improvise a Hercules figure before an audience, he would have drawn on his extensive past visual experience of the mythological character to fulfill the request at the moment he rendered the image. His so-called improvisatory performance would have produced a polished rhetorical drawing born of careful study, extended practice, and the skillful manipulation of that which was now stored in his memory.[49]

In nuce, Armenini's concept of improvisation as presented in *De' veri precetti della pittura*, assumes that drawing is the medium through which the act will be effected—and, more specifically, through that tradition of drawing generally associated with central Italy. Therefore, while improvisation could be employed as a studio technique which allowed the artist to begin developing his composition, the resulting *schizzi* were understood merely as stepping stones to more elaborately finished *disegni* which Armenini favored—consider, for example, Perino's rendering of *The Evangelist Luke* (fig. 3)—and which were increasingly produced by artists as demonstration pieces and collectors' items. In book 2, chapter 6, Armenini calls the most refined of this type of drawing the *ben finito cartone* (well-finished cartoon).[50] What is more, the mere

3. Perino del Vaga, *The Evangelist Luke*, c.1540. Black chalk with gray wash. Prepared for the Cappella del Crocifisso, San Marcello al Corso, Rome; painted by Daniele da Volterra. Paris, Musée du Louvre. Réunion des Musées Nationaux/Art Resource, N.Y.

existence of *schizzi* generated through such improvisation required justification by analogy to the poet's working method. And when the artist performed an improvisation before an audience, he was obliged to furnish a drawing exhibiting *fine* almost immediately. Hence, performed improvisation was to be a highly precise and conscious act; for Armenini, it was a virtuoso technique fraught with danger, forcing him to advocate that it remain in the domain of those very few artists capable of producing finished images without "false starts" or preliminary sketches. But if these requirements legitimized improvisation for the central Italian art community, they at once undermined the essential character of improvisation as defined by the Accademia della Crusca in its *Vocabolario*. To a great extent, these requirements led to a contradiction in terms which was nearly impossible to overcome as long as the hierarchy of values attached to central Italian drawing remained firmly entrenched. It is worth noting in this regard that the term 'improvisation' does not merit an entry in Filippo Baldinucci's *Vocabolario toscano dell'arte del disegno* (*Tuscan Dictionary of the Art of Design*), sponsored by the academy and published in Florence in 1681 nearly one hundred years after the appearance of *De' veri precetti della pittura*.[51]

When the hierarchy of values which constrained Armenini during the Renaissance finally fell away during the Modern period, an accord between improvisation as an artistic concept and improvisation in artistic practice became increasingly attainable. Yet recent (re)evaluations of improvisatory practice during this period and beyond have modified the traditional romantic and now stereotypical view which I presented at the outset of my inquiry with a more complex reading of its characteristics that, in some important respects, is not out of sympathy with Armenini. As Hazel Smith and Roger Dean have argued for the later twentieth century, improvisation is seldom a totally spontaneous act because it requires skill and practice. They recognize that "most improvisors have a bank of 'personal cliches' to which they resort" and contend that the success of the act depends on the size of the bank and the ability of the improvisor to reorganize and transfigure those cliches. Smith and Dean also distinguish between what they call "pure" or performed improvisation which engages an audience and "applied" improvisation which occurs in private and is but one step of several required to produce a work—"perhaps on a canvas," they suggest coincidentally.[52] If Armenini's attempt to identify and articulate the nature of visual improvisation in central Italy toward the close of the sixteenth century is awkward, contradictory, and even at times elusive, it nonetheless foreshadows the discussion which has again attached itself to the problem of artistic improvisation at a moment when the implications of these same characteristics are being championed. Thus at the beginning of the twenty-first century, the importance of Armenini's contribution lies both in the light it sheds on improvisation in the Cinquecento and in the context it may now offer for contemporary debate on the subject.

NOTES

[1]Wassily Kandinsky, *Über das Geistige in der Kunst*, introd. Max Bill (Bern: Bümpliz: Benteli, 1952), 142; translated as *Concerning the Spiritual in Art*, trans. M. T. H. Sadler (New York: Dover, 1977), 57. Kandinsky's *Improvisation* series, with ties to landscape painting, was begun in 1909.

[2]Surrealist automatism was defined by its earliest apologist, André Breton, in his "Manifeste du Surréalisme" (1924), collected in his *Oeuvres complètes*, 2 vols. (Paris: Gallimard, 1988), 1:311–46, esp. 328; for a translation, see *Manifestoes of Surrealism*, trans. Richard Seaver and Helen R. Lane (Ann Arbor: University of Michigan Press, 1969), 3–47, esp. 26.

[3]The photographs were initially published in 1951; the film, which Namuth produced with Paul Falkenburg, was first screened at the Museum of Modern Art in New York in June 1951. See Barbara Rose, "Hans Namuth's Photographs and the Jackson Pollock Myth: Part One: Media Impact and the Failure of Criticism," *Arts Magazine* 53, no. 7 (1979): 112–16, and "Hans Namuth's Photographs and the Jackson Pollock Myth: Part Two: *Number 29, 1950*," *Arts Magazine* 53, no. 7 (1979): 117–19. Pollock's improvised activity is more broadly situated in Daniel Belgrad, *The Culture of Spontaneity: Improvisation and the Arts in Postwar America* (Chicago: University of Chicago Press, 1998), *passim*.

[4]For Dada performance and its relationship to improvisation, see John D. Erickson, *Dada: Performance, Poetry, and Art* (Boston: Twayne, 1984), 5, 13, 72–73; and Jeanpaul Goergen, "Musik der Ironie und Provokation," *Neue Zeitschrift für Musik* 155, no. 3 (1994): 4–13. On Fluxus performance and its debt to Cage, see Douglas Kahn, "The Latest: Fluxus and Music," in *In the Spirit of*

Fluxus (Minneapolis: Walker Art Center, 1993), 102–08; and Ellsworth Snyder, "John Cage Discusses Fluxus," *Visible Language* 26, nos. 1–2 (1992): 59–68.

[5]Giorgio Vasari, *Le vite de' più eccellenti pittori scultori ed architettori nelle redazioni del 1550 e 1568*, ed. Rosanna Bettarini and Paola Barocchi, 6 vols. (Florence: Sansoni and S.P.E.S., 1960–87), 4:16, 24; translated as *Lives of the Painters, Sculptors and Architects*, trans. Gaston du C. de Vere, introd. and notes by David Ekserdjian, 2 vols. (New York: Knopf, 1996), 1:626, 631. Subsequent citations to this translation are given in parentheses following references to the Italian edition in my notes. For a fuller discussion of Leonardo's musical activity, see Emanuel Winternitz, *Leonardo da Vinci as a Musician* (New Haven: Yale University Press, 1982), esp. 25–38, who also provides discussion of the *lira da braccio* and improvisation.

[6]Vasari, *Le vite*, 4:84, 261, 269 (1:668, 776, 782).

[7]A surfeit of literature on this issue appeared during the early 1990s. See Paul Barolsky, *Why the Mona Lisa Smiles and Other Tales by Vasari* (University Park: Pennsylvania State University Press, 1991); Lynette M. F. Bosch, "Men, Myth and Truth," *Oxford Art Journal* 16, no. 2 (1993): 62–72; David Cast, "Reading Vasari Again: History, Philosophy," *Word and Image* 9, no. 1 (1993): 29–38; Carl Goldstein, "The Image of the Artist Reviewed," *Word and Image* 9, no. 1 (1993): 9–18; Patricia Rubin, "What Men Saw: Vasari's Life of Leonardo da Vinci and the Image of the Renaissance Artist," *Art History* 13 (1990): 34–46; and Catherine M. Soussloff, "*Lives* of Painters and Poets in the Renaissance," *Word and Image* 6, no. 2 (1990): 154–62.

[8]Giovanni Battista Armenini, *De' veri precetti della pittura*, ed. Maria Gorreri (Turin: Einaudi, 1988), 45, 126, 237; translated as *On the True Precepts of the Art of Painting*, ed. and trans. Edward J. Olszewski (New York: Burt Franklin, 1977), 102, 176, 278. Subsequent citations to this translation are given in parentheses following references to the Italian edition in my notes.

[9]In Renaissance Italy, the term *invenzione* was understood in two ways: the first emerged from the rhetorical tradition of the ancients and referred to content or subject matter; the second, derived from the poetic tradition, referred to the workings of the artist's imagination. See the discussion in Martin Kemp, "From *Mimesis* to *Fantasia*: The Quattrocento Vocabulary of Creation, Inspiration, and Genius in the Visual Arts," *Viator* 8 (1977): 348–61, 396–97. However, the two traditions were blurred in writing on art during the sixteenth century, and their relationship was complicated by the overlapping relationship between the poetic definition of *invenzione* and that of the process of *disegno* (outlined briefly in n. 20, below). In book 1, chap. 9, of *De' veri precetti della pittura*, Armenini puts the emphasis on the rhetorical definition of *invenzione* but does not exclude entirely the poetic definition.

[10]Armenini, *De' veri precetti della pittura*, 87–88 (142; elision marks in the quotation in my text appear where I have omitted the word "spontaneous" from Olszewski's translation because it does not appear in Armenini's Italian).

[11]Notwithstanding the documented existence of professional female artists in Cinquecento Italy, it is a given that Armenini imagines the artist as male. I employ the words *he*, *him*, and *his* exclusively throughout my text in recognition of this.

[12]Giovanni Andrea Gilio da Fabriano, "Dialogo nel quale si ragiona degli errori e degli abusi de' pittori circa l'istorie," in *Trattati d'arte del cinquecento fra manierismo e controriforma*, ed. Paola Barocchi, 3 vols. (Bari: Laterza, 1960–62), 2:3–115. Gorreri makes a similar but more limited observation in Armenini, *De' veri precetti della pittura*, 88, n. 5. For a more detailed review of Gilio's discussion of intelligibility and historical accuracy, see Leslie Korrick, "*Ut Pictura Musica*: Observations on the Reform of Painting and Music in Post-Tridentine Rome" (Ph.D. diss., University of Toronto, 1996), 80–85, 92–95. For further evidence of Armenini's commitment to the reform aesthetic, see Armenini, *De' veri precetti della pittura*, 173–74, 195–96 (217–18, 237–38).

[13]Pietro de' Crescenzio, *Trattato dell'agricoltura* (Florence: Cosimo Giunti, 1605), book 7, chap. 139, no. 7, as cited in *Vocabolario degli Accademici della Crusca* (1612; facs. reprint Florence: Licosa, 1974), 424. One of the primary goals of the Accademia della Crusca, founded in 1582, was to ensure the continued purity and primacy of the Tuscan language as presented in Pietro Bembo's *Prose della volgar lingua* of 1525; the *Vocabolario* was conceived for this purpose. Thus, following Bembo's contention that the vernacular was best preserved in the literary period defined by Dante and Boccaccio, the compilers of the dictionary relied heavily on source material more or less belonging to the fourteenth century for examples of usage. This is explicitly stated in the introduction of the *Vocabolario* and is reflected in the "tavola de'nomi degli autori o de'libri citati in quest'opera" ("table of names of authors or books cited in this work"). Because the first Tuscan translation of Crescenzio's erudite yet practical tome was produced in the mid fourteenth century, it fell into this category. In addition to the multiple manuscript copies which followed, no fewer than twenty-three Italian editions had been printed before 1600. For an overview of Crescenzio and the *Opus ruralium commodorum*, see Pierre Toubert, "Crescenzi, Pietro de'," in *Dizionario biografico degli Italiani* (Rome: Istituto della Enciclopedia italiana, 1960–), 30:649–57. On the history and activities of the Accademia della Crusca, see Severina Parodi, *Quattro secoli di Crusca 1583–1983* (Florence, 1983).

[14]Armenini, *De' veri precetti della pittura*, 88 (142).

[15]Relatively little has been published on *prestezza* to date, and most of these studies are narrowly focused. See Robert J. Clements, "Michelangelo on Effort and Rapidity in Art," *Journal of the Warburg and Courtauld Institutes* 17 (1954): 301–10; Tom Nichols, "Tintoretto, *Prestezza* and the *Poligrafi*: A Study in the

Literary and Visual Culture of Cinquecento Venice," *Renaissance Studies* 10, no. 1 (1996): 72–100; Tom Nichols, "Price, *Prestezza* and Production in Jacopo Tintoretto's Business Strategy," *Venezia Cinquecento* 6, no. 12 (1996): 207–33; and Robert Williams, "The Vocation of the Artist as seen by Giovanni Battista Armenini," *Art History* 18 (1995): 518–36, which includes an analysis of Armenini's judgment of *prestezza*. I am currently preparing a more wide-ranging article on the topic based on my paper "Making Quick Work: *Prestezza* in Cinquecento Art Theory and Practice," presented at the Sixteenth-Century Studies Annual Conference in Atlanta in 1998.

[16]Armenini, *De' veri precetti della pittura*, 88–89, 109, 131 (142–43, 161, 182); my translation.

[17]Ibid., 89 (144).

[18]For the standard analysis of the relationships between painting and poetry in the Renaissance and thereafter, see Rensselaer Lee, *Ut Pictura Poesis: The Humanistic Theory of Painting* (New York: W. W. Norton, 1967); reprinted from the *Art Bulletin* 22, no. 4 (1940): 197–269. At the outset of the sixteenth century, these relationships were most extensively codified by Leonardo, who then challenged their implications in order to place painting above poetry; see Claire J. Farago, *Leonardo da Vinci's* Paragone*: A Critical Interpretation with a New Edition of the Text in the* Codex Urbinas (Leiden: Brill, 1992), 196–241. On *ekphrasis*, see the pioneering article by Sveltana Alpers, "Ekphrasis and Aesthetic Attitudes in Vasari's *Lives*," *Journal of the Warburg and Courtauld Institutes* 23 (1960): 190–215; and, more recently, David Rosand, "*Ekphrasis* and the Renaissance of Painting: Observations on Alberti's Third Book," in *Florilegium Columbianum: Essays in Honor of Paul Oskar Kristeller*, ed. Karl-Ludwig Selig and Robert Somerville (New York: Italica, 1987), 147–65, who situates the practice at the outset of the early Renaissance; and Norman Land, *The Viewer as Poet: The Renaissance Response to Art* (University Park: Pennsylvania State University Press, 1994). On the shifting place of painting within the Renaissance hierarchy of the arts, see Claire J. Farago, "The Classification of the Visual Arts in the Renaissance," in *The Shapes of Knowledge from the Renaissance to the Enlightenment*, ed. Donald R. Kelley and Richard A. Popkin (Dordrecht: Kluwer, 1991), 23-48.

[19]Armenini, *De' veri precetti della pittura*, 90 (144). For further commentary by Armenini on relations between painting and poetry, see 39–40, 43–44, 63–64, 126 (97–98,101–02, 119, 176). Although it was of no interest to Armenini, the analogous working method which he attributes to the painter and poet could also be extended to include that of the composer; see Jessie Ann Owens, *Composers at Work: The Craft of Musical Composition 1450–1600* (New York: Oxford University Press, 1977), 135–96, who explores a compositional process documented consecutively on paper in the forms of sketches, drafts, and fair copies. Owens addresses the issue of improvised composition directly and provides evidence that sixteenth-century composers thought of it as akin to the poet's process (64–70).

[20]The distinction between *schizzo* (or *bozzo*) and *disegno* was widely employed during the Cinquecento, and these were distinguished in turn from *cartone* (cartoon), a detailed full-scale drawing prepared by the artist for transfer to the surface on which it would finally be painted. Armenini employs *schizzo*, *bozzo*, and *disegno* in book 1, chap. 9, maintaining for the most part the distinction outlined in my text, as well as the verb *disegnare* (to draw). Within this sequence, however, *disegno* carried with it a second meaning, often translated into English as "design," which encapsulated the process of elaborating and transferring a mental concept to paper through the act of rendering. For an incisive review of *disegno* as both "drawing" and "design," see Karen-edis Barzman, "Perception, Knowledge, and the Theory of Disegno in Sixteenth-Century Florence," in Larry J. Feinberg, *From Studio to Studiolo: Florentine Draughtsmanship under the First Medici Grand Dukes* (Oberlin: Allen Memorial Art Museum, Oberlin College, 1991), 37–48. When I want to highlight difference among drawing types in the remainder of my text, I maintain the Italian *schizzo* and *disegno*; when difference is clear through context or irrelevant, I use the English term 'drawing.'

[21]Leonardo da Vinci, *Treatise on Painting (Codex Urbinas Latinus 1270)*, trans. and annotated A. Philip McMahon, introd. Ludwig H. Heydenreich, 2 vols. (Princeton: Princeton University Press, 1956), 1:108–09, 2:62^{r}. The *Codex Urbinas Latinus 1270*, dated c.1550, contains the earliest known compilation of the *Trattato della pittura*. On its scope and critical fortune, see 1:xi–xliii.

[22]Leonardo's choice of media (which came to dominate in the Cinquecento) might be contrasted here with silver point (the dominant drawing medium in Quattrocento Italy). Once a mark is made with a silver point stylus, it cannot be in any way modified; this inflexible medium cannot create the painterly effects associated with chalk, charcoal, or pen and ink, and thus silver point drawings are typically composed of clean, discrete lines. Also, laborious preparation of the support surface is required before silver point drawing commences and hence further diminishes the possibility for spontaneous rendering. For additional discussion of Leonardo's sketching techniques contextualized with the drawing style of his contemporaries, see the classic 1952 article by Ernst Gombrich, "Leonardo's Method for Working Out Compositions," in his *Norm and Form: Studies in the Art of the Renaissance I*, 3rd ed. (London: Phaidon, 1978), 58–63. For a more recent analysis building on Gombrich's work, see Robert Zwijnenberg, *The Writings and Drawings of Leonardo da Vinci: Order and Chaos in Early Modern Thought*, trans. Caroline A. Van Eck (Cambridge: Cambridge University Press, 1999), 60–82.

[23]Vasari, *Le vite*, 4:6 (1:619). The reference appears in the *proemio* (preface) to pt. 3 which is not on drawing alone but also on painting and sculpture.

[24]Ibid., 5:60 (2:121).

[25]Armenini, *De' veri precetti della pittura*, 93 (147–48). Gombrich notes that

Leonardo also used a stylus to lift a single concept from "the welter of *pentimenti*" in a given drawing and cites the verso of the artist's *Study for the Virgin and Child with St. Anne and the Infant St. John the Baptist with Studies of Machinery* as evidence ("Leonardo's Method for Working Out Compositions," 58). For a detailed contextualization of the *calco* technique, see Carmen C. Bambach, *Drawing and Painting in the Italian Renaissance Workshop: Theory and Practice, 1300–1600* (Cambridge: Cambridge University Press, 1999), 1–32, 333–61.

[26]Armenini, *De' veri precetti della pittura*, 94 (148).

[27]I have deliberately chosen the term *pulito* to capture the aesthetic quality which Armenini attempts to describe in light of Vasari's assessment of Perino's decoration at the Vatican Loggie—"il più vago e pulito" ("the most charming and polished" [my translation])—among all the artists working there under Raphael between 1518 and 1519 (*Le vite*, 5:113). Interestingly, *pulito* is translated as "finish" in the translation which I cite in my text (*Lives*, 2:157). When Armenini writes of this same polish with reference to the poet's verse, he uses the word *limano* (*De' veri precetti della pittura*, 90). The issue of *ultimi finimenti* is taken up by Armenini in book 2, chap. 10, entitled "Quanto sia laudabile il finir bene l'opere sue e quanto sia dispiacevole il fare all'opposito" ("How Laudable It Is to Finish One's Works Well and How Displeasing to do the Opposite"). With the exception of a brief reference to some drawings of Leonardo he had seen "quali erano finiti con un modo . . . tanto straordinarii" ("which were finished in such an extraordinary manner"), Armenini's discussion is developed with reference to the completion of painting (*De' veri precetti della pittura*, 150 [198]). On the various applications of *finito* as an artistic term during the Cinquecento and the problems of interpretation today, see David Cast, "Finishing the Sistine," *Art Bulletin* 73 (1991): 669–84.

[28]Armenini, *De' veri precetti della pittura*, 93 (147). In his analysis of Michelangelo's drawings, Alexander Perrig offers support for the gist of Armenini's comment by observing "the optimal relation between kinetic effort and esthetic efficiency" (Perrig, *Michelangelo's Drawings: The Science of Attribution*, trans. Michael Joyce [New Haven: Yale University Press, 1991], 61).

[29]Vasari, *Le vite*, 6:108 (2:736); discussed in Michael Hirst, *Michelangelo and his Drawings* (New Haven: Yale University Press, 1988), 17–19; and Perrig, *Michelangelo's Drawings*, 1–4.

[30]Armenini, *De' veri precetti della pittura*, 92 (146).

[31]Ibid., 93 (147).

[32]Armenini's anecdote plays on the Cinquecento construction of Michelangelo as a generous individual, one established by Vasari in tandem with the artist himself; summarized in Paul Barolsky, *Michelangelo's Nose: A Myth and Its*

Maker (University Park: Pennsylvania State University Press, 1990), 58–60.

[33]If the story is not apocryphal, it would have taken place at least twenty-two years before the treatise was published since Michelangelo died in 1564.

[34]See James Haar, "*Improvvisatori* and Their Relationship to Sixteenth-Century Music," in *Essays on Italian Poetry and Music in the Renaissance, 1350–1600* (Berkeley and Los Angeles: University of California Press, 1986), 76–99; and Anthony M. Cummings, *The Politicized Muse: Music for Medici Festivals, 1512–1537* (Princeton: Princeton University Press, 1992), 37–41.

[35]Ascanio Condivi, *Vita di Michelangelo Buonarroti*, ed. Giovanni Nencioni with essays by Michael Hirst and Carolyn Elam (Florence: S.P.E.S., 1998), 15; translated as *The Life of Michelangelo*, trans. Alice Sedgwick Wohl, ed. Hellmut Wohl, 2nd ed. (University Park: Pennsylvania State University Press, 1999), 17. The content of this biography was largely controlled by Michelangelo and must be read as part of the artist's attempt to shape his life for posterity. Condivi refers to the musician as *Cardiere*; but see Cummings, *The Politicized Muse*, 39. Aspects of Cordier's life are discussed in Paul A. Merkley, "Patronage and Clientage in Galeazzo's Court," *Musica e storia* 4 (1996): 137–43; Reinhard Strohm, *Music in Late Medieval Bruges* (Oxford: Clarendon, 1985), 37–38; and Richard Walsh, "Music and Quattrocento Diplomacy: The Singer Jean Cordier between Milan, Naples and Burgundy in 1475," *Archiv für Kulturgeschichte* 60 (1978): 439–42.

[36]See Anthony M. Cummings, "The Sacred Academy of the Medici and Florentine Musical Life of the Early Cinquecento," in *Musica Franca: Essays in Honor of Frank A. D'Accone*, ed. Irene Alm, Alyson McLamore, and Coleen Reardon (Stuyvesant, N.Y.: Pendragon Press, 1996), 54–63. Migliorotti's position as *perpetuo cytharedo* is documented in a letter he received from the academy dated 27 April 1515; reproduced in Paul Oskar Kristeller, "Francesco da Diacceto and Florentine Platonism in the Sixteenth Century," in *Studies in Renaissance Thought and Letters* (Rome: Storia e letteratura, 1956), 335.

[37]Benvenuto Cellini, *La vita*, ed. Guido Davico Bonino (Turin: Einaudi, 1973), 69; *The Autobiography of Benvenuto Cellini*, trans. George Bull, rev. ed. (Harmondsworth: Penguin, 1998), 53–54. Pulci was a descendant of the Florentine poet Luigi Pulci (1432–84).

[38]The dual nature of artistic *grazia* during this period is succinctly described by David Summers, *Michelangelo and the Language of Art* (Princeton: Princeton University Press, 1981), 369, who writes that "grace was given to works of art by the artist who had grace." For a more general analysis of the term as it is employed in *Il libro del cortegiano* and especially in the passage to follow in my text, see Eduardo Saccone, "*Grazia, Sprezzatura, Affettazione* in the *Courtier*," in *Castiglione: The Ideal and the Real in Renaissance Culture*, ed. Robert W. Hanning and David Rosand (New Haven: Yale University Press, 1983), 45–67.

[39]Baldesar Castiglione, *Il libro del Cortegiano*, ed. Walter Barberis (Turin: Einaudi, 1998), 59; translated as *The Book of the Courtier*, trans. Charles Singleton (Garden City: Doubleday, 1959), 43.

[40]Castiglione, *Il libro del Cortegiano*, 63; *The Book of the Courtier*, 47.

[41]My thinking on virtuosic performance has been influenced by Thomas Carson Mark, "On Works of Virtuosity," *Journal of Philosophy* 72 (1980): 28–45 (the page numbering for this article is badly scrambled). Mark, whose discussion includes examples from a range of periods and geographies within the Western high art tradition though not sixteenth-century Italy, determines three essential requirements for works produced through virtuoso performance which, probably unbeknownst to him, are also reflected in Armenini's own writing: "(1) the artwork must require skill; (2) it must be about the skills that it requires; (3) it must display the skills it is about" (36).

[42]For further discussion with reference to *Il libro del cortegiano*, see Saccone, "*Grazia*, *Sprezzatura*, *Affettazione* in the *Courtier*," 61–63.

[43]Armenini, *De' veri precetti della pittura*, 93 (147–48). The impossibility of rendering entirely new forms was a view held by Armenini, who thus believed that the artist would inevitably be engaged in a process of recycling forms that had already been described (ibid., 95 [149]).

[44]Ibid., 90–91 (144–45).

[45]Ibid., 92 (146); my translation.

[46] Vasari, *Le vite*, 5:281–82 (2:313).

[47]Summarized in Alison Wright, "The Myth of Hercules," in *Lorenzo Il Magnifico e il suo mondo*, ed. Gian Carlo Garfagnini (Florence: Olschki, 1994), 323–39. The degree to which the Medici pursued Hercules for their own iconography is a matter of some debate. For a reading which is more committed to this interpretation than Wright's, see Leopold D. Ettlinger, "Hercules Florentinus," *Mitteilungen des kunsthistorischen Institutes in Florenz* 16, no. 2 (1972): 135–37. Regardless, the popularity of the painted and sculpted Hercules images which emerged from the studio of the Pollaiulo brothers in Florence during the 1460s at the behest of the Medici was such that they subsequently reappeared on ceramic work, marquetry, and prints (Patricia Lee Rubin and Alison Wright, *Renaissance Florence: The Art of the 1470s* [London: National Gallery Publications, 1999], 256).

[48] The marble Hercules statue, now lost, receives mention in Condivi, *Vita di Michelangelo Buonarroti*, 14; Condivi, *The Life of Michelangelo*, 15; and Vasari, *Le vite*, 6:12 (2:649). On the history, iconography, and critical fortune of the

Hercules and Cacus executed by Bandinelli, see Virginia L. Bush, "Bandinelli's Hercules and Cacus and Florentine Traditions," in *Studies in Italian Art and Architecture 15th through 18th Centuries*, ed. Henry A. Millon (Cambridge: MIT Press, 1980), 163–206. On the antique statues and relief panels of Hercules in Cinquecento Rome, see Phyllis Pray Bober and Ruth Rubenstein with contributions by Susan Woodford, *Renaissance Artists and Antique Sculpture: A Handbook of Sources* (London: Harvey Miller, Oxford University Press, 1986), 164–66, 170–73. For the reference to the wax *Hercules and Anteaus*, see Vasari, *Le vite*, 6:101 (2:727). On the drawing (and its relation to the lost statue), see Perrig, *Michelangelo's Drawings*, 111–14. On the bronze statuette, see Paul Joannides, "Michelangelo and the Medici Garden," in *La Toscana al tempo di Lorenzo il Magnifico: politica, economica, cultura, arte*, 3 vols. (Pisa: Pacini, 1997), 1:32–33.

[49]For Michelangelo's powerful memory, see Condivi, *Vita di Michelangelo Buonarroti*, 64; Condivi, *The Life of Michelangelo*, 107. In the second edition of the *Vite*, Vasari closely paraphrases Condivi. See Vasari, *Le vite*, 6:114 (2:741).

[50]Armenini, *De' veri precetti della pittura*, 120. Olszewski's translation (171) does not provide an equivalent for the term. For additional discussion of the *ben finito cartone* and its functions, see Bambach, *Drawing and Painting in the Italian Renaissance Workshop*, 257, 263–71, 276–77, 281. For a useful contextualization of the production of such drawings by an artist whom Armenini discusses, see Linda Wolk-Simon, "Fame, *Paragone* and the Cartoon: The Case of Perino del Vaga," *Master Drawings* 30, no. 1 (1992): 66–77.

[51]On Baldinucci's relationship to the Accademia della Crusca, see Edward L. Goldberg, *After Vasari: History, Art, and Patronage in Late Medici Florence* (Princeton: Princeton University Press, 1988), 110–13, 147–48.

[52]Hazel Smith and Roger T. Dean, *Improvisation, Hypermedia and the Arts since 1945* (Amsterdam: Harwood, 1997), 25–33.

Index